i

P9-BZF-640

# Uncle John's

# FAST-ACTING
# LONG-LASTING
# BATHROOM
# READER

By the
Bathroom Readers'
Institute

Bathroom Readers' Press
Ashland, Oregon

# OUR "REGULAR" READERS RAVE!

"I love to read your books. They make the world a better place."
—**Dan A.**

"I worship your books. They are the best. Congratulations on making the only book I've read in five years that I wasn't forced to read. Rock on!"
—**Vincent D.**

"My four children, ages 12 through 18, have learned more from the *Bathroom Readers* than any other book. Can't wait for the next edition to come flowing out of the bookstores! You deserve a seat on the throne. You have helped us freshen up our intellect!"
—**Linda L.**

"I have finally found a place of refuge in the worst of times. The BATHROOM. With your *Bathroom Reader* and an iPod, my bathroom experiences are great. Thanks. Keep bringing those books."
—**Tony C.**

"I learned a lot from *Bathroom Readers*. I only read two but it's like reading 500 regular information books."
—**Randy R.**

"My son is CRAZY for *Bathroom Readers*! Every October he says, 'Don't forget my new BR for Christmas, Mom.' And, of course, he gets one. (He got his buddies at work hooked on them, too.)"
—**Marie S.**

"I love the *Bathroom Reader* series. Your books are funny, clever, informative, and at times, quite touching. They're a cross between the *Encyclopedia Britannica*, *Poor Richard's Almanac*, and *Mad Magazine*. Keep up the great work!"
—**Your #1 celebrity fan, Eddie Deezen (The guy who played Eugene in *Grease*, Malvin in *WarGames*, Dopey in *Attack of the Killer Bimbos*, and has voiced dozens of cartoon characters)**

## UNCLE JOHN'S
## FAST-ACTING LONG-LASTING
## BATHROOM READER®

For information, write:
The Bathroom Readers' Institute,
P.O. Box 1117, Ashland, OR 97520
*www.bathroomreader.com*
888-488-4642

Cover design by Michael Brunsfeld,
San Rafael, CA (*Brunsfeldo@comcast.net*)
BRI "technician" on back cover: Larry Kelp

*Uncle John's Fast-Acting Long-Lasting Bathroom Reader*®
by the Bathroom Readers' Institute
ISBN-13: 978-1-59223-483-7
ISBN-10: 1-59223-483-6

Library of Congress Catalog Card Number:
2005929788

Printed in the United States of America

First Printing

1 2 3 4 5 6 7 8 9 09 08 07 06 05

\*     \*     \*

Miss Nevada, 1959, was Dawn Wells. Five years
later, she starred as Mary Ann on *Gilligan's Island*.

# THANK YOU!

*The Bathroom Readers' Institute sincerely thanks the people whose advice and assistance made this book possible.*

Gordon Javna
John Dollison
Thom Little
Jay Newman
Julia Papps
Brian Boone
John Gaffey
Jeff Altemus
Malcolm Hillgartner
Jahnna Beecham
Michael Brunsfeld
Angela Kern
Rain Thering
Sharilyn Hovind
Gideon Javna
Sydney Stanley
Paul Stanley
Allen Orso
Jenny Baldwin
Nancy Toeppler
JoAnn Padgett
Jolly Jeff Cheek
Scarab Media
Jef Fretwell
Kristine Hemp

Dan Schmitz
Connie Vazquez
Richard Staples
Jeremy Busch
Debi Taylor
Kyle Coroneos
Rad Welles
Jack Mingo
Erin Barrett
Jennifer Thornton
Jennifer Browning
Dan Mansfield
Maggie Javna
(Mr.) Mustard Press
Steven Style Group
Mana Monzavi
Keziah Veres
Shannon Kehle
Angela Worthington
Barb Porshe
Paula Leith
Chris Olsen
Rebecca Kaiser
Porter the Wonder Dog
Thomas Crapper

\*   \*   \*

"Life is like a roll of toilet paper. The closer it gets to the end, the faster is goes."

—**Andy Rooney**

**Huh? The word *school* comes from the Greek word for "leisure."**

# CONTENTS

Because the BRI understands your reading needs, we've
divided the contents by length as well as subject.
**Short**—a quick read
**Medium**—2 to 3 pages
**Long**—for those extended visits, when something
a little more involved is required
**\* Extended**—for those leg-numbing experiences

\*     \*     \*

**Consumed at the 2005 Super Bowl in Houston, Texas**
15,000 hot dogs, 9,000 gallons of soft drinks, 6,400 cookies,
4,000 baked potatoes, 3,000 barbecue sandwiches, and 261
gallons of chili. Super Bowl Sunday is the second biggest
food consumption day of the year (after Thanksgiving).

# A NOTE FROM YOUR FAVORITE UNCLE

Welcome one and all to our 18th edition, *Uncle John's Fast-Acting Long-Lasting Bathroom Reader*. We think the title is a pretty accurate description of the reading material you'll find in any *Bathroom Reader*. Our articles not only provide you with fun information that you can absorb fast, we hope the knowledge you gain will be long-lasting, remaining in your brain for years to come. For instance, did you know that houseflies hum in the key of F? Now you do (and you'll probably remember it for the rest of your life).

What's the most astonishing thing we've learned after 18 years of making *Bathroom Readers*? It's that there's still so much to write about, so many fascinating topics to be explored (and so many bad jokes to tell). Each year we have to dig a little deeper to find them, but once again, the remarkable BRI staff has uncovered a treasure trove of fresh new topics. So expect to find a lot of little-known historical happenings that have had a lasting impact on the future: the first African-American sea captain, the phonograph wars, and the man who gave us leaded gas. On a happier note, you'll also read about the person who may have saved a billion lives. How? Turn to page 445.

What else have we got in store for you? Loads:

• **Origins:** The boomerang, the clock, the spy novel, and nachos.

• **Curses!** From the Ice Man to the Little Rascals.

• **Pop Science:** Hiccups, canoe plants, modern maladies, mad scientists, and rigor mortis.

• **Sports:** The long-awaited conclusion to the history of football tells the story of what happened when the pros took over.

• **Duh!** Dumb crooks, dumb politicians, dumb celebrities, and a woman who called 911 because she was having a cheeseburger emergency at the drive-thru window.

- **Useful Information:** Audio treasures, video stinkers, and survival tips that will come in handy in an array of catastrophes.

- **The Strange:** A beauty pageant held in a Lithuanian women's prison, a tortoise that adopted an orphaned hippopotamus, and a toothless man who stole toothbrushes.

Now comes the part where I get to thank our dedicated staff for going the extra mile to bring you an extra-great book.

- To our in-house outhouse writers—John D, Thom, Brian, and Jay, all of whom spent hot summer days in the cool confines of our little, red house in Ashland, Oregon—great work! (And thanks for the laughs!)

- A 21-flush salute to our out-house outhouse writers—Malcolm, Jahnna, Jef Ef, Kyle, Ernest "No More Doughnuts" Cheek, Jack, Erin, Gideon, and Angie, whose feet adorn almost every page.

- To our fabulous production staff—John G., Jeff A., Jennifer's terrific team of conscientious copyeditors, Rain, whom we will miss, Michael B., who's always got us covered, and Julia, whose managing prowess actually makes this book possible—thanks for 522 pages worth of hard work and dedication.

- To Allen, Sydney, JoAnn, and our friends at Banta, thank you for the support.

- To Porter the Wonder Dog. You're simply the best dog...ever.

And finally, thank *you*, our faithful readers. Every day we get letters telling us how much our books mean to you. Well, you mean just as much to us. We're all just one big happy family keeping the bathroom reading movement alive. It brings a tear to my eye. (I have to go now, before I short out my computer.)

Keep on reading. And as always,

*Go with the Flow!*

**Uncle John and the BRI Staff**

P.S. Did we mention our Web site? It's *www.bathroomreader.com*

# YOU'RE MY INSPIRATION

*It's always interesting to find out where the architects of
pop culture get their ideas. These may surprise you.*

CHARLIE AND THE CHOCOLATE FACTORY. In the
1920s, England's two biggest chocolate makers, Cadbury
and Rowntree, tried to steal trade secrets by sending spies
into each others' factories, posed as employees. Result: both companies became highly protective of their chocolate-making process.
When Roald Dahl was 13, he worked as a taste-tester at Cadbury.
The secretive policies and the giant, elaborate machines inspired
the future author to write his book about chocolatier Willy Wonka.

MARLBORO MAN. Using a cowboy to pitch the cigarette brand
was inspired when ad execs saw a 1949 *Life* magazine photo—a
close-up of a weather-worn Texas rancher named Clarence Hailey
Long, who wore a cowboy hat and had a cigarette in his mouth.

NAPOLEON DYNAMITE. Elvis Costello used it as a pseudo-
nym on his 1986 album *Blood and Chocolate*. Scriptwriter Jeremy
Coon met a street person in New York who said his name was
Napoleon Dynamite. Coon liked the name, and unaware of the
Costello connection, used it for the lead character in his movie.

CHARLIE THE TUNA. The Leo Burnett Agency created
Charlie for StarKist Tuna in 1961. Ad writer Tom Rogers based
him on a beatnik friend of his (that's why he wears a beret) who
wanted to be respected for his "good taste."

THE ODD COUPLE. In 1962 TV writer Danny Simon got
divorced and moved in with another divorced man. Simon was a
neat freak, while his friend was a slob. Simon's brother, playwright
Neil Simon, turned the situation into *The Odd Couple*. (Neil says
Danny inspired at least nine other characters in his plays.)

"I DON'T GET NO RESPECT." After seeing *The Godfather* in
1972, comedian Rodney Dangerfield noticed that all the characters
did the bidding of Don Corleone out of respect. Dangerfield just
flipped the concept.

---

Psycho? Alfred Hitchcock had an extreme fear of eggs.

# A LAZY LUMP OF CHEESE

*BRI member Richard Staples sent us these real responses from Russian high school kids applying to come to America on a foreign-exchange program.*

**Tell us about yourself:**

"I'd like to be rich and famous. But it can hardly come true, I'm lazy and talentless."

"I don't want to write about my friends because I am afraid to fall over."

"I love to eat ice cream, apples, chocolate and my mother's plow."

"I have a medium body (not too fat and not weedy)."

"In my free time I like to write poems. They are not very nice but they are mental."

"My father reckons that I'm just a lazy lump of cheese."

"And then I will have a good job and I'll be happy and blah blah blah."

**Tell us about your family:**

"People often ask me, my appearance is like mother's or father's one. I can say proudly I'm hybrid."

"I felt safe, as safe as only can be when you are falling off a hill with a bicycle and a father."

**Tell us about your town:**

"My town is windy and full of stones."

"In the suburbs of our town we have stud factory."

**Do you have any pets?**

"I visit my dog's club. His name is Danil. He is an American Staff-teryer. I am proud of him because he is an American."

"Most of all I prefer to play with my cat and change his hairstyle in winter."

"My cat is a member of my family. I have special relations with her."

**Tell us about your school:**

"We had to learn stupid poems in English about cows and pigs."

"Exact sciences reach my brain with difficulty."

**Anything else to tell us?**

"Free cheese only in mouse-catching machine."

"Though my mother told me it was only a toy, I could not forgive the silence of the teddy bear."

---

**The degree sign ( ° ) is an ancient symbol representing the sun.**

# FIRSTS

*Q: What does everything in the world have
in common? A: There was a first one.*

**First brewery in North America:** opened in New Amsterdam (Manhattan) in 1612.

**First professional sports organization in the United States:** the Maryland Jockey Club, founded in 1743.

**First American to fly in a hot air balloon:** Edward Warren (1784).

**First American cookbook:** *American Cookery*, published by Amelia Simmons in 1796.

**First electric refrigerator:** invented by Thomas Moore in Baltimore, Maryland, in 1803.

**First flea circus performance:** took place in New York City in 1835.

**First American novel to sell a million copies:** *Uncle Tom's Cabin* by Harriet Beecher Stowe (1852).

**First drive-in movie theater:** opened in Camden, New Jersey, in 1933. (Picture shown: *Wives Beware*, starring Adolphe Menjou.)

**First female celebrity to wear pants in public:** Actress Sarah Bernhardt was photographed wearing men's trousers in 1876.

**First blood transfusion:** June 1667, by Jean-Baptiste Denys, a French doctor, to a 15-year-old boy. (He got lamb's blood.)

**First electric hand drill:** invented by Wilhelm Fein of Norwell, Massachusetts, in 1895.

**First tank:** built in 1916 and nicknamed "Little Willie," it could only go 2 mph and never saw duty in battle.

**First drink of Kool-Aid:** taken by chemist Edwin Perkins of Hastings, Nebraska, in 1927.

**World's first flight attendant:** Ellen Church, hired in 1930. (She wanted to be a pilot.)

**First coast-to-coast direct-dial phone call:** made from Englewood, New Jersey, to Alameda, California, in 1951.

**First *Uncle John's Bathroom Reader*:** went to press in 1988.

# BATHROOM NAMES

*The origins of some names you can see from where you're sitting.*

**K**OHLER. Named after John Michael Kohler, an Austrian immigrant who started a steel products company in New Jersey in 1873. In 1883 he applied enamel to one of his products, a horse trough, creating the company's first bathtub.

**PRICE PFISTER.** Founded in Los Angeles in 1910 by Emil Price and William Pfister. Their first plumbing product: a garden faucet. Over the decades they added indoor faucets, valves, and showerheads. (During World War II they made hand grenade shells.)

**ELJER.** In 1907 Raymond Elmer Crane and his cousin, Oscar Jerome Backus, bought an old dinnerware plant in West Virginia, where they made some of the earliest vitreous china toilet tanks. The name combines the "El" in Elmer and the "Jer" in Jerome.

**DELTA.** Owned by Masco Screw Corporation, which was founded in Detroit in 1929 by Armenian immigrant Alex Manoogian. In 1952 an inventor brought Manoogian his latest product—a one-handled faucet with a ball-valve to mix the hot and cold water. But it leaked. Manoogian bought the rights, perfected the valve, and released the "Delta" faucet, so named because the triangle-shaped cam resembled the Greek letter *delta* [Δ].

**HANSGROHE.** Named after Hans Grohe, who founded the plumbing products company in Shiltach, Germany, in 1901. Hansgrohe's innovations include the first handheld showerhead (1928) and the Selecta adjustable showerhead (1956). Today they're the world's largest showerhead supplier. (Not to be confused with Grohe, another German company, which was started by Friedrich Grohe in 1936 and makes futuristic-looking faucet sets.)

**AMERICAN-STANDARD.** It comes from two companies: the American Radiator Company, founded in 1872, and the Standard Sanitary Manufacturing Company, founded in 1875. They merged in 1929 to become the American Radiator and Standard Sanitary Corporation. In 1968 they changed it to "American-Standard."

# OOPS!

*Everybody enjoys reading about somebody else's blunders.*
*So go ahead and feel superior for a few minutes.*

## SMART CAR...DUMB TRUCK

"A truck driver hit a Smart car on a motorway then drove for two miles with the tiny vehicle wedged to the front of his HGV—and did not know it was there. Trucker Klaus Buergermeister only stopped when he was flagged down by police, allowing terrified driver Andreas Bolga, 48, to escape. Klaus, 53, said he had only felt a slight bump and added: 'I could not believe it when I got out and saw there was a car stuck on the front of my truck.'"

**—The Express (UK)**

## (P)OOPS

"A police sniffer dog caused a political stink in South Africa's parliament after leaving its excrement under of the seat of a prominent opposition leader. The dog feces found under the bench of Inkatha Freedom Party leader Mangosuthu Buthelezi provoked outrage among politicians as some believed it was left there as an insult. One member of parliament demanded a formal apology from the Speaker of Parliament. But a police spokesman said it amounted to a simple call of nature. 'It was one of our police dogs we use to sweep the premises,' said Inspector Dennis Adriao. 'The handler did try to clean it up but missed some of it. Obviously, we have apologized for any embarrassment caused.' "

**—Reuters**

## OOH, THAT STINGS

"A Pasadena, Texas, man who blasted a wasp's nest with a 12-gauge shotgun was jailed after an errant pellet injured a 5-year-old boy in a nearby apartment. Police Sgt. J. M. Baird said Romeo Gonzalez, 18, fired the gun to break up the nest which was hanging from a tree outside his second-floor apartment. The pellet entered a first-floor apartment and struck David Marban in the thigh. The boy was hospitalized but is expected to recover."

**—CBS News**

---

Technically speaking, coffee is a fruit juice.

## ONE OF THESE DAYS, ARNOLD, POW...

"Joe Scarborough, a political commentator for MSNBC, failed to check his facts when he recently reported that California Governor Arnold Schwarzenegger had advocated destroying the moon. Citing a British newspaper, Scarborough, a former congressman, quoted Schwarzenegger as saying: 'If we get rid of the moon, women—those menstrual cycles are governed by the moon—will not get PMS. They will stop bitching and whining.'

"Scarborough then chided Schwarzenegger for insensitivity, saying: 'I don't know how it works in Austria, but let me tell you something, friend. Jokes about such matters are not laughing subjects to women in America.' It turned out, however, that the remarks Scarborough attributed to the Austrian-born governor were actually made by a Schwarzenegger impersonator who regularly appears on the Howard Stern radio show. Eleven days later, Scarborough apologized to viewers and Schwarzenegger for 'my terrible mistake.'"

—Reuters

## WHAT'S COOKING?

"A married couple in Howard, Wisconsin, ducked behind a refrigerator when bullets began exploding in their oven. Police said the husband hid the ammunition and three handguns in the oven before the couple went on vacation out of fear that they would be stolen if someone broke into the house. Upon returning, the wife turned on the oven."

—USA Today

## BRAZIL NUTS

"A gang of prisoners in a Brazilian jail spent months digging a tunnel in a bid for freedom. But they emerged from the tunnel's end inside the prison yard. The underground escape route, which had reportedly taken the 67 men months to complete, ended just one foot short of the main perimeter wall. Prison guards promptly took the crestfallen prisoners back to their cells, *Journal da Globo* reported last week. 'They were so frustrated and we could not hold back our laughter, they were so dumb,' a guard told the newspaper."

—*The Australian*

# CHICKEN NUGGETS

*We pecked around our library and laid
this egg—a page of chicken trivia.*

- There are over 150 varieties of domestic chickens. The most common egg-layers are White Leghorns and Golden Comets. The most common poultry varieties are Cornish Cross and Plymouth Rocks.

- Chickens and turkeys can cross-breed. The result is called a *turkin*.

- The short-term egg-laying record was set in 1967 by a White Leghorn in Sri Lanka. She laid 17 eggs in six hours.

- If there's no rooster in a flock of chickens, one hen will stop laying eggs and crow, assuming the role of protector.

- The chicken is the closest living relative of Tyrannosaurus rex.

- The amount of waste a chicken generates in its lifetime could power a 100-watt light bulb for five hours.

- Chickens are native to Asia. They were spread around the world as an easy food source, and were first brought to North America by Christopher Columbus.

- World record: In 1930 a chicken in New Zealand laid 361 eggs in 364 days.

- Typically, it takes a hen 24 to 26 hours to lay an egg, which hatches in 21 days.

- A chicken's comb (the decorative head plumage) has a practical function: it keeps the bird cool. There are eight varieties: buttercup, pea, strawberry, V-shaped, silkis, cushion, rose, and single.

- Chickens can't swallow while they are upside down.

- If a chicken has a white earlobe, its eggs will be white. If it's earlobe is red, the eggs will be brown-shelled. An exception: Arucana chickens can lay green, pink, and blue eggs.

- Worldwide, chickens outnumber humans.

- World's largest chicken egg: 16 ounces, laid by a New Jersey White Leghorn in 1956.

- Chickens have 24 distinct cries to communicate to one another, including separate alarm calls depending on what kind of predator is near.

---

**Are you chicken when it comes to chickens? Then you have *alektorophobia*.**

# LIFE IN 1902

*It's amazing how much things have changed in 100 years.*

Average life expectancy in the United States: 46

Fourteen percent of American homes had a bathtub. Eight percent had a telephone.

Cost of a three-minute phone call from Denver to New York City: $11

There were 8,000 cars in the United States and 144 miles of paved road on which to travel.

Marijuana, heroin, and morphine were all legal and available over the counter at any drugstore.

Speed limit in most cities: 10 mph

Mississippi, Iowa, Tennessee, and Alabama all had larger populations than California.

Average hourly wage in the United States: 22 cents (the average worker made between $200 and $400 a year)

Population of Las Vegas: 30

Ninety percent of doctors in the United States hadn't attended college.

Leading causes of death in the United States: pneumonia, influenza, tuberculosis, heart disease, diarrhea, and stroke.

Crossword puzzles, canned beer, and iced tea hadn't been invented yet.

Only six percent of American adults were high school graduates. Ten percent of adults were illiterate.

There were 230 reported murders in the United States.

Ninety-five percent of all births took place at home.

Sugar cost 4¢ a pound, coffee was 15¢ a pound, and eggs were 14¢ per dozen.

Oklahoma, New Mexico, Arizona, Hawaii, and Alaska were not yet states.

Most women washed their hair once a month and used egg yolks or borax for shampoo.

Eighteen percent of American homes had a full-time servant.

The Eiffel Tower was the tallest structure in the world.

Charles Dickens's character Tiny Tim was originally called Small Sam.

# THEY ARE WHAT YOU EAT

*You eat these products and drink a few of them, too. But how much do you know about the people they're named for?*

## MRS. PAUL

In 1946 power plant worker Edward Piszek started selling deviled crab cakes in a local Philadelphia bar to earn money while the plant was on strike. "One Friday I prepared 172 and we only sold 50," he recalled later. "There was a freezer in the back of the bar, so we threw 'em in there. It was either that or the trash can." A week later the frozen crab cakes still tasted fine, so Piszek and a friend, John Paul, each chipped in $350 and started a frozen seafood business. Piszek's mother pressured her son to name the company after her...but instead they named it Mrs. Paul's Kitchens after John's mom. Piszek bought out his partner in the 1950s but kept the Mrs. Paul's name. In 1982 he sold the company to Campbell Soup for a reported $70 million.

## EARL GREY

In his day Charles Grey, the second Earl Grey (1764–1845) was best known as the prime minister of Great Britain who ended slavery throughout the British Empire. Today he's better known for the gift he received when a British envoy saved the life of a Chinese government official. The grateful official sent Grey a diplomatic gift of black tea flavored by the oil of a citrus fruit known as bergamot. Grey liked the tea and started serving it in his home; when his supply ran low, he asked his London tea merchant, Twinings, to make more. Guests who enjoyed the prime minister's tea and wanted some for themselves would go to Twinings and ask for "Earl Grey's tea." Today it's the most popular blend of tea in the world.

## DR. LOUIS PERRIER

In 1902 Sir St. John Harmsworth, an English aristocrat, was seriously injured in an auto accident and went to Vergeze, a spa town

...n France, to recuperate. While there, a local doctor named Louis
Perrier had him drink mineral water from Les Bouillens ("bubbling
waters"), a natural spring he owned. Its supposed health-giving
properties had been touted since the days of the Roman Empire;
Harmsworth thought it would make an excellent mixer for whiskey
for his friends back home. He bought the spring from Dr. Perrier,
renamed it in his honor (who'd drink a mineral water called
Harmsworth?), and started bottling it in green bottles shaped like
the Indian clubs that Perrier had him swing for exercise. By the
1980s, Perrier was the world's best-selling mineral water.

## RUSSELL STOVER

As we told you in The Best of Uncle John's Bathroom Reader, an
Iowa schoolteacher named Christian Nelson invented the world's
first chocolate-dipped ice cream bar in 1921, and at a dinner party
someone suggested calling it Eskimo Pie. Here's another part of
the story: The person who came up with the name was Clara
Stover, wife of Nelson's business partner, Russell Stover. The Nel-
sons and the Stovers made a fortune their first year in business,
but after 15 months, others began to copy their idea, nearly forcing them out of business. The Stovers sold their share for $25,000
and moved to Denver, Colorado, where they started making and
selling boxed chocolates out of their home. Today Russell Stover
Candies is the best-selling boxed chocolate brand in the United
States.

## DR. ANCEL KEYS

In 1941 the U.S. War Department asked Keys, a University of
Minnesota physiologist, to develop a non-perishable, ready-to-eat
meal that would be small enough to fit into a soldier's pocket.
Keys went to a local market and looked around for foods that
would fit the bill. He came up with hard biscuits, dry sausages,
hard candy, and chocolate bars; then he tested his 28-ounce,
3,200-calorie "meals" on six soldiers at a nearby Army base. The
meals rated it only "palatable" and "better than nothing," but
they did relieve hunger and gave the soldiers enough energy to
engage in combat. The Army threw in chewing gum, toilet paper,
and four cigarettes...and named the packets "K-rations" in honor
of their creator.

# TOO RISKY FOR GUINNESS

*If you make it into the Guinness Book of World Records and somebody breaks your record, your name gets taken out. Turns out there's another way to get booted from the book.*

## BY THE BOOK

If you published a book of world records, what kinds of records would you allow into your book? What kinds would you keep out? The people at the *Guinness Book of World Records* have been asking themselves those questions for more than 50 years.

Founding editors Ross and Norris McWhirter took a conservative approach from the start: anything having to do with hard liquor or sex was out. "Ours is the kind of book maiden aunts give to their nieces," the brothers once explained. Crime was out, too—the brothers didn't want readers breaking laws just to get in the book.

As the years passed and the *Guinness Book* grew into an international phenomenon, a new problem arose: Some categories that were pretty dangerous to begin with—sword swallowing, fire eating, etc.—became more so as the winning records climbed ever higher. Do you remember the "Iron Maiden" category? That's where a person lies down on a bed of nails, has another bed of nails placed down on top of him, then has hundreds of pounds of heavy weights piled on top of that. There's a physical limit to how many weights you can pile on a guy sandwiched between two beds of nails before he dies a horrible, crushing death. Sooner or later, somebody trying to get into the book in the Iron Maiden category was going to be killed in the attempt. "We feel that's something we shouldn't encourage," Norris McWhirter said in 1981.

## WRITTEN OUT

So in the late 1970s, the *Guinness Book of World Records* began to close the book on some records that had been around for years.

"This category has now been retired," the editors stated after some entries, "and no further claims will be entertained." A few years later, many such categories disappeared from the book altogether.

That might have been it if not for the fact that the *Guinness Book of World Records* had changed hands a few times since then, and each new owner has had their own ideas about what should be included in the book. Some categories that were once deemed too dangerous were brought back...though in a few cases the old world records were forgotten or ignored and replaced with new "world records" that didn't even beat the ones they replaced.

So who's back in? Who's still out? What else is new? Here's a look at how some of the more unusual categories have fared.

### IRON MAIDEN

**Record Holder:** Vernon Craig of Wooster, Ohio, who performed under the stage name "Komar"

**Details:** Craig set his world record on March 6, 1977, in Chicago, when 1,642½ pounds of weights were piled on top of him while he was sandwiched between two beds of nails.

**What Happened:** In the 1979 edition, Craig's record appeared with the following note: "Now that weights in Bed-of-Nails contests have attained ¾ of a ton it is felt that this category should be retired. No further claims for publication will henceforth be examined."

**Update:** By 2000 the record was reopened for competition; today it's held by Lee Graber of Tallmadge, Ohio, who beat Komar's record by 16½ pounds, for a total of 1,659 pounds on June 24, 2000. According to *Guinness*, the hardest part of Graber's attempt was controlling his breathing, "as he had a lot of weight on his chest and needed to relax to avoid bursting a blood vessel in his head." (Komar retired his Iron Maiden act in 2000 at the age of 68).

### THE LONG SHOWER

**Record Holder:** Arron Marshall of Rockingham Park, Australia

**Details:** On July 29, 1978, Marshall stepped into his shower, turned on the water, and did not leave again until August 12, setting a world showering record of 336 hours.

**What Happened:** In the 1982 edition, his world record appeared

---

Americans spend over 2 billion hours a year mowing their lawns.

with the following disclaimer: "Desquamination [skin peeling off in scales] can be a positive danger."

**Update:** The category was closed and unlike the Iron Maiden, as of 2005 it has not been reopened. (Apparently long showers are more dangerous than the Iron Maiden.)

## CAR JUMPING OFF A RAMP

**Record Holder:** Dusty Russell of Athens, Georgia

**Details:** In April 1973, Russell climbed into his 1963 Ford Falcon, sped up a ramp, and jumped more than 176 feet.

**What Happened:** The record was still there in the 1981 edition, but in 1982 it was gone.

**Update:** By 1998 the category was back, but with a slight modification: now a car has to "land on its wheels and drive on afterwards." On August 23, 1998, an Australian named Ray Baumann set a new record, jumping his car 237 feet.

## FIRE-EATING

**Record Holder:** Jean Chapman of Buckinghamshire, England

**Details:** On August 25, 1979, Chapman extinguished 4,583 flaming torches using only her mouth. It took her two hours.

**What Happened:** For the 1982 edition Chapman's entry was followed with the disclaimer: "Fire-eating is potentially a highly dangerous activity." The category was later dropped.

**Update:** By 2004 *Guinness* was accepting entries in a modified (and presumably safer) fire-eating category: most flaming torches extinguished in *one minute*. Current record holder: Robert Wolf, who extinguished 43 torches on July 30, 2004. According to press reports, Wolf "finished the very dangerous record attempt without any injury to others and sustained only minor burns to his mouth."

\*　　\*　　\*

## SIX BALD ROCK STARS

- Rob Halford (Judas Priest)
- Fred Durst (Limp Bizkit)
- Moby
- Michael Stipe (R.E.M.)
- Billy Corgan (Smashing Pumpkins)
- Sinead O'Connor

# THERE OUGHTA BE A LAW

*The syndicated TV show* Celebrity Justice *asked a slew of celebrities to finish this sentence: There oughta be a law…*

"…against people who scrape their silverware on plates. I hate that."
—Rebecca Romijn

"…against people who get into the '10 items or less' line with more than 10 items and use a credit card where it says 'cash only.'"
—Samuel L. Jackson

"…against people who make jokes that aren't jokes. Like when you say, 'Is today Tuesday?' And somebody says, 'All day!' That's not a joke. Not funny. Don't say it."
—Hank Azaria

"…that if you are a good driver, and you have a reasonable IQ, you should be able to drive any speed you want."
—Jenna Elfman

"…against honking your horn unless it's absolutely necessary. Otherwise you're going to drive everybody crazy, the stress level will come up, people will be fighting in the streets. Don't honk your horn!"
—Dick Clark

"…against people coming into a meeting, in close quarters, with bad breath."
—Coolio

"…against people that when they give you your change at the cash register, that they put the dollar down first, and then the change."
—Elizabeth Perkins

"…that if a guy gets dumped by a woman on national TV, he should get half of everything she owns. I mean that's how it works in the real world."
—Charlie, *The Bachelorette*

"…and a serious fine for people who don't pick up their dog turd, and I want them to be thrown in jail."
—Marg Helgenberger, *CSI*

"…that the whole world sort of adopts Spain's timetable, where you sort of take the whole day off to relax and have fun."
—David Arquette

"…that people smile at at least three people every day."
—Orlando Bloom

---

The Sun converts over 4,000,000 tons of matter into energy every second.

# APRIL FOOLS!

*It's not unusual to find odd-but-true stories in the newspapers these days. But if the date on the paper is April 1...you might want to think twice before assuming it's true.*

In 1998 Burger King ran a full-page advertisement in *USA Today* announcing the new Left-Handed Whopper. "The new left-handed sandwich will have all condiments rotated 180°, thereby reducing the amount of lettuce and other toppings from spilling out the right side of the burger."

• In 1993 a group calling itself "The Arm the Homeless Coalition" announced that volunteers dressed as Santa would be stationed outside local malls collecting donations to buy guns and ammo for the homeless citizens of Columbus, Ohio. "There are organizations that deal with food and jobs, but none that train homeless people to use firearms," a spokesperson told reporters. A few days later three Ohio State University students admitted they'd made the whole thing up.

• In 1959 the Indiana *Kokomo Tribune* announced that due to budget cuts, the city police department would now be closing each night from 6 p.m. to 6 a.m. Anyone who called the police after hours would have to leave a message on the answering machine, and in the morning a police officer would listen to the messages. "We will check the hospitals and the coroner, and if they don't have any trouble, we will know that nothing happened," the paper quoted a police department spokesperson as saying.

• In 1999, just four months after most of western Europe adopted the euro as a standard currency, England's BBC radio service announced that England was scrapping the national anthem, "God Save the Queen," in favor of a Euro anthem that would be sung in German. "There's too much nationalism," a spokesperson for the EU supposedly told the BBC. "We need to look for unity."

• In March 1998, the newsletter *New Mexicans for Science and Reason* published a story claiming that the Alabama state legislature had passed a bill changing the mathematical value of pi from 3.14159 to the "Biblical value" of 3.0. On April 1 a physicist named Mark Boslough came forward and admitted he wrote the article to parody legislative attacks on the teaching of the theory of evolution.

• At about the same time that Pepsi made a worldwide change from its traditional white soda cans to blue ones in 1996, England's Virgin Cola announced an "innovation" of its own: its red cans would turn blue when the cans passed their sell-by date. "Virgin strongly advises its customers to avoid ALL blue cans of cola," the company said in an April 1 newspaper ad. "They are clearly out of date."

• In 1996 America Online published a report that NASA's *Galileo* spacecraft had found life on Jupiter. The following day they admitted they made it up. "Yes, it is a hoax," an AOL representative told reporters, "but it's a good one, don't you think?"

• In 1993 the German radio station Westdeutsche Rundfunk in Cologne broadcast a report that the city had issued a new regulation requiring joggers to run no faster than 6 mph; running faster than that "could disturb the squirrels who were in the middle of their mating season."

• In 1981 the *Herald-News* in Roscommon, Michigan, printed a warning that scientists were preparing to release 2,000 "freshwater sharks" into three area lakes as part of a government-funded study.

• In 1980 the BBC broadcast a report that London's Big Ben was going to be remade into a digital clock and the clock hands would be offered for sale to the first listeners who called in. "Surprisingly, few people thought it was funny," a BBC spokesman told reporters.

• In 1993 San Diego's KGB-FM radio station announced that the space shuttle *Discovery* was being diverted from Edwards Air Force Base to a local airport called Montgomery Field. More than 1,000 people descended on the tiny airstrip, snarling traffic for miles. "I had to shoo them away with their video cameras," airport manager Tom Raines told reporters. "A lot of them were really mad."

• In 1981 England's *Daily Mail* newspaper published a story about a Japanese entrant in the London Marathon named Kimo Nakajimi who, thanks to an error in translation, thought he had to run for 26 *days*—not 26 miles. The paper reported that there had been several recent sightings of Nakajimi, but that all attempts to flag him down had failed.

Many residents of Troublesome Creek, Kentucky, have blue skin

# WORD ORIGINS

*Ever wonder where words come from?*
*Here are some interesting stories.*

E XPLODE
**Meaning:** Burst or shatter violently
**Origin:** "This word has a history in the theater, where its meaning was once quite different than it is today. Originally 'explode' meant to drive an actor off the stage by means of clapping and hooting. It is made up of the Latin prefix *ex-* (out) and *plauder* (to applaud). The word still retains the sense of rejection, such as in the act of exploding a theory—exposing it as false—and, in general use, there is still noise associated with things which explode." (From *Dictionary of Word and Phrase Origins, Volume II*, by William and Mary Morris)

**FILIBUSTER**
**Meaning:** The use of prolonged speeches to obstruct legislative action
**Origin:** "From the Spanish *filibustero*, meaning 'freebooter' (which is derived from the Dutch *vrijbuter*). It was first used in English to designate a pirate or buccaneer in the Caribbean. In the 1850s, the word was used to signify adventurers who took part in illegal expeditions against Cuba, Mexico, and Central America to set up local governments that would apply to the United States for annexation. It was first used as a political term in the U.S. Senate in the late 1800s." (From *An Avalanche of Anoraks*, by Robert White)

**GOD**
**Meaning:** Deity; creator of the universe; supreme being
**Origin:** "The term for the deity sometimes is said to derive from 'good,' and there is some overlap between the two words. The words have different Indo-European roots, however. God has been traced to *gheu-*, meaning 'to call,' 'to invoke,' or 'to offer sacrifices to.' Good derives from *ghedh-* and means 'to unite,' 'to join,' or 'bring together.'" (From *Devious Derivations*, by Hugh Rawson)

---

Sweet smell of success: The smell of peppermint improves the concentration of office workers.

## STRIKE

**Meaning:** To stop working as a form of organized protest

**Origin:** "First used to describe an event in 1768 when a group of angry British sailors demonstrated their refusal to work by 'striking' (taking down) their sails. As a labor term, it was first used in America in 1799 to describe a ten-week walkout by New York shoemakers." (From *Once Upon a Word*, by Rob Kyff)

## DOODLE

**Meaning:** Scribble absentmindedly

**Origin:** "Comes from the German word *dudeln*, meaning 'to play the bagpipe.' The notion seems to be that a person who spends his time playing bagpipes would be guilty of other frivolous time-wasting activities—like scribbling aimlessly on scraps of paper. Although the word has been around for several centuries, it did not come into widespread popularity in the United States until Gary Cooper used it in the famous film *Mr. Deeds Goes to Town* in 1936." (From *Dictionary of Word and Phrase Origins, Volume III*, by William and Mary Morris)

## MUMBO JUMBO

**Meaning:** Confusing language; nonsense

**Origin:** "The earliest references used capital initials, as Mumbo Jumbo was said to be an African deity. Unfortunately, no one since the 18th century has reported any such deity in any West African tribe. It is possible that mumbo jumbo is a corrupt form of *nzambi*, Congolese for 'god.'

"Many explorers dismissed any native god as ignorant superstition. A religious belief in Mumbo Jumbo, a god supposedly invented to scare the womenfolk, was seen as even more nonsensical. Presumably this gave rise to mumbo jumbo in its modern sense of 'obscure or meaningless talk.'" (From *Take Our Word for It*, by Melanie and Mike Crowley)

\* \* \*

**Dumb Joke:** A man walks into a bar with a slab of asphalt under his arm and says, "A beer please, and one for the road."

**18th-century English sailors wore skirts.**

# CAR TUNES

*Radios are so much a part of the driving
experience, it seems like cars have always had
them. But they didn't. Here's the story.*

## SUNDOWN

One evening in 1929 two young men named William Lear
and Elmer Wavering drove their girlfriends to a lookout
point high above the Mississippi River town of Quincy, Illinois,
to watch the sunset. It was a romantic night to be sure, but one
of the women observed that it would be even nicer if they could
listen to music in the car.

Lear and Wavering liked the idea. Both men had tinkered with
radios—Lear had served as a radio operator in the U.S. Navy during World War I—and it wasn't long before they were taking apart
a home radio and trying to get it to work in a car. But it wasn't as
easy as it sounds: automobiles have ignition switches, generators,
spark plugs, and other electrical equipment that generate noisy
static interference, making it nearly impossible to listen to the
radio when the engine was running.

## SIGNING ON

One by one, Lear and Wavering identified and eliminated each
source of electrical interference. When they finally got their radio
to work, they took it to a radio convention in Chicago. There
they met Paul Galvin, owner of Galvin Manufacturing Corporation. He made a product called a "battery eliminator," a device
that allowed battery-powered radios to run on household AC current. But as more homes were wired for electricity, more radio
manufacturers made AC-powered radios. Galvin needed a new
product to manufacture. When he met Lear and Wavering at the
radio convention, he found it. He believed that mass-produced,
affordable car radios had the potential to become a huge business.

Lear and Wavering set up shop in Galvin's factory, and when
they perfected their first radio, they installed it in his Studebaker.
Then Galvin went to a local banker to apply for a loan. Thinking
it might sweeten the deal, he had his men install a radio in the

banker's Packard. Good idea, but it didn't work—half an hour after the installation, the banker's Packard caught on fire. (They didn't get the loan.)

Galvin didn't give up. He drove his Studebaker nearly 800 miles to Atlantic City to show off the radio at the 1930 Radio Manufacturers Association convention. Too broke to afford a booth, he parked the car outside the convention hall and cranked up the radio so that passing conventioneers could hear it. *That* idea worked—he got enough orders to put the radio into production.

## WHAT'S IN A NAME

That first production model was called the 5T71. Galvin decided he needed to come up with something a little catchier. In those days many companies in the phonograph and radio businesses used the suffix "ola" for their brand names—Radiola, Columbiola, and Victrola were three of the biggest. Galvin decided to do the same thing, and since his radio was intended for use in a motor vehicle, he decided to call it the Motorola.

But even with the name change, the radio still had problems:

• When the Motorola went on sale in 1930, it cost about $110 uninstalled, at a time when you could buy a brand-new car for $650, and the country was sliding into the Great Depression. (By that measure, a radio for a new car would cost about $3,000 today.)

• In 1930 it took two men several days to put in a car radio—the dashboard had to be taken apart so that the receiver and a single speaker could be installed, and the ceiling had to be cut open to install the antenna. These early radios ran on their own batteries, not on the car battery, so holes had to be cut into the floorboard to accommodate them. The installation manual had eight complicated diagrams and 28 pages of instructions.

## HIT THE ROAD

Selling complicated car radios that cost 20 percent of the price of a brand-new car wouldn't have been easy in the best of times, let alone during the Great Depression—Galvin lost money in 1930 and struggled for a couple of years after that. But things picked up in 1933 when Ford began offering Motorolas pre-installed at the factory. In 1934 they got another boost when Galvin struck a deal with the B.F. Goodrich tire company to sell and install them in its chain of tire stores. By then the price of the radio, installation included, had dropped to $55. The Motorola car radio was off and running. (The name of the company would be officially changed from Galvin Manufacturing to "Motorola" in 1947.)

In the meantime, Galvin continued to develop new uses for car radios. In 1936, the same year that it introduced push-button tuning, it also introduced the Motorola Police Cruiser, a standard car radio that was factory preset to a single frequency to pick up police broadcasts. In 1940 he developed with the first handheld two-way radio—the Handie-Talkie—for the U.S. Army.

A lot of the communication technologies that we take for granted today were born in Motorola labs in the years that followed World War II. In 1947 they came out with the first television to sell under $200. In 1956 the company introduced the world's first pager; in 1969 it supplied the radio and television equipment that was used to televise Neil Armstrong's first steps on the Moon. In 1973 it invented the world's first handheld cellular phone. Today Motorola is one of the second-largest cell phone manufacturer in the world. And it all started with the car radio.

## WHATEVER HAPPENED TO...

The two men who installed the first radio in Paul Galvin's car, Elmer Wavering and William Lear, ended up taking very different paths in life. Wavering stayed with Motorola. In the 1950s he helped change the automobile experience again when he developed the first automotive alternator, replacing inefficient and unreliable generators. The invention led to such luxuries as power windows, power seats, and, eventually, air-conditioning.

Lear also continued inventing. He holds more than 150 patents. Remember eight-track tape players? Lear invented that. But what he's really famous for are his contributions to the field of aviation. He invented radio direction finders for planes, aided in the invention of the autopilot, designed the first fully automatic aircraft landing system, and in 1963 introduced his most famous invention of all, the Lear Jet, the world's first mass-produced, affordable business jet. (Not bad for a guy who dropped out of school after the eighth grade.)

# FLUBBED HEADLINES

*These are 100% honest-to-goodness headlines. Can
you figure out what they were trying to say?*

MASSACHUSETTS WOMAN
HAS EYE ON KERRY'S SEAT

Four Top Dogs Inducted Into
Meat Industry Hall of Fame

*Material in Diapers Could
Help Make the Deserts Bloom*

Study Shows Some
Denial From Par-
ents on Ecstasy

MAN KILLED
OVER PHONE

*Passengers Feeling
Airline Crew Cuts*

**Toronto Suspects
Hate Crime**

Waterskiing Accident
Ruled Accidental

***JUDGE NOT
CONVINCED MURDER
VICTIM IS ALIVE***

Men Who Make
Inappropriate Advances
Should Be Exposed

*11 HIGH STUDENTS
SCORE PERFECT GRADE*

*Bonus Permits Enable 809
Hunters to Kill Two Deer*

**Brief Cooking at Low Heat
Recommended For Diabetics**

Teacher Strikes Idle Kids

**POLICEMAN SHOOTS
MAN WITH KNIFE**

Astronomers See Colorful Gas
Clouds Bubble Out of Uranus

School Bans All Kinds
of Nuts on Campus

DEALERS WILL HEAR
CAR TALK AT NOON

MINERS REFUSE TO
WORK AFTER DEATH

HOSPITALS SUED BY
SEVEN FOOT DOCTORS

**Youth Steals Funds
For Charity**

MUSIC INDUSTRY
MEETS ON DRUGS

OIL BARGE
BREAKS OFF TEXAS

Dodge Says Probe Puts
Him in Awkward Position

# "I SPY"...AT THE MOVIES

*You probably remember the kids' game "I Spy, with My Little Eye..." Filmmakers have been playing it for years. Here are some in-jokes and gags you can look for the next time you see these movies.*

*T*HE INCREDIBLES (2004)
I Spy...The computers from 2001: A Space Odyssey
**Where to Find Them:** Animators paid homage to 2001 by making the computer screen displays on Syndrome's secret island replicas of the ones used in Stanley Kubrick's 1968 classic film.

*THE RETURN OF THE KING* (2003)
I Spy...Director Peter Jackson's arm
**Where to Find It:** In the tunnel of Shelob, when Sam's (Sean Astin) arm enters the frame and points the sword at the big spider, it's not Astin's arm, it's Peter Jackson's.

*MONKEY BUSINESS* (1931)
I Spy...Sam Marx, father of the Marx Brothers
**Where to Find Him:** When the brothers are being carried off the ship, dad can be seen behind them sitting on a crate.

*SCHINDLER'S LIST* (1993)
I Spy...A photograph of Anne Frank
**Where to Find It:** In the scene where the Nazis are gathering the Jews' belongings, the camera pans over a pile of photographs; the top one is a picture of Anne Frank, the girl who wrote the famous diary about hiding from Nazis with her family in Amsterdam.

*JAWS* (1975)
I Spy...Peter Benchley, author of the novel that inspired the film
**Where to Find Him:** He's the TV reporter on the beach talking about Amityville and the shark.

The flashing light on the Capitol Records Tower spells out HOLLYWOOD in Morse code.

## BIG FISH (2003)

**I Spy...**Props from earlier Tim Burton movies

**Where to Find Them:** During the bank robbery, the door to the vault is the same one that protected the Batsuit in *Batman* (1989). At the science fair, young Ed Bloom shows off a breakfast machine that first appeared in *Pee-wee's Big Adventure* (1985).

## FIGHT CLUB (1999)

**I Spy...**Starbucks coffee cups

**Where to Find Them:** In every shot, according to director David Fincher, who put the cups there to illustrate the pervasiveness of corporations in our society. "I don't have anything against Starbucks, per se," he says, "but do we need three on every corner?"

## THE SOUND OF MUSIC (1965)

**I Spy...**Maria von Trapp

**Where to Find Her:** The nanny who inspired the story worked as an extra in the scene where Julie Andrews (starring as Maria) sings "I Have Confidence." There are two Austrian peasant women standing in a doorway—von Trapp is the elder of the two.

## CATWOMAN (2004)

**I Spy...**Former Catwoman Michelle Pfeiffer

**Where to Find Her:** In a stack of photos labeled "catwomen of history" is a picture of Pfeiffer as Catwoman from the 1992 movie *Batman Returns.*

## SHREK 2 (2004)

**I Spy...**Justin Timberlake (boyfriend of star Cameron Diaz)

**Where to Find Him:** When Fiona (Diaz) visits her childhood bedroom, there's a poster of "Sir Justin" on the wall.

## MONTY PYTHON AND THE HOLY GRAIL (1975)

**I Spy...**Michael Palin's infant son William

**Where to Find Him:** In "The Book of the Film" scene, baby William is the photograph of Sir-Not-Appearing-In-This-Film.

# CAPITAL-ISM

*Small towns are flush with pride about their contributions
to the world. Here are some places that proudly
proclaim themselves "World Capitals."*

## SOCK CAPITAL OF THE WORLD
**Town:** Fort Payne, Alabama
**Story:** There are more than 150 sock mills in the Fort
Payne area. Half the local population—6,000 people—produces
12 million pairs of socks each week. It's estimated that one out of
every four feet in America is dressed in a Fort Payne sock.

## EARMUFF CAPITAL OF THE WORLD
**Town:** Farmington, Maine
**Story:** Chester Greenwood invented earmuffs here in 1873 (he
was 15 years old). He subsequently opened a factory in Farmington, and business took off when he won a contract to supply them
to World War I soldiers. Farmington celebrates Greenwood with a
parade on the first Saturday of every December. Everyone and
everything, including pets and police cars, wears earmuffs.

## COSTUME JEWELRY CAPITAL OF THE WORLD
**Town:** Providence, Rhode Island
**Story:** In 1794 a Providence resident named Nehemiah Dodge
developed a simple, low-cost method of gold-plating. Result: a
pirate's booty in expensive-looking jewelry that almost anyone
could afford. Today there are more than 1,000 costume jewelry
plants in Rhode Island, most of them in Providence.

## CASKET CAPITAL OF THE WORLD
**Town:** Batesville, Indiana
**Story:** Since 1884, the town has been home to Batesville Casket,
the country's most prolific coffin manufacturer. (The plant churns
out one casket every 53 seconds.) The town built around death
has a lot of life, including an annual Raspberry Festival and a
Music & Arts Festival...but no Casket Festival.

## COW CHIP THROWING CAPITAL OF THE WORLD
**Town:** Beaver, Oklahoma
**Story:** The World Championship Cow Chip Throw is held here every April. The town's registered trademark: King Cow Chip, a cartoon of a dried pile of cow poop wearing a crown.

## CORN CAPITAL OF THE WORLD
**Town:** Olivia, Minnesota
**Story:** Olivia has more corn seed research facilities and processing plants than any other place on earth, and it celebrated that fact in 1973 by erecting a 50-foot-tall statue of a cornstalk. In 2003, the Minnesota senate passed a resolution making Olivia's claim to the world title official. But don't confuse Olivia with its corny rival, Constantine, Michigan, which grows 20 percent of the nation's seed corn. In 2003 the Michigan legislature proclaimed Constantine the "*Seed* Corn Capital of the World."

## KILLER BEE CAPITAL OF THE WORLD
**Town:** Hidalgo, Texas
**Story:** Killer bees emerged in the 1950s when some African bees escaped from a South American lab and bred with the local bees, creating a volatile spawn that migrated north. In 1990 they crossed into the United States through Hidalgo. Did the town flee in horror? Nope. They used it to promote tourism. Hidalgo spent $20,000 to build the "World's Largest Killer Bee," a 10-foot-tall, full-color bee in the center of town.

## SPINACH CAPITAL OF THE WORLD
**Town:** Alma, Arkansas
**Story:** The Allen Canning Company, based in Alma, cans 65 percent of all American canned spinach—60 million pounds a year—so in 1987, Alma proclaimed itself the Spinach Capital of the World. Their claim was challenged by Crystal Springs, Texas, which said it already *was* the Spinach Capital, and had been since 1937, when Del Monte opened a spinach canning plant there. Proof: they have a statue of Popeye in the town square. Not to be outdone, Alma built its own Popeye statue, then painted its water tower green, and labeled it the "World's Largest Can of Spinach."

# THE WRIGHT STUFF

*Words of bizarre wisdom from one of the most original comics ever—and one of our all-time favorites—Steven Wright.*

"Do Lipton employees take coffee breaks?"

"I was stopped once for going 53 in a 35-mph zone, but I told them I had dyslexia."

"If you saw a heat wave, would you wave back?"

"When I was crossing the border to Canada, they asked me if I had any firearms with me. I said, 'Well, what do you need?'"

"I have an existential map. It has 'You are here' written all over it."

"If a person with multiple personalities threatens suicide, is it considered a hostage situation?"

"Imagine if birds were tickled by feathers. You'd see a flock of birds come by laughing hysterically."

"I'd kill for a Nobel Peace Prize."

"I stayed in a really old hotel last night. They sent me a wake-up letter."

"When I was a baby, I kept a diary. Recently I was rereading it. 'Day one: still tired from the move. Day two: everybody talks to me like I'm an idiot!'"

"I Xeroxed a mirror. Now I have two Xerox machines."

"I'm taking Lamaze classes. I'm not having a baby, I'm just having trouble breathing."

"I went to a 7-11 and asked for a 2 by 4 and a box of 3 by 5s. The clerk said, 'ten-four.'"

"I was sad because I had no shoes, then I met a man with no feet. So I said, 'Got any shoes you're not using?'"

"It may be that your sole purpose in life is simply to serve as a warning to others."

"I busted a mirror and got seven years bad luck. But my lawyer thinks he can get me five."

"I tried to hang myself with a bungee cord. I kept almost dying."

The wet look: Billy goats trying to attract a mate urinate on their own heads.

# TOY FADS

*It happens every few years: Some new toy becomes instantly popular, every kid wants it, parents push and shove to buy one, and a company makes millions of dollars. Then, just as quickly, the fad is over.*

**F**AD: Teddy Ruxpin

**LASTED:** 1985–1988

**BACKGROUND:** Ken Forsse was a pioneer in *animatronics* at Disneyland in the 1960s and '70s, where he designed such innovative robotic displays as the talking figure of Abraham Lincoln in the Hall of Presidents. In the early 1980s he spent $1 million (of his own money) to develop Teddy Ruxpin, a doll in the likeness of a bear that would move his mouth and eyes as he read pre-recorded stories. He got financial backers and started a company, Worlds of Wonder (WOW), specifically to make the dolls.

**RISE AND FALL:** Teddy Ruxpin debuted in 1985. Despite its high price ($70) WOW couldn't produce the dolls fast enough and sold $93 million worth of them in the first year alone. A hit TV cartoon show followed and by 1987 Worlds of Wonder had earned $330 million, making it the fastest-growing startup company—of any kind—to date. But by 1988 they were broke. Every toymaker in the business had come out with animatronic dolls by then, and just as quickly as the fad had exploded, it collapsed. By 1988, WOW was $312 million in debt; by 1989 it was out of business.

**FAD:** Pogs

**LASTED:** 1992–1996

**BACKGROUND:** Pogs has its roots in an Hawaiian game from the 1920s. Kids would take fruit juice lids—cardboard disks—and stack them up. Half were one player's; half the other's. One player would then toss a heavy coin at the stack, and all the disks that had turned over—landing label side up—were kept by the thrower. The game would continue until one player had all the disks. It was called "Pogs" because of what was printed on the label: P.O.G., an acronym for "*p*assion fruit, *o*range, *g*uava," a popular juice combination.

**RISE AND FALL:** The game was popular for a while, died out, and then came back in the early 1990s. When it started to spread from Hawaii to the rest of the United States and then to Canada, toy companies started making a version. Instead of a juice label, the pogs—still cardboard disks—were adorned with images such as cartoon characters and movie stars. Hundreds of kinds of pogs were available. Thanks to its simplicity and low cost, the game quickly became hugely popular, with sales of more than $1 billion. The "World Pog Federation" even held international championships. But because it was so simple, kids quickly got bored with it. By 1996 it was washed up.

**FAD:** Chatty Cathy
**LASTED:** 1959–1965
**BACKGROUND:** In the late 1950s, Mattel engineer Jack Ryan—previously a missile designer for the U.S. government—designed the first doll with a voicebox that worked by pulling a string. The pull-string activated a tiny record player that played one of 11 phrases at random, including "I love you," "I'm hungry," and "Please brush my hair." The doll was also different in that it didn't look like a baby—it looked like a little girl, complete with bangs, buck teeth, and freckles. Mattel owner Elliot Handler's wife, Ruth (the inventor of the Barbie doll), named her "Chatty Cathy."
**RISE AND FALL:** Introduced in 1959, Chatty Cathy was immediately a hit. The doll was redesigned in 1963 and given seven more phrases; a new version released in 1964 could speak over 120 phrases. But by then, pull-string talking toys were commonplace and no longer a novelty. An attempt to bring the doll back in 1969 (voiced by Maureen McCormick, Marcia on *The Brady Bunch*) failed. Chatty Cathy was gone by 1971.

## MORE TOY FADS

• **Slap bracelets** (1980s) Flexible strips of fabric- or plastic-covered metal. Kids "slapped" them on each other's wrists.

• **Super Soakers** (1990s) Huge, pump-driven water guns that shot water farther and with more pressure than previous squirt guns.

• **Tamagotchi** (1997) Handheld plastic eggs with screens that displayed virtual "pets." Kids had to feed them (by pressing buttons)...or they would "die."

# IRONIC, ISN'T IT?

*There's nothing like a good dose of irony to put the*
*problems of day-to-day life into proper perspective.*

## EYE SPY

William Foster of Tallahassee, Florida, was charged with a hit-and-run in 2004 after striking a pedestrian with his car. Foster says he doesn't remember seeing or hitting the pedestrian, but he does remember where he was going at the time: he was driving to an optometrist appointment.

## RUN FOR THE BORDER

In 2003 *Men's Fitness* magazine named Houston "America's Fattest City." In 2005 a local bike club tried to change the city's image by holding a 40-mile bike rally through downtown Houston. To get people to sign up, they offered free beer and tacos at the end of the race.

## LOOK WHO'S TALKING

In 2004, 76-year-old game show producer Ralph Andrews filed suit against Dick Clark for age discrimination when Clark refused to hire Andrews to work for his production company, calling him a "dinosaur." Clark's age at the time: 74.

## DID MY NAME GIVE ME AWAY?

Acting on an anonymous tip, Detroit police pulled over a suspected drug dealer in May 2005. They found 33 pounds of cocaine in the vehicle, for which the drug dealer faces several years in prison. What's ironic about that? Her name is Denise Coke.

## WEB OF DECEPTION

A family values watchdog group called United Confederacy Against the World Wide Web distributed a petition in 2005 with the specific mission of banning the Internet from all American homes. But there's only one way to sign the petition: by visiting the UCAWWW Web site.

---

Oregon's state flag is the only one with a different design on each side.

# WHAT DOES IT TAKE?

*It takes the average bathroom reader about two minutes to read this page*

- **It takes** 1,000 yards of linen to wrap an average mummy.

- **It takes** 50,000 words to use up the lead in one pencil.

- **It takes** 600 grapes to make one bottle of wine.

- **It takes** 30 to 40 gallons of maple tree sap to make one gallon of maple syrup.

- **It takes** 24 to 26 hours for a hen to produce an egg.

- **It takes** 72 muscles to speak one word.

- **It takes** eight weeks for the average man to grow a one-inch-long beard.

- **It takes** one acre of soybeans to produce 82,368 crayons.

- **It takes** a bushel of corn to sweeten 400 cans of soda pop.

- **It takes** 25 tomatoes to make one bottle of ketchup.

- **It takes** one acre of trees one year to remove 13 tons of dust and noxious gases from the air.

- **It takes** seven years for a lobster to grow to one pound.

- **It takes** 345 squirts of milk from a cow's udder to make one gallon of milk.

- **It takes** 18 hummingbirds to weigh an ounce.

- **It takes** 42,000 tennis balls for a Wimbledon tournament.

- **It takes** one bale of cotton to make 1,217 T-shirts.

- **It takes** one cherry tree to produce enough cherries for 28 pies.

- **It takes** 650 cherries to make a cherry pie.

- **It takes** 2 million visits to 2 million flowers for a honeybee to make one pound of honey.

- **It takes** five gallons of milk to make a five-pound wheel of cheese.

- **It takes** a mole one day to make a tunnel 300 feet long.

- **It takes** 23 seconds for blood to make a complete circuit of the human body.

- **It takes** a five-mile walk to burn off the calories of one chocolate sundae.

---

**Stop that! Children touch their mouths with their hands about once every three minutes.**

# CHEDDAR MAN

*Everyone wants to know about their family tree. Here's*
*a great-great-great-great-great-great story about how*
*someone found the longest-lost relative in history.*

### HOLES IN CHEDDAR

Richard Gough was a retired sea captain living in the village of Cheddar, England, in 1890. Cheddar was famous for its cheese, but it was also beginning to become famous for the beautiful limestone caves that are found inside Cheddar Gorge, an enormous canyon just outside the village. Gough's uncle had turned one of the caves into a profitable tourist attraction, and Gough wanted to find one to exploit, too. He had his eye on one in particular, but an old woman lived in it, and it wasn't until she moved away that Gough finally got a chance to explore it.

The cave didn't look promising at first; it was small and not very interesting. But one of the walls of the cave was made of mud and boulders, not solid rock, so despite knowing nothing about how limestone caves are formed, Gough started digging.

It turned out to be a pretty smart move.

### LUCKY STRIKES

Limestone caverns are formed over millions of years as water slowly dissolves underground limestone deposits and washes them away, leaving behind large caverns filled with stalactites, stalagmites, and other beautiful wonders. Underground rivers flow through these caverns, and just as with rivers on the surface, they carry boulders, rocks, silt, and other debris. In places where the caverns narrow, the material can pile up and form a clog, or "choke."

The wall in the old woman's tiny cave was just such a choke, and after Gough dug for a while it fell away, revealing a much larger cavern inside. Gough and his sons spent the next eight years excavating other chokes in the cave and uncovering more than a quarter mile's worth of magnificent chambers. "Gough's Cave," as it came to be known, became a huge tourist attraction.

Gough died in 1902, but his sons continued the business. When

---

TV's Flipper was played mainly by two female dolphins, Suzy and Cathy.

they started blasting part of the cave floor (to improve drainage) in 1903, they made another discovery: the skeleton of a Stone Age caveman that turned out to be more than 9,000 years old. To this day it remains the oldest intact human skeleton ever found in Great Britain. "Cheddar Man," as he came to be known, helped turn Gough's Cave into one of the most popular attractions in England (today it attracts more than 400,000 visitors per year).

## GETTING TO KNOW YOU

So how much is known about Cheddar Man? The original blasting obliterated whatever artifacts may have been with him, but scientists have learned a few things by studying his bones: Cheddar Man was about 23 years old when he died, stood 5'5", and had strong teeth, which indicates a healthy diet. There is evidence that he suffered several blows to the head before his death, one of which apparently broke off a tiny piece of bone on the inside of his skull between his eyes. Scientists speculate that the wound may have caused an infection that eventually killed him.

Today Cheddar Man's bones are in the Natural History Museum in London, where they have been studied repeatedly over the years. But the biggest discovery of all wasn't made until 1997, when Britain's HTV network decided to do a series of documentaries on archaeological subjects in the United Kingdom.

A filmmaker named Philip Priestley was hired to direct one of the documentaries, and decided to make Cheddar Man the subject of his film. To make it more relevant to contemporary audiences, he obtained a DNA sample from Cheddar Man's bones and compared it to DNA taken from villagers living in Cheddar.

## BACK TO SCHOOL

Priestley was on a tight budget, so he didn't want to test any villagers until Oxford University scientists had successfully extracted DNA from one of Cheddar Man's molars. By then he'd already shot some footage of an archaeologist speaking before an audience of Cheddar schoolchildren. So, to make that footage blend with the footage he still had to shoot, he decided to test the DNA of some of the schoolkids who'd been filmed sitting in the audience. Their history teacher, a man named Adrian Targett, helped Priestley identify which kids came from old Cheddar families.

Some of the kids were under the impression that the DNA test involved drawing blood. Targett explained that no big, scary needles were involved—the tester was just going to swab the inside of their cheek. To reassure the kids, Targett had his DNA tested, too.

When all the tests were completed, only one person tested was found to be related to Cheddar Man: Mr. Targett, the history teacher. And how much had the Cheddar Man's family changed over time? More than 9,000 years later, Mr. Targett still lives within walking distance of the cave.

## ALL IN THE FAMILY

Since the discovery Targett has managed to trace his ancestry all the way to 1807. From there his family tree spreads back more than 300 generations to Cheddar Man, who was born in about 7150 B.C. That's the world's oldest confirmed family tree, easily beating out the previous record holders—living descendants of the Chinese philosopher Confucius. They can trace their ancestry back 85 generations to Confucius' great-great-great-great grandfather, who lived in the eighth century B.C.

The discovery of a living descendant of Cheddar Man has ramifications beyond the Targett family, too. Cheddar Man was a member of a clan of hunter-gatherers, who later came into contact with farmers from continental Europe. Historians have long debated whether the hunter-gatherers were pushed aside by the farmers and died out, or whether they picked up farming skills and assimilated with the new arrivals from Europe. The discovery of a living descendant of a hunter-gatherer supports the assimilation theory.

## NO BIG DEAL

And what happened to Adrian Targett? One minute he was a history teacher living quietly in a small village in southwest England; the next minute he was making headlines all over the world as a living member of the world's oldest family tree. How's he taking it? In stride. "We all have 9,000-year-old ancestors," he says, "I just happen to know who mine is."

\*     \*     \*

**Chinese proverb:** "Every family has a skeleton in the cupboard."

Q: What are shaggy manes, inky caps, sulphur tufts, and pig's ears? A: Mushrooms.

# A TALE OF A WHALE

*A good sea yarn is always worth telling—but
even more so when it inspired one of the
great works of American literature.*

## CHASING HIS DREAMS

Owen Chase was a happy man. Only 23 years old, he was already first mate on a New England whaling ship, the *Essex*, out of Nantucket and bound for the South Seas. In 1819 fortunes were made hunting sperm whales and Chase intended to get his share. Led by captain George Pollard, the crew of 21 left port August 12; two years later, more than half the crew would be dead and the *Essex* a wreck on the bottom of the Pacific.

The voyage started ominously when, two days out of port, a sudden squall knocked the ship over on its side. Although it righted itself after a few minutes, many of the crew began muttering that the voyage was cursed. It took five long months to reach Cape Horn at the tip of South America, and then took five more weeks to sail the treacherous Straits of Magellan. By the time the ship reached the South Pacific, the crew was exhausted and morale was low. Little did they know their ordeal had just begun.

## THAR SHE BLOWS

On November 20, 1820, the *Essex* was sailing 1,500 miles west of the Galápagos Islands when a huge sperm whale appeared off the port bow. To the crew's stunned disbelief, the giant beast turned and charged the ship. The whale struck the hull with such force that every man was knocked off his feet. Then it swam ahead of the boat, turned around, and rammed full speed into the bow, crushing the thick hull like an eggshell.

In 100 years of American whaling, no ship had ever been attacked by a whale. These sailors were supposed to be the hunters; suddenly they were the prey. Dazed and bewildered, the crew lowered their whaleboats and rowed away from the *Essex* as quickly as they could, just before it sank. What became of the whale? It had already submerged; they never saw it again.

## DESPERATE CIRCUMSTANCES

The situation couldn't have been bleaker. Twenty men (one had died on the outward journey) bobbed in three small, open boats in the middle of the vast Pacific Ocean. The officers debated which direction to go. To the south and west lay the barely known islands of Polynesia, rumored to be populated by cannibals. To the east lay the Galapagos Islands and the Spanish-controlled coasts of Chile and Peru—civilization. They had about 56 days' worth of provisions. If all went well, they could just make it.

All did not go well. They ran into vicious storms that pummeled the small boats. Even worse were the dead calms, when they would drift for days at a time with no way to shield themselves from the intense sun. On December 20, they found a small deserted island, but it didn't have enough food or water to sustain them all. When Captain Pollard insisted they sail on for South America, three men refused and stayed behind. (They probably made the right decision: they were rescued by a passing ship in April.)

On January 12, 1821, Chase's boat was separated from the others. Two days later, Second Mate Joy became the first to die; four days later another crewman, Richard Peterson, died. Both were buried at sea. By the time Seaman Isaac Cole died on February 8, Chase's boat had been out of food for days. Chase and the other two remaining men on his boat, Benjamin Lawrence and Thomas Nickerson, decided to eat the dead man rather than throw the body to the fishes. The meat kept them alive for another 10 days, when the British brig (a two-masted ship) *Indian* rescued them.

## TAKE A NUMBER

Captain Pollard and the men on the other two boats were forced to make the same dire decision in order to stay alive: as each shipmate died of dehydration, the others ate his carcass. Four men were consumed in this fashion. Pollard was too weak to help when the other boat, commanded by Obed Hendricks, drifted away, never to be seen again.

By February 1, after weeks at sea, Pollard's boat ran out of "food" again. Faced with a slow, lingering death by starvation, two crew members suggested they draw lots to decide who should be eaten next. Pollard reluctantly agreed. To his dismay, the short straw was picked by his 17-year-old cousin, Owen Coffin, who was summarily shot by the man with the second-shortest straw. The next meal was provided by Brazillai Ray, who died on February 11. Now only Captain Pollard and crewman Charles Ramsdell were left.

## SAVED

On February 23, 1821, the lookout on the Nantucket whaler *Dauphin* spotted the drifting whaleboat. When the sailors came up alongside, they found Pollard and Ramsdell, living skeletons, sucking the bones of their dead mates, which, according to the captain of the *Dauphin*, "they were loathe to part with." Pollard and Ramsdell had spent 95 days in an open boat and had drifted 3,500 nautical miles.

The five survivors were taken home to Nantucket. Surprisingly, they all went back to the sea. Chase, Ramsdell, Lawrence, and Nickerson all became successful sea captains. Pollard did as well, but was shipwrecked again in 1823, survived again, and then spent the remaining 45 years of his life as a night watchman...on land. Chase not only became a captain, he became an author. In 1821 he wrote a pamphlet entitled *Narrative of the Most Extraordinary and Distressing Shipwreck of the Whale-Ship Essex*, chronicling his sea adventure. It was a modest success. Poor health forced him to retire from the sea in 1840, and he suffered from chronic headaches the rest of his life. Shortly before his death in 1869, he was found hoarding food in the attic of his home.

## CALL ME...HERMAN?

In 1841, 20 years after the wreck of the *Essex*, Owen Chase's son, William, was hunting whales in the South Pacific in the same area in which his father's ordeal had taken place. When a young whaler from another ship peppered him with questions about the whale that sank the ship, William Chase reached into his sea chest and gave the stranger a copy of his father's pamphlet to read.

The young stranger was Herman Melville. Ten years later he published an epic novel about a Nantucket whaling ship that was rammed and sunk by a huge sperm whale named Moby Dick.

\* \* \*

"Always be sincere, even if you don't mean it." —**Harry Truman**

# WELCOME TO TEN SLEEP

*Sometimes the story of how a place got its name
is more interesting than the place itself.*

**D**EADWOOD, SOUTH DAKOTA. Gold was discovered in a nearby gulch in 1875. The gulch's other feature: a grove of dead trees.

**BOWLING GREEN, KENTUCKY.** 19th-century lawyers who came to the county courthouse passed their free time playing lawn bowling.

**ZIP CITY, ALABAMA.** A local resident named it in the 1920s because of all the cars that rushed or "zipped" through it on the way to Tennessee, the nearest place to buy whisky legally.

**CASHTOWN, PENNSYLVANIA.** Named for the Cashtown Tavern, so-called because the owner accepted only cash.

**TEN SLEEP, WYOMING.** According to a method of measuring distance by local Indians, the settlement was 10 nights, or "sleeps," from Fort Laramie, Wyoming.

**LADIESBURG, MARYLAND.** Early 19th-century settlers were predominantly women, outnumbering men seven to one.

**HURRICANE, WEST VIRGINIA.** A tornado destroyed a nearby forest in 1774. So why "Hurricane?" Local legend: as the tornado neared, someone yelled to Cain, the town blacksmith, "Hurry, Cain."

**BARGAINTOWN, NEW JERSEY.** Named by a land developer to lure settlers with the promise of cheap land.

**NOVI, MICHIGAN.** The sixth stagecoach stop outside Detroit was marked by a sign reading "No VI." Most travelers thought it was a word (not an abbreviation and a Roman numeral).

**GALVESTON, INDIANA.** Probably got its name from Galveston, Texas, but local lore says the town's founder looked out his window while thinking up a name and saw a "gal with a vest on."

---

More romantic than they look: Alligators "snuggle" for days before mating.

# Q & A:
# ASK THE EXPERTS

*Everyone's got a question they'd like answered—basic stuff,*
*like "Why is the sky blue?" Here are a few questions,*
*with answers from the nation's top trivia experts.*

## WEIGHTY QUESTION

**Q:** *Why doesn't pound cake weigh a pound?*

**A:** "Traditionally, it was made with a pound of flour, a pound of sugar, and a pound of butter. That would make three— enough to shatter the pound barrier and cause a crash landing directly on your hips. Incidentally, the same name game is played with cupcakes. The original recipe called for one cup of each ingredient. And you thought it was because they're baked in those cute little paper cups." (From *Crazy Plates* by Janet Podleski)

## SICK OF IT ALL

**Q:** *Why do people get sick more often in the winter?*

**A:** "It is not cold feet and wet heads that are the problem, disease experts say, but the fact that human beings are warmth-loving social animals. At least in cold climates, widespread outbreaks of diseases like colds and influenza tend to start in winter months, when people spend more time together indoors in close quarters with the windows shut. The cold months also bring children, those well-known vectors of bacteria and viruses, together in the classroom, where they can pick up infections and take them home to the rest of the family." (From *The New York Times Second Book of Science Questions and Answers* by C. Claiborne Ray)

## GET A LEG UP

**Q:** *Why do male dogs lift their leg up to urinate?*

**A:** "It isn't to avoid 'missing' and squirting their legs by mistake. It's to mark territory. Most dogs are compulsive in their habits and have favorite 'watering holes.' By lifting a leg, the urine flows up and out much farther, extending the boundaries of the male's terri-

---

**Americans buy over 73,000 miles of neckties each year.**

tory. From a dog's point of view, evidently, the bigger the territory, the better." (From *Why Do Dogs Have Wet Noses?* by David Feldman)

## THERE'S THE RUB

**Q:** *How does an eraser erase pencil marks?*
**A:** "Look at a pencil mark under a microscope. You'll see that it's not continuous; it's made up of individual black particles, a few ten-thousandths of an inch big, clinging to the paper fibers. The eraser's job is to pluck them out. It can do that because (a) it is flexible enough to reach in between the fibers and (b) it is sticky enough to grab onto the black particles. But while the eraser is rubbing the paper, the paper's fibers are also rubbing off pieces of the rubber. The rubbed-off shreds of rubber roll up their collected black particles into those pesky crumbs that you have to brush away." (From *What Einstein Told His Barber* by Robert L. Wolke)

## TASTES LIKE...SPLEEN?

**Q:** *What's really in a hot dog?*
**A:** "All manufacturers must list their ingredients on the label. 'Beef,' 'pork,' 'chicken,' 'turkey,' etc. can only be used if the meat comes from the muscle tissue of the animal. If you see the words 'meat by-products' or 'variety meats,' the hot dog may contain snouts, stomachs, hearts, tongues, lips, spleens, etc. Frankfurters once contained only beef and pork but now can legally contain sheep, goat, and up to 15% chicken. Hot dogs are made by grinding the meat with water, seasoning, sweeteners, preservatives, salt, and binders. (From *Why Does Popcorn Pop?* by Don Voorhees)

## CAN I DRIVE 55?

**Q:** *When a speed limit sign is posted, does that speed take effect when the driver sees it or when the driver passes it?*
**A:** "Speed limit signs, whether decreasing or increasing the speed limit, take effect at the time that you pass the sign and not a car length sooner. Yellow speed limit signs are there to warn drivers of potentially dangerous situations, such as sharp curves, requiring a reduction in speed. They are considered 'advisory,' but should you crash while maneuvering through one of these areas, you may be cited for reckless driving." (*First Coast News*, by Linda Mock)

# OPRAH'S INSIGHTS

*Oprah Winfrey's rise from poverty to wealth, fame, and influence are the source of these inspirational words. (Maybe this will get us in her Book Club.)*

"Real integrity is doing the right thing, and knowing that nobody's going to know whether you did it or not."

"I don't think of myself as a poor, deprived ghetto girl who made good. I think of myself as somebody who from an early age knew I was responsible for myself, and I had to make good."

"Excellence is the best deterrent to racism or sexism."

"The big secret in life is that there is no big secret. Whatever your goal, you can get there if you're willing to work."

"They say getting thin is the best revenge. Success is much better."

"Think like a queen. A queen is not afraid to fail."

"Though I am grateful for the blessings of wealth, it hasn't changed who I am. My feet are still on the ground. I'm just wearing better shoes."

"My idea of heaven is a great big baked potato and someone to share it with."

"Be thankful for what you have; you'll end up having more. If you concentrate on what you don't have, you will never, ever have enough."

"I'm black. I don't feel burdened by it. It's part of who I am; it does not define me."

"What we dwell on is who we become."

"Everyone wants to ride with you in the limo, but what you need is someone who will take the bus with you when the limo breaks down."

"I always knew I was destined for greatness."

"Do the one thing you think you cannot do. Fail at it. Try again. Do better the second time. The only people who never tumble are those who never mount the high wire. This is your moment. Own it."

# FOUNDING FATHERS

*You know the names. Here's a look at the people behind them.*

## HOWARD DEARING JOHNSON

In 1925 Johnson opened a soda fountain and pharmacy in Wollaston, Massachusetts. He sold a lot more sodas than pharmaceuticals, so he added beachfront ice cream and hot dog stands. Then in the late 1920s, he remade the business into a restaurant—the first Howard Johnson's. By 1952 he'd built it into the world's largest restaurant franchise, with more than 350 around the country (the restaurants' orange roofs were as famous as McDonald's golden arches are today). Two years later he opened his first motel. Today the restaurants are gone, the victim of bad management, changing times, and the rise of the fast-food industry. But the hotel chain is still going strong: as of 2005 there are nearly 500 Howard Johnson's hotels in 14 countries around the world.

## JOSEPH BULOVA

In 1875 Joseph Bulova, a 23-year-old immigrant from Bohemia (part of the modern-day Czech Republic), opened a jewelry store in New York City. In 1911 he expanded into clocks and pocket watches, and the following year he opened a watchmaking factory in Switzerland. When Bulova noticed during World War I that pocket watches were beginning to fall out of favor with soldiers, he introduced the product that would eventually make his name a household word: the Bulova *wrist*watch.

## PAUL JULIUS REUTER

In 1849 the telegraph was only ten years old, and there was still no direct telegraph line between the two largest European cities, Berlin and Paris. The German line ended in the city of Aachen; the Paris line ended in Brussels, Belgium, 77 miles away. That year, a German named Paul Julius Reuter came up with the idea of using 45 carrier pigeons to fly stock prices from the Paris stock exchange across the gap to Berlin. The pigeons were fast, delivering news to Reuter's clients six hours before the trains could. That's how Reuters News Service began, but even back then Reuter understood that the real money was in sending news by telegraph,

---

Child-care guru Dr. Benjamin Spock won the 1924 Olympic gold medal in rowing.

not by carrier pigeons. When a cable across the English Channel connected London and Paris in 1851, Reuters transmitted news and stock prices between the two capital cities. Newspapers that subscribed to his service reprinted the information in their papers. As the telegraph system grew, so did Reuters News Service; today it provides news and other information to more than 150 countries and is one of the largest news organizations in the world.

## DR. JULES BENGUE

In the late 1800s, Dr. Bengue, a French pharmacist, came up with a strong-smelling salve that helped ease muscle pain (the smell comes from menthol and wintergreen oil). In France it sold under the name Baume Bengue, but when it was introduced to the United States in 1898, the spelling was Americanized to Ben-Gay.

## JOE JUNEAU

On October 3, 1880, Joe Juneau and another prospector, Richard Harris, made the first major gold discovery in Alaska—they found nuggets "as large as peas and beans" in a stream that came to be known as Gold Creek. The men established a 160-acre town site on the beach alongside the creek, and named it Harrisburgh, after Harris. But at the first town meeting, held the following February, it was decided that there were already too many Harrisburghs in the United States. So they changed the name to Rockwell, in honor of Navy commander Charles Rockwell, whom the government sent to the area to maintain order once the gold had been found. *That* name lasted until Joe Juneau started complaining that nothing in the area had been named after him, even though he was one of the guys who had discovered the gold. He rallied other miners to his cause, and in 1882 the name of the town was changed to...Juneau.

\*     \*     \*

### LOVED BY ANYONE?

**Patient:** Doc, I can't stop singing "The Green, Green Grass of Home."
**Doctor:** That sounds like Tom Jones Syndrome.
**Patient:** Is it common?
**Doctor:** It's not unusual.

---

A little early for spring cleaning? The word *February* comes from Latin for "to cleanse."

# IT'S ALL ABOUT ME

*Uncle John wants to know why none of these
people ever says anything about him.*

"I thank you in advance for the great round of applause I'm about to get."
—**Bo Diddley**

"Every morning when I awake, the greatest of joys is mine: that of being Salvador Dalí ."
—**Salvador Dalí**

"I have the stardom glow."
—**Jennifer Lopez**

"I am hip-hop. Hip-hop does not happen until I do it."
—**KRS-One**

"I'm the stuff men are made of."
—**John Wayne**

"Every relationship I've been in, I've overwhelmed the girl. They just can't handle all the love."
—**Justin Timberlake**

"I don't mean to be a diva, but some days you wake up and you're Barbra Streisand."
—**Courtney Love**

"My name is Ted f***ing Williams and I'm the greatest hitter in baseball."
—**Ted Williams**

"You got to believe in yourself. Hell, I believe I'm the best-looking guy in the world and I might be right."
—**Charles Barkley**

"I am beautiful, famous, and gorgeous."
—**Anna Kournikova**

"I'm very secure with the fact that I'm not black. I'm white, pink, and rosy. But I've got soul."
—**Bono**

"I never lie. I believe everything I say, so it's not a lie."
—**Mark Wahlberg**

"I'm the high-priced dog meat that everybody wants, the Alpo of the NBA."
—**Shaquille O'Neal**

"To the people I forgot, you weren't on my mind for some reason and you probably don't deserve any thanks anyway."
—**Eminem**

"After the holocaust, there will still be cockroaches and Cher."
—**Cher**

---

Eeek! The longest one-syllable word in the English language is *screeched*.

# BAD MUSICALS

*Plenty of weird concepts make it to the Broadway
stage. Some are really successful. Not these.*

**M**USICAL: *Rockabye Hamlet* (1976)
**TOTAL PERFORMANCES:** 7
**STORY:** Adolescent angst and rebellion are major
themes in rock music—and in Shakespeare's *Hamlet*. So that
would make Hamlet the perfect inspiration for a rock musical,
right? Wrong. Originally written as a radio play (under the title
*Kronberg: 1582*), *Rockabye Hamlet* hit Broadway in 1976 with hundreds of flashing lights and an onstage band. Writers followed
Shakespeare's storyline but abandoned his dialogue. They opted
instead for lines like the one Laertes sings to Polonius: "Good son,
you return to France/Keep your divinity inside your pants."
**Notable Song:** "The Rosencrantz and Guildenstern Boogie."

**MUSICAL:** *Bring Back Birdie* (1981)
**TOTAL PERFORMANCES:** 4
**STORY:** A sequel to the 1961 hit *Bye Bye Birdie*. In the original,
teen idol Conrad Birdie sings a farewell concert and kisses a lucky
girl before joining the military (it was inspired by Elvis Presley
being drafted in the 1950s). *Bring Back Birdie* takes place 20 years
later and couldn't have been farther from the real Elvis story—
Birdie has settled down as mayor of a small town when somebody
talks him into making a comeback. The only problem: audiences
didn't come back.
**Notable Moment:** One night during the show's brief run, when
actor Donald O'Connor forgot the words to a song, he told the
band, "You sing it. I hate this song anyway," and walked off stage.

**MUSICAL:** *Via Galactica* (1972)
**TOTAL PERFORMANCES:** 7
**STORY:** A band of hippies (led by Raul Julia) travel through
outer space on an asteroid in the year 2972, searching for an unin-
habited planet on which to settle "New Jerusalem." The weightlessness of space was simulated by actors jumping on trampolines

---

Q: What was the Lone Ranger's name? (Hint: his first name isn't Lone.) A: John Reid.

r the entire show. A rock score would have suited the 1970s counterculture themes, but for some reason songwriters Christopher Gore and Galt McDermot chose country music.
**Notable Name:** The original title for the show was *Up!*, but producers changed it because it was being staged at the Uris Theatre and the marquee would have read "*Up! Uris.*"

## MUSICAL: Carrie (1988)
**TOTAL PERFORMANCES: 5**
**STORY:** Based on Stephen King's gory novel about a telekinetic teenager who kills everybody at her high school prom, *Carrie* was full of bad taste and bad ideas. It's regarded by many critics as the biggest flop (it lost $8 million) and worst musical of all time:

• *Newsday* called *Carrie* "stupendously, fabulously terrible. Ineptly conceived, sleazy, irrational from moment to moment, it stretches way beyond bad to mythic lousiness."

• *The Washington Post* likened it to "a reproduction of 'The Last Supper' made entirely out of broken bottles. You can't help marveling at the lengths to which someone went to make it."

**Notable Songs:** Carrie's mother sings about being sexually molested in "I Remember How Those Boys Could Dance," and Carrie serenades a hairbrush in "I'm Not Alone."

## MUSICAL: Breakfast at Tiffany's (1966)
**TOTAL PERFORMANCES: 0** (Closed in previews)
**STORY:** It had the highest advance sales of any show in 1966, primarily because of its cast—TV stars Mary Tyler Moore and Richard Chamberlain—but also because audiences expected a light, bouncy stage version of the popular movie. Unfortunately, they got a musical more like Truman Capote's original novella: dark and tragic. After a disastrous trial run, playwright Edward Albee was hired to rewrite the script. He did little to improve it, removing nearly all the jokes and making Moore's character a figment of Chamberlain's imagination. Audiences were so confused that they openly talked to and questioned the actors on stage. The show ran for four preview performances before producer David Merrick announced he was closing it immediately to save theatergoers from "an excruciatingly boring evening."

# STRANGE LAWSUITS

*It seems people will sue each other over practically anything. We can't always find the verdicts for these real-life lawsuits, but they're so funny, we knew they'd make great bathroom reading, anyway.*

**P**LAINTIFF: Norreasha Gill of Lexington, Kentucky
DEFENDANT: Kentucky radio station WLTO-FM
LAWSUIT: In June 2005, Gill was listening to the station when she heard the host offer to give "one hundred grand" to the tenth caller at a specified time. Gill listened for several hours, called at the right time…and won! The next morning she went down to the station to pick up her $100,000, but was told by the station manager that she hadn't won $100,000—she'd won one Nestle's 100 Grand candy bar. Obviously, Gill was upset. After numerous complaints, the station offered to give her $5,000, but Gill refused and filed suit, demanding the $100,000 (she'd already promised her kids a minivan). "What really hurts me," Gill said, "is they were going to get me in front of my children, all dressed up, and hand me a candy bar."

PLAINTIFF: Luiz Fernandes Peres
DEFENDANT: The Taverna Pub Medieval Bar in Natal, Brazil
LAWSUIT: When Peres got sick and threw up in the bar's restroom, the bartender added a "puke tax" to his bill. So Peres sued the bar for charging him the extra fee. "I consider this extortion," he told the local newspaper. The bar's owner defended the fee, saying they've been charging it to people who vomit on the premises for years.

PLAINTIFF: Marina Bai, a Russian astrologist
DEFENDANT: NASA
LAWSUIT: In July 2005, NASA sent a car-sized probe, dubbed "Deep Impact," on a successful collision course with Tempel 1, a comet that passes Earth every $5\frac{1}{2}$ years. Scientists were hoping to determine the makeup of the ancient comet, and possibly learn the makeup of the solar system billions of years ago. Bai sued the American space agency for $300 million, claiming that the colli-

sion had changed her horoscope. "It is obvious," Bai told Russia's *Izvestia* newspaper, "that elements of the comet's orbit, and correspondingly the ephemeris, will change after the explosion, which interferes with my astrology work and distorts my horoscope."

**PLAINTIFF:** Patricia Frankhouser of Jeannette, Pennsylvania
**DEFENDANT:** The Norfolk Southern Railway
**LAWSUIT:** Frankhouser sued the railroad in 2004 after she was hit by a train...while walking on the tracks. Frankhouser's suit blamed the railroad company for her injuries, claiming it should have posted warning signs, notifying people that the train tracks were being used by trains. (She wasn't badly hurt.)

**PLAINTIFF:** Bernd Naveke of Rio de Janeiro, Brazil
**DEFENDANT:** The Brahma Brewery
**LAWSUIT:** Naveke, 40, worked as a brewer and beer taster for 20 years until being forced to leave his job because he had become an alcoholic. In 2000 he sued the company, saying that for the 20 years in their employ he had to drink eight liters (about two gallons) of beer daily and even more during holiday seasons. "I left work drunk every day," Naveke said. Was it the brewery's fault that he was an alcoholic? The court thought so: Naveke was awarded $30,000 and a monthly pension of $2,600 for the rest of his life. But he thought it wasn't enough. In 2004 the appeals court agreed...and awarded him a lump sum of $2 million.

**PLAINTIFF:** Jesus Christ
**DEFENDANT:** West Virginia Department of Motor Vehicles
**LAWSUIT:** A man who changed his name to Jesus Christ sued the West Virginia DMV in 2005 because they wouldn't issue him a driver's license with the name on it. Officials said they couldn't issue the license because his birth certificate shows his birth name, Peter Robert Phillips Jr., and he never obtained a legal name change. He did, however, have a passport, a Social Security card, and a Washington D.C. driver's license, all of which showed the name "Jesus Christ." His attorney said he had changed his name 15 years earlier and had never had a problem. When asked if his client would comment on the case, his lawyer said, "Christ is not speaking to the press at this time."

# WACKY TV

*Every year TV executives hear hundreds of ideas
for new shows. We all know the great ones;
here are a few of the clunkers. Believe it or
not, these actually made it to the tube.*

## S IT OR MISS (1950)

A fast-paced daytime game show in which five contestants competed for cash and prizes by playing musical chairs.

## TONI TWIN TIME (1950)

Basically a 15-minute commercial trying to pass itself off as a talent show. Hosted by a young Jack Lemmon, it featured pairs of teenage twin girls. First came the talent portion: girls would sing a song, perform a dramatic recital, or play an instrument. Next, though completely unrelated to the talent portion, the audience would guess which girl had had her hair done professionally and which had used a Toni Home Permanent kit. The program aired in prime time.

## THE UGLIEST GIRL IN TOWN (1968)

In order to stay in London with his British girlfriend, an American man dresses in drag and lands work as a fashion model. Despite looking nothing like a woman (his face wasn't even shaved), he becomes the toast of the swinging '60s fashion world because of his "unique" appearance. It ran for 20 episodes.

## LANCELOT LINK / SECRET CHIMP (1970)

A parody of secret-agent shows like *The Man From U.N.C.L.E.* but with an all-chimpanzee cast. The plot: the members of a chimpanzee rock band, the Evolution Revolution, have a sideline--*they're spies!* So, cut between footage of chimps "playing" guitars and drums are scenes of chimp gun battles, chimps jumping out of airplanes, and chimps crashing cars. Special effects weren't used to make the chimps "talk"; producers gave them gum to chew to mimic talking and voices were dubbed by humans. A goofy show like this would have worked fine on Saturday mornings as a

---

Most school buses in America are painted "National School Bus Chrome Yellow."

kids' show, but *Lancelot Link* was broadcast in prime time. And it bombed. So it was moved to Saturday mornings, where it thrived. (It was also successful on Nick at Nite as a rerun in 1988.)

## THE BRADY BUNCH VARIETY HOUR (1977)

Three years after their sitcom went off the air, the cast of *The Brady Bunch* returned in this weekly hour of songs, skits, and water stunts (yes, water stunts), performing in character as the Brady family. The original Jan (Eve Plumb) didn't want to do the show and was replaced with actress Geri Reischl, who didn't look like her. It lasted nine episodes.

## GREAT DAY (1977)

Al Molinaro ("Al" in *Happy Days*) and Billy Barty play two homeless alcoholics trying to survive on the streets of New York City. A compelling tragic drama? No—*Great Day* was a comedy. It aired only once.

## MANIMAL (1983)

An animal behavior studies professor can turn himself into any animal he wishes, whenever he wishes, and uses his power to fight crime. What was an intriguing premise didn't work. Why? Because the special effects needed to turn man into animal turned out to be very expensive. So producers cut corners, using poorly trained animal actors. Result: the show's handful of episodes featured birds, tigers, dogs, snakes, and cougars moving the wrong way, attacking the camera, looking directly into the camera, or sitting completely still when they should have been running. NBC's most-hyped show of 1983 was gone after eight episodes.

## THE CHARMINGS (1987)

Premise: Snow White, Prince Charming, a magic mirror, and some dwarves are accidentally transported through time to 1980s Burbank, California. The show featured live actors, not animation, and the comedy arises mostly from Snow White's difficulty in dealing with the 20th century—especially modern appliances. It ran for 20 episodes.

## WOOPS! (1992)

Back in Fox's early days it liked to experiment with edgy concepts. Here's one they came up with: A nuclear holocaust instantly kills everyone on Earth except for six Americans: a teacher, a feminist, a yuppie stockbroker, a homeless man, a doctor, and a ditzy blonde. They manage to find each other and try to come up with ways to rebuild civilization. Sound familiar? Basically, they just took the premise for *Gilligan's Island* and changed the island to a barren post-apocalyptic wasteland after billions of people died. Funny, huh? Viewers didn't think so. *Woops!* lasted only 10 episodes.

## FATHER OF THE PRIDE (2004)

Produced by animation studio Dreamworks (they made the *Shrek* movies) this prime-time cartoon was for kids, right? Wrong. It was about the private lives of the jungle animals in Siegfried and Roy's Las Vegas show and was strictly adults only, with lots of frank sexual dialogue and depiction of drugs. The fact that prior to the show's debut Roy Horn was critically mauled by one of his tigers couldn't have been a good omen. But since each episode took nine months and $1.6 million to produce, NBC went ahead and aired the show anyway, despite the tragedy. They should have heeded the omen—*Father of the Pride* lasted only seven episodes.

\*     \*     \*

## JEWEL THIEF

"Two thieves who tried to rob two elderly women in the Lithuanian city of Klaipeda, thinking they were easy prey, got more than they bargained for. The two would-be thieves rang the doorbell and attacked the women as soon as they opened the door. But Zoja Popova, 93, brought one of the robbers to his knees—she grabbed the thief by the family jewels and squeezed. 'I pressed as hard as I could and he squealed like an animal,' said Popova. Neighbors came running to find out what all the shouting was about. The robbers tried to escape through a window, but were caught by private security guards and handed over to the police."
—*Mail & Guardian* UK)

It may not look like it, but a violin contains about 70 separate pieces of wood.

# WRONG WAY CORRIGAN

*While rummaging through our "Dustbin of History" file recently, we discovered the story of this colorful character. He snookered his way into the hearts of people on both sides of the Atlantic by heading in the wrong direction and ending up in the right place*

## THAT'S MY STORY...

On the foggy morning of July 17, 1938, a 31-year-old pilot named Douglas Corrigan took off from Brooklyn's Floyd Bennett Field on a solo, nonstop trip to California. Twenty-eight hours later, he landed in Ireland...with a lot of explaining to do. He had no passport or papers of any kind, nor had he received permission from U.S. officials to make the transatlantic flight.

Safely on the ground, Corrigan offered this explanation to Irish customs: Heavy fog in New York had forced him to navigate using only his compass. The fog continued all that day and into the night; there was never good visibility. When the sun rose the next morning—26 hours into his flight—he was surprised to find himself over an ocean. Taking a closer look at his compass, Corrigan realized he'd been following the wrong end of the needle—heading due east instead of west! But by now he was almost out of fuel; he couldn't turn around. His only hope was to continue east and hope to reach land before he ran out of gas. Two hours later he saw fishing boats off a rocky coast and knew he was safe. From there, he made his way to Baldonnel Airport in Dublin. His first words upon exiting the plane were "Just got in from New York. Where am I?"

## ...AND I'M STICKING TO IT!

He repeated the story to the American ambassador and then to Ireland's prime minister. By this third telling—to the Irish cabinet—the European and American press had got wind of the story and ran with it. When he got to the part about misreading his compass, the cabinet ministers all laughed and Corrigan knew that things would work out. Ireland graciously sent him home without penalty.

---

J. Edgar Hoover once gave his mother a canary bred by the "Birdman of Alcatraz."

When he got back to New York, Corrigan was amazed to find out he'd become a folk hero. In the bleak days of the Great Depression, Corrigan's achievement and amusing explanation lifted people's spirits. Over a million well-wishers turned out for a ticker-tape parade in his honor (more than had turned out to honor Charles Lindbergh after his transatlantic flight). The *New York Post* even ran a backward headline that read "!NAGIRROC YAW GNORW OT LIAH!" ("Hail To Wrong Way Corrigan!").

## THE TRUTH

So what really happened? It's no secret that Corrigan's dream was to fly solo across the Atlantic. He got his start in the airplane business in 1927 working for the company that built Lindbergh's *Spirit of St. Louis*. Corrigan helped assemble the wing and install the instrument panel on the famous plane. His greatest honor was meeting Lindbergh. ("Even more than if I had met Abraham Lincoln himself!") After Lindbergh made the first solo transatlantic flight in 1927, Corrigan vowed to follow in his footsteps.

He spent the early 1930s barnstorming the country, landing near small towns and charging for airplane rides to pay for gas. In 1933 he bought a secondhand Curtiss Robin J-6 monoplane for $310, which he named *Sunshine*, and began overhauling it for a trip across the ocean. In 1936 and again in 1937, Federal Aviation officials denied Corrigan's requests to attempt the Atlantic flight.

So it's unlikely that when Corrigan took off from New York in 1938, he didn't know where he was going. Not only was he an accomplished pilot and navigator who had a history of flying without the proper paperwork, but he'd been working 10 straight years toward his dream of flying nonstop to Europe. Wrong Way Corrigan knew one end of a compass from the other.

## COME ON, JUST ADMIT IT

For the rest of his life (he died in 1995), people tried to get Corrigan to come clean—but he never did, not even in his autobiography. In 1988 Corrigan took *Sunshine* on a national tour to celebrate the 50th anniversary of his famous flight. He was continually asked the same question: "Were you *really* trying to fly to California?" "Sure," he answered. "Well, at least I've told that story so many times that now I believe it myself."

In the Middle Ages, dead bodies were often used as ammunition in catapults.

# UNSUNG HEROES

*You may not recognize their names, but you've heard their music more times than you know. These teams of studio musicians have played on hundreds of hit records over the last 50 years.*

## THE WRECKING CREW

That's the nickname these musicians from the 1960s gave themselves after the old line studio players, who hated rock, complained that they were "wrecking the business." The band, which included Hal Blaine (drums), Joe Osborne (bass), Larry Knechtel (keyboards), Glen Campbell (guitar), and Leon Russell (piano), were producer Phil Spector's "go-to" guys.

♪ The Wrecking Crew played on six consecutive Record of the Year Grammy winners: "A Taste of Honey" by Herb Alpert and the Tijuana Brass (1966), "Strangers in the Night" by Frank Sinatra (1967), "Up, Up and Away" by the Fifth Dimension (1968), "Mrs. Robinson" by Simon and Garfunkel (1969), "Aquarius/Let the Sunshine In" by the Fifth Dimension (1970), and "Bridge Over Troubled Water" by Simon and Garfunkel (1971).

**Selected Hits:** "Be My Baby" by the Ronettes • "Surf City" by Jan and Dean • "You've Lost That Lovin' Feeling" by the Righteous Brothers • "I Got You, Babe" by Sonny and Cher • "Mr. Tambourine Man" by the Byrds • "California Dreamin'" by the Mamas and the Papas • "This Diamond Ring" by Gary Lewis and the Playboys • "Good Vibrations" by the Beach Boys • "I'm a Believer" by the Monkees • "River Deep, Mountain High" by Ike and Tina Turner

## MUSCLE SHOALS RHYTHM SECTION

Jimmy Johnson (guitar), Roger Hawkins (drums), David Hood (bass), Barry Beckett (keyboards), and Donny Short (lead guitar) are known as the "Swampers" by the music legends who've come down to Muscle Shoals, Alabama, to record with them since 1967.

♪ The musicians were given the nickname "Swampers" during a recording session with Mick Jagger because of the swampy land in Muscle Shoals. They were referenced by name in Lynyrd Skynyrd's "Sweet Home Alabama."

---

**Dust from the Sahara desert has been carried by the wind as far as Chicago.**

♪ The Muscle Shoals Sound Studios were founded in 1969 in an old casket warehouse. Their first client was Cher.

**Selected Hits:** "Mustang Sally" by Wilson Pickett • "Old Time Rock 'n' Roll" by Bob Seger • "Respect" by Aretha Franklin • "High Time We Went" by Joe Cocker • "Tonight's the Night" by Rod Stewart • "Kodachrome" by Paul Simon • "When a Man Loves a Woman" by Percy Sledge • "Sweet Soul Music" by Arthur Conley • "The Harder They Come" by Jimmy Cliff • "Chain of Fools" by Aretha Franklin • "Wild Horses" by the Rolling Stones • "Land of a Thousand Dances" by Wilson Pickett • "Lay Down Sally" by Eric Clapton

## THE A TEAM

Immortalized by John Sebastian in his song "Nashville Cats," these superpickers—including Bob Moore (bass), Buddy Harman (drums), Grady Martin, Hank Garland, Chet Atkins, Harold Bradley (guitar), Hargus "Pig" Robbins, Floyd Kramer (piano), Pete Drake (steel guitar), and Charlie McCoy (harmonica)—have played on hundreds of country hits of the past half century.

**Selected Hits:** "Oh, Pretty Woman" by Roy Orbison • "Stand By Your Man" by Tammy Wynette • "Just Like a Woman" by Bob Dylan • "Crazy" by Patsy Cline • "Battle of New Orleans" by Johnny Horton • "King of the Road" by Roger Miller • "El Paso" by Marty Robbins • "Big Bad John" by Jimmy Dean • "Jingle Bell Rock" by Bobby Helms • "I'm Sorry" by Brenda Lee

## THE MEMPHIS SOUND

In 1958 the Royal Spades were a band of white kids from Memphis who loved black music. When sax player Packy Axton's mother opened a studio called Satellite Records (later Stax-Volt) to record local talent, they changed their name to the Mar-Keys and became the house band. Local black musicians soon joined, led by keyboard player Booker T. Jones, drummer Al Jackson Jr., and sax man Andrew Love. In 1962 guitarist Steve Cropper and bassist Donald "Duck" Dunn split off from the Mar-Keys to join Jones and Jackson as Booker T. and the MGs ("Memphis Group"), and Love and trumpeter Wayne Jackson still play as the Memphis Horns. But together this assembly of black and white musicians wrote the book on what came to be called classic Southern soul.

**Selected Hits:** "Try a Little Tenderness" by Otis Redding • "Soul Man" by Sam and Dave • "Midnight Hour" by Wilson Pickett • "Knock on Wood" by Eddie Floyd • "Dock of the Bay" by Otis Redding • "Son of a Preacher Man" by Dusty Springfield • "Suspicious Minds" by Elvis Presley • "Let's Stay Together" by Al Green • "Shaft" by Isaac Hayes • "I'll Take You There" by the Staples Singers • "Born Under a Bad Sign" by Albert King • "Cry Like a Baby" by The Box Tops • "Mercury Falling" by Sting • "Storm Front" by Billy Joel

## THE FUNK BROTHERS

They worked in a basement called the "Snake Pit" and churned out legendary Motown hits hour after hour from 1958 to 1973. The band included Benny Benjamin (drums), James Jamerson (bass), Joe Messina, Larry Veeder (guitar), Earl Van Dyke, Joe Hunter (piano), Hank Crosby (saxophone), Paul Riser (trombone), and Herbie Williams (trumpet). They claim to have played on more hit records than the Beatles, Elvis, and Frank Sinatra combined.

♪ Recording sessions began at 10 a.m. and were over at 1 p.m. The musicians were on call seven days a week.

♪ Originally, each band member was paid $10 per song. It usually took about an hour to record each song, but sometimes less.

**Selected Hits:** "Dancing in the Street" by Martha and the Vandellas • "Stop! In the Name of Love" by the Supremes • "My Girl" by the Temptations • "I Can't Help Myself" by the Four Tops • "Ain't That Peculiar" by Marvin Gaye • "Reach Out, I'll Be There" by the Four Tops • "Do You Love Me" by the Contours • "Tears of a Clown" by Smokey Robinson and the Miracles • "My Guy" by Mary Wells • "Please Mr. Postman" by the Marvelettes • "Cloud Nine" by the Temptations • "I Want You Back" by the Jackson Five • "Going to a Go-Go" by the Miracles • "What's Going On" by Marvin Gaye

**Random Session Notes:**
• Drummer Hal Blaine of the Wrecking Crew played a set of tire chains in Simon and Garfunkel's "Bridge Over Troubled Water."
• Billy Joel played piano on the Shangri-Las' teenage angst classic "Leader of the Pack." He was 16.

# WEIRD CANADA

*Canada: land of beautiful mountains, clear lakes...and some really weird news reports.*

## HOME COOKING

Health inspectors in Granby, Quebec, shut down the Comme Chez Soi restaurant in 2000 when the owners were caught re-serving foods such as tartar sauce, coleslaw, bread, and fondue that had been discarded from previous customers' plates. They'd even used bread slices with bites out of them to make bread crumbs. They were also caught reusing discarded food from rooms in a motel they owned. (*Comme chez soi* means "just like home.")

## STEP RIGHT UP

In 2005 the Canadian postal service notified Christine Charbonneau of Orleans, Ontario, that they would no longer be delivering mail to her door. Reason: her front steps were 30 cm (12 inches) high, and regulations say that mail carriers are not required to climb steps higher than 20 cm (8 inches). Charbonneau said that the mail had been delivered to her door for the last 17 years and added that her 77-year-old mother-in-law—who is on oxygen—uses the stairs regularly.

## BEAUZEAU LE CLOWN

In 2001 Quebec Premier Bernard Landry proposed the province spend $11 million to increase the number of clowns and other performers graduating from Quebec's National Circus School. The school was only graduating ten students a year, and when it comes to clown training, said Landry, Quebec must "maintain and enhance its leadership position."

## UH, DOCTOR?

Rebecca Chinalquay of Saskatoon, Saskatchewan, sued the Meadow Lake Hospital after she was left alone in the delivery room while in labor. She called for help, but no one came, and she ended up having the baby by herself. The hospital's excuse: Chinalquay was being uncooperative and wouldn't allow nurses to monitor her condition, preventing them from knowing that the baby was coming.

---

Lemons and strawberries do not ripen after being picked. Avocados and bananas do.

## SHOW ME THE MONEY

The Toronto-Dominion Bank loaned businessman Edward Del Grande $3.5 million in 1990. In 1995, when he didn't pay them back, they sued him. Del Grande countersued...for $30 million. His charge: the bank ruined him by loaning him too much money. Case dismissed.

## LOTT O' LUCK

A man from Sherbrooke, Quebec, sued the provincial lottery, Loto-Quebec, for fooling him into believing he could actually win. He said that they sold only losing tickets, something he could prove by showing the $840 worth of losing tickets he'd bought in the month of March alone. The man, who is on welfare, sued the lottery for $879.58. Lawyers predicted an out of court settlement.

## DWV

In 2004 a 54-year-old man was pulled over by Ontario Provincial Police on Highway 400 in Toronto because he was playing the violin while driving. He said he was on his way to a performance and needed to warm up.

## CANADIAN ACHIN'

• A Saskatchewan wildlife officer was attempting to "mercy kill" a wounded moose when the slug from his rifle missed, hit a tree, and ricocheted into a fellow officer's leg. The wounded moose was put down; the wounded officer was not—he made a full recovery.

• In 1952, Stan Long, 23, of the Victoria Cougars hockey team in British Columbia, had his left thigh completely pierced by a hockey stick. The defenseman had collided with another player whose stick had just broken and was saved only by the fact that there was a doctor in the stands. He recovered from the wound and eventually played hockey again.

• A 19-year-old woman from Ontario was injured in 2005 when her car collided with a Molson Beer truck. The crash on Toronto's Highway 401 caused the truck to flip over. Both drivers received only minor injuries, but 2,184 cases of beer spilled onto the highway in the middle of the morning rush hour. Traffic was held up for hours in what one officer described as a "sea of beer."

To introduce them to European ways, missionaries gave Native Americans flannel underwear.

# HISTORY'S MYTH-STORIES

*Hereth thum thtuff the hithtory bookth methed up.*

**M**yth: The United States first began to fight the threat of Soviet communism just after World War II, during the Cold War.

**Truth:** In August 1918, just after the end of World War I, President Woodrow Wilson sent 3,000 American troops into Russia to fight the communist Bolsheviks who had overthrown the czar in 1917. Civil war had broken out in the wake of the revolution. So, a coalition of British, French, Japanese, and American troops fought in two major divisions: one in Archangel (in northern Russia) and another near Vladivostok (in Siberia). But the allied fighting force was too small to defeat the Bolsheviks and prevent them from establishing a communist regime. Wilson pulled out all of his troops in 1920. Total American fatalities: 275.

**Myth:** Lincoln's Emancipation Proclamation freed the slaves.

**Truth:** Lincoln opposed slavery but thought it would die naturally without government interference. In any event, Lincoln's goal during the Civil War was preserving the Union, not abolishing slavery. The Emancipation Proclamation of 1862 didn't free slaves—it was an exertion of federal authority over the Southern states. (Although a futile one, since the Confederate states had declared themselves an independent nation, and weren't about to abide by the document.) Meanwhile, the Proclamation allowed Union-loyal slave states—Kentucky, Missouri, West Virginia, Maryland, and Delaware—to keep their slaves. Slavery wasn't eliminated until the passage of the Thirteenth Amendment to the Constitution in December 1865.

**Myth:** Julius Caesar was the first baby delivered by cesarean section, giving the procedure its name.

**Truth:** The idea that even as an infant, Caesar was so special he couldn't be born in the standard way may add to his mystique, but

---

Charles Darwin's *The Origin of Species* sold out its entire first edition (1,250 copies) in one day.

most historians agree that caesarean section, by any name, was not
practiced in ancient Rome. The act of delivering a baby via an
incision to a mother's abdomen gets its name from the Latin word
*caedere*, which means "to cut."

**Myth:** World War I was the first "world" war.
**Truth:** Historians cite at least six wars prior to World War I that
could be called "world wars." Based on the definition of a world
war as one large conflict that's fought simultaneously on multiple
fronts by numerous world powers, here's their list:

• The Nine Years War (1688–1697), in which the League of
Augsburg—England, Spain, Portugal, the Netherlands, Sweden,
and the Holy Roman Empire—fought against France. Battles were
fought all over Europe, as well as in the American colonies
(Native Americans fought on the French side).

• Queen Anne's War (1701–1714) saw France, Rome, England,
the Netherlands, and Austria battle for control of Spain.

• The War of Austrian Succession (1740–1748) and the Seven
Years' War (1756–1763), in which England, France, Bavaria,
Spain, Saxony, the Netherlands, Prussia, Russia, Sweden, Portugal,
and the houses of Hanover and Saxony fought over Austria.

• The French Revolution (1792–1802), in which French com-
moners overthrew the king, leading England, Prussia, Austria,
Spain, and the Netherlands to step in to restore the monarchy.

• The Napoleonic Wars (1803–1815), in which every European
power resisted Napoleon's attempt to conquer all of Europe.

World War I wasn't even called World War I until much later.
During the actual conflict it was called "the Great War."

\*　\*　\*

## THANK YOU, NEW ORLEANS, FOR...

Oysters Rockefeller, Fats Domino, shrimp scampi, jazz, the cock-
tail, jambalaya, Jelly Roll Morton, Cajun crawfish, Southern Comfort, the po' boy sandwich, dental floss, Anne Rice, poker, brunch
(started in the French Quarter), bananas Foster, the drum set, the
Neville Brothers, gumbo, the Higgins boat (landing craft used by
allied troops on D-Day), Mardi Gras, and Louis Armstrong.

# UNCLE JOHN'S STALL OF FAME

*Uncle John is amazed—and pleased—by the unusual ways
people get involved with bathrooms, toilets, toilet paper,
and so on. That's why he created the "Stall of Fame."*

**H**onoree: State Senator Al Lawson of Florida
**Notable Achievement:** Coming up with a "pay-as-you-go"
plan to help growing towns upgrade their sewer systems.
**True Story:** Lawson introduced a bill to place a tax of two cents
per roll on toilet paper. The money was to be used to fund the
sewer system improvements and to help fast-growing Florida communities cope with increasing demands on infrastructure. Lawson
estimated the tax could raise as much as $50 million a year. "Two
cents is not going to hurt families at all," he said. "People don't
mind paying for it." Governor Jeb Bush would not commit one way
or the other, but said that if toilet paper is taxed, people might use
less of it. "That's not necessarily a good thing," said the governor.

**Honoree:** Marcel Duchamp, one of the most important modern
artists of the 20th century
**Notable Achievement:** Elevating a restroom urinal to high art
**True Story:** In 1917 Duchamp paid $6 to enter one of his pieces
in the Society of Independent Artists exhibit in New York. But
rather than enter a painting or some other standard work of art,
Duchamp entered what he called a "ready-made": he took an
everyday object, in this case a restroom urinal, gave it the title
*Fountain*, and entered it unchanged. He signed the work "R. Mutt."

Exhibit organizers tried to block Duchamp's entry, but the rules
did not allow them to prevent an artist from showing his work.
Still, they wanted to know why they should consider a urinal a
piece of art. "Because I said so," Duchamp told them. That remark
is considered emblematic of the attitude of an entire generation of
artists. Because of this, in a 2004 survey of top artists, *Fountain*
beat out works by Pablo Picasso, Henri Matisse, and Andy Warhol
to be voted the most influential work of art of the 20th century.

**Honoree:** A pet dog living in the village of Mundhaghar, India

**Notable Achievement:** Surviving a night locked in a bathroom with a leopard...without suffering a scratch

**True Story:** Think finding a spider in your bathroom is bad? One morning in 2005 some villagers in Mundhaghar heard a leopard growling in theirs. Somehow it had gotten in during the night. They called the police, who opened the door and were stunned to see the family's dog in there, too. "By some miracle, the leopard hadn't harmed the dog, even as they spent the night together in the small room," a police inspector told reporters. The leopard now lives in a zoo; at last report the dog was healthy but "still terrified."

**Honoree:** An Australian bus driver who wishes to remain anonymous

**Notable Achievement:** Turning a pit stop into a jackpot

**True Story:** The bus driver was in the middle of his route when he needed to take a bathroom break. There were no customers on the bus, so he pulled into a local casino to make use of their restroom (no word on why a casino and not a gas station). While there he played a couple of games of Keno—a numbers game similar to lotto—and won! Now, thanks to his bathroom break, he's $2.2 million richer.

**Honoree:** Anthony Stone, a worker at the Corus steel plant in Port Talbot, Wales

**Notable Achievement:** Taking a bathroom break that saved his life

**True Story:** On November 8, 2001, Stone was working at the plant when he had a sudden urge to go to the bathroom. It wasn't the kind of urge that could be put off, so Stone excused himself. As he was rounding the corner next to the restroom, the blast furnace he'd just been standing next to exploded, killing three people and injuring 12 more. "It was like an atomic bomb going off," Stone said. "I would not be here if I had been five seconds later."

\*　　　\*　　　\*

"Always go to the bathroom when you have the chance."

—**King George V (England)**

---

Don't have a ruler? Don't worry—a dollar bill is exactly six inches long.

# EARTH'S GREATEST HITS

*Every so often a hunk of rock hurtles out of the sky and slams into our planet, creating a gigantic hole and wreaking havoc. Here are some of the more impressive cosmic splats.*

## CHICXULUB, YUCATÁN

About 65 million years ago, a giant meteor six miles wide splashed down in the Caribbean region of Mexico. It probably split in two shortly before impact. The result: *two* craters that are a combined 102 miles in diameter. The meteors fell in a sulfur-rich area of the Yucatán Peninsula, kicking up billions of tons of poisonous dust. The sky all over the world was dark for six months, making global temperatures drop below freezing. That climate change, according to most scientists, caused the extinction of half the Earth's existing species…including the dinosaurs.

## GRAND TETONS, WYOMING

In 1972 a 1,000-ton meteor entered the Earth's atmosphere high above the Grand Tetons at a very shallow angle and then skipped back out into space like a stone skipping off the surface of a lake (but not before being recorded by Air Force and tourist photographers). If it had gone all the way through the atmosphere, it would have hit Canada and the impact would have rocked the area with a blast the size of the Hiroshima A-bomb.

## TUNGUSKA, SIBERIA

On June 30, 1908, Russian settlers north of Lake Baikal saw a giant fireball streak across the sky. Moments later a blinding flash lit up the sky, followed by a shock wave that knocked people off their feet 40 miles away. The blast was estimated to be more than 10 megatons, toppling 60 million trees over an area of 830 square miles. What was startling about the Tunguska blast was that there was no crater, which led to speculation about the blast: A black hole passing through the Earth? The annihilation of a chunk of antimatter falling from space? An exploding alien spaceship? Research ultimately revealed that the devastation was caused by a meteor about 450 feet in diameter that exploded four to six miles above the ground. If it had landed on a city, no one would have survived.

---

Wal-Mart's annual income is nearly equal to that of Russia.

## ARRINGER METEOR CRATER, ARIZONA

Located in the middle of the desert, this crater is important because it was the first one on Earth positively identified as the result of a falling meteor. The meteorite that made the crater was about 150 feet in diameter, weighed about 300,000 tons, and was traveling at a speed of 40,000 mph when it landed. The crater is three quarters of a mile wide and was named for D. M. Barringer, the mining engineer who correctly identified it. He also believed that the actual meteorite was still lodged below the Earth's surface and could be mined for its iron content. (He died before studies revealed that it had vaporized on impact.) Scientists say a meteor of this size can be expected to hit the Earth every 50,000 years. Since this one fell to Earth about 49,000 years ago, we could be due for another one soon.

## METEOR FACTS

• So far 150 impact craters have been identified on the Earth's surface.

• Oldest crater on Earth: Vredefort Crater in South Africa. It's two billion years old.

• Meteors the size of a basketball hit Earth once a month.

• More than 25,000 meteors bigger than 3.5 ounces hit every year.

• Meteors as large as the one that hit Tunguska impact the Earth every 100 years or so. Bigger explosions, the size of the largest H-bombs, take place about once every 1,000 years.

• Terminology: in space it's a *meteor*; on the ground, it's a *meteorite*.

• A large meteorite is always cold to the touch. The outer layers are burned off from its trip through the atmosphere; the inner layers retain the cold of deep space.

• Preview of the big one? In 1994 the comet Shoemaker-Levy 9 slammed into the atmosphere of Jupiter, generating an explosion the equivalent of 300 trillion tons of TNT. The comet was estimated to be three miles in diameter; the hole it made was larger than Earth. If it had hit our planet instead of Jupiter...well, you do the math.

# NAME THAT VOICE

*You hear these voices all the time—on TV, at the movies, on your computer, even on the telephone. But you probably don't know anything about the people behind them.*

## DON PARDO

D Born Dominick Pardo in 1918 in Westfield, Massachusetts, his voice-over career began on NBC Radio in 1944, and he's been working for the network ever since. He moved to NBC-TV in 1950 and over the next 25 years was the announcer for some of the most popular game shows. He was the first to say, "It can be yours...if the price is right!" and worked an 11-year stint on the original *Jeopardy!* Pardo was also the first person to tell the nation that President Kennedy had been shot, reading the bulletin at 1:32 p.m. on November 22, 1963.

In 1975 Lorne Michaels was putting together *Saturday Night Live* and asked NBC if he could use Pardo to announce the show. He thought a trusted and familiar voice would add credibility to a show that was going to feature otherwise unknown talent. NBC agreed, Pardo took the job, and he's still there, having worked more years on *SNL* than anyone else...including Lorne Michaels. Now in his 80s, Pardo has slowed down somewhat (when he's not up to doing the opening, *SNL* cast member Darrell Hammond pitches in by impersonating Pardo's voice), but he still works as often as he wants. Pardo is one of only two people who have been given a lifetime contract by NBC; the other was Bob Hope.

## ELWOOD EDWARDS

Edwards was a professional voice-over man in the 1980s, working mostly in local Ohio markets. In 1987 he was in one of cyberspace's first-ever chat rooms and met a woman with whom he began a correspondence. The two soon fell in love and got married. Edwards's new bride just happened to work at a company called Quantum Computer Services. In 1989 she overheard her boss saying that he wanted to add a human voice to their new e-mail software. She suggested her husband for the job, so they had him make a tape. From his living room, Edwards recorded a few phrases: "Welcome," "You've got mail," "File's done," and

"Good-bye." Shortly after, the company changed its name to America Online. For the past 15 years, millions of people a day have been greeted by Edwards's voice on AOL.

## DON LAFONTAINE

Don LaFontaine has lent his deep, throaty voice to more than 4,000 movie trailers over the past 40 years—in fact, he single-handedly *invented* the modern movie trailer. Before LaFontaine came along, movie trailers were quickly thrown together by the film's editors as more of an afterthought than a solid marketing tool, and they came *after* the feature (hence the term "trailer"). In 1962 LaFontaine was working as a recording engineer in New York when he was given the task of creating some promotional spots for the movie *Dr. Strangelove*. He enjoyed the process, and his boss, Floyd Peterson, liked the result. So the two men formed a company whose sole purpose was to create movie trailers. Most of the now-cliché phrases ("In a world where…" and "Nowhere to run. Nowhere to hide. And no way out…") were written by LaFontaine. Although he no longer writes the copy, he still records several trailers a week and jokes that when friends ask him to recommend a movie, he describes it as "the white-knuckle rollercoaster ride of the summer," or as "a very special motion picture that speaks to the soul of every man and every woman who's ever been in love."

## BILLY WEST

As a child, West's hero was Mel Blanc, the man behind dozens of cartoon voices. He spent hours trying to imitate all of Blanc's characters and discovered that he had a natural talent. He tried a career as a stand-up comic but gave it up in 1978 and dedicated himself full-time to creating cartoon voices. It took West a decade in the business before he landed his first big role as Cecil on the 1988 cartoon *Beany and Cecil*. Cartoonist John Kricfalusi directed it and thought West would be perfect for the voice of a dim-witted cat he was creating. West took the job and eventually voiced both main characters on the cult Nickelodeon cartoon *The Ren & Stimpy Show*. From there, he landed one great role after another, voicing some of the most popular characters of our time: Bugs Bunny (originally done by Mel Blanc) and Elmer Fudd in the feature film *Space Jam*; George Jetson for a Radio Shack advertising campaign; the red M&M on the M&M commercials; and several main characters on Fox's *Futurama*, including Fry, Professor Farnsworth, Doctor Zoidberg, and Captain Zapp Brannigan.

## JANE BARBE

Very few people who knew Jane Barbe had any idea how famous she was. Her normal speaking voice had a friendly Southern drawl, quite different from the way she spoke to over 20 million people a day: "Your call cannot be completed as dialed. Please check the number and dial again." Or, "At the tone, the time will be…"

The one-time professional singer (she once toured with the Buddy Morrow Orchestra) began making telephone announcements in the mid-1960s for an Atlanta, Georgia, phone company. Over the next 40 years she recorded automated messages for phone companies, hotel chains, corporations, and cell phone voice mails. Barbe passed away in 2003 at age 74, but her voice lives on—even if it sometimes isn't hers. Most new voice-mail systems hire women who sound like Barbe to record their menu options.

## DON MESSICK

Messick was an out-of-work ventriloquist in the late 1940s when he got his start at MGM. One day, the regular voice actor for the cartoon character Droopy Dog wasn't available, and neither was another voice actor, Daws Butler. Butler recommended his friend Don Messick to the director, and Messick did so well in the role that he eventually took it over. In 1957, when Hanna-Barbera broke off from MGM and started their own company, Messick and Butler went with them as the two main voice talents. Butler got the lead parts such as Yogi Bear or Huckleberry Hound, while Messick was relegated to mostly sound effects, supporting roles such as Boo-Boo Bear or Ranger Smith, and narration for all the old Hanna-Barbera cartoons.

His most famous role came in 1969 when he was asked to create a voice for a scaredy-cat dog named Scooby-Doo. "I had to come up with what I call 'growl talk,'" he later recalled. Messick played Scooby until his death in 1997. Other characters he voiced along the way: Scrappy-Doo, Astro the Dog, Bamm-Bamm Rubble, Papa Smurf, and Hamton J. Pig from *Tiny Toon Adventures*.

Q: Where do you keep your *vibrissae*? A: In your nose (they're nose hairs).

# GO, GRANNY, GO!

*The good, the bad, and the grandma.*

## TAKE MY WHAT?

In June 2005 91-year-old Katherine Woodworth was walking through the parking lot of a Toledo, Ohio, department store when a young man approached her. "I didn't have my hearing aid in," she told reporters later, "and I thought he said he was going to take my *pulse*, and I said, 'No, you're not.'" Woodworth proceeded to whack the would-be robber with her purse and continued hitting him until he finally ran to a car and sped off. Another shopper got the license plate number and a short time later, 20-year-old Matthew Spradlin was arrested. The arresting officer, Sgt. Tim Hanus said he was surprised (and amused). Woodworth was too. "I'll be 92 in August," she said, "and I guess I've got more nerve now than when I was younger."

## WALK SOFTLY, AND CARRY A BIG SHOVEL

One April day, 90-year-old Mildred Luce looked out her window to a horrifying scene: a bobcat had the head of her cat, Smudge, in its mouth. Luce, who lives alone in northern Maine, ran out the door, grabbed a snow shovel, and clamped it down on the bobcat's neck. But it wouldn't let go of her cat. So, what did she do? "I took hold of its head with my hand and pulled on its tail—and Smudge popped out." The kitty immediately bolted into the house…and the bobcat ran in after her. Luckily, it became confused, and Luce (with a neighbor's help) was able to lock it in the bathroom, where it was later snared by police. Asked what it felt like to grab a bobcat by the tail, Luce told reporters, "I had no fear of it. I was just interested in saving Smudge."

## KEEP-A-GOIN'

Eighty-year-old Marian Foulkes of Melbourne, Australia, wanted to renew her driver's license but was denied. Her husband, Tom, also in his 80s, had already lost his license, and they were angry. So they got in their car and hit the road. Over the next two weeks the unlicensed duo evaded police on a 1,400-mile joy ride from southern to northern Australia and halfway back again. At that point they were stopped by a policeman and had their keys taken away...so they got on a bus and continued the trip. A few days later, they were finally located in a hotel in Canberra. The couple's son, Paul, told Reuters that his parents were afraid of losing their freedom. "The desire to be independent, it's the human spirit isn't it? They said they had had a good time—they called it a holiday."

## SHE'S STILL SHARP(SHOOTER)

Janet Grammer is a great-great-grandmother...and a pretty good shot. In April 2005 she was working in a convenience store in Jacksonville, Florida, when a man walked in, fired two shots at the back wall, and demanded money. Instead of giving him the cash, she grabbed a pistol from under the counter and shot the thief in the chest. He fell to the ground, then got up and ran out of the store. Police later arrested him (he'd checked into a hospital). The mother of 10, grandmother of 32, great-grandmother of three, and great-great-grandmother of three wasn't happy about shooting the man. "All I could think about was his poor parents," she told police.

## DO THE BUMP

A 77-year-old German woman was standing at a street corner in Dresden waiting for the light to change when a man walked by, bumped her with his backpack, and continued walking across the street. That ticked her off. She yelled at the man and ran after him, then grabbed him by the hair and tackled him. A passerby called the police, and the woman sat on the man until they arrived. The judge ignored the assault...and fined the man for jaywalking.

## UH-OH, IT'S SNEAKY GRANNY

Florida resident Margaret Anderson was arrested at Fort Lauderdale Airport in November 2004 because of a "book" she had in her tote bag. It was actually a gun case with a pistol and seven bullets nestled inside. Anderson claimed that she had forgotten the cleverly hidden single-shot Colt derringer was there. Freed on $1,000 bond, the 79-year-old faced felony charges that could put her in jail for five years. "I'm awful sorry," she said when released, "I wouldn't harm a soul."

The 1900 Paris Olympics included events in billiards, checkers, and fishing.

# WARNING LABELS

*Some things in life should go without saying, but it seems there's always somebody who needs to be told not to eat a mattress.*

**On a can of insect spray:**
"Harmful to bees."

**On a life-saving device:**
"This is not a life-saving device."

**On children's cough syrup:**
"Do not drive car or operate machinery."

**On a motorcycle mirror:**
"Objects in the mirror are actually behind you."

**On garden furniture:**
"Keep away from damp and sunlight."

**On a box of sleeping pills:**
"May cause drowsiness."

**On a milk bottle:**
"After opening, keep upright."

**On a bag of peanuts:**
"This product contains nuts."

**On a water heater:**
"If building in which heater resides is on fire, do not go into building."

**On a mattress:**
"Do not attempt to swallow."

**On a TV remote control:**
"Not dishwasher safe."

**On a garden hose:**
"May cause cancer in California."

**On an iron:**
"Never iron clothes on the body."

**On a graduation gown:**
"Do not wash or dry clean."

**On a video game console:**
"Do not attempt to stick head inside deck, which may result in injury."

**On a bottle of aspirin:**
"Do not take if allergic to aspirin."

**On a chainsaw:**
"Do not attempt to stop chain with hands or genitals."

**On a birthday card:**
"Not suitable for children aged 36 months or less."

**On a wristwatch:**
"This is not underwear. Do not put in pants."

**On a hammer:**
"Do not use to strike any solid object."

**On a curling iron:**
"For external use only."

---

Winston Churchill once designed greeting cards for Hallmark.

# BRAND NAMES

*We all know these businesses—many are a part of our
everyday lives. Here's where their names came from?*

## IKEA

Even when he was a kid growing up in Agunnaryd, Sweden, in the 1930s, Ingvar Kamprad had a head for business. He started out buying matches in bulk in Stockholm and selling them at a profit back in Agunnaryd. With the money he made, he expanded into pencils, pens, flower seeds, and anything else he thought his neighbors might want to buy. By the time he was 17, he was ready to give his business a name. He added his own initials (I.K.) to the first letter of the farm he grew up on (Elmtaryd), and the first letter of the village of Agunnaryd. In 1947 Kamprad added furniture to his product line; it sold so well that he stopped selling anything else. Today he has 200 stores in 32 countries around the world and sells more than $15 billion worth of furniture a year.

## BLUE CROSS & BLUE SHIELD

As late as the 1920s, the American health-care system was organized on a pay-as-you-go basis: If you got sick, you had hospital bills. If you didn't get sick, you didn't. Then in 1929 former Dallas school superintendent Justin Kimball was hired to run Baylor University's school of medicine in Dallas. One of his first challenges: a stack of unpaid hospital bills from former schoolteachers, who were poorly paid and couldn't afford medical care.

Kimball knew that hazardous industries like mining, logging, and railroads paid for medical care in advance by paying doctors a regular monthly fee for their services. He decided to develop the same kind of plan for workers in a *non*-hazardous profession. In exchange for a monthly payment of 50 cents, the 1,300 teachers in the Dallas school system could receive up to 21 days of hospitalization per year at Baylor's hospital. Bonus: the system improved the overall quality of medical care by guaranteeing hospitals a regular stream of income, instead of one that dried up whenever the economy tanked and people couldn't afford to go to the doctor.

The idea was copied all over the country, and in 1934 a Minnesota organization wanted to come up with a logo that symbolized their emphasis on helping people, kind of like the American Red Cross. How about a *blue* cross? Five years later a Buffalo, New York, health-care provider adopted a blue *shield* as their symbol. (Blue Cross and Blue Shield merged in 1982.)

## STAPLES

In the summer of 1985 a supermarket executive named Tom Stemberg lost his job and had to look for a new one. He spent the July 4th weekend writing up a business plan...and then his type-writer ribbon broke. He was stuck—it was a holiday weekend, and the local stationery store was closed. The experience caused him to scrap his original business plan and write one for an entirely new kind of business: a supermarket that sold office supplies and nothing else. Instead of going to small stationers with limited inventory and high prices, his customers could grab a shopping cart and wander aisles crammed with affordably priced office sup-plies. Stemberg wanted a simple name for his stores, and he decid-ed to name it after one of the simplest office supplies of all—the staple.

## HOLIDAY INN

In the summer of 1951, a Memphis real estate developer named Kemmons Wilson and his wife packed their five kids into their car and hit the road for a two-week trip to Washington, D.C. The trip was fun—except for the hotels they stayed in. They were usually dirty, didn't have restaurants, and there was nothing for the kids to do.

Where others saw grimy walls and cigarette butts extinguished on bathroom floors, Wilson saw a business opportunity. By the time the trip was over he was already planning a chain of clean, affordable, family-friendly hotels, crammed with freebies like air-conditioning, parking, ice machines, and swimming pools, all at no extra charge. Wilson was a big Bing Crosby fan, so when it came time to pick a name for his hotels, he decided to name them after the crooner's 1942 film, *Holiday Inn*. Today there are more than 1,000 Holiday Inns around the world; the company estimates that 96 percent of all Americans have stayed in one at least once in their lives.

# A BARREL OF LAUGHS

*This letter is a classic piece of American humor. It's been around
in various forms for nearly a century, appearing in dozens of books
and movies, and even in a* Saturday Night Live *sketch in 2004. This
version is a memo to an insurance company, but there are many others.
The tale has now been passed around so often that it's achieved urban
legend status—in other words, some people believe it's true. It's
not. In fact, it was written in 1902 by Will Rogers. (Not
really, we just thought we'd add to the legend.)*

D ear Sir:
I am writing in response to your request for
additional information in Block 3 of the
accident report form. I put "poor planning" as the
cause of my accident. You asked for a fuller
explanation, and I trust the following details
will be sufficient.

I was alone on the roof of a new six-story
building. When I completed my work, I found that I
had some bricks left over which, when weighed
later, were found to be slightly more than 500
pounds. Rather than carry the bricks down by hand,
I decided to lower them in a barrel by using a
pulley that was attached to the side of the building on the sixth floor.

I secured the rope at ground level, climbed to
the roof, swung the barrel out, and loaded the
bricks into it. Then I climbed back down and
untied the rope, holding tightly to ensure a slow
descent of the bricks.

You will notice in Block 11 of the accident
report form that I weigh 135 pounds. Due to my
surprise at being jerked off the ground so suddenly, I lost my presence of mind and forgot to let
go of the rope. Needless to say, I proceeded at a
rapid rate up the side of the building.

Somewhere in the vicinity of the third floor, I

---

Well, at least the wings taste good: The longest recorded flight of a chicken is 13 seconds.

met the barrel, which was now proceeding downward at an equally impressive speed. This explains the fractured skull and the broken collar bone, as listed in section 3 of the accident form.

Slowed down slightly, I continued my rapid ascent, not stopping until the fingers on my right hand were two knuckles deep into the pulley.

Fortunately, by this time I had regained my presence of mind and was able to hold tightly to the rope—in spite of beginning to experience a great deal of pain. At approximately the same time, however, the barrel of bricks hit the ground and the bottom fell out of the barrel. Now devoid of the weight of the bricks, the barrel weighed approximately 50 pounds.

(I refer you again to my weight.)

As you can imagine, I began a rapid descent down the side of the building. Somewhere in the vicinity of the third floor, I met the barrel coming up. This accounts for the two fractured ankles, the broken tooth, and the lacerations of my legs and lower body.

Here my luck began to change slightly. The encounter with the barrel seemed to slow me enough to lessen my injuries when I fell on the pile of bricks; fortunately, only three vertebrae were cracked.

I am sorry to report, however, that as I lay there on the pile of bricks—in pain and unable to move—I again lost my composure and presence of mind and let go of the rope; I could only lay there watching as the empty barrel begin its journey back down towards me. This explains the two broken legs.

I hope this answers your questions.

Sincerely,

Thomas L.

# WHAT SIDE ARE YOU ON?

*Which side is the right side of the road?*

**B**ACKGROUND
For most of known human history, people have traveled on the left side of the road. Historians think there's a simple explanation: since most travelers were right-handed, bearing left kept their sword arm between them and any oncoming threat. Here are some important landmarks on the road to the decision: Left side or right side?

• The first known drive-side regulation dates from the Zhou Dynasty's *Book of Rites*, 1100 B.C., although it appears to be more about social protocol than traffic flow: "The right side of the road is for men, the left side for women, and the center for carriages."

• The Romans were probably left-side drivers. Researchers determined this after examining a well-preserved Roman road going in and out of a stone quarry in England and noting that the deeper ruts were on the left side. Why does that make the Romans left-side drivers? It's assumed that the carts went in empty and came out full.

• In 1300, Pope Boniface VIII ordered all pilgrims traveling to Rome to keep to the left.

• In 1756 the British passed the first modern keep-left rule.

• Pennsylvania countered with a keep-right rule in 1792. France followed suit in 1794, New York in 1804. Why the divergence? Drivers wanted to sit close to the center of the road so that they could see the wheels of oncoming wagons and steer clear. Teamsters in the United States and France drove large wagons drawn by more than one team of horses. The driver sat on the left rear horse so he could reach the entire team with his whip. The English used smaller wagons. Drivers sat on the right side of the wagon, so their whips wouldn't get caught on the load behind them.

• Napoleon enforced the keep-right rule in every country he con-

---

For centuries, many Europeans refused to eat potatoes. (They're not mentioned in the Bible.)

quered, which by 1814 was most of Europe. It's thought he insisted on the change because he was left-handed, which made the right side of the road the advantageous side. Even after his defeat and exile, Napoleon's former dominions kept to the right.

• The states that resisted Napoleon—England, Austria, Hungary, Russia, Portugal, Denmark, and Sweden—clung to the left side of the road rule. Denmark went right in 1793 but otherwise the left/right division of Europe stayed intact until after World War I.

• European countries brought their left- or right-side driving practices to the lands they colonized. That's why drivers in Morocco, Algeria, Senegal, the Ivory Coast, and all of Latin America drive on the right. Those in India, Kenya, Uganda, Australia, and New Zealand hug the left.

• By the American Civil War, every state in the Union and the Confederacy drove on the right.

• Japan officially went left in 1859, due, some scholars say, to pressure from the British. But historical evidence shows that the Japanese were always left-siders and unlike Westerners, they still bear to the left when they walk on the streets today.

• The emerging dominance of the U.S. automobile industry in the early 20th century pushed more and more countries into adopting right-side drive. Canada, which had previously gone both ways (French-speaking provinces were righties; English, lefties) finally succumbed to the economic pressure from its southern neighbor. Newfoundland was the last province to go right, in 1947.

• When the Nazis invaded Austria, Czechoslovakia, and Hungary during World War II, Hitler forced them to change overnight to right-side drive. The change created havoc because drivers couldn't see traffic signs.

• Sweden was the most recent European country to switch from left to right. It made the move in 1967. Only four European countries still drive on the left—the United Kingdom, Ireland, Malta, and Cyprus.

• As of 2005, 168 countries drive on the right, 75 on the left. That comes to four billion people on the right, two billion on the left.

---

Ernest Hemingway read his own obituary in papers after his plane crashed in 1954.

# BRITS VS. YANKS

*As playwright George Bernard Shaw said, "England and America are two countries separated by a common language." See if you can match the British words to their American counterparts. (Answers on page 519.)*

| BRITISH | AMERICAN |
|---|---|
| 1) Trainers | a) Potato chips |
| 2) Boot | b) Zucchini |
| 3) Plaster | c) Naked |
| 4) Wireless | d) Car hood |
| 5) Courgette | e) Sweater |
| 6) Rubber | f) Apron |
| 7) Estate car | g) Lawyer |
| 8) Bonnet | h) Car trunk |
| 9) Nappy | i) Speed bump |
| 10) Crisps | j ) Bandage |
| 11) Jumper | k) Vest |
| 12) Pinny | l) Swimsuit |
| 13) Cozzy | m) Liquor store |
| 14) Gum | n) Bacon slice |
| 15) Pram | o) Doctor's office |
| 16) Rasher | p) Pharmacist |
| 17) Starkers | q) Eraser |
| 18) Surgery | r) Radio |
| 19) Chemist | s) Glue |
| 20) Solicitor | t) Diaper |
| 21) Waistcoat | u) Sneakers |
| 22) Off-license | v) Baby carriage |
| 23) Sleeping policeman | w) Station wagon |

Bathrooms in British Ramada Inns are stocked with complimentary rubber duckies.

# POLITALKS

*Politicians don't get much respect these days—but then,
it sounds like they don't deserve much, either.*

"I believe what I said yesterday. I don't know what I said, but I know what I think, and, well, I assume it's what I said."
—**Donald Rumsfeld**

"You bet we might have!"
—**Sen. John Kerry, asked if he would have invaded Iraq**

"I have a few flaws—people sometimes have to correct my English. I knew I had a problem when Arnold Schwarzenegger started doing it."
—**George W. Bush**

"Instead of 'closing,' I meant 'securing.' I think maybe my English, I need to go back to school and study a little bit."
—**Arnold Schwarzenegger, on saying the U.S. should close its borders**

"If I could only go through the ducts and leap out onstage in a cape—that's my dream."
—**Ralph Nader, on missing the presidential debates**

"As I was telling my hus—as I was telling President Bush…"
—**Secretary of State Condoleezza Rice**

"Get some devastation in the background."
—**Sen. Bill Frist, posing for a photo in tsunami-ravaged Sri Lanka**

"I'm undaunted in my quest to amuse myself by constantly changing my hair."
—**Hillary Clinton**

"'Ever' is a very strong word."
—**Rep. Tom DeLay, asked if he had ever crossed the line of ethical behavior**

"It's been a great ride, but I know how quickly these fads can pass. You all remember the pet rock, the mood ring, Howard Dean."
—**Sen. Barack Obama, after being elected**

"I wish we lived in the day where you could challenge a person to a duel."
—**Sen. Zell Miller**

"My vision is to make this the most diverse state on Earth, and we have people from every planet on Earth in this state."
—**California Governor Gray Davis**

General appearance: The social status of a Roman was indicated by the stripes on his toga.

# ANIMAL SCIENCE

*We can't duck this issue—so we'll have to grin and bear it. We're dog tired, so we're going to take a cat nap. (We're not lion.)*

## NOT ALL DUCKS QUACK ALIKE

**Study:** British researcher Victoria de Rijke wondered whether all ducks quacked exactly the same way or if their "speech" varied from location to location. So she started studying one group in downtown London and another living in the countryside near Cornwall in southwest England.

**Findings:** "There are definite differences," de Rijke says. "The London ducks are noisier, laughing raucously; the Cornish ones are soft and chilled out." She speculates that London ducks quack louder because they have to fight to be heard over the noise of the city.

## DOGS CAN DETECT CANCER

**Study:** Anecdotal evidence of cancer-sniffing canines dates back centuries, but scientists didn't get serious about testing the phenomenon until recently. In 2004 the British medical journal *BMI* published the results of a study in which dogs were tested on their ability to detect bladder cancer by sniffing urine samples. Six dogs were trained to lie down next to a sample from a person with bladder cancer. Then each dog was presented with seven different urine samples: six from healthy people and a seventh from a person with bladder cancer. The study was a "double blind" experiment, meaning neither the dogs nor the people administering the study knew which urine samples were which.

**Findings:** If the dogs had no ability to detect bladder cancer, the odds that they would pick the correct sample would only be one in seven, or just over 14 percent. The dogs were able to pick out the cancerous sample 40 percent of the time, and two of the dogs were correct 60 percent of the time. "The results are unambiguous," *BMI* reported. "Dogs can be trained to recognize and flag bladder cancer."

**Note:** The CBS TV show *60 Minutes* asked the researchers to recreate the study on camera. This time the dogs did poorly—they kept identifying a particular non-cancerous urine sample as being cancerous. "But," says Andy Cook, their trainer, "the hospital had confidence in our dogs, so they sent the sample off for further tests. And they were completely blown away when it came back that this patient not only had cancer on his kidney but also had bladder cancer."

## BEARS PREFER HONDAS

**Study:** In the mid-1990s, Yosemite National Park spent more than $1 million on "bear safes"—bear-proof food lockers for the park's campsites. The idea was to teach bears that the food in the campgrounds was beyond reach. Instead, campers got the idea that if food was safe in a metal locker, it would be safe in their metal cars, too. Wrong. Cars are much flimsier—bears can easily smash the windows and even peel car doors right out of their frames. After the lockers went in, the number of car "cloutings" went up 600%.

**Finding:** Park rangers kept statistics on the cars that are broken into, and the bears seem to show a particular preference for certain brands, namely Hondas and Toyotas. In a two-month study of "bear incidents," they broke into 26 Hondas and 21 Toyotas, but only two Buicks and one Lexus. What is it about these cars that makes the bears prefer them over others? No one knows for sure.

## ELEPHANTS DO IMPRESSIONS

**Study:** Mlaika is a 10-year-old female African elephant who lives in a stockade in Tsavo, Kenya; Calimero is a 23-year-old male African elephant who lives with two Asian elephants at the Basel Zoo in Switzerland. When both animals were observed making unusual sounds—Mlaika "rumbled" and Calimero "chirped"—an international team of scientists started studying them to try to understand what was happening.

**Findings:** After carefully studying the acoustics of the sounds of the elephants and their surrounding environments, the scientists concluded that both animals were mimicking sounds they heard around them: Mlaika was imitating the sound of trucks passing by on a highway about two miles away, and Calimero was copying the sounds made by the Asian elephants he lived with. Until now, African elephants have never been known to make the chirping sounds of Asian elephants. In fact, Mlaika and Calimero are the first non-primate land mammals ever to exhibit an ability to mimic.

Howdy, cousin: A dolphin's closest relatives on land are horses and cows.

## DOLPHINS ARE SOCIAL BUTTERFLIES

**Study:** Researchers from the University of Aberdeen (Scotland) and the University of Michigan traveled to New Zealand to study the social behavior of dolphins.

**Findings:** It has long been known that dolphins live in "pods," clans of about a dozen dolphins each. They exhibit sophisticated social interactions, such as playing together, hunting in groups, and coming to the aid of other dolphins who are injured or in danger. But the New Zealand researchers observed a type of behavior never noted before: some dolphins act as "liaisons" between different pods. When these liaisons were present, the pod socialized regularly with other pods nearby. But when those dolphins went away, the pods stopped socializing with each other until the liaison dolphins returned, at which time they started socializing again.

## DO LOBSTERS FEEL PAIN?

**Study:** It's a question that many a seafood lover has asked as a live lobster is being dropped into a pot of boiling water. To answer it, the Norwegian government commissioned a scientific study headed by Dr. Wenche Farstad of the University of Oslo. The country was in the process of revising its animal welfare laws and wanted to find out if lobsters should be protected. The team didn't spend a lot of time boiling lobsters—instead, they researched all available scientific literature on invertebrates, including crabs, worms, slugs, snails, clams (and lobsters); then in 2005, the team presented its findings.

**Findings:** It's very unlikely that lobsters feel any pain when they're being cooked—their brains are too small to read the information as pain. The same goes for worms that are used as fish bait. "The common earthworm has a very simple nervous system," Farstad says. "It seems to be only reflex curling when put on the hook. They might sense something, but it is not painful and does not compromise their well-being."

Will this study change any minds about lobster boiling? Animal rights groups like People for the Ethical Treatment of Animals (PETA) point out that Norway has a large fishing industry and isn't exactly unbiased when it comes to studying lobsters. "This is exactly like the tobacco industry claiming that smoking doesn't cause cancer," says PETA spokeswoman Karin Robertson.

# DOUBLE TROUBLE

*It might be great to have an identical twin—you could*
*switch places in school, on dates, on the job, etc. But as these*
*sets of twins demonstrate, it's not always twice as nice.*

**TWINS:** Brian and Ryan Clausen of Greenville, Texas

**BACKGROUND:** At only two months of age in 1983, Brian and Ryan were more alike even than most identical twins: they were not only the same height and weight, but both also had the same birthmark on their foreheads and a smaller middle toe on their right feet. So how did their parents, Butch and Gwyen Clausen, tell them apart? By labeling their clothing and being very, very careful.

**DOUBLE TROUBLE:** That system worked great…for a while. But one day in December, Butch got their clothes mixed up and Gwyen's sister changed the babies' diapers before Butch could straighten them out. Then Gwyen changed the babies' diapers a second time; that's when things really got confusing. Was the kid wearing Ryan's clothes Ryan or Brian? Was "Brian" Brian or Ryan?

**WHAT HAPPENED:** Some people probably would have just started over, picking one of the kids to be Brian and one to be Ryan; Butch and Gwyen hired a private detective. He took the case to the district attorney's office, and after poring over dozens of sets of maternity ward footprints, they got a match: the baby wearing Ryan's shirt was Ryan, and the other baby was Brian.

**TWINS:** John and Glen Winslow, 38

**BACKGROUND:** If you were an identical twin *and* had a warrant out for your arrest, what would you do if you got pulled over for speeding? When John Winslow was pulled over in Council Bluffs, Nebraska, in July 2004, he didn't have his license with him, and he knew he had a misdemeanor warrant for damaging someone's property. So rather than admit who he was, he identified himself as *Glen* Winslow.

**DOUBLE TROUBLE:** What John didn't know at the time was that Glen was wanted by the police, too—for first-degree sexual assault. When John identified himself as Glen, the police immedi-

ately slapped the cuffs on him and hauled him off to jail.
**WHAT HAPPENED:** John confessed to furnishing false information to the police, but they weren't taking any chances. They held him until a fingerprint check confirmed that he really was John. Then he did 10 days in jail for the original property damage charge, for not having a driver's license, and for providing false information to police. A new arrest warrant went out for Glen; he was taken into custody in Omaha five days later.

**TWINS:** Angela and Sharon Statton, 19
**BACKGROUND:** In April 1997, Angela got into a heated argument with her boyfriend and called the police.
**DOUBLE TROUBLE:** When they arrived on the scene, the boyfriend lied and told them that Angela wasn't Angela, she was her sister, Sharon, who had a warrant out for her arrest for failing to appear in court on a shoplifting charge. Angela insisted she really *was* Angela, and to prove it she pleaded with the police to drive her to her mother's house to talk to the real Sharon.

Even after talking to the *real* Sharon, the police weren't convinced. They still suspected that Angela might really be Sharon and considered arresting both sisters, but decided they couldn't because they had only one arrest warrant. In the end they arrested Angela on Sharon's warrant and took her to jail.
**WHAT HAPPENED:** Angela spent four nights in jail before she got her day in court. Then she and Sharon appeared together and convinced the judge that Angela really was who she said she was. "I kept telling people, 'My name is not Sharon. It's Angela,'" Angela says. "They thought I was playing with them, but I wasn't. I sat in jail for nothing. But I'm just glad I'm out." Sharon was ordered to reappear at a later date to answer for the shoplifting and failure-to-appear charges, but no word on whether she showed up (or somebody else did).

\*　　\*　　\*

### COWBOY WISDOM
• Don't squat with your spurs on.
• Never slap a man who's chewin' tobacco.
• There's two theories to arguin' with a woman. Neither one works.

---

Russian Czar Ivan the Terrible once had an elephant killed because it did not bow to him.

# STRANGE TOURIST ATTRACTIONS

*Planning a vacation? Looking for something a little unusual? Next time you're traveling, you might want to consider one of these attractions.*

## FIELD OF DREAMS
**Location:** Dyersville, Iowa

**Background:** Every year more than 50,000 people visit the baseball field from the 1989 movie *Field of Dreams*. It actually straddles two farms: Al Ameskamp owns left and center field; Don Lansing owns the infield, right field, and the bleachers. Both have their own access roads and gift shops (they sell the same stuff).

**Be sure to see:** One Sunday a month, a local minor league baseball team dresses in early 1900s uniforms, hides in the cornfield, and then emerges to play catch with visitors.

## UNCLAIMED BAGGAGE CENTER
**Location:** Scottsboro, Alabama

**Background:** When airport luggage goes unclaimed, it eventually ends up at this facility—part thrift store, part vacation destination. Anything in good shape that's clean and legal is put on sale here, very cheap: books, jewelry, electronics, sports equipment, and clothes (cleaned and pressed). Lost something on a previous vacation? Come here on your next one—you might recover it.

**Be sure to see:** The glass-encased "UBC Museum" of rare or valuable salvaged items, including a violin from 1770, some ancient Egyptian artifacts, a 40.95-karat emerald, and a gnome from the movie *Labyrinth*.

## BEN & JERRY'S FLAVOR GRAVEYARD
**Location:** Behind the Ben & Jerry's factory in Waterbury, Vermont

**Background:** The specialty ice-cream company is always coming up with new flavors. Some, like Chunky Monkey or Cherry Garcia, do very well; others don't. So every year Ben & Jerry's discontinues eight to ten of its worst sellers and retires them in the

---

Why did French women wear high heels in the 1600s? To show they were too rich to walk.

"Flavor Graveyard." It's a real graveyard, covered with lush green grass and surrounded by a white picket fence. There are currently 56 dead flavors in the cemetery. Each one has a real tombstone with an illustration of its lid, topped with a winged cone ascending upward.

**Be sure to see:** The graves of Peanut Butter & Jelly, Sweet Potato Pie, Lemon Peppermint Carob Chip, and Ricotta.

## THE CENTER OF THE WORLD

**Location:** Southeastern California, near the Arizona border

**Background:** In 1985 Jacques André Istel, author of an obscure children's book called *Coe: The Good Dragon at the Center of the World*—and recipient of two votes in the 2003 California gubernatorial election—bought a chunk of desert just off Interstate 8, incorporated the town of Felicity (named after his wife), and declared himself mayor. Then he built a 21-foot-tall pink marble pyramid. On the floor of the pyramid is a bronze plaque, and on the plaque is a tiny dot. That, according to Istel, is the center of the world.

**Be sure to see:** A 25-foot-high section of spiral staircase from the Eiffel Tower. Istel bought it at auction for $200,000; it now sits at the entrance to the pyramid, spiraling upward to nowhere in particular. And don't miss the Wall for the Ages, a 100-foot-long granite wall where visitors can have their names inscribed. Cost per name: $200. (It's tax-deductible.)

## SWEATSHOP TOUR

**Location:** Los Angeles

**Background:** This educational and political tour, offered by the Communist Revolutionary Party of California, takes visitors through L.A.'s garment district. Highlights include visits to actual textile factories and sweatshops and classes on profit earnings distribution and working conditions. Visitors may also peer through locked, grated doors at rows of heads bent over sewing machines.

**Be sure *not* to see:** Government agents raiding the premises, looking for illegal immigrants. (Tour organizers recommend running shoes and loose-fitting clothing for a quick escape.)

---

**Serve yourself: In a feeding frenzy, a shark may eat parts of its own body.**

# FAMOUS LAST WORDS

*We're all going to go, but it would be nice to
have something clever to say when we do.*

"To die, to sleep, to pass into nothingness, what does it matter? Everything is an illusion."
—**Mata Hari**

"I don't need bodyguards."
—**Jimmy Hoffa**

"All the damn fool things you do in life you pay for."
—**Edith Piaf, singer**

"I believe we must adjourn this meeting to some other place."
—**Adam Smith, economist**

"Shakespeare, here I come."
—**Theodore Dreiser, author**

"What is the answer? In that case, what is the question?"
—**Gertrude Stein**

"So much mortality still clings to me; I wanted most desperately to live and still do."
—**Thomas Wolfe, author**

"What? The flames already?"
—**Voltaire**

"My design is to make what haste I can to be gone."
—**Oliver Cromwell**

"God, don't let me die. I have so much to do."
—**Huey Long, Louisiana governor**

"Let not my end disarm you, and on no account weep or keen for me, let the enemy be warned of my death."
—**Genghis Khan**

"I am still alive!"
—**Caligula,** *Roman emperor*

"Kill me, or else you are a murderer!"
—**Franz Kafka, author,** *begging his doctor for an overdose of morphine*

"Everybody has got to die, but I have always believed an exception would be made in my case. Now what?"
—**William Saroyan, author**

"Bless you sister. May all your sons be bishops."
—**Brendan Behan, author,** *to his nurse, a nun*

"Tomorrow, I shall no longer be here."
—**Nostradamus**

# CURSES!

*In previous* Bathroom Readers *we've told you about famous curses like the curse of the Hope diamond and the curse of King Tut. Here are a few you may not have heard of.*

## THE CURSE OF THE DEVIL MONKEY

**Background:** In 2000 a Ghanian witch doctor mailed a wooden statue of a monkey to Great Britain and then flew there to get it. Why didn't he just take it with him on the plane? Because, as suspicious customs officials discovered when they examined the statue closely, it was hollow—and stuffed with 666 grams of marijuana.

**Cursed!** When the witch doctor showed up to collect the statue, police arrested him. As he was being led off to jail, he placed a curse on the statue. Dubbed the "devil monkey," it has been blamed for inflicting dozens of injuries to workers at the customs warehouse, where it's still being held as evidence. Workers have received nasty splinters from it, tripped over it, and even been hit on the head by it when it mysteriously falls off shelves as people walk by. "It is cursed," customs spokesman Nigel Knott told reporters in 2001, "and very dangerous."

## THE LIVERMORE SEWER CURSE

**Background:** In 1969 Chippewa Indian Adam Fortunate Eagle Nordwall carved a 20-foot totem pole, which he donated to the city of Livermore, California, as part of the city's centennial celebration. The city accepted the gift but then "desecrated" it by sawing several feet off the bottom before installing it in a park.

**Cursed!** Nordwall was furious. He insisted that the city reattach the bottom part of the totem pole. When officials refused, he went to a city council meeting and placed a curse on the city's sewer system. Less than two weeks later, the sewers backed up. Did the curse work? City officials didn't take any chances—they reattached the bottom of the pole...and the sewer problems cleared up.

**Update:** More than 30 years later, Nordwall still hasn't lifted the curse. He says he's waiting for an official apology. Meanwhile, other Indians in the area have complained to the city about Nord-

---

Q: What's the scientific name for heavy winter fog containing ice crystals? A: Pogonip.

wall. They accuse him of making a mockery of a Native American art form—totem poles—by tying them to a silly curse. Nordwall, who comes from what he calls a "teasing clan," says he isn't going to apologize either. "I use humor in a way some Indians don't understand," the 73-year-old told the *San Francisco Chronicle* in 2002. "It's called serious joke medicine."

## THE CURSE OF THE ABBEY WALL

**Background:** In 1534 England's King Henry VIII broke from the Roman Catholic Church and established the Church of England. Two years later he began to disband Catholic monasteries in England and seize their property, including the 12th-century Margam Abbey in Port Talbot, Wales.

**Cursed!** As one of the last monks was being thrown out of the abbey, he pointed a finger at one of the walls and said, "If this wall doth fall, then so will all that surrounds it." Neither the new owner, Sir Rice Mansel, nor any of the property's subsequent owners dared challenge the curse. Over the years, as the abbey buildings were demolished and replaced, the wall was preserved.

**Update:** Today Margam Abbey is long gone. A steel plant now occupies the site...but a 20-foot portion of the nearly 1,000-year-old wall still stands, lovingly preserved by its owner, Corus Group. Why? The company says it has a responsibility to preserve this unique piece of British heritage...but they also don't want to mess with the curse. "We're not superstitious," says a company spokesman, "but we like to hedge our bets."

## THE MUNDA BABY CURSE

**Background:** Ask your parents—did your first baby tooth break through your upper or your lower gum?

**Cursed!** If you're female and your first tooth broke through on top, be glad you're not a member of one of the Munda tribes of India. According to them, you are cursed and will someday be devoured by wild animals. The Munda ward off the curse by literally marrying their infant daughters to dogs, who will protect them from the wild animals. Two such weddings were performed in 2005 in a village outside the Indian city of Bhubaneswar. "All the wedding rituals are carried out," one beaming father of the bride told the *Hindustan Times*. "The groom (dog) comes in a marriage procession and the bride's family welcomes him. Then all the rituals are followed like an original marriage. We cannot take a risk with our daughter's future."

**The Good News:** Though the infant-dog wedding is considered as real as a wedding between a normal bride and groom, when the girl grows up she is free to marry again, without having to divorce the dog.

## THE CURSE OF LADY MACDOUGALL

**Background:** One Sunday morning in the 1550s, members of the MacCallum clan gathered at their church in Kilbride, Scotland, for Sunday Mass. Members of the MacDougall clan also attended services there, but by the time they arrived the church was so full of MacCallums that there was no place for them to sit.

**Cursed!** It made Lady MacDougall so mad that she put a curse on the MacCallum clan: the sons and their descendants would die unless they moved off the family farm at Cologin.

The twelve MacCallum brothers who lived on the Cologin farm ignored the curse...until, one by one, over the next few years, nine of them died. The surviving three got the message—they moved off the farm and their descendants survive to this day. The story of the curse, which was never lifted, has been passed down in both clans for more than 400 years.

**Update:** Finally in July 2002, American members of the two clans met at the annual Highland Games at Grandfather Mountain in North Carolina and performed a "lifting of the curse" ceremony in front of the beer tent (there was no church handy). Just as they had done in the 16th century, a group of MacCallums blocked the entrance. But this time, when the MacDougalls tried to enter, the MacCallums parted and let them pass.

\*     \*     \*

## REAL CLASSIFIED ADS

**Wanted:** Cleaning and Janitorial help. Please leave mess.

**Physiotherapist required** for orthopedic rehab clinic. $80,000/hour.

**Wanted:** Desk clerk and housekeeping help at Best Western PLEASE NO PHONE CALLS!!! (760) 375-2311

# ODD PROMOTIONS

*Sometimes ad campaigns do more than sell a product—sometimes they make us laugh.*

The R.J. Reynolds Tobacco Company tried to market Salem cigarettes in Japan using the American slogan "Salem— Feeling Free." They had to change it: it translated into Japanese as "When smoking Salem, you feel so refreshed that your mind seems to be empty."

• Swedish furniture manufacturer IKEA issued an apology after it advertised its children's "Gutvik" bunk beds in Christmas catalogs in Germany. Reason: In German, *Gutvik* translates into an explicit sexual reference. (*Gut* means "good"—you'll have to figure out the rest.) An IKEA spokeswoman explained that "Gutvik is the name of a tiny Swedish town. We didn't realize that it could also be taken as something obscene."

• Family and religious groups in Michigan protested a series of beer ads that appeared on billboards in 2004. Sechs Beer put up ads with messages like "As long as you're 21, it's OK to pay for Sechs" and "It's OK to have Sechs by yourself." The brewer, Walton Sechs Brewery of Wisconsin, explained that *sechs* is the German word for "six" and refused to remove the billboards.

• Dirt Cheap Cigarettes & Beer, a store in Fenton, Missouri, runs commercials on late-night television. They feature a man dressed as a chicken running around the store yelling, "Cheap cheap fun fun!" while the owner tells male viewers that they should buy beer from him because "the more she drinks, the better you'll look."

• In 2004, WCAT, a country music radio station in Pennsylvania, changed its format. They announced the change by playing the children's song "Pop Goes the Weasel" non-stop, 24 hours a day, for four straight days. After the four days, CAT Country was gone, and Cool Pop 106.7—a pop-music station—was born.

• Family members of the late Johnny Cash refused to allow one of Cash's signature songs to be used for a TV commercial. Producer Sula Miller wanted to use the song "Ring of Fire" in a commercial for a hemorrhoid medication.

# PUDGE GOES PRO

*In our Supremely Satisfying Bathroom Reader, we told you how football started. Well, halftime is over. (We hope you enjoyed the show.) Here's the story of the very first pro football player.*

C OLLEGE GAME
Football was invented at Ivy League colleges in the 1870s, combining rugby with some other ball games popular at the time. For more than 50 years the college game was the dominant form of the sport, both in terms of the number of teams and the number of fans. College football *was* football. But what about people who didn't go to college, or grads that wanted to relive their glory days? They wanted to play, too, and they wanted teams they could root for. So in the 1890s local sports clubs and businesses began to organize teams.

These sports clubs, such as the YMCA, had an agenda: their members saw them as stepping-stones to get into even more exclusive clubs and a great way to do that was to belong to a club with a successful sports team. So the pressure was on from the beginning to recruit the best men possible.

One problem: it was against the rules to pay athletes for playing. Amateurism was seen as a noble quality; getting paid to play was seen as crass. So instead of breaking the rules, the clubs bent them. San Francisco's Olympic Athletic Club, for example, promised to find a job for any athlete that joined the club. Even if this didn't technically violate the rules, it certainly violated the spirit of amateurism. But the practice was so widespread that, rather than condemn it, in 1890 the Amateur Athletic Union, which governed amateur clubs, created an entirely new category for that kind of athlete—the "semiprofessional."

## LORD OF THE RINGERS
William "Pudge" Heffelfinger was a former All-American for Yale University. One of the best players of his time, Heffelfinger was famous for hurling himself over the heads of interlocked offensive linemen and cannonballing knee-first into the ball carrier's chest. (Needless to say, the rules of football were quite different back then.)

---

Botulism bacteria are so toxic that one pound could kill every human on Earth.

A popular practice at the time was to cheat by hiring ringers, skilled college players who posed as average Joes and played under assumed names. Heffelfinger was sorely needed by two rival clubs in Pittsburgh, Pennsylvania: the Allegheny Athletic Association and the Pittsburgh Athletic Club. After playing to a 6–6 tie in the citywide championship game in October 1892 (highly contested because Allegheny had stolen some of Pittsburgh's best players), a rematch was set for three weeks later. Both clubs scrambled to field the best teams possible; both clubs secretly met with Heffelfinger.

**GAME DAY**

More than 3,000 people turned out for the rematch on November 12, even though it was snowing. The Allegheny crowd cheered when Pudge took the field with their team. The Pittsburgh side cried foul—Allegheny was using *ringers*, after all. They refused to play unless Allegheny agreed that all bets placed on the game were off. (Gambling was another big part of the early game.) After nearly an hour, Allegheny agreed.

For all the hoopla that led up to it, the game itself was pretty uneventful. Pudge scored the only touchdown, and Allegheny won 4–0 (back then, a touchdown only counted for four points—today it counts for six). Even with the low score and the bitterly cold weather, the crowd was entertained by the brutal play and carnage on the field. Several players were injured—three had to be carried off on stretchers.

Today, Pudge Heffelfinger is just a footnote in professional football. He wouldn't even be that, were it not for a single scrap of paper that survived among the Allegheny Athletic Association's financial records for the 1892 season. Today that scrap of paper— an expense sheet for the November 12 game—is on display in the Pro Football Hall of Fame. On it is an entry showing that, in addition to being reimbursed for his expenses, Heffelfinger received a $500 "game performance bonus for playing." And in those days, $500 was about what a schoolteacher made in a year. Although neither Pudge nor Allegheny ever admitted to the transaction, the expense sheet speaks for itself: Heffelfinger was the first documented professional football player in the history of the game.

*Cut left and go long to page 221
for "The Birth of the NFL."*

It takes 630 silkworm cocoons to make a single silk blouse.

# BAGPIPER'S FUNGUS

*Recent studies have found that professional musicians often suffer from some very real—but very odd—ailments. Here are a few.*

F IDDLER'S NECK
The name might sound silly, but according to a study of regular violin and viola players by Dr. Thilo Gambichler of Oldchurch Hospital in London, the friction of the instrument's base against the left side of the neck (for right-handed players) can cause lesions, severe inflammation, and cysts. What's worse, said the study, published in the British medical journal *BMC Dermatology*, it causes *lichenification*—the development of a patch of thick, leathery skin on the neck, giving it a "bark-like" appearance.

## GUITAR NIPPLE

A similar report issued in the United States cited three female classical guitarists who suffered from *traumatic mastitis*—swelling of the breast and nipple area—due to prolonged friction from the instrument's body. The condition can strike male players, too.

## BAGPIPER'S FUNGUS

Recent medical reports have detailed the dangers of playing Scotland's national instrument. Bagpipes are traditionally made of sheepskin coated with a molasses-like substance called treacle. That, the report said, is a perfect breeding ground for various fungi, such as *aspergillus* and *cryptococcus*. Bagpipers can inadvertently inhale fungal spores, which, according to Dr. Robert Sataloff of Thomas Jefferson University Hospital in Philadelphia, can lead to deadly lung—and even brain—diseases.

## TUBA LIPS

Many long-term tuba players develop an allergic reaction to nickel, an ingredient in brass. The allergy can result in dermatitis of the lips and can sometimes develop into chronic eczema. Strictly speaking, the condition can also affect the chin and hands, and can be contracted from any number of brass instruments (but "tuba lips" is more fun to say).

# HAPPINESS IS...

*"Happiness is a good quote page."* —Uncle John

"Happiness is nothing more than good health and a bad memory." —Albert Schweitzer

"Happiness is perfume you cannot pour on others without getting a few drops on yourself." —Ralph Waldo Emerson

"The grand essentials of happiness are: something to do, something to love, and something to hope for." —Allan K. Chalmers, artist

"Happiness is a Swedish sunset—it is there for all, but most of us look the other way and lose it." —Mark Twain

"Happiness is your dentist telling you it won't hurt and then having him catch his hand in the drill." —Johnny Carson

"Happiness is unrepentant pleasure." —Socrates

"Happiness is a wine of the rarest vintage, and seems insipid to a vulgar taste." —Logan Pearsall Smith

"Happiness is a way station between too little and too much." —Channing Pollock

"Happiness is as a butterfly which, when pursued, is always beyond our grasp, but which if you will sit down quietly, may alight upon you." —Nathaniel Hawthorne

"Happiness, at my age, is breathing." —Joan Rivers

"Happiness is never stopping to think if you are." —Palmer Sondreal

"Happiness is when what you think, what you say, and what you do are in harmony." —Mohandas K. Gandhi

"The fact is always obvious much too late, but the most singular difference between happiness and joy is that happiness is a solid and joy a liquid." —J. D. Salinger

"Real happiness is cheap enough, yet how dearly we pay for its counterfeit." —Hosea Ballou, minister

Abraham Lincoln and Paul Revere were distant relatives.

# ORIGIN OF NACHOS

*Readers sometimes ask if we'll ever run out of things to write about.
No way. Origins are a good example: as we recently discovered, even
lowly snack foods can have fascinating (and delicious) origins.*

## SNACK

In 1943 Ignacio Anaya, or "Nacho" as he was nicknamed, was working as the maitre d' at a restaurant called the Victory Club in Piedras Negras, Mexico, just across the border from Eagle Pass, Texas. According to Anaya's son, Ignacio Jr., one night the restaurant's cook disappeared just as a group of officers' wives from Fort Duncan Air Base arrived for dinner. Thinking fast, Anaya went into the kitchen and improvised a meal by taking some tostadas and topping them with shredded cheddar cheese, then putting them in a broiler, and serving them garnished with jalapeño peppers. The women were impressed. One of them, Mamie Finan, named them "Nachos Especiales" in honor of Anaya's nickname.

The recipe soon became a specialty of many local restaurants, but remained unknown outside of southern Texas until a man named Frank Liberto saw the potential of nachos as a concession-stand item. In 1977 he figured out how to process the cheese to keep it soft all the time, and started selling nachos at Arlington Stadium, then home of the Texas Rangers baseball team. He later replaced the tostadas with tortilla chips, and modern-day nachos were born.

## CRUNCH TIME

But nachos might have remained a Texas specialty if not for Howard Cosell and *Monday Night Football.* Someone gave Cosell nachos before a game. He loved them…and liked the funny-sounding name. That night (and for weeks after), Cosell and the broadcast team worked references to nachos into the game analysis as often as possible. Cosell loved describing great plays by calling them "nachos," giving the food national recognition, making the term an acceptable adjective for spectacular events, and forever securing its spot as one of the sport watcher's favorite finger foods.

*Taco is Spanish for "plug."*

# CELEBRITY GOSSIP

*Here's the latest edition of the BRI's cheesy tabloid
section—a bunch of gossip about famous people.*

## MICHAEL JACKSON

During his 2005 trial, a lot of information came to light about the King of Pop—even his favorite food: "Colonel Sanders's KFC original fried chicken (breasts) with mashed potatoes, corn, and biscuits with spray butter," according to police records. For his toddler son, Prince Michael II: "crackers, grapes, juice or milk, and KFC cut up into pieces." On his plane, Jackson bans broccoli "or any other strong-scented food."

## PARIS HILTON

While dining at a fancy restaurant with Pamela Anderson, Hilton threw a temper tantrum when handed the menu. "I hate reading! Someone tell me what's on the menu!" Anderson told the story to GQ magazine, concluding, "I'm blonde, too. But c'mon."

## WILLIAM SHATNER

Want to know what your favorite star smells like? On the set of the show *Boston Legal*, which Shatner starred in with James Spader, they filmed a "love scene" in which the two "spooned" in bed together. Spader recalled the experience: "You can tell a lot about a person by that first impression, that first smell. Bill had a very sort of, a strangely very attractive sort of pungent sort of gamey, sort of a venison or a lamb sausage scent." Ironic twist: Shatner is a vegetarian.

## OPRAH WINFREY

After undergoing DNA tests, Winfrey proudly declared that she is a Zulu, descended from the race of warriors who once ruled South Africa. How did the modern day Zulus react? They snubbed her. African-Americans, they claim, are descended from *West* Africans. South Africans ended up in Asia and South America. Prince Mangosuthu Buthelezi, leader of the seven-million-strong tribe, said, "I hate to tell Oprah this, but she is sorely mistaken."

## HUGH GRANT

In a book about how people deal with their loved ones getting cancer, Grant recounted his relationship with his mother during her final days. "I got bored and went back to tormenting her," he said. "My personal favorite being secretly activating her hospital bed so that the head and legs both lifted to put her in an amusing jack-knife position. I blow-dried her hair on the day before she died, which was frankly not the success I had hoped for, and which may—I now concede—have finished her off."

## GEORGE H.W. BUSH

In 1989 President Bush was giving a speech in Poland when it started to rain. He ordered a Secret Service guard—who was holding Bush's raincoat—to give it to an old woman on the other side of the fence. The press praised the president for his selfless generosity. Sixteen years later, Bush admitted that the raincoat wasn't his; it belonged to the guard…who was just about to put it on.

## HOWIE MANDEL

The wacky comedian was expelled from his Toronto high school. Why? For pretending to be a member of the school board and convincing a construction company to start work on an addition to the school.

## CHRISTINA AGUILERA

In 2005 the pop singer was about to record a song written by "Aurora Lynne"…until Aguilera found out that Aurora Lynne was actually a pen name for Britney Spears, who wrote the song. Aguilera refused to record it—keeping a feud going that started early in their careers when the two were Mouseketeers.

## TOM JONES

Trying to maintain a hip image, 65-year-old Jones recently returned to wearing his trademark tight leather pants and open shirt on stage. But his son (and manager), Mark Woodward, told him: "Dress your age." Fearing that fans may have stopped taking the Welsh singer seriously, Woodward banned his father's new outfit. Also on the "Don't do that anymore" list: picking up women's panties that are thrown onto the stage.

# SPY HUNT: GRAY DECEIVER, PART I

*Everyone loves a spy thriller—especially when it's real life. Here's an amazing tale that a BRI operative recently uncovered.*

## THE MOLE

In February 1994, FBI agents arrested a 30-year veteran of the CIA named Aldrich Ames. The charge: spying for the Soviet Union. In the nine years that Ames was an active spy, he exposed more than 100 sensitive operations and revealed the name of every CIA intelligence source in the Soviet Union. At least 10 of them were executed; many others were sent to prison. Ames was paid more than $2.5 million for his efforts and was promised another $1.9 million, making him the highest-paid double agent in history, not to mention one of the most damaging.

Yet as pleased as the FBI and the CIA were to have caught and convicted Ames (he received a life sentence), disturbing signs soon began to emerge that there might be one, and possibly even more moles hiding elsewhere in various U.S. intelligence agencies. Some secrets known to have been compromised couldn't be traced back to Ames—he simply didn't know about them.

So both the CIA and the FBI set up new mole-hunting teams and set to work looking for spies. The FBI gave the investigation the code name GRAYSUIT; each time a new suspect was identified they were given a code name with "GRAY" as a prefix. The new mole hunt dredged up two more relatively minor spies: an FBI agent named Earl Edwin Pitts and a CIA agent named Harold J. Nicholson. Both men were arrested in 1996 and sentenced to more than 20 years in prison.

## BIG SECRETS

Neither arrest answered the question of who was responsible for giving the two biggest intelligence secrets to the Russians:

● **The Tunnel.** Someone told the Soviets about the secret eavesdropping tunnel that the FBI and the National Security Agency (NSA) had dug beneath the new Soviet embassy in Washington,

D.C. The tunnel program cost more than $100 million but never produced a single piece of useful intelligence, because the Russians were told of its existence in 1994—five years before they moved in.

• **The Spy.** As we told you in *Uncle John's Slightly Irregular Bathroom Reader*, in 1989 the FBI was hot on the trail of a senior U.S. diplomat named Felix Bloch, who was suspected of spying for the KGB. Someone tipped off his handler, a KGB spy named Reino Gikman. Gikman then tipped off Bloch, blowing the FBI's investigation before they could collect enough information to indict him. To date Bloch has never been charged with espionage.

## MYSTERY MAN

Both the spy tunnel and the Bloch investigation were FBI operations, but early on the FBI concluded that the mole was more likely to be a CIA official, so that's where they focused their efforts.

For years tips had been coming in from U.S. sources in Russia, describing a spy who had a thing for "exotic dancers," sometimes liked to be paid in diamonds, and was said to make "dead drops" (leave packages and pick up money) in Nottoway Park in Vienna, Virginia. None of the Russian sources knew the man's identity—as far as anyone knew at the time, the man had never revealed his real name to his handlers or even told them which intelligence agency he worked for. Apparently he'd never met with his Russian handlers, either. No one even knew what he looked like.

## THE MATRIX

One of the ways intelligence agencies hunt for spies is to make what is called a "matrix." They compile a list of all the intelligence secrets that have been betrayed, and then make a list of the people who had access to those secrets. Then, using whatever other clues they have, they try to rule suspects in or out. The FBI mole hunters used just such a matrix to narrow a list of 100 suspects down to seven and then down to just one: a CIA agent named Brian Kelley. They gave him the nickname GRAY DECEIVER.

Kelley specialized in exposing Soviet "illegals," spies who do not pose as diplomats and thus have no diplomatic immunity if they are caught. One illegal that Kelley had uncovered was Reino Gikman, the KGB agent who tipped off Felix Bloch. Kelley was a distinguished agent—he'd been awarded five medals for his work at the CIA, including one for the Felix Bloch case. But the FBI was now convinced that he'd been a spy all along. Uncovering Gikman and then warning him about Bloch was the perfect cover—who would ever suspect that a decorated CIA officer would blow his own case?

## DIGGING DEEP

In late 1997 the FBI arranged for Kelley to be given a new assignment: to review the Felix Bloch files to see if any clues had been missed. The real purpose of the assignment was to isolate him and keep him at CIA headquarters, making it easier for FBI mole hunters to keep an eye on him until enough evidence was collected for him to be arrested.

In the meantime, the FBI placed Kelley on round-the-clock surveillance and secretly searched his home. They also tapped his phone lines, sifted through his garbage, searched his home computer, and planted listening devices all over the house. On one occasion they even tailed him all the way to Niagara Falls, only to lose him near the Canadian border. That suggested that Kelley was "dry cleaning"—taking evasive action to lose anyone who might be following him, so he could slip over the border into Canada, presumably to meet with his Russian handlers.

## ONE TOUGH COOKIE

It was then that the mole hunters realized just how difficult it was going to be to catch Kelley red-handed. Sure, they knew about the dry cleaning incident at the border, and they also knew that Kelley shopped at a mall where SVR operatives had been seen in the past (the KGB was renamed the SVR after the collapse of the Soviet Union). But after all the bugging, searching, and garbage sifting, the only incriminating piece of physical evidence they were able to find was a single hand-drawn map of nearby Nottoway Park, with various times written at different locations on the map. To the mole hunters it could only be one thing: a map of various dead drops, complete with a schedule of different drop-off times. With the exception of the map, though, Kelley seemed to be an expert at erasing nearly every trace of his double life.

In fact, to the untrained eye, he didn't seem like a spy at all.

*Who was the mole? Covertly flip to Part II on page 342.*

*Who was the mole? Covertly flip to Part II on page 342.*

---

Tough guy: A 100-pound cougar can take down an 800-pound elk.

# MOLES AND MICE

*Who says you have to be a spy to talk like one? Here's*
*a look at some of the expressions real spies use*
*when they're on the job. (Don't tell anyone.)*

• **Black-bag job:** Sneaking into a home or office and searching it, leaving no evidence that you were there.

• **Floater:** A waiter, bellhop, or other low-level employee who occasionally freelances for a spy agency when needed.

• **Dog drag:** A device which, when a spy drags it behind him, releases a scent to throw bloodhounds off his trail.

• **L pill:** A suicide pill. ("L" stands for *lethal.*)

• **Notional agent:** A non-existent secret agent who is identified as the source of secret information in order to protect the real source.

• **Sheep dipping:** Obscuring the true identity or origin of individuals and equipment so they can be sent out on secret missions.

• **Dry clean:** To make sudden U-turns or other evasive driving maneuvers to spot and hopefully lose enemy agents who are tailing you.

• **Operation slammer:** The U.S. program of interviewing convicted spies in prison to learn their motives and prevent spying in the future.

• **Foots:** Members of surveillance teams who ride as passengers in pursuit cars and then follow suspects on foot after they leave their cars.

• **Wet affairs:** A Russian term for spy operations that involve killing people ("wet" refers to blood).

• **Walk the cat:** Retrace the steps of a "blown" secret agent or operation in an attempt to figure out what went wrong.

• **Piano:** A spy radio. The person who operates it is the "pianist."

• **M.I.C.E.** The four most common reasons people turn against their own country and spy for a foreign power: 1) Money; 2) Ideology; 3) Compromise (they've been *compromised* by incriminating information); 4) Ego.

---

Eat 'em before they spoil: 65% of American candy brands are over 50 years old.

# THE POLITICALLY CORRECT QUIZ #1

*Here are some real-life examples of "politically correct" and "politically incorrect" behavior. How sensitive are you? Guess which answer is the "correct" one. Answers are on page 515.*

**1.** In 1994 Great Britain's Gateway supermarket chain changed some of the baked goods sold in its stores out of fear they might offend customers. What kind of baked goods and why?

**a)** Hot cross buns. It removed the "Christian" crosses—buns *without* crosses "better reflect the cultural and religious diversity of modern Britain," said a spokesperson.

**b)** Gingerbread men. It renamed them gingerbread *persons* "to promote gender parity."

**c)** Bear claws. It dropped the "bear." Now they're just "claws." "The imagery of an amputated bear claw was rather demeaning to bears," said a spokesperson.

**2.** After a 10-year battle, in 2004 commissioners in Jefferson County, Texas, voted to change the name of a street that some community members found offensive. Which street?

**a)** Liberal Lane. (Jefferson County is 70 percent Republican).

**b)** Sissy Street, named in honor of county founder Jefferson Davis Sissy. "I don't care if he died at the Alamo," local resident Shelby Jones told reporters. "I'm tired of living on Sissy Street."

**c)** Jap Road. Ironically, the street was named in *honor* of Yasvo Mayumi, a Japanese immigrant and farmer who introduced rice farming to the area in the early 1900s.

**3.** In 1999 a former employee of Play It Again Sports in Sydney, Nova Scotia, filed a complaint alleging that her employer "created a poisoned environment" by giving her a demeaning nickname. What was the nickname?

**a)** Hot Pants. (The woman resented the sexual innuendo.)

**b)** Kemosabe. (The woman is a member of an Indian tribe.)

**c)** Big Girl. (The woman was sensitive about her weight.)

---

Ain't it grand? Rachmaninoff could cover 12 white keys on the piano with one hand.

**4.** In 2004 a student named Yvan Tessier was denied admission to a college course in Canada's University of New Brunswick. What was the course, and why was he denied admission?

**a)** History of the Animal Rights Movement. The class had a "cruelty free" dress code, and Tessier refused to leave his leather shoes outside in the hallway.

**b)** History of Sex Discrimination. Tessier is a man, and the class admits only women. "He has no context for understanding the subject. Besides, as a typical male, he probably just wants to gather information to use against women," said the professor, Sarah Pearsson.

**c)** Immersion English. The course requires that only English be spoken in the classroom and Tessier, who is blind, has a guide dog that responds only to French commands.

**5.** In the spring of 2004 a Lexington, Kentucky, high school student was barred from going to her own prom because she was wearing a dress the school considered "inappropriate." What was wrong with the dress?

**a)** Instead of sequins, it was decorated with condoms.

**b)** It was styled to look like a Confederate flag.

**c)** It was an old-fashioned hoop skirt with a petticoat. (Too traditional). "Why even have a feminist movement if women are going to dress like we never won the right to vote?" one school official told reporters.

**6.** In 2005 Oklahoma State Senator Frank Shurden proposed lifting the ban on cockfighting in his state by making the following reform to the blood sport:

**a)** Put tiny boxing gloves on the roosters.

**b)** Use radio-controlled robot roosters instead of real roosters.

**c)** Have them wear "uniforms" of protective padding similar to those worn by professional football players.

\*     \*     \*

"Life is uncertain. Eat dessert first."

—**Ernestine Ulmer**

# ROYAL PURPLE

*Today clothing comes in a wide variety of colors and shades, but that wasn't always the case. Read on to find out how people first made purple clothes.*

THE LAND OF THE PURPLE

According to an ancient Greek legend, the god Hercules was walking his dog on a beach one day when he suddenly noticed that the dog's snout had turned brilliantly purple. Upon investigating, Hercules discovered that the dog had been eating some sea snails. He gathered some of the snails himself, crushed them, spread the juice on some cloth—and was amazed by the vibrant color. So he dyed an entire robe with the color and sent it to the king of Canaan, declaring that the brilliant purple should be the color of his royal house. The king agreed.

Fable or not, purple dye was first used in Canaan (modern-day Lebanon). Around 1800 B.C., people in the port city of Tyre discovered that certain glands of the murex—a small, spiral-shelled mollusk—when extracted, produced a purple substance that could be used to dye cloth. Humans had been making dyes for thousands of years, but no one had never seen a color like this. The Canaanites started making the dye in their colonies all around the Mediterranean Sea, beginning the world's first chemical dye industry. The color became known as "Tyrian purple" and was so famous that it and the murex "fish" are mentioned in many ancient texts, including the Torah and the Bible. And "Canaan" was later known as Phoenicia—which means "the land of the purple" in Greek.

PURPLE GOLD

The dyeing process: Gather several thousand murex, crack them open, use a sharp tool to extract the glands and veins, mix well, and spread the substance on a piece of silk or linen. Place the fabric in the sun, and in a few days it will turn purple. Sounds simple, but it took more than *12,000 murex* to make just 1.4 grams of dye—less than a teaspoonful! At its peak, a pound of dyed cloth cost ten to twenty times its weight in gold.

Only the extremely wealthy could afford such a luxury, which meant royalty—that's how the color got the name "royal purple." In fact, another name for being born of royal blood was to be "born in the purple."

Some purple extravagances:

• Legend says that in the first century B.C., Cleopatra sailed to battle in a ship with a huge purple sail to show off her wealth.

• In the first century A.D., Roman emperor Nero made it a law that only emperors could wear royal purple. The punishment for violating the law: death. (Some historians believe the law was enacted to protect the shellfish, which were already in danger of extinction due to aggressive harvesting for the dye industry.)

## A NEW PURPLE

The mollusk-based dye industry changed hands several times as various empires—Egyptian, Persian, Greek, and Roman—took control of the lands around the Mediterranean. Yet purple remained the color of royal houses until the fall of the Eastern Roman Empire in 1453. Popes and high church officials had also worn royal purple through the ages, but in 1464 Pope Paul II made a less expensive dye, known as "cardinal's purple," the new official color of the church. That brought an end to the Mediterranean murex dye industry—which had survived for over 2,500 years.

The new purple was made from another very ancient process, one that used insects. Small, pea-sized kermes bugs infest a type of oak tree common in southern Europe and the Middle East. The insects were gathered from the trees, killed by exposure to heat (sometimes by the steam of boiling vinegar), dried and crushed into a powder that could be mixed with water, and applied to cloth. Cardinal's purple, which was actually more scarlet than purple, became the luxury dye of the Middle Ages, just as royal purple before it. Did it last? Yes: Catholic cardinals still wear the color today.

## BETTER LIVING THROUGH CHEMISTRY

In 1856, 17-year-old student William H. Perkin was given an assignment at the Royal College of Chemistry in London: produce a synthetic form of quinine, which is naturally produced in the bark of the *cinchona* tree in South America (quinine was used by Europeans to fight malaria). One experiment, with by-products of coal tar and aniline, led to a purple sludge. Perkin liked the color so much that he dyed some silk with it, and was so impressed with the result that he quit school and opened a dye factory.

Perkin called his color "mauve" (the French name for the purple mallow flower), but marketed it as "Tyrian purple." This new dye was affordable enough for the masses, and it quickly became hugely popular in Europe. Just as royal purple had marked the birth of the chemical dye industry 3,000 years earlier, mauve began the synthetic dye industry, which would go on to replace virtually all handmade dyes. The new color even got a nod from royalty: Queen Victoria wore a mauve silk robe to the Royal Exhibition of London in 1862.

## UNCLE JOHN'S FAVORITE PURPLE

There were other ways of making purple (or nearly purple) dye in ancient times, but they didn't produce the brilliant color that the murex dye did. One was known as Orchil dye, also known as "poor man's purple" because it used a cheaper base and was much easier to make. The important ingredient in Orchil dye was lichen—mossy fungi that grow on rocks and tree trunks. Another vital ingredient was uric acid. Where did ancient people get uric acid? From urine. Recipes from the time instructed how much was needed to get the desired color. Here's one from the *Plictho de L'Arte de Tintori*, from the 1540s:

> Take one pound of the Orselle of the Levant, very clean; moisten it with a little urine; add to this sal-ammoniac, sal-gemmae, and saltpetre, of each two ounces; pound them well, mix them together, and let them remain so for 12 days, stirring them twice a day; and then to keep the herb constantly moist, add a little urine, and let it remain eight days longer, continuing to stir it; afterwards add a pound and a half of pot-ash well pounded, and a pint and a half of stale urine. Let it remain eight days longer, stirring as usual; after which you add the same quantity of urine, and at the expiration of five or six days, two drachms of arsenic; it will then be fit for use.

\*    \*    \*

"Time's fun when you're having flies."

—Kermit the Frog

# UNLIKELY BEST SELLERS

*Recipe for a best seller: author writes great book, a publisher buys it, book is hyped and promoted, and sells a lot of copies. Except that it doesn't always happen that way. Take these books, for example.*

## THE ANARCHIST COOKBOOK

It was 1968. Nineteen-year-old William Powell was peripherally involved in the "counterculture" movement, smoking marijuana and attending anti-war protests. But he longed to do something *really* subversive, something to promote violence and chaos as a vehicle for social change. So, using military manuals and other sources that he got from the public library, he began compiling instructions for such activities as how to build pipe bombs, how to pick locks, how to manufacture LSD, and how to counterfeit money. He interlaced the "recipes" with anti-government rantings, put it all in book form, and under the pseudonym "Jolly Roger," shopped *The Anarchist Cookbook* to publishers. One (but only one) was interested: Lyle Stuart, who published it, unedited, in 1970.

By 1976 *The Anarchist Cookbook* had sold more than 800,000 copies...but Powell had changed. Radically. He'd graduated college, married, embraced religion, and was teaching high school. And although many of the "recipes" were inaccurate and didn't work, Powell now considered *The Anarchist Cookbook* the dangerous creation of an irresponsible youth, so he asked Lyle Stuart to take the book out of print. But Stuart refused, citing a loophole in Powell's original contract: Powell had refused royalties, so the copyright was taken out in the name of the publisher, not the writer, as is the usual practice. In other words, Lyle Stuart owned the book. In 1990 Stuart sold the rights to another publisher, Barricade Books. The book remains in print and has sold more than two million copies to date.

## THE BRIDGES OF MADISON COUNTY

In 1990 Robert James Waller, a University of Northern Iowa economics professor, spent 14 days writing a short romantic novel about a lonely housewife who engages in a brief love affair with a

---

Bird brains: In the 12th century, many Europeans believed that trees gave birth to birds.

photographer who comes to Madison County, Iowa, to photograph covered bridges. Waller printed a few copies and sent them as gifts to a handful of friends and family, one of whom liked it so much that he sent it to a friend of his: a literary agent. A few weeks later, Waller received a surprise phone call from the agent. "Robert," he said, "where have you been all my life?" Warner Books published it in 1992.

Warner's strategy for *The Bridges of Madison County:* target independent small-town bookstores. It worked. Bookstores recommended it to customers, who passed it along to friends. It didn't matter that it was a romance novel, either—the book was a hit with women *and* men. It slowly grew into a cultural phenomenon. Thousands of fans made pilgrimages to Iowa. Waller got dozens of calls and letters every day. He recorded *The Ballads of Madison County*, an album inspired by his book, and even released a book of photographs of Madison County's bridges. A 1995 film version of the book starring Clint Eastwood and Meryl Streep made $176 million. But at the center of it all was the book, which stayed on the *New York Times* best-seller list for 164 weeks and sold 12 million copies.

## MAUS

In 1978 illustrator Art Spiegelman began interviewing his father, Vladek, about his experiences during World War II in Poland, running from the Nazis, and eventually surviving the Auschwitz concentration camp. Spiegelman turned the interviews into *Maus* (German for "mouse"), a harrowing first-person account told in comic book form. Jews were depicted as mice; the Nazis as cats.

Most book publishers wanted nothing to do with it. They thought a long comic book about World War II and concentration camps with cats and mice trivialized the Holocaust. But when Pantheon Books finally published *Maus* in 1986, nobody thought it was trivial. It sold 50,000 copies in its first month and eventually over 300,000 (comic books usually sell under 100,000 copies) and even made the *New York Times* best seller list for three months.

*Maus* was the first successful "graphic novel," a novel told entirely in panel cartoons. It showed that comics could be literary works aimed at adults. Following the release of *Maus II* in 1991, Spiegelman was awarded the Pulitzer Prize.

# UNCLE JOHN'S CREATIVE TEACHING AWARDS

*Our yearly commendations to those teachers who make school special.*

**SUBJECT:** Conflict resolution
**WINNER:** Paulette Baines
**CREATIVE TEACHING:** In April 2005, Baines, who teaches high school in Dallas, went to the classroom of Mary Oliver, who was teaching a science class. She walked up to Oliver, yanked her out of her chair by her hair, and proceeded to drag her across the room to the door while punching her in the face. What caused the rage? Apparently Oliver had told Baines's daughter, who attends the school, to stop loitering at her locker and get to class. Baines was arrested and charged with assault; school officials put her on administrative leave.

**SUBJECT:** Sex education
**WINNER:** Several kindergarten teachers in Cisnadie, Romania
**CREATIVE TEACHING:** The teachers were suspended after school officials found a film of them having an after-hours sex party in the classroom. The film showed several semi-naked teachers smoking, drinking, and playing "sex games" in the children's classroom. (The children had gone home.)

**SUBJECT:** Creative writing
**WINNER:** A teacher in Louisiana (name withheld by the school)
**CREATIVE TEACHING:** A fourth-grade teacher at Norbert Rillieux Elementary in Waggaman, Louisiana, gave his students an assignment to write a 200-word essay. Along with the assignment, he gave each student an essay *he'd* written...about how much he disliked his job. "I hate my class," read one section, "because anytime I try to do something fun, they ruin it." Another part asked, "Are these children or animals?" Some of the "animals" were even identified by name. Outraged parents demanded the teacher be fired. One said, "You shouldn't be a teacher if you hate kids." The school disagreed, but promised to look into it.

---

In 1981 Turkish scientists concluded that disco music made mice homosexual.

**SUBJECT:** Physical education
**WINNER:** Bow High School, Bow, New Hampshire
**CREATIVE TEACHING:** In the fall of 2004, senior Isabel Gottlieb was informed that she still needed one class to graduate. They recommended that she drop one of her other classes—calculus or advanced placement biology—and take the required class: gym. Gottlieb (who holds varsity letters in three different sports) refused, asking, "Why would I drop AP Biology to take P.E.?" When the situation still hadn't been resolved at the end of the school year, Bow High advised Gottlieb that they weren't giving her a diploma. Gottlieb didn't care: she'd already been accepted to Trinity College in Connecticut, and Trinity was willing to accept her GED. Meanwhile, Gottlieb's mother planned a "non-graduation" party.

**SUBJECT:** Anatomy
**WINNER:** "Ingrid"
**CREATIVE TEACHING:** A teacher at the Holdersnest high school in Harkema, Holland, became the talk of the small town after she posed nude in the Dutch magazine *Foxy* under the pseudonym "Ingrid." Although parents were outraged, the school district said the teacher would not be fired or even suspended (but asked that she stay home for a week "in order to calm rumors down"). *Foxy* spokespeople said the magazine didn't understand what the fuss was about, adding that they'd be publishing more photos of Ingrid in the future. An employee of a local supermarket reported that they'd sold out of the magazine.

\*　　\*　　\*

## OOPS!

Melvyn Reed of Kettering, England, had an emergency heart bypass operation in August, 2005. His wife rushed in to see him. Then his wife rushed in to see him. Then his wife rushed in to see him. The three women, from different parts of England, quickly realized that their 58-year-old, car-salesman husband had been living secret lives. Result: he was sued for divorce (three times) and charged with bigamy (twice).

# WEIRD BEAUTY PAGEANTS

*If you think the Miss America contest is a little strange, put on your bikini and high heels and read about these ones.*

**TITLE:** Miss Artificial Beauty

**BACKGROUND:** When 18-year-old Yang Yuan was barred from competing in the 2004 Miss Beijing pageant because she was "an artificial beauty" (the Chinese expression for someone who has had plastic surgery), she sued pageant organizers and lost. Consolation prize: they created the 2004 Miss Artificial Beauty pageant.

**THE PAGEANT:** To qualify, entrants had to provide a doctor's certificate as proof that they had actually undergone plastic surgery. There were 19 finalists, ranging from age 17 to 62, including one transsexual. They competed in several different categories, including "Best Body" and "Biggest Physical Change." (The transsexual, 21-year-old Liu Xiaojing, won in the "Most Newsworthy" category.)

**AND THE WINNER IS:** Feng Qian, 22, a medical student, underwent four procedures—eyelid surgery to get "Western eyelids," facial sculpting, Botox injections, and liposuction on her cheeks and waist—not only to look beautiful, but also to "understand the psychology of someone who does this." Feng won $6,000 and a trip to Japan to attend a plastic surgery conference.

**TITLE:** Miss Beauty in Epaulettes

**BACKGROUND:** This pageant is for women in the Russian army. (An "epaulette" is a shoulder ornament on military uniforms.)

**THE PAGEANT:** Sixteen finalists from army posts all across Russia participated in the 2003 pageant. Beauty was only one area of competition—in addition to modeling evening gowns and combat fatigues, the women also competed in cooking, ballroom dancing, and target shooting.

**AND THE WINNER IS:** Junior Sergeant Tatyana Posyvnina, a radio engineer from the St. Petersburg military district.

---

Longest one-word palindrome: *Saippuakivikauppias*...Finnish for "lye merchant."

**TITLE:** Miss Captivity

**BACKGROUND:** Probably the world's first beauty pageant held in a women's prison: Lithuania's high-security Panevezys Penal Labor Colony. TV producer Arunas Valinskas, who came up with the idea in 2002, says he wanted to prove that you can "find beauty even where you might think there isn't any."

**THE PAGEANT:** Thirty-eight inmates competed in a wedding dress competition, a formal dress competition, and two bikini swimsuit competitions (one with a black leather theme and a second one featuring exotic furs). Contestants used pseudonyms instead of real names and details of their criminal records were not released to the press.

**AND THE WINNER IS:** "Samanta," a 24-year-old inmate who hopes to start a modeling career when she gets out of prison. She won a silver crown and about $2,000, which will be held for her until she is released. What are her hopes for the future? "I'd like to get out of prison right now." Stay tuned: A Hollywood movie is in the works and there's even talk of a Miss Captivity Europe pageant.

**TITLE:** Miss Besieged Sarajevo

**BACKGROUND:** When Bosnia-Herzegovina declared independence from Yugoslavia in 1992, the Serbian separatists placed the Bosnian capital under virtual siege. People trapped in Sarajevo were under constant threat of sniper and artillery attack. Yet for many this only made them more determined to live life as normally as possible. Hence the Miss Besieged Sarajevo beauty pageant, held in May 1993.

**THE PAGEANT:** Thirteen semifinalists, some with shrapnel scars, competed in two events: evening dress and swimsuit competitions. Reminders of the siege were everywhere: whizzing bullets and exploding artillery shells could be heard in the background. When the contestants came onstage during the swimsuit competition, they unfurled a banner that read, "Don't let them kill us."

**AND THE WINNER IS:** Seventeen-year-old Imela Nogic, who won a trip to Madrid. (She had to wait until the siege ended in 1995 to redeem it.) When asked by a reporter what her plans were after the pageant, she replied, "Plans? I have no plans. I may not even be alive tomorrow."

# RANDOM ORIGINS

*Once again, the BRI asks—and answers—the*
*question: Where does all this stuff come from?*

## CHEERLEADING

In the late 1870s, the Princeton University football team (the Tigers) had a male pep squad that supported them from the stands with chants of "Ray, ray, ray! Tiger, tiger, sis, sis, sis! Boom, boom, boom! Aaaah! Princeton, Princeton, Princeton!" In 1884, football was introduced to the University of Minnesota, where a student named Johnny Campbell became the world's first cheerleader: he got up in front of a crowd and urged them to chant "Rah, rah, rah" along with him to help motivate the team. Soon Campbell led five other male cheerleaders (the college was all-male). As college football spread in the early 20th century, cheerleading spread, too. The first female cheerleaders hit the sidelines in 1927 at Marquette University. (Paper pom-poms were introduced in the 1930s.)

## THE KAZOO

Similar instruments, called *mirlitons*, had been used in Africa for hundreds of years, either to imitate the sounds of animals when hunting or in religious rituals. The sound comes from the user humming (not blowing air) across a membrane, which causes it to vibrate. An African-American named Alabama Vest based the modern kazoo on these instruments. He invented his in Macon, Georgia, in the 1840s. They were mass-produced to Vest's specifications by German clockmaker Thaddeus von Clegg and were first demonstrated at the 1852 Georgia State Fair.

## HEIMLICH MANEUVER

Throat surgeon Dr. Henry Heimlich had long noticed the high number of deaths that resulted from simple choking incidents. In the early 1970s, the common method used to relieve choking was a slap on the back. Though it sometimes worked, it often forced food farther into the windpipe, making the choker's situation worse. Heimlich had a theory: a sudden burst of air pressure up through the esophagus would expel an obstruction. He tested it on dogs and

---

Q: What's the technical name for a kazoo? A: A *membranophone*.

found that it worked. Heimlich's "maneuver" forced any food caught in the throat *up*, rather than down, the way a back slap sometimes did. The technique: the person applying the maneuver stands behind the victim with interlocked fingers held below the rib cage and above the navel, and pulls upward. Heimlich published his findings in 1974. Within a week, the Heimlich maneuver was used to save a person from choking. It has saved tens of thousands since.

## MAD LIBS

In November 1953, TV writer Leonard Stern was stuck trying to describe the appearance of a new character he'd created for *The Honeymooners*. His friend, game-show host Roger Price, was in the next room and Stern called out, "Give me an adjective." But before Stern could finish his sentence—he'd needed a word to describe "nose"—Price responded, "Clumsy." The two found the idea of "a clumsy nose" absurdly funny and spent the rest of the day writing short stories, then removing certain words and replacing them with blank spaces, prompting the reader for a certain part of speech: a noun, adjective, verb, etc. When the stories were read back with all the blanks filled, the results were hilarious. For the next five years, Price and Stern tried, in vain, to get *Mad Libs* published. Finally, in 1958, they printed up 14,000 copies themselves. By then, Stern was writing for *The Steve Allen Show* and convinced his boss to use Mad Libs as a comedy bit. All 14,000 copies sold out in a week.

## CONTROL-ALT-DELETE

David Bradley was on the team that developed IBM's first personal computer, or PC, in 1981. Given the assignment of coming up with a way to restart the computer (simply turning it off and turning it back on damaged the hardware), he came up with what he called "the three-finger salute": the computer would restart if the "control," "alt," and "delete" buttons were all pressed simultaneously. Why those three buttons? Bradley figured it was nearly impossible to press that combination of keys by accident.

\* \* \*

**Afghani proverb:** "The right answer to a fool is silence."

# THE DAWN OF FERTILIZATION

*We're proud to present an example of the important
role the bathroom has played in the most pivotal
moments of human evolution.*

## ON THE GO

In prehistoric times, all humans were nomadic hunter-gatherers. That meant they never stayed in one place for very long. And when they had eaten all the food available in one place, they moved to a new place where they could find more food. This went on for hundreds of thousands of years.

But very recently—about 11,000 years ago—something happened in the area known as the Fertile Crescent, today called the Middle East. The nomads stopped moving. Instead, they found a way to replenish the land after they used up its resources: they learned how to cultivate wild plants, including wheat, peas, and olives.

Exactly how our ancestors discovered farming is one of the great mysteries of archaeology. One of the most compelling theories (from the BRI's perspective) comes from Pulitzer Prize–winning biologist Jared Diamond, who theorizes that the agricultural revolution began in the bathroom. And it makes sense when you consider the life cycle of a plant.

## THE BIRDS, THE BEES, AND THE BATHROOM

In order to successfully reproduce, a plant must be able to spread its seeds. Ever found burrs on your socks (or on your dog) after walking through a field? That's a plant using you to disperse its seeds. Or those fuzzy white things floating in the wind? Another method of seed dispersal.

But those two methods are hit or miss—there's no telling where those seeds will end up.

One of the best ways that nature has devised to sow wild seeds is to grow them inside an edible fruit. That way when birds and other animals (including humans) eat the fruit in one place, they

---

Hold on tight! The Tonga Islands in the South Pacific move nearly 3/4 of an inch per year.

digest everything except the seeds, and then...deposit the seeds somewhere else. It's a great system—the seeds are even "planted" inside a nice batch of fresh fertilizer.

## SETTLING DOWN

Back to 11,000 years ago in the Fertile Crescent.

When our ancient ancestors moved into a new area, they gathered and ate the best examples of their favorite food crops and then moved on. When their descendants (or other groups) came back year after year, generation after generation, they found the descendants of those choice plants growing in and around their old camp sites—particularly in the latrine areas.

In his book *Guns, Germs, and Steel*, Diamond theorizes that these sites "may have been a testing ground of the first unconscious crop breeders." It was this discovery, Diamond says, that gave the wanderers a reason to stop wandering and start experimenting with farming. Over subsequent generations, the people who inhabited these places became aware of their power to alter the evolution of wild plants, and, with practice, learned how to plant and harvest food on their own schedule.

And that changed everything.

Farming led to a food surplus, which meant that people could stay put for a while. That led to more permanent settlements, which became the first towns and cities. That led to culture, government, music, theater, writing, and finally to the pinnacle of human innovation—*Uncle John's Bathroom Reader*. All because of...poop.

\*　　\*　　\*

## A RIDDLE

Whoever makes it, tells it not.
Whoever takes it, knows it not.
And whoever knows it, wants it not.
What is it?

**A:** Counterfeit money

# WIDE WORLD OF WEIRD SPORTS

*Tired of baseball, basketball, and football?*
*Your worries are over—we've found*
*some unusual alternatives for you.*

## MAN VERSUS HORSE MARATHON

**Where They Do It:** Llanwrtyd Wells, Wales (the same village that invented "bog snorkeling").

**How It's Played:** Just like it sounds: people and horses run a cross-country race, on the theory that given enough distance over twisting, uneven terrain, a man can run as fast as a horse. The 21.7-mile race (real marathons are 26.22 miles), which has been run each June for more than 25 years, grew out of a bar bet. Who won the bet? The guy who bet on the horses...at least until 2004, when a man named Huw Lobb beat 40 horses and 500 other runners to win first prize. (His time: 2 hours, 5 minutes, 19 seconds.)

## REAL ALE WOBBLE

**Where They Do It:** Would you believe Llanwrtyd Wells, Wales?

**How It's Played:** It's a grueling 35-mile mountain bike race in the rugged terrain around Llanwrtyd Wells, with three checkpoint/watering stations along the route. The only difference between this race and a regular bike race is that the checkpoints put out cups of beer for the riders instead of water. (Bikers may consume no more than 1½ quarts of beer during the race, and if you're under 18 you need a parent's permission to enter.) "Beer gets down to the parts that you don't get down to with water," says race organizer Gordon Green. "It fortifies the cyclists."

## FATHER CHRISTMAS OLYMPICS

**Where They Do It:** In Gallivare, Sweden, 60 miles north of the Arctic Circle. (Not to be confused with the Santa Olympics held in—you guessed it—Llanwrtyd Wells, Wales.)

**How It's Played:** Fifty or more contestants dressed as Father

Christmas come from all over Europe to compete in several different Santa-related categories, including sled riding, reindeer riding, chimney climbing, and gift wrapping (with points for speed and beauty). Contestants are also rated on generosity, jolliness, and their ability to Ho-Ho-Ho. Any Santa caught smoking or drinking in front of children is automatically disqualified.

## HUMAN TOWER BUILDING

**Where They Do It:** Barcelona, Spain, during the Festa de la Merce each September

**How It's Played:** Large groups climb one another to form human towers as tall as nine people high. Then, when they've stacked themselves as high as they can, a small child climbs all the way to the top to make it just a little bit taller. According to one account, "horrific collapses are common and many participants have ended up in the hospital."

## UNDERWATER HOCKEY

**Where They Do It:** All over the United States

**How It's Played:** Teams of six players wearing fins, masks, snorkels, gloves, and helmets use 12-inch-long hockey sticks to push a puck across the bottom of a swimming pool. Most players can stay under water for about 20 seconds before they have to surface to breathe. The secret to winning is timing your snorkeling with your teammates so that you don't all swim to the surface at once, leaving the playing field wide open to the opposing team. Twenty-one teams competed in the 2005 U.S. Nationals in Minneapolis, Minnesota.

## CRICKET SPITTING

**Where They Do It:** At the Bug Bowl festival, held every April at Purdue University in Lafayette, Indiana

**How It's Played:** Thousands of contestants compete to see who can spit a dead, intact cricket the farthest. If the cricket loses its legs, wings, or antennae, the spit doesn't count. The world champion is Dan Capps, a mechanic at a meat-packing factory, who spit his cricket 32 feet in 1998. "It's just a matter of blowing hard," he says. "Crickets aren't very aerodynamic."

# BUT WAIT!
# THERE'S MORE!

*If you buy this Bathroom Reader right now for just $17.95,
we'll include this amazing Book-O-Matic—free of charge! Here's
the story of the Popeil family and their world of gadgets.*

**Y**OURS FREE IF YOU ACT NOW!
Since the 1950s, the name Popeil has been synonymous with
gadgets sold on television, in either breathless commercials
for plastic food choppers or in 30-minute "infomercials" for spray-
on hair. But Ron Popeil, the guy who sells the Showtime Rotisserie
("Set it...and...forget it") on TV, is actually a third-generation
pitchman. His great-uncle, Nat Morris, started in Asbury Park, New
Jersey, in the early 20th century. Like other pitchmen, Morris would
set up a table at county fairs, carnivals, or along the beach and sell
inexpensive items, usually kitchen utensils, to passersby. Morris was
so successful at it that by the 1920s, he'd become wealthy enough
to open his own metal kitchen products factory.

In 1932 Morris's nephew, Samuel Popeil, stepped in for a sick
relative to demonstrate kitchen utensils at Macy's in New York
City and discovered that he, too, had a natural ability for selling.
Like Morris, Popeil became a master of "the pitch," honed over
years of selling and performing product demonstrations at department stores, fairs, street corners, and boardwalks.

### ISN'T THAT AMAZING!
Sam Popeil and his brother Raymond earned their living in the
1930s and '40s by selling products that were made at their Popeil
Brothers factory. Eliminating the middleman associated with selling other companies' products meant more profits for the Popeil
brothers. Raymond oversaw factory production and Sam came up
with new gadgets, mostly graters and slicers that cost under a dollar. They gave the products names designed to evoke power and
efficiency, like "Kitchen Magician" or "Slice-a-Way." These simple
items were presented so enthusiastically by the Popeils that consumers bought them by the millions.

---

In Japan, apple farmers use turkeys to guard their orchards against monkeys.

In the late 1940s, the Popeil brothers fully embraced the plastics revolution. They sold plastic versions of common kitchen items such as breadboxes, flour sifters, cookie presses, and storage canisters. They were pleasing to the eye, looked modern, and were inexpensive to make.

## AS SEEN ON TV

But as television took hold in the 1950s it threatened the Popeils' usual circuit of fairs, carnivals, and department store demonstrations. In 1956 the Grant Company, an early TV advertising agency based in Chicago, asked Popeil to sell the new Chop-O-Matic food chopper in a TV commercial. It would essentially be a four-minute, taped version of the Popeil's department store pitch.

But Grant didn't choose Sam or Raymond to appear in the ad. They picked Sam's 21-year-old son, Ron Popeil, to be the pitchman. (He'd spent the previous five years doing demonstrations of Popeil products around the Midwest.)

Despite good sales for the Chop-O-Matic, the Popeils weren't convinced of television's power. They went back to in-store demonstrations and made more Chop-O-Matic-like products, which they contracted other companies to sell on TV. They wouldn't make their own ad until 1961, for the Veg-O-Matic. On the strength of that TV ad (featuring Raymond Popeil), the product sold 11 million units. *That* convinced them.

Other Popeil Brothers items Americans couldn't live without:

- **Automatic Egg Turner** (1948). A metal spatula that could flip an egg or a pancake perfectly
- **Toastie Pie** (1950). A toasted-sandwich maker
- **Citrex Juicer** (1951). A tiny juicer that plugs into the fruit and allows the juice to pour into a glass
- **Plastic Plant Kit** (1957). Molds liquid plastic to make plastic plants, which were very exotic at the time
- **Chop-O-Matic** spawned these slicers, dicers, peelers, and mixers: **Dial-O-Matic** (1958), **The Amazing Veg-O-Matic** (1961), **Corn-O-Matic** (1964), **Mince-O-Matic Seven** (1965), **Peel-O-Matic** (1965), and **Whip-O-Matic** (1974).

The Popeils churned out new products and commercials well

into the 1970s. Their downfall: themselves. By being an early proponent of TV advertising, they actually demonstrated its lucrative potential to other companies, which drove up ad rates and commercial production costs. Meanwhile, the introduction of more sophisticated electric kitchen appliances was making their simple plastic and metal gadgets look cheap and dated. The Popeil Brothers company was sold in 1979; it was dissolved and liquidated within two years.

But there was still Ronco.

*But wait, there's more! For the rest of the Popeil story, turn to page 453. Act now! Operators are standing by!*

*   *   *

*Here are some of Samuel Popeil's surefire sales tactics. (His son, Ron, uses many of the same methods on TV today.)*

• Sales booths should be situated near makeup aisles or women's restrooms to ensure a receptive—and captive—audience.

• Get one or two people to stop and listen. That will pique the interest of others passing by.

• Tout the product's indispensability. Show how the item is a value because it performs multiple tasks. Memorize the spoken part of the pitch so you can deliver it flawlessly while you demonstrate the product. That will show how easy it is to use.

• Describe the product's usefulness repeatedly, using words like "magic," "fantastic," and "miracle." Ask rhetorical questions like "Isn't that amazing?" when demonstrating the product.

• Never reveal the price until the end of the pitch. This builds suspense. Say to the audience, "You're probably asking yourself what a product like this costs." Then give a high round number, like $40. Then say that the item is well worth that price, but right now it's much cheaper. Progressively move the price down: It's not $10; it's not $5. It's the low, low price of $3.98! To encourage immediate purchase, tell the crowd that "supplies are limited."

• But wait, there's more! Before allowing anyone to purchase it, suddenly introduce and demonstrate a smaller product, noting its "retail" value, and give it away for free with purchase.

---

Artist Paul Cézanne taught his parrot to say "Cézanne is a great painter."

# DUMB CROOKS

*Here's proof that crime doesn't pay.*

## SAY WHAT?

"In 2002 Blair MacKay, 32, was fined $600 for invasion of privacy by a court in Dingwall, Scotland. The court had heard testimony that he had barged into a female neighbor's apartment and asserted, 'I don't listen to phone conversations!' The woman testified that she had just told her friend over the phone that MacKay was probably listening to them."

—*The Scotsman*

## MAZDA *LIGHT POLE* 3000

"It wasn't the Mazda RX-7's speed that caught the eye of Redondo Beach Police Officer Joseph Fonteno. It was the hood ornament— a 9-foot light pole draped across the hood. Minutes earlier, the car's driver had clipped a three-phase traffic signal from its concrete base and proceeded about seven miles to Pacific Coast Highway, where Fonteno pulled him over. When the officer asked about the traffic signal, the driver replied. 'It came with the car when I bought it.' The motorist was booked on charges of drunk driving, hit-and-run, and 'excessive sarcasm,' said police."

—*Los Angeles Times*

## STUPID FOR 15 MINUTES

"A day after they told their tale of buried treasure on national television, two men were charged with stealing the 1,800 antique dollar bills (estimated value: more than $100,000) they said they found in their back yard. As Timothy Crebase, 24, and Barry Billcliff, 27, of Methuen, N.H., recounted their story on *Good Morning America*, *Today*, Fox, and CNN, police noticed the details changed with each appearance. There were discrepancies about when they found the money, how deep it was buried, why they were digging, and the exact site.

"When Crebase and Billcliff returned from the New York media blitz, police and the Secret Service were waiting to question them. When it turned out they had found the bills in a barn they were

---

roofing, the two were charged with receiving stolen property and conspiracy to commit larceny. Ironically, the men were unable to raise the $5,000 cash bail."

—*Manchester* (N.H.) *Eagle-Tribune*

## FEELING WANTED

"A suspect in two taxicab robberies walked into a New York City police station and failed to notice his picture in a 'wanted' photo on the wall, giving cops an opportunity to make one of their easiest busts ever. An alert detective noticed the resemblance and immediately arrested Awiey 'Chucky' Hernandez, 20. Hernandez had gone to the station to inquire about a friend, Huquan 'Guns' Gavin, who had been arrested in another investigation, said Det. Sgt. Norman Horowitz of the New York Police Dept., adding that he had 'never seen anything like it in 30 years on the force.' "

—**Reuters**

## HE BLEW IT

"A Warrensburg man burned himself and is facing criminal charges after he used a lighter to check on his efforts to steal gasoline from a dump truck, causing a fire that destroyed a forklift. Glen Germain, 19, suffered minor burns in the blaze when he lit a lighter to see how full the gas can he was filling had become, sheriff's investigators said. The lighter ignited gas on his hands and in the can; the gas can fire then spread to the forklift, destroying the vehicle. Germain admitted he was responsible for the fire, telling investigators he was trying to see the progress of the siphoning process."

—*Post Star* (N.Y.)

## QUICKIES

• A couple rushing to make a high school graduation ceremony led police on a high speed chase that ended when they sped through a train crossing and crashed into a nearby home (no one was hurt). The wrecked car was going to be a surprise present for the graduate.

• A five-time burglar from Detroit found himself back in the can, charged with yet another burglary. How'd they catch him? He played with some Silly Putty in the home he'd just robbed and left his fingerprints.

---

Scientists have revived 250-million-year-old bacteria.

# D. B. COOPER

*Modern-day Robin Hood? Or high-flying robber?*
*He hijacked an airplane, stole a small fortune, then*
*parachuted out of sight…and straight into legend.*

**DAREDEVIL**

On Thanksgiving Eve, November 24, 1971, a nondescript man wearing a conservative dark suit, white shirt, narrow black tie, and sunglasses stepped up to the Northwest Orient Airlines ticket counter in Portland, Oregon. He paid $20 in cash for a one-way ticket to Seattle on Flight 305.

Once the 727 was airborne, the man summoned the flight attendant, Tina Mucklow, introduced himself as "Dan Cooper," and handed her a note. It said he had a bomb in his briefcase and would blow up the plane if they didn't grant his demands. He wanted two parachutes and $200,000 in $20 bills. When the plane landed in Seattle, Cooper kept the pilot and crew hostage but let the passengers off in exchange for the chutes and the loot. Then he ordered the pilot to take off again and set a course for Mexico with some special instructions: Keep the landing gear down, and the flight speed under 170 mph. Somewhere over the Lewis River, 25 miles northeast of Portland, Cooper strapped on a parachute, tied the money around his waist, and jumped out the rear stairway of the plane. He was never seen or heard from again.

**THE BIGFOOT OF CRIME**

In the ensuing investigation, the FBI questioned a man named Daniel B. Cooper. Although that person was never a serious suspect, the FBI reported to the press that they'd interrogated a "D. B. Cooper." And those initials became forever linked with the skyjacker.

The FBI manhunt that followed was unprecedented in scope and intensity. It was a showcase investigation, meant to display the competency and professionalism of the world's greatest law enforcement agency. Every inch of ground in the vicinity of the purported landing site was searched from the air and land, with teams of trackers and dogs, for 18 days. So it was a humbling moment when, after weeks of tracking down leads, the FBI admitted that they had come up with…nothing. No credible suspect. No trace of the loot or the parachute. No further leads to follow. A complete dead end. One frustrated FBI agent referred to Cooper as the "Bigfoot of crime" because there was no proof of his existence anywhere.

If Cooper survived, he'd pulled off the crime of the century.

## A STAR IS BORN

Something about the hijacking caught the public imagination, as the media reports raved about the audacity of the crime and the calm, competent way in which Cooper carried it out. According to the flight attendants, Cooper behaved like a gentleman throughout the ordeal, even requesting that meals be delivered to the crew while they were stuck on the ground in Seattle, waiting for the ransom money to be delivered.

He became a folk hero, a latter-day Jesse James. Songs were written about him, and a movie was made, starring Treat Williams as Cooper and Robert Duvall as the FBI agent on his trail. Half a dozen books, mostly by former FBI agents, published theories about what happened to him. He was living the high life on a beach in Mexico. Or he'd slipped back into his former life somewhere in the States, undetected, unnoticed, and forgotten.

On February 13, 1980, a family picnicking on the Columbia River, 30 miles west of Cooper's landing area, found three bundles of disintegrating $20 bills ($5,800 total). The serial numbers were traced to the ransom. The rest of the cash has never been found.

## …SO WHO DUNNIT?

• *Possible Suspect #1.* On April 7, 1972, four months after Cooper's successful hijacking, another hijacker stole a plane in Denver, using the same M.O. as D. B. Cooper. The Denver flight was also a 727 with a rear stairway, from which the hijacker made his getaway by parachute. A tip led police to Richard McCoy Jr., a man with an unusual profile: married with two children, a former Sunday school teacher, a law enforcement major at Brigham Young University, a former Green Beret helicopter pilot with service in Vietnam, and an avid skydiver. When FBI agents arrested McCoy two days after the Denver hijacking, they found a jumpsuit and a duffel bag containing half a million dollars. McCoy was convicted and sentenced to 45 years.

In August 1974 McCoy escaped from prison (he tricked the guards into letting him out of his cell with a handgun made from toothpaste and then crashed a garbage truck through the prison gate). The FBI tracked him down and three months later killed him in a shootout in Virginia.

In 1991 former FBI agent Russell Calame wrote a book titled *D. B. Cooper: The Real McCoy*, in which he claimed McCoy and Cooper were the same person. He quoted Nicholas O'Hara, the FBI agent who tracked down McCoy, as saying, "When I shot Richard McCoy, I shot D. B. Cooper at the same time." But there's no conclusive evidence. In fact, McCoy's widow sued for libel and won.

**Possible Suspect #2.** In August 2000, a Florida widow told *U.S. News and World Report* that her husband was D.B. Cooper. Jo Weber claimed that shortly before his death in 1995, her husband, Duane, told her, "I'm Dan Cooper." Later she remembered he'd talked in his sleep about jumping out of an airplane. She checked into his background and discovered he'd spent time in prison near Portland, Oregon, then found an old Northwest Airlines ticket stub from the Seattle-Tacoma airport among his papers. She found a book about D. B. Cooper in the local library—it had notations in the margins matching her husband's handwriting.

She relayed her suspicions to FBI Agent Ralph Himmelsbach, chief investigator on the D. B. Cooper case. To this day he insists Weber is one of the likeliest suspects he's come across. More recently, facial recognition software was used to find the closest match to the composite picture of D. B. Cooper. Of the 3,000 photographs used (including Richard McCoy's), Duane Weber's was identified as the "best match."

**Possible Suspect #3.** Elsie Rodgers of Cozad, Nebraska, often told her family about the time she was hiking near the Columbia River in Washington in the 1970s and found a human head. They never really believed her until, while going through her things shortly after her death in 2000, they found a hatbox in her attic...with a human skull in it. Could that have been the remains of D. B. Cooper? And if so, what happened to the ransom money? Thirty years later, his fate remains a mystery.

# UNCLE JOHN HELPS OUT AROUND THE HOUSE

*Impress your family with these strange household tips.*

• Having trouble removing a stubborn splinter? Squirt some Elmer's Glue on the area. When it dries, peel it off—the splinter will come off with it.

• To protect fine china from getting scratched, put a coffee filter between each dish or teacup when you stack them.

• Telephone getting grimy? Wipe it down with a soft cloth dipped in rubbing alcohol.

• Lose a contact lens in your carpet? Cover the end of a vacuum hose with a stocking and secure it with a rubber band. Then vacuum, holding the hose about an inch off the carpet. The stocking will prevent the lens from being sucked in.

• In a pinch, olive oil makes an effective (but greasy) substitute for shaving cream.

• Used fabric softener sheets are excellent for wiping dust off computer and TV screens.

• Adding a cup of coarse table salt to a load of wash helps prevent colors from fading.

• You can use Silly Putty to clean the gunk off your computer keyboard (and when you're finished you can use it to remove lint from clothes).

• Spy tip: Mailing a sensitive document? Seal the envelope with egg white—it's nearly impossible to steam open.

• Wash windows on a cloudy day: sunlight makes the cleaner dry more quickly, which can cause streaks.

• Kitty litter is good for soaking up oil and other fluids your car drips on your driveway.

• Spice drops (similar to gum drops) make an effective bait for mousetraps.

• To unclog a metal showerhead, unscrew it, remove the rubber washer, and simmer the showerhead in equal parts water and vinegar for about five minutes. (*Soak*—do not boil—plastic showerheads.)

• If you freeze candles before you use them, they will burn slower and last longer.

---

Barely half of women say color is an important factor when buying a car (60% of men do).

# YOU YELL, WE SHELL!

*Every branch of the armed services has its own set of official inspirational mottoes. And behind the scenes, they've got some unofficial ones, too. Here are some examples of both.*

## MARINE CORPS

**Official Line:** *Semper Fidelis* ("Always Faithful"), "Whatever It Takes," "Make Peace or Die," "Hell in a Helmet," *Mors De Contactus* ("Death on Contact")

**Off the Record:** "Uncle Sam's Misguided Children" (USMC), "You Yell, We Shell," "Muscles Are Required, Intelligence Not Essential, SIR!" (spells MARINES)

## ARMY

**Official Line:** "It Will Be Done," "This We'll Defend," "Duty, Honor, Country," "The Sword of Freedom," "Over, Under, and Through," "Hell on Wheels," "Heaven sent. Hell bent."

**Off the Record:** "Yes My Retarded A** Signed Up" (U.S. ARMY spelled backward)

## NAVY

**Official Line:** "Can Do," "Honor, Courage, Commitment," "Always ready, always there," "Lead, follow, or get out of the way."

**Off the Record:** "We've been to Hell…and it snows there too," "You didn't see me, I wasn't there, and I'm not here now," "In God we trust. All others, we monitor." (Naval Intelligence)

## AIR FORCE

**Official Line:** *Uno Ab Alto* ("One over All"), "Attack to Defend," "Fire from the Clouds," "These things we do that others may live"

**Off the Record:** "We were going by there anyway," "Nobody goes until we pass them the hose" (Fuel troops), "Without weapons, it's just another airline." (Weapons troops)

## COAST GUARD

**Official Line:** *Semper Paratus* (Always Ready)

**Off the Record:** "Support Search and Rescue—Get Lost"

---

American soldiers in Vietnam sometimes used Slinkies as radio antennas.

# STRANGE INVENTIONS

*Necessity is the mother of invention. These are its weird uncles.*

ONLINE CHICKEN PETTER

Ever feel the need to pet a chicken but there just wasn't one handy? Good news: the University of Singapore has invented the Touchy Internet system. "We understand the perceived eccentricity of a system for humans to interact with poultry remotely," says developer Adrian Cheok. "But this has a much wider significance." The device will allow people at zoos to scratch otherwise dangerous animals, such as lions or bears, and also enable people with allergies to touch their pets via the Internet.

How it works: Users pet a chicken-shaped doll that's hooked up to their computer, while watching a webcam image of a real chicken on the screen. Sensors on the doll relay the petting location to another computer, which then activates tiny motors in a lightweight jacket that the real chicken wears. The motors' vibrations mimic the sensation of being petted exactly as the user at home is petting the doll. "This is the first human-poultry interaction system ever developed," says Professor Cheok.

## BOVINE URINE NEUTRALIZER

A New Zealand agricultural company, Summit-Quinphos, has developed a device that fits under a cow's tail and automatically sprays a nitrate-inhibiting compound onto the ground every time she urinates. Cow urine is very high in soil-damaging nitrates, and farmers must regularly treat entire fields with expensive chemicals to neutralize it. The device is activated when the cow lifts its tail and sprays the ground where the cow has just peed. It could potentially save farmers a lot of money and labor.

## MOBILE MORNING ANNOYER

Gauri Nanda, a research associate at MIT, has come up with a unique alarm clock. The device (he calls it "Clocky") has two rubber wheels and is covered in thick shag carpet. When the sleepy person hits the "snooze" button, a motor is activated and the clock rolls off the bedside table and around the room, bumping into

---

A woman wearing stiletto heels exerts 552 pounds of pressure per square inch at the heel.

things until a built-in computer chip randomly decides when it will stop. Minutes later the alarm goes off again, forcing the sleeper to get up and look for it. "In designing Clocky," Nanda writes, "I was in part inspired by kittens I've had that would bite my toes every morning." He said it's "less of an annoying device than it is a troublesome pet that you love anyway. It's also a bit ugly."

## REMOTE HUGGER

Francesca Rosella, the owner of an Italian design company called CuteCircuit, has developed a T-shirt that she says can send a hug to a faraway loved one. The "F+R shirts" (Rosella's initials) employ built-in sensors that store information such as the body temperature and heart rate of a distant loved one. Using a cell phone, the caller "calls" the shirt, and the sensors, located in the upper arms, shoulders, back, and hips, cause small pads to inflate and deflate, as well as heat up, mimicking a hug. Rosella says the shirts are perfect for people in long-distance relationships.

## MARRIAGE-SAVING WASHER

In 2005 Spanish inventor Pep Torres invented a washing machine designed to help create equality between spouses. The "Your Turn" has a fingerprint sensor that must be touched before the washer will start…and it won't let the same person start the machine two times in a row. "I thought it would be good for the macho man who doesn't do anything around the house except drink beer," the Barcelona designer told the BBC's *Everywomen* TV show. The washer was expected to go on sale in time for Father's Day.

## AUTOMATIC ENTERTAINER

In 2004 Jimmy Or, a student at Waseda University in Tokyo, invented a robot that belly dances. He says he was inspired by actress Lucy Liu in the movie *Charlie's Angels*. Her movements reminded him of the eel-like lamprey as it swims through the water. "I decided to work on my idea secretly," he said. He built a computer program that mimics the lamprey's primitive neural network, which controls its slithery movement. Result: the Waseda Belly Dancer No. 1, a short, squat robot with a flexible spine. The WBD #1 wears a low-hanging skirt while it dances; Or says he's looking for some jewelry for it, too.

---

Times change: Until about 100 years ago, jump rope was considered a boy's game.

# UNPLANNED WORLD RECORDS

*Some people try their entire lives to make it into the pages*
*of the* Guinness Book of World Records; *other people*
*get in without even trying...and wish they hadn't.*

**RECORD:** Only person in recorded medical history to have been both a dwarf and a giant
**STORY:** Born in Austria in 1899, Adam Rainer was just under 3' 11" tall when he turned 21, which classified him as a dwarf. But then he started growing...rapidly. By his 32nd birthday he had topped out at 7' 2" tall. The strain was too much on his body—he spent the rest of his life in bed and died at the age of 51.

**RECORD:** Longest fall without a parachute (and surviving)
**STORY:** Twenty-three-year-old Vesna Vulovic was working aboard a Jugoslovenski Aerotransport on January 26, 1972, when it exploded over Srbska Kamenice, Czechoslovakia, while travelling at 33,330 feet. Vulovic was knocked into the tail section of the plane and plummeted all the way to the ground. She spent 23 days in a coma and another six months in the hospital, but she survived.

**RECORD:** Most bombs defused
**STORY:** From 1945 to 1957, Werner Stephan, a member of the West Berlin bomb squad, is documented to have defused more than 8,000. (He was killed by a grenade explosion in August 1957.)

**RECORD:** Worst kidney blockage
**STORY:** Ever heard of a condition called *hydronephrosis?* That's when your kidney becomes enlarged due to an obstruction in urine flow. In June 1999 a 35-year-old Egyptian man checked into a Saudi Arabian hospital with the complaint. Doctors removed 5.8 *gallons* of obstructed urine from the diseased kidney. (Three weeks later the kidney had to be removed, too.)

**RECORD:** Least successful published author.

**STORY:** Over a period of 18 years, William A. Gold wrote eight books and seven novels for a total of 3 million words before making his first sale to a newspaper in Canberra, Australia. Gold's total career earnings: 50 cents. "Until this bonanza," *Guinness* notes, "his closest approach to success has been the publication in 1958 of a 150-word book review in the *Workers Education Association Bulletin* in Adelaide, Australia, on the clear understanding that it would be published only if he did not demand a fee."

**RECORD:** Longest survival adrift at sea

**STORY:** Captain Oguri Jukichi and a sailor named Otokichi were sailing off the Japanese coast in October 1813 when their ship was disabled in a storm. They floated all the way across the Pacific and were rescued by an American ship off the California coast on March 24, 1815. Total time at sea: 484 days.

**RECORD:** Worst electric shock (and surviving)

**STORY:** On November 9, 1967, 17-year-old Brian Litasa touched a live "ultra-high-voltage" power line in Los Angeles and lived to tell the tale. Estimated shock: 230,000 volts.

**RECORD:** Fastest-flopping play

**STORY:** Lots of plays die after just one performance. *The Intimate Revue*, which opened at London's Duchess Theater on March 11, 1930, died after only half of one. The production was so unwieldy that the management scrapped seven scenes to ensure that the play would end at midnight. The play was never staged again.

**RECORD:** Deepest ocean escape without equipment

**STORY:** On September 28, 1970, Richard Slater had just finished raising a sunken boat near California's Catalina Island when the boat broke loose from the surface ship and plunged back into the sea. Slater, in a submersible, was still on the seabed 225 feet beneath the surface when the boat crashed into his vessel, breaching the hull. He was able to open the hatch and float to the surface, which took an estimated 2½ to 3 minutes. He was found floating face-down, unconscious, and not breathing, but was revived and went on to make a full recovery.

The original Guinness Brewery in Dublin, Ireland, has a 6,000-year lease.

# THE FIRST BLACK AMERICAN SEA CAPTAIN

*Born into bondage, Robert Smalls rose from slavery to the halls of Congress. In between, he helped the Union win the Civil War by doing what no black American had ever done before—he commanded a naval vessel.*

## AT HOME ON THE WATER

Robert Smalls was born a slave on April 5, 1839, in the coastal town of Beaufort, South Carolina. His first taste of a sailor's life came at 12 years old when his master hired him out to work at a shipyard in Charleston Harbor. Smalls took to it, displaying a natural talent for seamanship. By 19, he had risen to the highest sea rank available to a slave: a ship's pilot. Although Smalls could neither read nor write, his photographic memory recalled every bar, shoal, and current in Charleston Harbor.

In 1858 Smalls married another slave, Hannah Jones, and two years later they had a son, Robert Jr. Being a respected sea pilot, Smalls's life was better than that of most slaves...but he was still a slave. Longing to be his own master, he set out to buy his family's freedom. And he almost did it—Smalls had saved $700 of the $800 purchasing price when the Civil War broke out in 1861. Then everybody's life was put on hold.

## STEALING A SHIP

The Confederate army immediately put the 22-year-old Smalls to work doing what he did best: piloting a vessel. He was given the wheel of the CSS *Planter* (formerly the USS *Planter*), a 147-foot-long steamboat. With Smalls at the helm taking orders from Captain Charles Relyea, the ship hauled ordnance and supplies to the rebel forts guarding Charleston. A few miles offshore lay a fleet of blockading Union ships, and Smalls knew that freedom awaited him in that blockade. He formed a plan.

First, he studied the voice and speech patterns of Captain Relyea. Smalls was raised speaking "gullah," a creole dialect of English indigenous to the Sea Islands of South Carolina. Captain

Relyea, on the other hand, spoke in the "propuh Suthuhn" dialect. After spending weeks secretly mimicking his captain, Smalls was ready.

On May 12, 1862, Captain Relyea attended a party and decided to spend the night ashore. With the captain and white crew land-locked, the black crew was left in charge of the ship, which was not uncommon—they were well within Southern strongholds, protected by the guns of Fort Sumter. Smalls had counted on this; he smuggled his wife, his son, and 13 other slaves aboard. On May 13 at 3 a.m., the ship slowly pulled away from the dock, supposedly to take its place as a picket ship guarding the harbor. Smalls put on the captain's uniform—including the broad-brimmed hat, which shadowed his dark face—and sounded the proper whistle signals when the *Planter* passed Confederate forts. At 4 a.m., as the ship passed under the guns of Fort Sumter, he was ordered to halt and state his destination. Smalls mimicked Relyea's voice, said all the right things, and was allowed to continue. When they were out of range of the rebel batteries, Smalls lowered the Confederate flag.

As the sun came up, the CSS *Planter* was sailing right into the Union blockade. The first ship she approached was the USS *Onward*—and her captain was preparing to fire on the Confederate vessel. But Smalls put their fears to rest when he waved a large white flag and shouted out a friendly greeting: "Good morning, sir! I have brought you some of the old United States guns!"

## WAR HERO

The daring escape made headlines in the North, hailing Smalls for his cunning and guile. This led to a meeting with President Lincoln in August. Smalls so impressed the Union leader that Lincoln took the politically dangerous step of authorizing 5,000 blacks to be recruited for military service. Before the war ended three years later, more than 180,000 black American volunteers would serve in Lincoln's army—most of them former slaves.

The federal government awarded Smalls $1,500 for capturing the *Planter*, but he still chose to enlist and fight for the Union. After making a recruiting tour of New York, Smalls was sent back to South Carolina and commissioned as 2nd Lieutenant, Company B, 33rd Regiment, United States Colored Troops. He was once again given the wheel of the renamed USS *Planter*, now part

---

Going down: The Washington Monument is sinking at a rate of six inches per year.

of the Union blockading fleet.

## PROMOTION

In November 1863, the *Planter* took part in a futile attack on Fort Sumter with Smalls as pilot under the white Captain James Nickerson. When the ship was caught in a deadly crossfire from Confederate shore batteries, the captain deserted his post and ran below deck, hiding in the coal bin. Smalls took command, keeping the guns firing while he used his encyclopedic knowledge of Charleston Harbor to maneuver the damaged ship to safety.

A Naval Board of Inquiry dismissed Nickerson for cowardice, but Smalls was again regarded as a hero...and was given his first command. His ship: the *Planter*, the same ship on which he had escaped two years earlier. In combat, Captain Smalls fought in 17 naval engagements; off duty, he studied with tutors to learn to read and write, skills which had been forbidden him as a slave.

## CONTINUING THE FIGHT

When the war ended Smalls returned to Beaufort. Using the money he earned, he purchased the house in which he was born and moved his family into it (which now included two daughters and his recently freed mother). Smalls entered politics and served five non-consecutive terms in Congress. In 1897 the government belatedly recognized his wartime service by awarding him a $30-per-month veteran's pension.

Robert Smalls died in Beaufort on February 23, 1915. His home has since been designated a National Historic Landmark. A naval cargo vessel, the USS *Robert Smalls*, was named in his honor. Beside Smalls's grave is a statue with an inscription that sums up his life's work: "My people need no special defense, for the past history of this country proves them to be the equal of any people, anywhere. All they need is an equal chance in the battle of life."

\*　　\*　　\*

"Those who make peaceful revolution impossible will make violent revolution inevitable."
—John F. Kennedy

The odors of gardenia and orange blossoms, combined together, have no smell.

# A ROOM OF HER OWN

*Words of wisdom from worldly women.*

"The first time Adam had a chance he laid the blame on a woman."
—**Lady Nancy Astor**

"God gave women intuition and femininity. Used properly, the combination easily jumbles the brain of any man I've ever met."
—**Farrah Fawcett**

"The great and almost only comfort about being a woman is that one can always pretend to be more stupid than one is and no one is surprised."
—**Freya Stark, writer**

"Women are the only oppressed group in our society that lives in intimate association with their oppressors."
—**Evelyn Cunningham**

"I'm not denyin' that women are foolish: God Almighty made 'em to match the men."
—**George Eliot, writer**

"When you belong to a minority, you have to be better in order to have the right to be equal."
—**Christine Collange, writer**

"Women are like tea bags; you never know how strong she is until she gets into hot water."
—**Eleanor Roosevelt**

"Why are women so much more interesting to men than men are to women?"
—**Virginia Woolf**

"There is a growing strength in women—but it's in the forehead, not the forearm."
—**Beverly Sills**

"Women might start a rumor, but not a war."
—**Marga Gomez, artist**

"A man's got to do what a man's got to do. A woman must do what he can't."
—**Rhonda Hansome, actor**

"All women want from men is a partner who will share his hopes, his thoughts, his dreams. And if you don't, we're going to bitch at you until the day you die."
—**Stephanie Hodge, actor**

"Until all women have made it, none of us have made it."
—**Rosemary Brown**

---

A hummingbird's heart rate drops from 500 beats a minute to 10 when it goes to sleep.

# THE WOMAN EMPEROR

*In a civilization ruled by men for thousands of years, only one woman ever made it to the top in imperial China—Empress Wu.*

## HIGH CHINA

China hasn't had a monarchy since the Communist Revolution of 1949. But for more than 4,000 years before that, it was a ruled by 308 different emperors spanning 14 dynastic periods. Of those 308, only one was a woman.

It happened during the T'ang Dynasty, which ruled China from A.D. 618–907, an era commonly considered the height of Chinese art, literature, philosophy, trade, and technology. The capital city, Chang'an (modern-day Xi'an), was the largest and most culturally advanced city in the world, with a population of more than a million. This was also a rare era of freedom for women in China; women had long been treated as inferior but now enjoyed such freedoms as the right to be educated, to divorce, to own land, and to take part—to a degree—in politics. But no one could have expected a woman to take as large a role as the girl known as Wu Zhao.

## LUCKY GIRL?

Wu Zhao was born in 624 into a noble and wealthy family, and was educated from an early age in music, art, literature, and philosophy. That education would help her immensely. When she was 13 years old, her family's connections allowed her the great privilege of becoming a *Cairen*, one of nine "fifth-tier" concubines of the Emperor Tai-tsung. Her education, her musical talent, her beauty, and her wit made her stand out from the other girls, and she soon became one of the emperor's favorites. He gave her the title *Meiniang*, or "Charming Lady," and assigned her to work in the imperial study. There she would add to her knowledge the workings of government—knowledge she would put to great use in the coming years.

In 649, when Wu Zhao was 25, Emperor Tai-tsung died—not a good thing for a concubine: in keeping with tradition, all the concubines were sent to a Buddhist convent, where they were to spend the rest of their lives. But Tai-tsung's son, Kao-tsung, became emperor and soon began visiting Wu at the convent. Many historians believe that Wu Zhao had been having an affair with the prince for a number of years, possibly because she knew he could get her out of the convent when his father died. True or not, two years later the new emperor broke tradition and had Wu Zhao returned to the palace, where she became Wu Zhaoyi, *Zhaoyi* signifying the highest rank of the second-tier concubines. There were now only two women above her in what became her quest for the throne: Kao-tsung's wife, Empress Wang, and his first consort, Xiaoshu.

## HEIR REPLACEMENTS

Within a few years, Wu Zhaoyi had two sons by the emperor—two possible heirs to the emperor's throne if she got rid of the two women in her way. And she soon did.

When Wu Zhaoyi's newborn daughter died during childbirth, Wu accused Empress Wang of infanticide. Some versions of the story say that Wu actually killed her own daughter, then blamed it on the empress. In any case, in 655 the emperor imprisoned his wife and made Wu Zhaoyi empress. She quickly used her new power to have the former empress and the first concubine, Xiaoshu, executed. Wu Zhao now became Empress Wu Zetian. But she still wanted more.

Emperor Kao-tsung allowed Wu Zetian to take an active role in the government, and historians say she did it very well. Implementing such changes as improved agricultural practices, tax reductions, and increased efficiency in government administration, the empress helped bolster an already thriving empire. She also began to eliminate people who dared oppose her, replacing them with her supporters. Emperor Kao-tsung became aware of what she was doing, but historians believe he was either afraid of her or powerless to stop her. In 660 Kao-tsung, just 32 years old, had a debilitating stroke. He survived, but Empress Wu now essentially took his place, becoming the actual, if not the named, ruler of China. That still wasn't enough.

## ONE MORE STEP

Wu now began a brutal purge of the royal court. Anyone who opposed her was imprisoned, exiled, or executed—including family members. When the emperor finally died in 683, Wu's eldest son, Hung, would have been first in line for the throne. (By this time she had four sons.) But he was already gone, having died mysteriously a year earlier after complaining about his mother's rule. Her second son was also out of the picture; he had once complained about an affair his mother was having, so she had him exiled (he eventually committed suicide). The third son, Li Xian, was put on the throne…and was exiled 54 days later, apparently too difficult for the empress to control. That left the fourth son, Li Dan, to become emperor—in name only—and to carry out his mother's wishes.

By 690 Wu Zetian had eliminated enough of her enemies to do what had never been done by a woman in Chinese history: she deposed her puppet son and declared herself the sole ruler of China—giving herself the male name Emperor Shengshen.

## BIG WU

Emperor Shengshen declared the end of the T'ang Dynasty and a return to the Zhou Dynasty (Wu Zetian believed herself to be descended from the ancient Zhou emperors). She ruled China for the next 15 years. It was an ironically brutal rule during which she spread the compassionate teachings of Buddhism while ruthlessly butchering her enemies. In 695 she expanded her royal name, taking the Buddhist title Emperor Tiance Jinlun Shengshen—the Divine Emperor Who Rules the Universe. In 705, now 80 years old, her rule was ended by a successful palace coup. Her third son once again became emperor, ending the Zhou Dynasty after having just one ruler and restoring the T'ang Dynasty. She died nine months later.

Wu Zetian was vilified by Chinese scholars for centuries after her rule. Stories of her brutality and "immoral behavior" may even be false histories written by her critics in the centuries following her death. Many historians point out that her actions as ruler stand out only because she was a woman and were not very different from the actions of male emperors of the time. In all, the former concubine ruled China for nearly 45 years, 15 of them as emperor. No woman would ever rule China again.

# HOAX!

*Everything you read on this page is true. Or is it?*

## SHOPPING FOR ATTENTION

**Background:** A new piece of ancient artwork turned up in the British Museum in 2005. The artifact was a rock bearing painted images of animals, a man, and an unusual tool. The sign beneath it read: "Early man venturing towards the out-of-town hunting grounds."

**Exposed!** The "tool" in the picture was a shopping cart; the "artifact" had been secretly placed there by British hoax artist Banksymus Maximus, also known as "Banksy." He designed it to look like the authentic ancient pieces in the museum—and it stayed up for three days before "experts" at the museum noticed it. (The sign on the piece also dated it to "the Post-Catatonic era.") The museum took the hoax in good humor, and even returned the piece to the artist. It quickly went up at Banksy's latest show at another museum, with the label "On loan from the British Museum."

## HE NEEDS HELP

**Background:** A desperate Austrian man called police to his home in January 2005. He claimed the house was haunted. For weeks he had continually heard footsteps in the hallways and doors slamming through the night. He begged the police for help.

**Exposed!** Police put video cameras in the house and for the next few weeks compiled footage of the "ghost"—the 42-year-old wife of one of the man's employees. She was charged with creating a nuisance and jailed for four months. Why she did it remains a mystery.

## BUT IT SOUNDED GOOD

**Background:** Massachusetts Institute of Technology student Jeremy Stribling submitted an academic paper to a leading technology conference. The paper, entitled "Rooter: A Methodology for the Typical Unification of Access Points and Redundancy," was accepted, and he was invited to speak at the World Multiconference on Systemics, Cybernetics and Informatics in Orlando, Florida.

**Exposed!** The paper was nothing but gibberish generated by a

---

*Now you know: A white flag means surrender; a yellow flag means infectious disease.*

computer program. The program, written by Stribling and two fellow students, automatically spit out important-sounding nonsense, such as: "We can disconfirm that expert systems can be made amphibious" and "We concentrate our efforts on showing that the famous ubiquitous algorithm for the exploration of robots by Sato et al. runs in $\Omega((n + \log n))$ time [22]." Stribling later admitted to the hoax, adding that they'd done it because they were tired of being inundated with e-mail spam soliciting research papers for the conference. His conference credentials were subsequently revoked.

## IRONING OUT HIS PROBLEMS

**Background:** In 1999 Marcus Danquah, 41, of Kirton Lindsey, England, sued British appliance maker Morphy Richards, seeking $300,000. He claimed that a faulty clothes iron had given him an electric shock and a heart attack.

**Exposed!** During the course of the trial the court heard that Danquah, an engineer, had rewired the iron so that it shocked anyone who touched it. The company also charged that Danquah faked his heart attack with a homemade electric device. "They say it was hidden in his underpants," Judge Donald Hamilton reported, "and that he referred to the device as his 'electric underpants.'" Danquah, who'd already spent more than $20,000 in legal fees, was ordered to pay the company's court costs.

## FLOWER CHILD

**Background:** The "Flower Portrait" is probably the best-known painting of William Shakespeare. The familiar portrait, showing the Bard looking slightly to his right, wearing a wide white collar pressed tight up to his chin, has been reproduced countless times. (It is often printed on the cover of programs for Shakespeare plays.) It was named for one of its owners, Sir Desmond Flower, who donated it to the Royal Shakespeare Company in 1911. According to the date on the reverse side of the picture, it was painted in 1609—while Shakespeare was still alive.

**Exposed!** In 2005 experts at London's National Portrait Gallery conducted a four-month study of the painting, using X-rays, ultraviolet light, paint sampling, and microphotography. Their conclusion: It's a fake. It was painted between 1814 and 1840, 200 years *after* Shakespeare's death. They have no idea who painted it.

# WHAT DREAMS MEAN

*Psychologists say dreams reflect our waking lives. Although translations will vary with each individual, researchers say everybody's dreams share some common themes. Here are some examples.*

• **If you're naked,** you're dreading an upcoming event because you feel unprepared, ashamed, or vulnerable.

• **If you're falling,** it's a subconscious response to real-life stress. However, some experts say the "stress" could be something as simple as a mid-sleep leg or arm spasm.

• **If you die,** it doesn't portend death (yours or anybody else's)—it suggests insecurity or anxiety.

• **If you dream about a dead relative,** you've come to terms with the loss. Dream psychologists say we only dream about deceased loved ones when the grief process is complete.

• **If you see a car wreck,** a big undertaking in your life may feel bound for failure.

• **If you're being chased,** you're probably running away from something in real life. Being unable to run in a dream indicates feeling overwhelmed by daily pressures.

• **If your teeth fall out or crumble,** you're unhappy with your physical appearance. It may also mean you're excessively concerned about how others perceive you.

• **If you're giving birth,** great change is unfolding. Dreaming about babies indicates a desire to behave more maturely.

• **If you can fly,** you've just conquered a stressful situation. If you dream that you're able to control where you fly, it's a sign of confidence. Flying aimlessly suggests you're cautiously optimistic about your success.

• **If you dream about water,** it represents a general sense of your emotional state. Clear water means satisfaction with work and home. Muddy water is a sign of skepticism and discontent.

• **If you're urinating,** you may be expressing desire for relief from a difficult situation. Or you may really have to pee. Or you may be doing so already.

---

**Author Anne Rice's real name is Howard O'Brien. (She was named after her father.)**

# THE LITTLE RASCALS

*With 221 episodes filmed over more than two decades, Our Gang/Little Rascals is the most successful, longest-running film series in Hollywood history. Here's how the Little Rascals found their way onto the silver screen.*

## STICKS AND STONES

One day in 1921, a Hollywood producer named Hal Roach spent a frustrating morning auditioning girls for a part in one of his movies. It wasn't going well—the kids sounded too rehearsed and their stage makeup made them look like little grown-ups. In those days child actors were supposed to act like adults, not like normal kids. They were usually well scrubbed and well behaved, and because the adult characters were almost always the center of the story, the kids interacted with grown-ups more than they did with each other. They were often little more than props.

That afternoon when the auditions ended, Roach sat in his office and stared out at the lumberyard across the street. He noticed a group of kids that had snatched a few sticks to play with, and were now arguing over them—the smallest kid had grabbed the largest stick, and the biggest kid wanted it.

Roach was fascinated. "I knew they would probably throw away the sticks as soon as they walked around the block," he recalled more than 60 years later, "but the most important thing in the world right then was who would have which stick. All of a sudden I realized I had been watching this silly argument for over fifteen minutes because they were real kids."

## FORMING THE GANG

Roach thought movies about "kids doing the things that kids do" might make interesting viewing. As he told Leonard Maltin in *The Life and Times of the Little Rascals: Our Gang,* "I thought if I could find some clever street kids to just play themselves in films and show life from a kid's angle, maybe I could make a dozen of these things before I wear out the idea."

Roach started putting together a cast of archetypal kids that audiences would be able to relate to: the leader of the pack, the

---

Q: What is a group of 12 or more cows called? A: A *flink.*

pretty girl who gets teased by the boys, the tomboy, the nerdy smart kid, the chubby kid, the spoiled rich kid, etc.

Roach also decided to cast black kids in some of the parts. That may not sound like a big deal, but in the 1920s it was unheard of. In fact, he was the first Hollywood filmmaker to depict black kids and white kids playing together, treating each other as equals, even going to the same schools. (The integrated school scenes were cut out whenever the films played in the South.)

Characters like Farina, Stymie, and Buckwheat have since been criticized for perpetuating ethnic stereotypes, and ethnic humor was common in the series, especially in the early days. But the fact that the cast was integrated at all was a milestone. Hollywood films of the 1920s *never* portrayed blacks and whites as social peers, and they wouldn't for years to come. But Roach was determined that his kids would be peers.

Casting that first group of little kids was a snap—Roach just asked around the studio lot. Everybody, it seemed, either had a kid or knew one they thought would be good for a part. An eight-year-old black child actor named Ernie "Sunshine Sammy" Morrison was already appearing in Roach comedies, and his family knew of a one-year-old named Allen Hoskins. (Allen, better known as "Farina," would go on to appear in 105 *Our Gang* comedies—more than any other kid.) Photographer Gene Kornman's five-year-old daughter Mary was interested; so was her friend Mickey Daniels. Roach also hired a six-year-old child actor named Jack Davis, a three-year-old named Jackie Condon, a chubby four-year-old named Joe Cobb, and a few other kids as well.

## TESTING THE WATERS

The very first film, titled *Our Gang*, was shot twice with a different director each time because Roach didn't think the first version was funny enough. The second film, a 20-minute silent short, directed by an ex-fireman named Bob McGowan, was a hit with test audiences, critics, and movie exhibitors alike. When Roach received repeated requests for "more of these *Our Gang* comedies," he decided that would be the name for his series. The kids themselves were billed as "Hal Roach's Rascals"; the name "Little Rascals" came much later.

The fourth *Our Gang* movie to be filmed, *One Terrible Day*, was actually the first one released to the public; it hit the theaters in September 1922. *Our Gang* (the first film) was released two months later.

These films were unlike any that audiences had seen before. Kids were the stars, but the films were designed to appeal to people of all ages. And they were a hit from the start—kid actors were acting like real kids, arguing, getting dirty, and getting into all kinds of mischief. The acting was so natural that audiences forgot they were watching a movie.

## ACT NATURALLY

How was *Our Gang* director Bob McGowan able to coax such authentic performances out of actors as young as two years of age? He didn't have many options—reading scripts and memorizing lines was out, since many of the kids were too young to read. So McGowan made acting a game: he explained the scenes to the kids as carefully as he could, then he filmed them as they play-acted their parts. (One unintended consequence: as the kids grew older and became more aware of themselves as actors, their acting style sometimes became less natural.)

Because the *Our Gang* films were so successful, it wasn't long before every child star in Hollywood—not to mention thousands of aspiring kid stars all over the country—started clamoring for a part in the series. Mickey Rooney came to Hollywood just to audition for *Our Gang*. He didn't make the cut, and neither did the biggest child star in Hollywood history, Shirley Temple.

## SHOW BUSINESS

• A kid could be cast in an *Our Gang* film as young as two or three years of age (infants and toddlers were sometimes used as extras), and the average age was around seven. Most started out as supporting players and were promoted to more central roles as they got older. Spanky was a notable exception—he was cast in starring roles from the very beginning.

• The youngest actors weren't allowed to be on the lot more than six hours a day, and they spent at least half that time playing off camera, not working on the films. Once actors reached the age of six, however, they were expected to put in a full nine-hour shift (five hours of acting, three hours of school, and one for lunch).

- By the time most of the actors hit 11 or 12, they were starting
to look too old for the series, so they were phased out. Kids who
matured early had to leave sooner than that.

## MAKING NOISE

The Hal Roach Studios shot 88 silent *Our Gang* films between
1922 and 1929. In 1928 they started releasing their films with
phonograph records containing music and sound effects that were
synchronized with the films—but no dialogue. The first real
"talkies" followed a year later. Then from 1929 to 1937 Roach
made another 73 *Our Gang* shorts. Most film buffs consider these
later years to be the best of the series, with the most popular characters—Farina, Jackie, Chubby, Spanky, Buckwheat, Darla, and
Alfalfa—delivering their best performances.

## DOUBLE TROUBLE

*Our Gang* films were 20 minutes long until 1936. Around then,
theater owners started to drop short-subject comedies from their
schedules to make room for double features. In addition, the big
Hollywood studios like Columbia, Warner Brothers, and MGM
were bundling their own short-subject films with their feature
films and forcing theater owners to take them as a package—if an
owner wanted to show an MGM blockbuster like *Mutiny on the
Bounty* (1935), he had to show the MGM shorts with it.

The future for independent short-subject producers like Hal
Roach looked grim, so Roach switched gears and started making
feature-length films. Any short-subject that didn't work as a feature was discarded, and soon the *Our Gang* series was the only one
left at the studio. Roach ordered up a feature-length *Our Gang*
film called *General Spanky*. When it died at the box office, the
fate of the *Our Gang* series was sealed...or was it?

It turned out that Louis B. Mayer, the head of MGM, was an *Our
Gang* fan, and he thought there was still a lot of demand for the
films. Mayer promised Roach that if he cut the films down to 10
minutes in length, he'd see to it that they got distribution. Roach
agreed and made another 23 shorts over the next two years. But
even with MGM's support, demand for short comedies kept falling,
and so did the profits. In 1938 Roach sold the *Our Gang* unit to
MGM, including all of the films made between 1927 and 1938.

## THE SHOW'S OVER

The quality of the *Our Gang* series suffered terribly at MGM. Instead of assigning a single top-notch director to film the shorts, the studio used the series to prepare inexperienced directors for feature film work. As Leonard Maltin and Richard Bann write in *The Life and Times of the Little Rascals: Our Gang*, "Hal Roach Studios was geared to making nothing but good comedy shorts, while MGM was geared to make everything but. The result was a strictly-for-kids mixture of ten minute morality plays and pep talks pushing American virtues during wartime."

As the quality deteriorated so did audience interest; after 16 years of solid profits the films started losing money. MGM ended production in 1944; the last original *Our Gang* film, *Tale of a Dog*, was released in April 1944.

## LIVING ON

The era of first-run *Our Gang* shorts may have ended, but the age of reruns was just around the corner. In 1949 Hal Roach bought back the rights to his *Our Gang* shorts and began licensing them for television (MGM kept the rights to the ones they made). The only problem: MGM kept the rights to the *Our Gang* name in case they ever decided to make more films. Roach had to come up with another name for his films. Since the kids were already known as "Hal Roach's Rascals," he decided to name the series *The Little Rascals* for television.

Thanks to TV, by the mid-1950s the classic films were more popular than they'd ever been, entertaining a new generation of kids and bringing back fond memories for people old enough to remember them from the first time around. *The Little Rascals* has been airing almost continuously since then and is now available on video as well.

*Do you have a favorite* Little Rascals *character? Visit the "Little Rascals Hall of Fame" on page 508 to learn more about them. For a darker view, see "The Curse of the Little Rascals" on page 337.*

# IT'S A WEIRD, WEIRD WORLD

*Proof that truth is stranger than fiction.*

## HI-HO, HI-HO, IT'S OUT OF WORK WE GO

"Snow White had to make do with just four dwarfs due to cost-cutting at a theater in the German town of Stendal. The Altmark Stendal theater said it could afford only six actors for its Christmas rendition of *Snow White and the Seven Dwarfs*, which led to protests from theater-goers from the nearby city of Hanover who wanted to see all seven dwarves.

"The theater attached two puppets in dwarf outfits to a background wall to give the production six dwarfs. And the actor playing the prince was supposed to double as the seventh dwarf, but only made one brief appearance on stage. 'That dwarf wasn't on stage the whole time,' theater spokeswoman Susanne Kreuzer told reporters, 'because he was stuck down in the mine working overtime.'"

—*Gold Coast Bulletin* [Australia]

## LIFE'S UPS AND DOWNS

"For months, 14-year-old David Mossmann constructed a roller coaster in the back yard of his parents' house in Offenburg, Germany. Now he must tear it down. The roller coaster stands about 325 feet long and 16 feet high, and can reach a speed of 30 mph, but according to city officials, the wood construction does not comply with safety regulations, and it must be demolished.

—*N-TV* [Germany]

## NEIGHBOR'S PLOT FOILED

"A home in a Sacramento, California, neighborhood is surrounded by sheet metal, and neighbors are calling it an eyesore. But the residents, the D'Souza family, say the aluminium pieces are necessary to protect them from neighbors who have been bombarding them with radio waves and making them sick. 'It's a protective measure,' Sarah D'Souza said. The family claims the bombardment

Women of the Warramunga tribe in Australia don't speak for a year after their husbands die.

began after the first anniversary of the Sept. 11, 2001, terrorist attacks, and that the radio waves have caused them health problems ranging from headaches to lupus. Sacramento officials have ordered the family to remove the metal and they say they will comply with the order, but also plan to gather evidence to show city officials the problem with radiation."

—*Wall Street Journal*

## TIME TO GET UP

"After Bill DiPasquale was dismissed from his waiter's job at Abe & Louie's steakhouse in Boston because of a booze problem, he locked himself in his home and drank himself unconscious. Relatives found him near death and took him to Massachusetts General Hospital, where he was put on life support, but with hope fading, last week they decided to pull the plug. When the dying man's ex-boss, Charles Sarkis, heard about it, he barked, 'You tell him to wake up and get his a** back to work!' DiPasquale's friend Ralph Nash figured there was nothing to lose, so he delivered the message, whispering into his pal's ear, 'Charlie says to get out of bed and get your a** back to work.'

"Five minutes later, DiPasquale suddenly awoke and uttered, 'I've got to get to work.' And he began a quick recovery. DiPasquale believes God is giving him a second chance. 'He's telling me, 'If you want to be struck out, have another drink.' It will not happen. The show must go on.'"

—*New York Post*

## LAKE WHOA BE GONE!

"A Russian village was left baffled Thursday after its lake disappeared overnight. NTV television showed pictures of a giant muddy hole bathed in summer sun, while fishermen from the village of Bolotnikovo looked on disconsolately. Officials in Nizhegorodskaya region, on the Volga river east of Moscow, said water in the lake might have been sucked down into an underground cave system, but some villagers had more sinister explanations. 'I am thinking, well, America has finally got to us,' said one old woman, as she sat on the ground outside her house."

—**Reuters**

---

Instant makeover: Ribbon worms can turn themselves completely inside out.

# BRAINTEASERS

*BRI stalwart Maggie McLaughlin collected these puzzles and dared us to solve them. Uncle John immediately took them straight to our "research lab." We now pass them along to you. (Answers are on page 518.)*

## 1. A Thousand Squares

A rich old lady died and left a precious diamond to her family, but first they had to find it. She gave them one clue: "It is inside a cylinder surrounded by a thousand squares."

Where did she hide it?

## 2. Horse Sense

The dying king wanted to pass his crown on to the wiser of his two sons, so he held a horse race. He told them: "The son whose horse rides to the lake and returns to the castle *last* will inherit my kingdom." The younger son immediately jumped on a horse and rode away. Instantly, the king knew the younger son would inherit the kingdom.

How did he know?

## 3. Wrong Way Corrigan

A truck driver named Corrigan traveled three blocks down a one-way street—in the wrong direction. Along the way, he waved at a passing cop, who did not arrest him.

Why not?

## 4. Holed Up

Down at the city park, a baby bird fell into a hole that was four feet deep but only eight inches wide. Some kids who were playing on the swings nearby came over to help the bird, but just couldn't reach it. Their parents, who were sitting on a bench, couldn't reach, either. They wanted to try using a stick but were afraid it would hurt the bird. Little Julia, who was playing in the sandbox, came over and said, "I can save this bird, but it will take some time."

What did she do?

## 5. Dollars to Dogs

You have a dime and a dollar; you buy a dog and a collar. The dog is a dollar more than the collar. How much is the collar?

## 6. Pressing Riddle

I have keys but no locks.
I have space but no room.
I can be entered, but you can't come in, even though I am your type.

What am I?

---

Meteorologists' definition for drizzle: "No more than 14 drops per square foot per second."

# FABULOUS FLOP: THE DELOREAN, PART I

*Stainless steel. Gull-wing doors. Back to the Future. A big-time drug bust and $250 million in investment capital down the tubes. Here's the story behind one of the most spectacular flops of the 20th century.*

## THE TURNAROUND KID

In 1956 a 31-year-old engineer named John Z. DeLorean quit the Packard Motor Car Company and went to work for the troubled Pontiac division of General Motors. In those days Pontiac had a reputation for selling stodgy mid-market cars that didn't appeal to young people. Sales were down and getting worse.

DeLorean was instrumental in changing Pontiac's image with the introduction of the first muscle car, the GTO. Sales soared and so did DeLorean's career. In 1961 he was promoted to chief engineer; four years later he was named Pontiac's general manager. At just 40 years old, he was GM's youngest division head ever.

Pontiac's sales continued to rise, and in 1969 DeLorean was promoted to general manager of GM's largest division, Chevrolet. By 1972, Chevy's market share was on its way to record earnings when DeLorean was promoted to GM's corporate headquarters.

Only 47 years old, DeLorean was the hottest executive in Detroit—thought to be one of the only members of GM's senior management who understood what the public wanted and how to give it to them. He seemed a shoo-in for the presidency of GM.

Six months later, he was out of a job.

## MAKING CHANGES

According to DeLorean, he quit GM. But his detractors at GM say he was shown the door, reportedly because he was steering contracts to suppliers in which he had a financial interest. DeLorean had also begun to clash with GM's conservative corporate culture: In recent years he'd gotten a facelift and started dyeing his hair black. He grew long sideburns and took to wearing bell bottoms to the office in a company where everyone else wore business suits. In an even bigger shock to GM's culture, in 1969

DeLorean dumped his wife of 15 years and married 19-year-old Kelly Harmon just six months later.

## DREAM CAR

Whatever it was that caused the falling-out between DeLorean and GM, once he was on his own it wasn't long before he started contacting the company's auto dealers around the country to see if they'd be interested in carrying a new car—one completely different from anything GM had to offer. For some time DeLorean had wanted to start his own company and build his dream car: a two-seat luxury sports car that would be light years ahead of its time. It was just the kind of car that GM *wasn't* interested in producing—the market was too small to be worth the investment.

Building an auto company from scratch wasn't going to be easy. The last person to pull it off was Walter P. Chrysler, formerly the president of Buick, who founded his namesake company in the 1920s. Other companies had tried and failed: the Tucker Automobile Company folded in 1948 after producing only 51 cars, Kaiser-Frazer failed in 1956 after losing $100 million, Packard went under in 1958, and Studebaker followed in 1966. But inspired by Walter Chrysler's example, DeLorean was determined to try and immediately set about raising money for his corporation.

He got his first infusion of cash from a handful of wealthy investors, and then raised more money from auto dealers, who paid $25,000 each for the right to sell DeLoreans when the car went into production. This early money was used to design and build three prototypes. Raising money for manufacturing would come later.

## CAR OF THE FUTURE

In addition to its famous gull-wing doors (which open up, not out), the DeLorean as it was originally conceived would have two other features to set it apart from other American cars:

✔ It was going to be a "mid-engined" car, with the engine directly behind the driver and passenger seats instead of under the hood. This placement would improve the car's performance.

✔ It would have a high-strength plastic frame instead of a conventional steel one. Using a revolutionary new process known as elastic reservoir molding (ERM), the frame would be stronger than steel but would weigh half as much, making the car faster. Bonus: ERM plastic was a lot cheaper to work with because the parts were made using simple plastic molds instead of the massive, very expensive stamping machines used for steel parts. (There was one drawback: ERM panels couldn't be painted. DeLorean turned that to his advantage by giving the car a stainless-steel outer skin, which added to its mystique.)

## BACK TO THE DRAWING BOARD

That was how the DeLorean was *supposed* to turn out, but things didn't quite work out as planned:

✔ The four-cylinder engine used in the early prototype turned out to be underpowered, so it was scrapped in favor of a larger, heavier six-cylinder engine. But the new engine was too big to fit where the old one had gone, so it was moved to the rear, which hurt the car's performance.

✔ ERM proved to be impractical, so it was abandoned in favor of a much heavier steel-and-fiberglass frame. Fiberglass could be painted, which made the heavy stainless-steel outer skin unnecessary, but DeLorean insisted on keeping it. By the time all the changes were made, the car was 900 pounds overweight, hurting its performance even further. Now the DeLorean accelerated more slowly than the Chevy Corvette, the Porsche 911, and even the much cheaper Mazda RX-7.

The DeLorean still *looked* like it was ahead of its time, but underneath its shiny skin and gull-wing doors it was pretty ordinary.

## SUPPLY AND DEMAND

Even worse, by the time DeLorean was ready for production in 1979, the purchase price had soared to nearly $28,000, making it around $9,000 more expensive than the competing Corvette and $18,000 more expensive than the average car.

These figures should have been alarming because DeLorean was gearing up to manufacture 20,000 vehicles a year. A marketing study he had commissioned found that he would be able to sell that many cars only if it kept the price under $18,000. At $28,000, demand plummeted to less than 4,000 cars.

John DeLorean ignored the study and continued on.

*For Part II of the DeLorean story, steer to page 440.*

Goofy? Mickey? Nope—Walt Disney's middle name was Elias.

# COMMIE CRABS & THIRD-REICH RACCOONS

*Two strange tales of nature's revenge.*

**S**TRANGE TALE #1
In the 1930s, Soviet leader Josef Stalin started a transplantation program for Kamchatka crabs, known in the West as Red King crabs. The crabs—whose claws can span five feet and can weigh as much as 25 pounds—are native to the northern Pacific between Russia and Alaska. Stalin had them shipped by train 5,000 miles east to the Barents Sea, off the Scandinavian Peninsula. Red King crabs are a delicacy, known for large quantities of succulent white meat, and Stalin thought they would provide food and create a local industry. But with no natural predators in their new home, there are an estimated 15 million of the Red King crabs in the Barents now. Biologists say the crabs are decimating local fish and shellfish populations, turning the seafloor into an underwater desert. The crabs are also invading neighboring countries, already in huge numbers hundreds of miles up Norway's coast. Norwegians now fear an environmental disaster from what the media calls the invasion of "the new red army."

**STRANGE TALE #2**
In 1934 Hermann Goering, the head of Nazi Germany's Luftwaffe (air force), began a program of importing raccoons from the United States and releasing them into the wild in Germany. Raccoons aren't native to Europe; Goering said he wanted to "enrich the fauna of the Reich." Reports vary as to how many he imported—anywhere from one pair to 100—but what Goering didn't consider is that the raccoons would have no natural enemies in the country. Today there are more than a million of them in Germany alone, and they're spreading to neighboring countries. To counter the exponential growth of the invasive nocturnal creatures, in 2004 Germany announced that they would begin trapping and killing them. One town even hired a special wildlife officer to deal with the problem. They call him the "raccoon man."

---

Celebrity beauty secrets: Cleopatra's eye makeup was blue-black (upper lid) and green (lower).

# FICTIONARY

*The Washington Post runs an annual contest asking readers to come up with alternate meanings for various words. Here are some of the best we found (plus a few by the BRI).*

**Oyster** (n), one who sprinkles his conversation with Yiddish expressions.

**Counterfeiter** (n), a craftsman who installs fake kitchen cabinets.

**Derange** (n), where de buffalo roam.

**Heroes** (v), how a man moves a boat through the water.

**Pokemon** (n), a Jamaican proctologist.

**Subdued** (n), a guy who, like, you know, works on one of those, like, submarines.

**Baloney** (n), where your shin is located.

**Car battery** (n), auto abuse.

**Abalone** (n), shellfish nonsense.

**Bernadette** (n), the act of torching a mortgage.

**Relief** (v), what trees do in the spring.

**Jocular** (adj), to be funny *and* good at sports.

**Discovery** (n), a fancy CD case.

**Parasites** (n), what tourists see from the top of the Eiffel Tower.

**Spice** (n), the plural of "spouse."

**Pharmacist** (v), to help out on the farm.

**Willy-nilly** (adj), impotent.

**Dilate** (v), reaching old age.

**Barium** (v), what we do to our loved ones when they die.

**Chinese checkers** (n), cashiers at the Beijing Piggly Wiggly.

**Dogmatic** (n), a pooch that walks and feeds itself.

**Dialogue** (n), Help for your tree is just a phone call away.

**Avoidable** (v), what a bullfighter tries to do.

**Burglarize** (n), what a robber sees with.

**Polarize** (n), what a polar bear sees with.

**Ostracize** (n), what an ostrich… oh, you get the idea.

# HAMBURGER 911

*This may sound unbelievable, but it comes from the transcript of an actual 911 call made in Orange County, California.*

**Dispatcher:** Sheriff's department, how can I help you?

**Woman:** Yeah, I'm over here at Burger King right here in San Clemente.

**Dispatcher:** Uh-huh.

**Woman:** Um, no, not San Clemente—sorry—I *live* in San Clemente. I'm in Laguna Niguel, I think. That's where I'm at.

**Dispatcher:** Uh-huh.

**Woman:** I'm at a drive-through right now.

**Dispatcher:** Uh-huh.

**Woman:** I ordered my food three times. They're mopping the floor inside, and I understand they're busy...they're not even busy, okay? I'm the only car here. I asked them four different times to make me a Western Barbeque Burger. They keep giving me a hamburger with lettuce, tomato, and cheese, onions, and I said, "I'm not leaving..."

**Dispatcher:** Uh-huh.

**Woman:** I want a Western Burger because I just got my kids from Tae Kwon Do. They're hungry, I'm on my way home, and I live in San Clemente.

**Dispatcher:** Uh-huh.

**Woman:** Okay, she gave me another hamburger. It's wrong. I said four times, I said, "I want my hamburger right." So then the lady called the manager. She...well, whoever she is, she came up and she said, "Do you want your money back?" And I said, "No, I want my hamburger. My kids are hungry, and I have to jump on that freeway." I said, "I am not leaving this spot," and I said, "I will call the police because I want my Western Burger done right!" Now is that so hard?

**Dispatcher:** Okay, what exactly is it you want us to do for you?

**Woman:** Send an officer down here. I want them to make me...

**Dispatcher:** Ma'am, we're not going to go down there and enforce your Western Bacon Cheeseburger.

**Woman:** What am I supposed to do?

**Dispatcher:** This is between you and the manager. We're not going to enforce how to make a hamburger; that's not a criminal issue. There's nothing criminal there.

**Woman:** So I just stand here...so I just sit here and block...

**Dispatcher:** You need to calmly and rationally speak to the manager and figure out what to do between you.

**Woman:** She did come up, and I said, "Can I please have my Western Burger?" She said, "I'm not dealing with it," and she walked away. Because they're mopping the floor, and it's also the fact that they don't want to...they don't want to go and...

**Dispatcher:** Then I suggest you get your money back and go somewhere else. This is not a criminal issue. We can't go out there and make them make you a cheeseburger the way you want it.

**Woman:** Well, you're supposed to be here to protect me.

**Dispatcher:** Well, what are we protecting you from, a wrong cheeseburger?

**Woman:** No...

**Dispatcher:** Is this like...a harmful cheeseburger or something? I don't understand what you want us to do.

**Woman:** Just come down here. I'm not leaving.

**Dispatcher:** No ma'am, I'm not sending the deputies down there over a cheeseburger. You need to go in there and act like an adult and either get your money back or go home.

**Woman:** She is not acting like an adult herself! I'm sitting here in my car; I just want them to make my kids a Western Burger.

**Dispatcher:** Ma'am, this is what I suggest: I suggest you get your money back from the manager, and you go on your way home.

**Woman:** Okay.

**Dispatcher:** Okay? Bye-bye.

---

Croaker curfew: A Memphis, Tennessee, ordinance bans frogs from croaking after 11 p.m.

# FOOD OF THE GODS

*As Mrs. Uncle John always says, be sure to look at your food before you eat it. (You might want to put it on eBay.)*

**H**OLY CHAPATI
Shella Anthony of Bangalore, India, baked a chapati bread (an Indian staple) with what looked like an image of Jesus on it. She brought it to a local church, where more than 20,000 people from all over India flocked to see the "miracle" bread. Said Father Jacob George, "People are feeling blessed on witnessing it."

## HOLY GRILLED CHEESE

Diana Duyser of Miami kept half a grilled cheese sandwich with a bite out of it on her nightstand for ten years because she thought it bore an image of the Virgin Mary. In 2005 she sold it on eBay for $28,000, issuing a statement saying: "I would like all people to know that I do believe that this is the Virgin Mary Mother of God."

## HOLY PRETZEL

Machell Naylor's 12-year-old daughter, Crysta, of St. Paul, Nebraska, found a Rold Gold honey-mustard pretzel that looked like the Virgin Mary holding the baby Jesus. "We had a feeling of spirituality and warmth when holding it," Naylor said. She sold it on eBay for $10,600; the money went to charity (Crysta got a pony).

## HOLY CHICKEN BREAST

Edward Rouzin-Moy, a freshman at Eastern Illinois University, ordered a chicken breast in the school cafeteria. "I was about to dig in, and I looked at it," he said. "I turned to my buddy and said, 'It looks like the pope.'" Pope John Paul II had died just two weeks earlier. He put the breast on eBay, where it sold for $232.50.

## HOLY POTATO CHIPS

Rosalie Lawson of St. Petersburg, Florida, found a Lays potato chip that looks like Jesus. When her husband saw it he said, "Well, we can't eat that!" But take it with a grain of salt, warned Ms. Lawson, because "you only know what you think he looks like from pictures." She added that she might be selling the chip on eBay.

---

According to zoologists, a tiger's scent markings smell like buttered popcorn.

# LOCAL HERO: LEROY GORHAM

*Here's the story of a man who suffered a family tragedy and then went on a mission to save other families from the same fate.*

## TERRIBLE LOSS

In the summer of 1946 a fire broke out in LeRoy and Lillian Gorham's house in The Bottom neighborhood of Chapel Oaks, Maryland. It took firefighters a very long time to arrive. Too long. By the time they put out the fire, all three of the Gorhams' children—Ruth, 4, Jean, 3, and LeRoy Earl, 2—had perished in the blaze.

There's no way to know if the Gorham children could have been saved had the fire department arrived sooner, and for that matter, no one knows exactly why it took the fire department so long to get there. But The Bottom is a black community, and residents there claim that the all-white fire departments of surrounding communities were always slow to respond to emergencies in black neighborhoods...if they came at all.

"It's just the way it was," says resident Luther Crutchfield. "If they got a call for a fire in a black neighborhood, they either came or they didn't. Sometimes they came, but they took their time." Further complicating matters, The Bottom didn't have running water in the 1940s, so even when firefighters did respond, there was no place to hook up their hoses. Fires were fought with bucket brigades, using water drawn from nearby wells and streams.

## A NEW BEGINNING

Gorham was devastated by the loss of his children. He wanted to do anything he could to see to it that no other families in his neighborhood or the surrounding communities ever had to suffer the same fate. So he and a group of his friends decided to found the Chapel Oaks Volunteer Fire Department, the first all-black volunteer fire company in the state of Maryland.

Less than a year after the fire, the department opened its doors.

It wasn't easy—the organizers didn't receive any funding from Prince George's County, so they took up a collection in the surrounding black community and used these funds to buy an old pumper, which they kept in an old garage that served as the fire station. There wasn't enough money for proper firefighting gear, so the Chapel Oaks firefighters made do with surplus helmets, coats, and boots they got from the U.S. military. They had no breathing equipment, either—if the men had to enter burning buildings, they simply held their breath or tied wet handkerchiefs over their mouths. Since they didn't have access to professional training, the volunteers trained themselves by setting fires in abandoned buildings and putting them out.

"We weren't in the county fire association, because they had a white male–only clause," remembers Crutchfield, who joined the department in 1949. And the discrimination continued even when firefighters battled a blaze. "The white firefighters would take our lines out and put theirs in," Crutchfield says. "They wouldn't recognize the authority of our chief on the scene. But we wouldn't play those games. We were professional men who were there to save lives, and that's what we did."

## HEALING

Change came slowly in the decades that followed. When a fire destroyed the garage that served as Chapel Oak's first fire station, the volunteers raised enough money from the community to build their first proper fire station nearby and laid the bricks themselves. The county fire association eventually dropped its whites-only clause and Chapel Oaks joined in 1960; then in 1979, the county built them a new fire station.

Gorham and his wife had three more children. He was a volunteer with the department for 54 years, serving as chief for 17 of those. And when he wasn't at the station, he was listening to his radio scanner. "The only time his scanner wasn't on was when he was at church," his daughter Tanya says.

Even when he became too old to fight fires, Gorham continued to visit the fire station every day, and did so until the day before he died in July 2000. "LeRoy wanted to be sure," his friend and fellow firefighter Roy Lee Jordan remembers, "that no other children died like his did."

# WHEN REAL LIFE BECOMES *REEL* LIFE

*Movies that are "based on a true story" often stray from the truth. Hollywood has a tendency to embellish some facts, while omitting others. Here are some inconsistencies we found in major motion pictures.*

## SEABISCUIT (2003)

**Reel Life:** Red Pollard (Tobey Maguire) was neither a great jockey nor a great prizefighter, but he tried hard at both. When he's paired up with a racehorse who, like him, has never amounted to much, Pollard overcomes his weakness and starts winning races using little more than pure heart and guile.

**Real Life:** The film doesn't touch on Pollard's life-long battle with drinking, which started as a way to ease the pain suffered from his many injuries, but then became a habit he was unable to kick until much later in life.

**Reel Life:** Pollard is painted as a true American hero whose courage gives hope to a nation mired in the Great Depression.

**Real Life:** The movie left out the fact that he was Canadian.

## APOLLO 13 (1995)

**Reel Life:** On the second day of the ill-fated 1970 mission to the Moon, the three-man crew hears a loud bang. Warning lights begin flashing on the instrument panel. Commander Jim Lovell (Tom Hanks) says into his microphone, "Houston, we have a problem."

**Real Life:** It wasn't quite that dramatic. After checking the instrument panel, Swigert—not Lovell—said, "Okay, Houston, we've had a problem here." Mission Control responded, "This is Houston. Say again please." And *then* Lovell said, "Houston, we've had a problem. We've had a main B bus undervolt."

**Reel Life:** After the accident, tensions run high between crew members, especially after Fred Haise (Bill Paxton) accuses John Swigert (Kevin Bacon) of causing the explosion.

**Real Life:** "The crew conflict was something that Hollywood added to make us seem more human," admits the real Haise.

---

A 1946 FBI memo denounced the movie *It's a Wonderful Life* as communist propaganda.

## RAY (2004)

**Reel Life:** Ray Charles (Jamie Foxx) and his loyal wife, Bea (Kerry Washington), go to Georgia in 1979 to celebrate the end of his 17-year ban from performing there.

**Real Life:** He did go to the Georgia State Legislature in 1979, but it was so lawmakers could proclaim "Georgia on My Mind" the state song. That's it. There was never a ban against Charles performing in Georgia. And Bea didn't go with him. In fact, they'd been divorced for two years by that time.

## A BEAUTIFUL MIND (2001)

**Reel Life:** Mathematician John Forbes Nash Jr. (Russell Crowe) is a brilliant man, but he suffers from paranoid schizophrenia that gives him frightening hallucinations. Through sheer determination—along with the love of his faithful wife, Alicia (Jennifer Connelly)—Nash overcomes his illness, makes a groundbreaking mathematical discovery, and is awarded the Nobel Prize.

**Real Life:** In their book *Based on a True Story*, Jonathan Vankin and John Whalen rip into this film for its rampant lack of historical accuracy. Here are a few of the more glaring inconsistencies:

• Alicia did not stay by Nash's side; she divorced him three years into his illness. She got back together with Nash after he recovered.

• Completely removed from the film was the fact that Nash fathered a child with another woman and abandoned it.

• Another fact of his life left out of the movie: Nash was bisexual.

So why the changes? "The real events of Nash's life," write Vankin and Whalen, "were unacceptably unpleasant. The movie wouldn't sell."

## FINDING NEVERLAND (2004)

**Reel Life:** J. M. Barrie (Johnny Depp) befriends a widow named Sylvia Davies (Kate Winslet). His relationship with her four sons, especially 10-year-old Peter, inspires the 1904 play *Peter Pan*.

**Real Life:** Sylvia's husband, Arthur, was alive when Barrie met them, and the two men were friends for ten years before Arthur died. (Although the timeline of the movie is about a year, the events that it's based on happened over the course of 13 years.) And there were five kids, not four.

# THE FOGGIEST PLACE ON EARTH

*To "Newfies," the Canadian island province of Newfoundland is home sweet home. It's also the site of many firsts, feats, and claims to fame.*

- **Oldest City in North America.** St. John's, the capital of Newfoundland, was founded in 1497. It's also the home of the continent's oldest street, Water Street.

- **First Smallpox Vaccine.** In 1800 Dr. John Clinch of Trinity, Newfoundland, was the first doctor in North America to administer the smallpox vaccine.

- **World's Longest Squid.** The longest giant squid ever caught was netted in Glover's Harbour, Newfoundland, on November 2, 1878. It was 55 feet long.

- **Oldest Sporting Event.** The Royal St. John's Regatta has been held every year since 1825, making it the longest-running sporting event in North America.

- **First Transatlantic Wireless Radio Transmission.** In 1901 Guglielmo Marconi sent the first successful wireless radio transmission from Cornwall, England, to St. John's, Newfoundland.

- **First to Respond to the *Titanic*.** Wireless operators Walter Gray, Jack Goodwin, and Robert Hunston of Cape Race, Newfoundland, were the first to hear and respond to the *Titanic*'s distress signal on April 14, 1912.

- **First Transatlantic Flight.** British pilots John Alcock and Arthur Whitten flew from Newfoundland to Ireland in June 1919. It took them 16 hours to cross the Atlantic.

- **Longest Running Daily Radio Show in North America.** *The Fisheries Broadcast* (nicknamed "The Broadcast") has aired from St. John's since March 5, 1951.

- **Foggiest Spot.** The Grand Banks, off the southeast coast of Newfoundland, was named "the foggiest place on Earth" by the

---

What do you get when you cross a four-leaf clover with poison ivy? A rash of good luck.

*Guinness Book of World Records*. In winter it's shrouded in fog 40 percent of the time; in summer, 84 percent.

- **Only Province to Have Been a Nation.** Newfoundland was an independent country (part of the British Commonwealth of former colonies) from 1907 to 1934. It became part of Canada in 1949.

- **Oldest Known European Settlement in North America.** Ruins of Viking sod houses still stand at L'Anse aux Meadows in Newfoundland. The area was settled around A.D. 1000.

- **Most Places to Drink.** George Street in St. John's has the most pubs per square foot in all of Canada. The most popular drink is Newfoundland Screech, a local brand of rum.

- **Most Scary Creatures.** Columnist and paranormal researcher Dale Jarvis says Newfoundland is "blessed with more fairies, devils, old hags, phantoms, and sea monsters than any other spot in Canada." (He may have had too much Screech.)

## OTHER NIFTY NEWFIE NEWS

- There are no snakes, skunks, deer, porcupines, or groundhogs on the island. Moose were introduced to the island in 1878, chipmunks in 1962, and squirrels in 1963.

- Newfoundland has its own time zone: Newfoundland Standard Time. It's $1\frac{1}{2}$ hours ahead of Eastern Standard Time.

- The province consists of Newfoundland, an island, and Labrador, on mainland Canada. Though still informally called Newfoundland, the provincial government has referred to itself since 1964 as the Government of Newfoundland and Labrador. In 2001 the Constitution of Canada also made the name change.

- The names of some Newfoundland towns: Come by Chance, Tickle Cove, Heart's Content, and Dildo.

- The Iceberg Corporation of St. John's harvests icebergs to produce Iceberg water, Iceberg beer, and Iceberg vodka.

- The Grand Banks, an underwater plateau off Newfoundland, is home to one of the world's largest oil-drilling rigs, the Hibernia Platform, which is designed to withstand a collision with a million-ton iceberg.

# UNCLE JOHN'S PAGE OF LISTS

*Random bits of interesting information from the BRI files.*

**5 Songs on George W. Bush's iPod**
1. "Brown Eyed Girl" by Van Morrison
2. "Centerfield" by John Fogerty
3. "(You're So Square) Baby, I Don't Care" by Joni Mitchell
4. "Alive 'n' Kickin'" by Kenny Loggins
5. "My Sharona" by The Knack

**5 Types of Cars**
1. 4-door sedan
2. 2-door coupe
3. Station wagon
4. Convertible
5. Sports car

**6 Stars Who Took Karate Lessons from Chuck Norris**
1. Bob Barker
2. Priscilla Presley
3. Steve McQueen
4. Michael Landon
5. Marie Osmond
6. Donny Osmond

**Top 5 Inventions (1998 survey)**
1. Toilet
2. Computer
3. Printing press
4. Fire
5. Wheel

**5 Foreign Names for Colonel Mustard (from Clue)**
1. Oberst Von Gatow (Germany)
2. Si. Mustardas (Greece)
3. Colonel Moutarde (France, Belgium)
4. Oberst Gulin (Norway)
5. Madame Curry (Switzerland)

**8 Most Shoplifted Items**
1. Pain relievers
2. Pregnancy tests
3. Disposable razors
4. Film
5. Baby formula
6. Preparation H
7. Decongestant
8. Laxatives

**5 Entertainers Who Had Airports Named After Them**
1. Bob Hope
2. John Wayne
3. Ronald Reagan
4. John Lennon
5. Will Rogers

**13 Cigarette Additives**
1. Yeast
2. Coffee
3. Honey
4. Rum
5. Fig juice
6. Cognac oil
7. Chocolate
8. Carrot oil
9. Caffeine
10. Apple skins
11. Nutmeg powder
12. Ammonia
13. Vinegar

**3 Poems by Jimmy Carter**
1. "A Motorcycling Sister"
2. "My First Try for Votes"
3. "Of Possum and Fatback"

# FOOTBALL NAMES

*Every football team has a storied history. So do their names.*

**P**ITTSBURGH STEELERS. Originally named the Pirates after Pittsburgh's professional baseball team, in 1940 owner Al Rooney renamed the team for the city's steel industry.

**HOUSTON TEXANS.** The Dallas Texans were one of the original AFL teams. They moved to Kansas City in 1963, so when Houston got an expansion team in 2002, they revived the name.

**KANSAS CITY CHIEFS.** Dallas Texans owner Lamar Hunt was reluctant to relocate to Kansas City until Mayor H. Roe "Chief" Bartle promised to enlarge the city's stadium and guarantee high season ticket sales. Hunt showed his appreciation by naming the team after him.

**BALTIMORE RAVENS.** Selected by fans (via a telephone poll) from a list of 100 NFL-approved names. Baltimore was once the home of poet Edgar Allan Poe, author of "The Raven."

**ATLANTA FALCONS.** In 1965 the new team held a contest to name the franchise. A teacher from Griffin, Georgia, suggested Falcons: "The falcon is proud and dignified, with great courage and fight. It is deadly and has a great sporting tradition."

**MINNESOTA VIKINGS.** General manager Bert Rose came up with the name as a nod to the area's large Nordic population.

**INDIANAPOLIS COLTS.** Originated as the Baltimore Colts in 1947, the name recognizes Baltimore's long tradition of horse breeding and racing.

**SAN FRANCISCO 49ERS.** The name is a reference to the gold rush prospectors who came west in 1849, the year after gold was discovered at Sutter's Mill in the mountains east of San Francisco.

**TENNESSEE TITANS.** Formerly the Tennessee Oilers (after a move from Houston), owner Bud Adams picked the name from Greek mythology. He thought it was appropriate because the team played in Nashville, nicknamed "the Athens of the South."

# THE WIND EAGLE

*Here is an American Indian legend from the Abenaki people,
who once inhabited the area that is now New England. After
the Europeans arrived, those who survived went north to
Quebec, where their culture and stories are carried on.*

Long ago, **Gluscabi** lived with his grandmother, Woodchuck, in a small lodge beside the big water. One day Gluscabi said, "I think it is time to hunt some ducks." So he took his bow and arrows and got into his canoe. As he paddled out into the bay, he sang:

> *Ki yo wah ji neh*
> *yo hey ho hey*
> *Ki yo wah ji neh*
> *Ki yo wah ji neh*

But just then the wind came up and blew him back to shore. Gluscabi tried to paddle out again, but the wind blew harder. He sang again—louder still. But the wind blew even harder. Four times he tried to paddle out into the bay, and four times he failed.

Gluscabi was unhappy. He went to the lodge of his grandmother and asked her, "What makes the wind blow?"

Grandmother Woodchuck looked up from her work. "Ah, Gluscabi," she said.

"Whenever you ask such questions I feel there is going to be trouble. But I know that you are very stubborn and will never stop asking. So, I shall tell you. If you walk always facing the wind you will come to the place where Wuchowsen stands."

"Thank you, Grandmother!" said Gluscabi as he left the lodge and began to walk into the wind.

**Gluscabi walked across** the fields, and through the woods, and the wind blew hard. Through the valleys and into the hills and the wind blew harder still. Up into the mountains and the wind blew even harder. It was so strong that it blew off Gluscabi's moccasins. But being very stubborn, he kept on walking. Now the wind was so strong that it blew off all his clothes and he was naked, but he still kept walking. Now the wind was so very strong that it blew off his hair and eyebrows.

Gluscabi had to pull himself along by grabbing hold of the boulders. But there, on the peak ahead of him, he could see a great bird flapping its wings. It was Wuchowsen, the Wind Eagle.

**Gluscabi took a deep breath.** "Grandfather!" he shouted.

The Wind Eagle stopped flapping his wings and looked around. "Who calls me Grandfather?" he said.

Gluscabi stood up. "I do. I came up here to tell you that you do a very good job making the wind blow."

The Wind Eagle puffed out his chest with pride. "You mean like this?" he said and flapped his wings even harder. The wind was so strong that it almost blew Gluscabi right off of the mountain.

"You do a very good job of making the wind blow, Grandfather. This is so. But it seems to me that you could do an even better job if you were on that peak over there."

The Wind Eagle replied, "Perhaps...but how would I get from here to there?"

Gluscabi smiled. "I will carry you. Wait here." Then he ran back down the mountain until he came to a big

basswood tree. He stripped off the bark and braided a strong carrying strap, which he took back up the mountain.

"Here, Grandfather," Gluscabi said, "let me wrap this around you so I can lift you more easily." Then he wrapped the strap so tightly around Wuchowsen that his wings were pulled to his sides and he could hardly breathe.

"Now, Grandfather," said Gluscabi, picking the Wind Eagle up, "I will take you to a better place."

Gluscabi began to walk toward the other peak but stopped at a large crevice. As he stepped over it, he let go of the Wind Eagle, who slid down into the crevice, upside down, and was stuck.

"Now," Gluscabi said, "it is time to go hunt some ducks."

**Gluscabi walked and walked** until he got back to the lodge by the big water, and by now all his hair had grown back. And the wind did not blow.

He got some new clothing and took his bow and arrows and went back to the bay. As he paddled out into the water he sang his canoeing song:

*Ki yo wah ji neh*
*yo hey ho hey*

---

**Sickening fact:** Americans spend $957.3 billion on health care every year.

*Ki yo wah ji neh*
*Ki yo wah ji neh*

But the air was so still and hot that it was hard to breathe. Soon the water began to grow dirty and smell bad, and there was so much foam that he could hardly paddle.

**Gluscabi was not pleased** at all and went back to his grandmother's lodge. "What is wrong?" he asked. "The air is hot and still, and it is hard to breathe. The water is dirty and covered with foam. I can-not hunt ducks at all."

Grandmother Woodchuck said, "Gluscabi, what have you done now?"

Sheepishly, he told her.

"Oh, Gluscabi," she said, "Will you never learn? Tabal-dak, the Owner, set the Wind Eagle on that mountain to make the wind because we need the wind. The wind keeps the air cool and clean. It brings the clouds that give us rain to wash the Earth. It moves the waters to keep them fresh and sweet. With-out the wind, life will not be good for us, for our children, or our children's children."

Gluscabi nodded his head.

"I understand, Grandmother." He walked all the way back to the crevice. There was Wuchosen, the Wind Eagle, wedged upside down.

"Uncle?" Gluscabi called.

The Wind Eagle looked up as best he could. "Who calls me Uncle?" he said.

"I'm up here. But what are you doing down there?"

"Oh," said the Wind Eagle, "a very ugly naked man fooled me and trapped me here. And I am so uncomfortable."

"Ah, Grandfath…er, Uncle, I will get you out." Then Gluscabi climbed down into the crevice. He pulled the Wind Eagle free and placed him back on the mountain and untied his wings.

**"Uncle," Gluscabi said,** "it is good that the wind should blow sometimes and that it should be still at other times."

The Wind Eagle looked at Gluscabi and then nodded his head. "Grandson," he said, "I hear what you say."

And so it is that sometimes there is wind and sometimes it is very still to this very day.

\* \* \*

**Yiddish proverb:** "If triangles had a God, He'd have three sides."

In 2002, paleontologists discovered 160-million-year-old fossilized dinosaur vomit.

# MUSICAL NOTES

*Here's some trivia about the structure and history of music.*

• There are more than 42,000 playable guitar chords.

• The first modern piano was built in 1700 by Bartolomeo Cristofori in Italy. The instrument's real name: *piano et forte*, which means "soft and loud."

• Since 1955 piano keys have been made of plastic, not ivory.

• In 1987 Missouri named the fiddle its official state instrument. In 1990 San Francisco named the accordion its official instrument.

• Purdue University had the first collegiate marching band (1886). They were also the first to play on a sports field and make a formation—they formed a giant "P" (1907).

• Most recognizable piece of Western music: the opening of Beethoven's *Fifth Symphony* (duh-duh duh-duuuh).

• Clarinets are made from the wood of the granadilla tree.

• Most frequently sung songs in English: "Happy Birthday," "For He's a Jolly Good Fellow," and "Auld Lang Syne."

• Written music as we know it today, originated in the 1200s

• Mozart wrote the opera *Don Giovanni* in one sitting. It was first performed the very next day with no rehearsals.

• The trombone is based on a medieval instrument with a much better name: the *sackbut*.

• Florida state song: Stephen Foster's "Old Folks Home."

• For an album to go "gold" in the United States, it must sell 500,000 copies. For England it's 100,000; Canada, 50,000; Australia, 30,000; New Zealand, 7,500.

• Oldest piece of music found: a choral work from 408 B.C. used in a performance of the Greek play *The Orestia*.

• "Guitar" comes from *kithara*, the name of an instrument popular in ancient Greece.

• There are more than 10 million pianos in the U.S.

• The first flutes originated 20,000 years ago. They were made of reindeer antlers.

• British scientists say chickens produce more eggs if they listen to easy listening or Top 40 radio. (They hate heavy metal, opera, and jazz.)

# ACCORDING TO THE LATEST RESEARCH

*It seems as though practically every day there's a report on some scientific study with dramatic new info on what we should eat...or how we should act...or who we really are underneath it all. Some are pretty interesting. Did you know, for example, that science says...*

## E-MAIL ROTS YOUR BRAIN

**Study:** In 2004 scientists at the King's College, London University were commissioned by Hewlett-Packard to see what toll compulsive e-mail checking and Internet chatting have on a worker's "functioning IQ." Eighty volunteers participated in clinical trials and another 1,100 people were interviewed for the study.

**Findings:** Sixty-two percent of the interviewees were "addicted" to checking e-mail and exchanging text messages, which they did not only at their desks, but also "during meetings, in the evenings, and on weekends." The scientists dubbed this phenomenon "info-mania."

• Info-mania takes a noticeable toll on productivity. "An average worker's functioning IQ falls 10 points when distracted by ringing telephones and incoming e-mails...more than double the four-point drop seen in studies on the impact of smoking marijuana," the scientists concluded. A 10-point drop is the equivalent of trying to put in a full day of work after missing an entire night of sleep.

## TRAFFIC JAMS CAN KILL YOU

**Study:** Researchers with Germany's National Research Center for Environment and Health interviewed 691 people who'd suffered heart attacks between 1999 and 2001. The researchers asked them to describe all of their activities in the four days leading up to their heart attacks. The results of the study were published in the November 2004 issue of the *New England Journal of Medicine*.

**Findings:** People who've been stuck in traffic in the past hour are nearly three times more likely to suffer a heart attack than people

---

BOOM! The sound of thunder travels at about 1,100 feet per second.

who haven't been stuck in traffic. Overall, nearly 1 in 12 heart attacks was linked in some way to traffic congestion. Men are at a greater risk than women, and people over age 60 are at a greater risk than those under 60.

• If you have to be stuck in traffic, you're actually better off in a car than you would be riding the bus, the subway, or a bicycle. Heart attacks were 2.6 times more likely for people stuck in a car, 3.1 times more likely for people on public transportation, and 3.9 times greater for bike riders. "Because the association was also observed for persons who used public transportation, it is unlikely that the effect is entirely attributable to the stress linked with driving a car," researchers say.

• So is it the stress associated with being stuck in traffic that causes heart attacks, or is it the exhaust fumes—or some other factor? Who knows? "Given our current knowledge, it is impossible to determine the relative contribution of risk factors such as stress and traffic-related air pollution," the researchers say.

## DUDES SAY "DUDE" MORE THAN DUDETTES DO

**Study:** In 2004 University of Pittsburgh linguist-dude Scott Kiesling published a paper in the journal *American Speech* on the word "dude" and its many uses.

**Findings:** Blame it on Spicoli, dude: Kiesling traces the current popularity of the word "dude" to the 1982 movie *Fast Times at Ridgemont High*, featuring that Sean Penn dude.

• Men are more likely to use the word "dude" than women are. They're also more likely to use it with men than with women. When they do use it with women, the woman is usually just a friend; women with whom dudes are intimate are rarely if ever referred to as "dude."

• According to Kiesling, "dude" owes much of its popularity to the fact that it connotes "cool solidarity"—young men use it to express friendship or closeness, without being so close as to invite suspicion that they are gay. Dude!

\*　　\*　　\*

"Every kind of music is good, except the boring kind."

—Gioacchino Rossini, composer

The phrase "United we stand, divided we fall" was a moral in one of Aesop's fables.

# A PEACH OF AN ELECTION

*The strange events surrounding the 1946 Georgia gubernatorial election may read like the plot of a Marx brothers movie. But this really happened.*

## IT ENDS IN A DEAD HEAT

In November 1946, Democrat Eugene Talmadge won a fourth (nonconsecutive) term as governor of Georgia, defeating the unpopular incumbent, Ellis Arnall. But on December 21, 1946—a month before he was supposed to be sworn in—governor-elect Talmadge died of cirrhosis of the liver. As of January 1947 Georgia would have no governor...or perhaps it would have three.

**Governor #1: Herman Talmadge.** Eugene Talmadge's son, Herman, knew before the election what the public didn't—his father was dying. Herman wanted his father's job, so he had organized a write-in campaign for himself in the 1946 election. He knew that if his father won and then died before taking office, there'd be a runoff election between the next two highest vote getters. Herman aimed to finish in the top three and then win the runoff based on public love and sympathy for the elder Talmadge. It worked: He came in second to his father.

**Governor #2: M. E. Thompson.** In many states, when a governor dies, the lieutenant governor assumes the executive office. Georgia had only created the post of lieutenant governor in 1945 and the first lieutenant governor was to be elected in the 1946 general election. The winner: Talmadge rival M. E. Thompson. His position was that even though he hadn't yet been sworn in as lieutenant governor-elect, technically he was next in line for the governor's job.

**Governor #3: Ellis Arnall.** Arnall, who lost to Eugene Talmadge, actually was the sitting governor, and as such, refused to vacate his office until the Georgia Supreme Court could decide who the new governor would be.

Put down that swatter! 80% of the world's food crops are pollinated by insects.

## THERE OUGHTA BE A LAW

But it wasn't up to the Supreme Court; it was in the hands of the Georgia General Assembly (the legislature), which had the constitutional authority to decide contested elections. When the Assembly met in January 1947, the majority of members were against the idea of having another election—they favored giving the governorship to Herman Talmadge because he'd finished second in votes. Furthermore, Talmadge supporters argued, the new lieutenant governor, M. E. Thompson, had no claim to the office because he hadn't yet taken office himself, and therefore couldn't be a successor.

Thompson wasn't going down without a fight. His supporters plied pro-Talmadge legislators with drinks that were laced with knockout drops. Thompson figured that if the Talmadge faction fell asleep, they couldn't very well vote for Talmadge, giving Thompson backers an easy win. But the vote never took place. It was prevented when Talmadge supporters found out about Thompson's scheme and stormed the capitol building. "There were several thousand people there, 90 percent of them my friends—some of them armed," Talmadge later recalled. "And some of them drunk."

## MINOR SETBACK

Meanwhile, ballot recounts showed that Herman Talmadge hadn't finished second in the election after all. He'd actually finished third, making him ineligible for any claim at governor. Did that eliminate him from the running? Nope. Later that week, a bunch of ballots from Telfair County (Talmadge's home county) were suddenly "discovered" and sent to the Capitol. That put Talmadge back into contention for what looked to be a runoff vote with Arnall. (Historians later found that all the late ballots were written in the same handwriting and cast in alphabetical order by deceased voters.)

Amazingly, the Assembly opted against a runoff and hurriedly appointed Talmadge governor on January 15, 1947. The only problem: the incumbent, Ellis Arnall, refused to acknowledge Talmadge's appointment. He locked himself inside the governor's office and would not leave...until a Talmadge mob stormed the office, broke the door down, and forcibly removed him. As Arnall later recalled, "The lock splintered with a crash and the mob poured into the office. A pathway opened in the crowd, and the young son of the dead governor-elect of Georgia was led through the office on the arm of his chief advisor. Behind them trailed a committee of legislators and a giant professional wrestler who had been the strong-arm man for the faction."

## BACKROOM BARGAIN

As the mob escorted Arnall from the governor's office, he changed his plan. He would no longer focus on remaining governor, but on unseating Talmadge. Still declaring himself the acting governor, Arnall worked out a deal with the now sworn-in lieutenant governor, M.E. Thompson: Arnall would "resign" and Thompson would become governor. Now the number of potential governors was down to two...and Arnall would get what he really wanted: The debacle would be decided by the Georgia Supreme Court.

At this point, Talmadge and Thompson each claimed to be the rightful governor. But who actually was the governor? Georgia Secretary of State Ben Fortson didn't know, but he wasn't taking any chances—he began sitting on or sleeping with the state seal, which was needed by the governor (whoever it was) to make certain documents legal. With neither man able to perform the functions of the job, they took the fight to court.

## DISORDER IN THE COURT

In March 1947, the Georgia Supreme Court declared Thompson acting governor. Their reasoning: the General Assembly had acted improperly in its January sessions. According to the court, they should have declared Eugene Talmadge the governor-elect, even though he was dead. That would mean the next in line, the lieutenant governor-elect, Thompson, would be the successor.

Or would he? The court also ordered a special election to be held in 1948, mostly to avoid any more Talmadge-organized mobs and riots. Thompson would serve until then. The legitimate winner of the 1948 election was Herman Talmadge. In the final analysis, all three men vying for the office—Talmadge, Thompson, and Arnall—served as governor of Georgia. Although the controversy seems comical today, at the time it was a great embarrassment for Georgia, and it still ranks as one of the weirdest political moments in American history.

Boom boom: Athens, Georgia, is home to the only double-barreled cannon ever made.

# PLOP, PLOP, QUIZ, QUIZ

*Since this is our* Fast-Acting, Long-Lasting Bathroom Reader, *we thought it might be fun to test our ad slogan IQ. How many products and brands can you recognize by their slogans? Answers are on page 518.*

1. "Good to the last drop."

2. "You're in good hands."

3. "It takes a tough man to make a tender chicken."

4. "A little dab'll do ya."

5. "When it absolutely, positively has to be there overnight."

6. "The beer that made Milwaukee famous."

7. "We answer to a higher authority."

8. "Plop, plop, fizz, fizz."

9. "When it rains, it pours!"

10. "Don't leave home without it."

11. "Ask the man who owns one."

12. "I liked it so much I bought the company."

13. "Takes a licking and keeps on ticking."

14. "Reach out and touch someone."

15. "Let your fingers do the walking."

16. "It keeps going, and going, and going."

17. "Come to where the flavor is."

18. "It helps the hurt stop hurting."

19. "It does a body good."

20. "It's what's for dinner."

21. "We love to fly and it shows."

22. "And we thank you for your support."

23. "Rich Corinthian leather."

24. "Celebrate the moments of your life."

25. "Manly, yes, but I like it, too."

26. "Generation Next."

27. "We'll leave the light on for you."

28. "Better living through chemistry."

---

Better people…or better criminals? Only 12% of those arrested for murder are women.

# ROCKING-CHAIR ROCKERS

*It's easy to say "hope I die before I get old" when you're 20. But what about when you're 50 or 60? Here's what these golden oldies have to say.*

"Don't talk to me about getting old, 'cause I'm not old yet."
—**Tina Turner, 67**

"People love talking about when they were young and heard 'Honky Tonk Women' for the first time. It's quite a heavy load to carry the memories of so many people. I like it but I must be careful not to get trapped in the past. That's why I tend to forget my songs."
—**Mick Jagger, 62**

"Somebody said to me this morning, 'To what do you attribute your longevity?' I don't know. I mean, by all accounts I should be dead."
—**Ozzy Osbourne, 51**

"Music is forever; music should grow and mature with you, following you right on up until you die."
—**Paul Simon, 63**

"Getting old is fascinating. The older you get, the older you want to get."
—**Keith Richards, 62**

"In this business it takes time to be really good—and by that time, you're obsolete."
—**Cher, 52**

"Neil Young doesn't like the old groups getting together. He goes on about all us dinosaurs digging out our old songs forever. But as John Lennon said, 'It takes a hypocrite to know a hypocrite.'"
— **Pete Townshend, 60**

"I guess I don't so much mind being old, as I mind being fat and old."
—**Peter Gabriel, 55**

"People still think I wear bright glasses and high-heeled shoes. That's not happened since the '70s. But you know, you create a persona and you are going to have to live with it whether you like it or not."
—**Elton John, 58**

"Musicians don't retire; they stop when there's no more music in them."
—**Louis Armstrong, 69**

In 1990 the French government created a new cabinet position: Le Ministry du Rock 'n' Roll.

# NAME YOUR POISON

*What's the difference between Scotch and bourbon?*
*Vodka and gin? Port and sherry? We've always*
*wondered, so we looked them up.*

## WHERE ALCOHOL COMES FROM

Ethyl alcohol (the kind you can drink) is created by a process known as *fermentation*. Yeast is added to fruit juice or a "mash" (a cooked mixture of grain and water), and the yeast consumes the sugars, creating two by-products: carbon dioxide and alcohol. But there's a natural limit to this process. When the alcohol content of the mixture reaches about 15 percent, the yeast loses its ability to convert any more sugars into alcohol. If you want alcohol with a stronger kick than that, you have to continue on to a second process: *distillation*.

Distilled spirits are made in a device called a *still*, which consists of a boiler, a condenser, and a collector. The fermented liquid is heated in the boiler to at least 173°F, the boiling point for alcohol. All the alcohol (and some of the water) boils off in the form of vapor. The vapor flows into the condenser, where it cools back to liquid form and is collected in the collector. The process can be repeated to increase the alcohol content even further.

All distilled liquor is colorless when it is first made, but it can darken during the aging process, especially when aged in wooden barrels or casks. Some manufacturers use caramel or artificial coloring to darken their spirits.

### BAR CODES

• **Whiskey.** The word comes from the Gaelic *usquebaugh*, meaning "water of life." It's alcohol distilled from fermented grains such as barley, rye, corn, wheat, or a combination. In Ireland and the United States, whiskey is spelled with an "e." In Scotland, Canada, and Japan, it's spelled *whisky*.

• **Scotch.** Whiskey made in Scotland. According to international law, only whiskey made in Scotland may be called Scotch.

• **Bourbon.** American whiskey of the type originally made in

Bourbon County, Kentucky, typically made from 70 percent corn and 30 percent wheat, rye, or other grains. Tennessee whiskey is similar to bourbon, except that it's produced in—you guessed it—Tennessee. It is filtered through a ten-foot layer of maple charcoal, which gives it a milder, distinctive flavor.

• **Brandy.** Alcohol distilled from fermented fruit juices. Brandy is short for brandywine, which comes from the Dutch *brandewijn*, which means "burnt wine." It can be made from grapes, blackberries, apples, plums, or other fruits. Cognac is a type of brandy produced in the Cognac region of France.

• **Gin.** Distilled grain alcohol flavored with juniper berries. Sloe gin is gin flavored with sloe berries from the blackthorn bush instead of juniper berries.

• **Rum.** Alcohol distilled from molasses and sugarcane juice, both of which are by-products of the process used to turn sugarcane into refined sugar.

• **Vodka.** Distilled alcohol originally made from potatoes, but today mostly made from grain. "Vodka" is the diminutive form of *voda*, the Russian word for water, and means "little water." All vodka produced in the United States is required by law to be colorless, odorless, and nearly tasteless, which accounts for its popularity in mixed drinks.

• **Sherry.** White wine that has been fortified by the addition of distilled spirits. It gets its name from *Shareesh*, the Arabic name for the town of Jerez in southwestern Spain, where it originated.

• **Port.** Fortified red or white wine. It gets its name from the city of Porto in northern Portugal, where it originated.

• **Vermouth.** Fortified white wine flavored with aromatic herbs and spices. It's no longer true, but the flavorings were originally used to mask the flavor of inferior wines. Vermouth gets its name from *wermut*, German for wormwood, one of the traditional flavors.

• **Cordials.** Distilled spirits combined with sweetened fruit pulp or fruit juices. Liqueurs are similar to cordials, except that the flavoring is provided by flowers, herbs, seeds, roots, or the bark of plants. Many traditional cordial and liqueur recipes are centuries old and started out as medicinal products.

# ANATOMY OF A HICCUP

*Have the...hic...hiccups? Reading this page won't cure them...hic...but at least...hic...you'll have a better idea of what you're...hic...dealing with.*

W**HAT YOU MIGHT NOT KNOW**
• A hiccup occurs when a stimulus causes an involuntary contraction of the diaphragm, the muscle separating the lungs from the abdomen. The contraction makes the sufferer take a quick breath, causing the glottis (located in the voice box) to close, which makes the "hic" sound.

• Technical term for hiccups: a diaphragmatic spasm, or *singultus*.

• Unlike other body reflexes (coughs, sneezes, vomiting), hiccups serve no useful purpose.

• Most common causes: too much alcohol, spicy food, cold water, carbonated drinks, indigestion, or asthma. They can also be caused by liver or kidney problems, abdominal surgery, or a brain tumor.

• The word "hiccup" may come from the French *hocquet*, which was used to describe the sound of a hiccup. The earliest known version in English is *hicket*, dating from the 1500s.

• Hiccup lore: In ancient Greece, a bad case of the hiccups meant an enemy was talking about you. To get rid of them one had to guess the enemy's name. The Scots thought holding your left thumb (or your chin) with your right hand while listening to someone singing a hymn would stop the hiccups.

• Some forms of *encephalitis* (swelling of the brain) can cause hiccuping. During the encephalitis pandemics of the 1920s, several cities reported cases of mass hiccuping.

• Fetuses hiccup in the womb.

• Charles Osborne of Anthon, Iowa, holds the title of "World's Longest Hiccuper." It started in 1922, hiccuping as often as 40 times per minute. Sometimes he hiccuped so hard his false teeth fell out. In 1987—nearly 70 years later—the hiccups stopped.

• Folk cures: eat peanut butter, eat Wasabi, drink vinegar, eat Lingonberry jam, drink a glass of water while urinating.

# BATHROOM NEWS

*All the latest information from the news stream.*

## LOO ALERT

Dyno-Rod, England's largest emergency plumbing service, issued a warning in late 2004: Luxury toilet papers are causing an increase in blocked commodes. The company funded a study to see how long different TPs took to disintegrate in water. Their finding: "Modern products, including double quilted, pre-moistened, and aloe vera–impregnated tissue can take several days to disintegrate while others take just three minutes." Result: a 10 percent rise in emergency calls to plumbers. One brand, Kandoo, was still intact after five days in water. Said Dyno-Rod spokesman Alan McLaughlin, "The explosion in luxury paper is placing toilets under considerable strain."

## SUPER BOWL

When a maintenance worker arrived at a highway rest stop in Valle, Norway, she was probably happy to discover that there was one toilet she would not have to clean...because it had been stolen. Helga Homme, an employee of Mesta, the company that services rest stops, immediately reported the theft to the Public Roads Administration (PRA). A Mesta manager reported that although he had seen plenty of thefts from rest stops over the years, things like lightbulbs and toilet paper, he had never heard of someone stealing a toilet. It cost the PRA more than $3,000 to replace the stainless-steel toilet, which appeared to have been carefully removed. "They had a disgusting job," said Homme.

## WRONG KIND OF SNAKE

In February 2005, Shannon Scavotto of St. Petersburg, Florida, was getting ready for work when he lifted the lid of his toilet to discard a tissue...and a snake stuck its head out of the bowl. Scavotto quickly called local animal control. When they told him it would cost $150 to have the snake removed, he decided to make his own snake-catching device out of PVC pipe and string. Scavotto lassoed the snake around its head and started pulling... and pulling...and pulling... "It was one of those five levels of realization," he told the St. Petersburg Times. "How big is this snake?" It turned out to be a six-foot African python. Scavotto has no idea how it got there, but it has given him a new worry in life: "Makes me wonder now when I go to the restroom." (Us, too.)

## POLICE LOG

Police officer Craig Clancy walked into a public bathroom stall at a San Antonio auto auction, pulled his pants down...and accidentally dropped his gun, shooting the man in the next stall. The falling pistol, which the officer tried to grab, somehow went off...*twice*. The victim was hospitalized but not seriously injured, according to police.

## PAY TOILET

A 29-year-old German man was taking some money to the bank for his boss in June 2005. On the way, he stopped at a public restroom to relieve himself, then continued on to the bank. Five minutes later he realized he'd left the money—36,000 euros (almost $43,000) which he was carrying in a plastic bag—behind. He ran back to get it but, not surprisingly, it was gone. Police said the man's story appeared to be genuine, since he was not insured for such a situation and he would probably have to repay the money to the company himself.

## LOADED

Fifty-three-year-old John Jenkins, an operator at a power plant in Morgantown, West Virginia, entered a portable toilet at work, sat down, and lit a cigarette. Bad idea. The ensuing explosion threw him off the toilet and out the door. "When I struck the lighter, the whole thing just detonated," he said. "The whole top blew off." The explosion was apparently caused by a faulty pipe beneath the unit that had collected methane gas inside it. Jenkins suffered burns on his legs, arm, and face, and sued the plant for $10 million.

\* \* \*

**Newsflash:** This just in. Hundreds of wigs were stolen from a local factory last night. Police are combing the area.

# ALTERNATE TV GUIDE

*Some actors are so closely associated with a specific role
or TV series that it's hard to imagine he or she wasn't
the first choice. But it happens all the time.*

**T**HE BRADY BUNCH. Gene Hackman almost got the part of Mike Brady. Producers cast Robert Reed instead—they didn't think Hackman was well-known enough.

**GILLIGAN'S ISLAND.** Among the actors almost cast: Jayne Mansfield as Ginger, Dabney Coleman as the Professor, and Raquel Welch as Mary Ann.

**THE DICK VAN DYKE SHOW.** Writer Carl Reiner originally sold this show about a TV comedy writer and his young wife as *Head of the Family*. Reiner's choice for the lead role: Johnny Carson.

**BEWITCHED.** When baby Tabitha got old enough to be played by a toddler, two child actresses were initially considered: Helen Hunt and Jodie Foster. (The part went to twins Diane and Erin Murphy.)

**THE DUKES OF HAZZARD.** Dennis Quaid almost landed the part of Luke Duke, but it went to Tom Wopat instead.

**MURDER, SHE WROTE.** The role of Jessica Fletcher was written with Jean Stapleton (Edith in *All in the Family*) in mind. She turned it down (so did Doris Day), so it went to Angela Lansbury.

**THE MONKEES.** Producers originally wanted to build a sitcom around an existing band. When the Dave Clark Five and the Lovin' Spoonful turned down the chance, unknown actors and musicians were sought.

**DESPERATE HOUSEWIVES.** Calista Flockhart, Heather Locklear, Sela Ward, and Mary-Louise Parker were all almost cast in the role ultimately given to Teri Hatcher.

The alphabet, arranged by frequency of use: ETAISONHRDLUCMFWYPGVBKJQXZ.

**THREE'S COMPANY.** Billy Crystal auditioned for the part of Jack Tripper, which eventually went to John Ritter.

**CHARLIE'S ANGELS.** They were almost Angels: Kim Basinger, Michelle Pfeiffer, and Kathie Lee Gifford.

**DYNASTY.** Elizabeth Taylor, Raquel Welch, and Sophia Loren were all passed over for the part of Alexis; Angie Dickinson was offered the role of Krystal. The roles went to Joan Collins and Linda Evans.

**THE A-TEAM.** For the part of Hannibal, producers nearly cast James Coburn. They went with George Peppard instead.

**THE PARTRIDGE FAMILY.** After four seasons, David Cassidy was exhausted and wanted to leave the show. Rick Springfield was scheduled to replace him—until the network decided not to renew the show for a fifth year.

**FRIENDS.** Jon Cryer was offered the role of Chandler. He turned it down and it went to Matthew Perry.

**HAPPY DAYS.** Robby Benson was considered for the role of Richie Cunningham, but lost out to Ron Howard. (Former Monkees Mickey Dolenz and Michael Nesmith both auditioned to play Fonzie.)

**STAR TREK.** Martin Landau turned down the part of Spock. It went to Leonard Nimoy, who would later replace Landau when he quit *Mission: Impossible.*

\*     \*     \*

## OOPS

In 2005 *Money* magazine named its 100 best places to live. At #28 was Wexford, Pennsylvania. Only problem: Wexford doesn't exist. It's a postal designation for parts of four real Pittsburgh suburbs, but it has no boundaries, government, or taxes (which may be why it's considered such a great place to live).

---

Author Alexandre Dumas (*The Three Musketeers*) kept a pet vulture on a leash.

# THE GREAT PIG WAR

*San Juan Island is one of many islands that dot Puget Sound,
which separates Washington and Canada. Today, it's a popular
tourist destination, most notably for whale watching. But more
than a century ago, it was not a whale but a pig that thrust
San Juan Island to the center of the world stage.*

## RUDE AWAKENING

Lyman Cutlar was a potato farmer who lived on San Juan Island. On the morning of June 15, 1859, he was startled out of bed by the sound of grunts coming from his potato patch. He got up, grabbed his rifle, and went to investigate. What Cutlar saw incensed him: In the middle of his field was a giant black boar munching on his newly planted tubers. Next to the fence stood a man laughing at the spectacle. Cutlar was mad. He raised his rifle, took aim, and shot. The pig fell dead; the man ran into the woods.

That would be the only fatality in a tense standoff that nearly brought the United States and England into a full-scale war.

## THIS LAND IS OUR LAND

After winning the Revolutionary War against England in 1783, the United States started expanding west, embracing the idea of Manifest Destiny, a belief that Americans had a divine right to all lands from the Atlantic to the Pacific. The Louisiana Purchase of 1803 added more than 800,000 square miles, extending from the Mississippi River to the Rocky Mountains. The Mexican-American War of 1846 extended the nation out to California.

That same year, America and Great Britain signed the Oregon Treaty, which set the international boundary between the United States and western Canada, at the time governed by the British. According to the treaty: "The boundary shall be continued westward along the forty-ninth parallel of north latitude to the middle of the channel which separates the continent from Vancouver's Island, and thence southward through the middle of said channel, and of Fuca's Straight, to the Pacific Ocean."

Although this wording may sound thorough, it wasn't—especially the phrase "in the middle of the channel." San Juan Island sat in the middle of that channel, and there were two navigable channels on opposite sides of it: the Haro on the west and Rosario to the east. Britain claimed Rosario as the border, making the island British territory. The Americans claimed it was the Haro, making the island American territory.

## TENSION MOUNTS

While the diplomats argued, both sides staked their claims. Hudson's Bay Company, owned by England, turned the verdant, 55-square-mile island into a giant sheep ranch. Sixteen Americans also settled on San Juan, one of whom was Lyman Cutlar. The governor of Oregon Territory had (mistakenly) assured him that San Juan belonged to the United States. Therefore, as an American citizen, Cutlar (mistakenly) thought he was entitled to 320 acres of free land under the Donation Land Claim Act of 1850. But because the ownership of the island was under dispute, the Claim Act did not apply.

Cutlar's nearest neighbor was Charles Griffin, an Englishman who managed Hudson's Bay's giant sheep ranch. Griffin also owned a few pigs, which he allowed to roam freely. After all, as far as he was concerned, the island belonged to the British.

The two sides shared an uneasy peace for a few years...until Cutlar killed Griffin's pig. The American farmer offered $10 compensation for the deceased pig, but Griffin scoffed at the paltry price and demanded $100. Cutlar wasn't about to pay such a huge sum for a pig that trespassed on *his* land. He replied: "Better chance for lightning to strike you than for you to get a hundred dollars for that hog!" Both men took their complaints to their respective governments.

## SETTING THE PIECES

Griffin called on Sir James Douglas, governor of British Columbia, who sided with his countryman. Years earlier, Douglas had publicly opposed the Treaty of Oregon, believing that the Columbia River—which lies many miles to the south and now separates Washington from Oregon—should have been the border between the two countries. Unhappy with the upstart Americans living on "his" island, Governor Douglas ordered Cutlar to pay the $100.

Cutlar told the governor where he could stick his order and

walked away. He was, after all, an American citizen, and San Juan Island was in the United States of AMERICA! Douglas issued a warrant for the potato farmer's arrest.

Cutlar ignored the warrant (he was never arrested) and complained bitterly to General William S. Harney, commander of the U.S. Army's Department of Oregon. Harney was a hothead. According to biographer George Rollie Adams, Harney was "excitable, aggressive, and quick to react to any affront, insult, or attack, whether real or imagined." And General Harney hated the British as much as Governor Douglas hated the Americans. Harney sent his best officer to occupy the island—Captain George Pickett, another hothead who earlier had been cited for "reckless bravery" in the Mexican War. Pickett landed on San Juan Island in July of 1859 with 461 soldiers. They built a fort, brought in their artillery, and prepared for battle. Pickett proclaimed (without federal authority) that the island was United States territory and appointed himself the sole authority. "No laws, other than those of the United States," would be recognized.

Meanwhile, Governor Douglas warned the British Foreign Office: "The whole of San Juan Island will soon be occupied by a squatter population of American citizens if they do not receive an immediate check."

## CHECK

The British sent five warships and 2,000 soldiers. Undeterred, Harney ordered Pickett to stop the British from landing, and if they tried, to open fire. Pickett pledged that if he had to, he would "make a Bunker Hill out of it" and fight to the last man.

Governor Douglas ordered his navy to take San Juan by force, but British Rear Admiral Robert L. Baynes, who commanded the fleet, was the only one of the bunch with a knack for diplomacy. "I refuse to involve two great nations in a war over a squabble about a pig!" So Baynes kept his men on the ships, their guns pointed at the American fort. Both sides were ready to fight, but neither wanted to fire the first shot. So there they stayed, facing each other's guns, waiting.

Back in Washington, D.C., the standoff—now more than two months old—was treated with the utmost importance. With the threat of a civil war looming at home, no one wanted to go to war

---

A single square inch of skin on the human hand contains 72 feet of nerves.

with England...again. President Buchanan dispatched his best negotiator, General Winfield Scott, who had previously mediated two disputes over the U.S.–Canadian border, one at Aroostook, Maine, and the other at Niagara Falls.

## TO THE RESCUE

General Scott arrived in October to find Captain Pickett and his men tired, anxious, and with itchy trigger fingers. He met with General Harney and told him, "Resign or get fired." Disgraced, Harney left the island, having fired not a single shot.

Now in sole charge of the situation, General Scott met with Governor Douglas. They came to a stalemate as to the true owner-ship of San Juan Island, but agreed on a joint occupancy until an international arbiter could be brought in to settle the matter. The British fleet sailed away, and most of the American troops with-drew, as did Lyman Cutlar, who found that living on San Juan Island was far more trouble than it was worth. Each side left a symbolic token force, encamped on opposite ends of the island. They shared a second, uneasy peace for more than a decade.

## THE FINAL OINK

Thirteen years passed before the matter was finally settled. So who did England and the United States get to solve the problem? Kaiser Wilhelm I, of Germany. He agreed to serve as their neutral arbiter and appointed three experts to examine the evidence. In October 1872, the German leader finally rendered his verdict: "The boundary line shall be drawn through the Haro Channel." The kaiser gave San Juan Island to the United States.

As for the wayward pig that started the whole fiasco... it's as-sumed he ended up on either Cutlar's or Griffin's dinner table.

\*      \*      \*

### IS IT TOO LATTE?

It turns out too much caffeine can kill you. How much is too much? According to *www.energyfiend.com*, it would take 435 cans of A&W Creme Soda to kill a 185-pound man. Brewed coffee: 117 cups. Red Bull energy drink: 157 cans. Snapple Decaffeinated Lemon Tea: 2805 bottles.

# RATHERISMS

*Anchorman Dan Rather may be known as a serious
journalist, but we love him for these odd phrases,
ad-libbed during election night coverage.*

"This race is hotter than a
Times Square Rolex."

"The presidential race is
swinging like Count Basie."

"This race is humming along
like Ray Charles."

"Bush is sweeping through the
South like a big wheel through
a cotton field."

"In southern states, Bush beat
Kerry like a rented mule."

"You know that old song: It's
delightful, it's delicious, it's
de-lovely for President Bush
in most areas of the country."

"His lead is as thin as turnip
soup."

"Keep in mind they are teeto
tally meetmortally convinced
they have Ohio won."

"The re-election of Bill Clinton is as secure as a double-
knot tied in wet rawhide."

"We don't know whether to
wind a watch or bark at the
moon."

"These returns are running
like a squirrel in a cage."

"This race is as tight as a too-
small bathing suit on a too-hot
car ride back from the beach."

"Bush is sweeping through the
South like a tornado through
a trailer park."

"This race is as tight as the
rusted lug nuts on a '55 Ford."

"This race is spandex-tight."

"This race is shakier than
cafeteria Jell-O."

"When it comes to a race like
this, I'm a long distance run-
ner and an all-day hunter."

"The Michigan Republican
primary is tighter than Willie
Nelson's headband."

"His lead is as thin as November ice."

"A lot of people in Washington
could not be more surprised if
Fidel Castro came loping
through on the back of a hippopotamus this election night."

There is an underground church in Poland carved from solid salt.

# THE DEATH OF SUPERMAN

*In 1992 the world's most famous superhero was "killed"—and he nearly took the entire comic book industry down with him*

## WRITERS OF STEEL

It was 1990. The writers of the Superman comic books wanted to do something new with their character. So that July, after a courtship that began in *Action Comics* in 1938, they had Clark Kent finally pop the question to Lois Lane. With tears in her eyes, Lois accepted. "Clark," she said, "I've already decided...Yes. I want to share my life with you." A few months later, in *Action Comics* #662, mild-mannered Clark revealed to Lois his true "super" identity.

With all of these plot developments, comic fans were energized. And as they awaited the "wedding of the century," comic book sales skyrocketed. Some newspapers even treated it as real news, printing articles about the famous couple's impending nuptials. But despite all the hoopla, the brass at DC Comics suddenly instructed their writers to put the story on hold. There was a problem.

ABC was working on a new Superman television show, *Lois and Clark: The New Adventures of Superman*, and production was behind schedule. The premiere had to be postponed: Instead of debuting in the fall of 1992 as originally planned, ABC had to move it back a year to 1993. But producers were excited about the media exposure generated by the Man of Steel's marriage and felt that if it coincided with the new TV show, it would translate into strong ratings. They wanted "the wedding" to be postponed, too.

## BACK TO THE DRAWING BOARD

Every year, the writers and editors of Superman comics hold a meeting they call the "Super Summit" to plot, a year in advance, the stories for each of the four different Superman comic books: *Superman*, *The Adventures of Superman*, *Action Comics*, and *Superman: The Man of Steel*. The meetings are essential because each of the titles are linked, and the events of one book help to shape what happens in the others.

When they met in the fall of 1991 to create the stories for the upcoming year, suddenly they had to start from scratch. With the wedding scrapped, how would they keep fans interested? Faced with pressure from all sides, the writers decided they had to do something extreme—Superman would die. "At every single meeting we've ever had, as a joke, somebody would say, 'Let's kill him.' It never failed," revealed longtime Superman editor Mike Carlin. "But then we actually did it."

## SAY IT ISN'T SO

When the news was leaked to the media six months later, it created a storm of publicity—even more than the wedding had. The writers at DC knew the death of Superman would be a big deal to comic fans, but they had no idea how big the public's reaction would be. Comic book controversy was nothing new—in fact, earlier that same year, a Marvel Comics character named Northstar had made news when he "revealed" he was gay. But he was just a minor character; Superman was...Superman.

The story broke on the June 16, 1992, cover of *Newsday*, and it spread like wildfire, appearing in newspapers all over the United States, Canada, and even as far away as Germany and Australia. The publicity department at DC Comics, meanwhile, remained tight-lipped, refusing to address any questions pertaining to Superman's death.

## IT'S A BIRD! IT'S A PLANE! IT'S...DEAD!

So what could kill the Man of Steel? It wasn't longtime nemesis Lex Luthor or even kryptonite. It was Doomsday—a giant green monster whom writer Dan Jurgens referred to as "primal rage incarnate." Doomsday leveled skyscrapers, spawned chaos, and crushed innocent bystanders. Appearing first in *Superman: The Man of Steel* #18, he ravaged the streets of Metropolis over the course of a storyline that spanned seven comic books.

Finally, on November 18, 1992, in *Superman* #75, after a savage fistfight between Superman and Doomsday, both fell to the ground...dead. The comic book was packaged in black plastic and included a poster and a black armband.

The first printing flew off the shelves, prompting DC Comics to publish a second edition (but without the promotional items). When that one sold out, DC published the entire seven-issue story in a trade paperback. In the end, they sold more than 6 million copies of the comic book in its various printings, making the "Death of Superman" one of the best-selling comics of all time.

## RESURRECTION

Despite what the readers believed, Superman's death was never meant to be permanent. DC issued an eight-issue story titled "Funeral for a Friend," in which friends and superheroes mourned Superman (who appeared in every issue as a corpse). The subsequent series, "Reign of the Supermen," involved four superheroes (a child, an alien, a robot, and a man in an iron suit), each claiming to be Superman's heir. Readers were left to guess whether there was a connection between any of the new characters and Superman. (There wasn't.) Finally, in *Superman* #82, released in October 1993, a benevolent alien reinserts life into Superman's dead body.

The death of Superman represented the last real boom of the comic book industry. The Man of Steel was everywhere. *Saturday Night Live* ran a sketch that featured several superheroes attending Superman's funeral. On December 31, 1992, Roseanne Arnold appeared on *The Tonight Show*. Her New Year's resolution: to hunt down Superman's killer and "make him pay for what he did."

## POSTMORTEM

Superman the cultural icon recovered, and the Superman TV show was a hit for ABC (it lasted until 1997). But Superman the comic book hero? When Superman was revived, fans felt ripped off, and most of them never went back. Result: *all* comic-book sales went down—1993 had been the biggest-selling year ever, topping $1 billion, but since then they've declined almost 70 percent. Today, both DC and Marvel Comics make most of their money from movies, such as *Spider-Man*, *Batman*, and *X-Men*. Doomsday seems to have struck a fatal blow from which the comic book industry, unlike Superman, has never quite recovered.

**One Last Thing:** The wedding that started it all didn't happen until 1996, when Lois and Clark got married on the screen and in the comic. The TV episode was a hit; the comic book wasn't.

# ODD FACTS ABOUT CHARLES DICKENS

*"It was the best of times, it was the worst of times, it was the age of wisdom, it was the age of foolishness…" wrote Charles Dickens, whose life was a rich mixture of all the above*

W**HAT THE DICKENS?** Charles Dickens was the first literary superstar—his popular works reached a wider audience than any writer before him. With classics like *Oliver Twist, A Christmas Carol, Great Expectations, A Tale of Two Cities,* and *David Copperfield,* Dickens dominated the literary life of 19th-century England and the United States. But like many remarkable people, Dickens was a complex, multi-layered individual, full of peculiar quirks and odd habits.

- **OBSESSIVE-COMPULSIVE.** Dickens was preoccupied with looking in the mirror and combing his hair—he did it hundreds of times a day. He rearranged furniture in his home—if it wasn't in the exact "correct" position, he couldn't concentrate. Obsessed with magnetic fields, Dickens made sure that every bed he slept in was aligned north–south. He had to touch certain objects three times for luck. He was obsessed with the need for tidiness, often cleaning other homes as well as his own.

- **NICKNAME-IAC.** Just as some of his most endearing characters had odd nicknames (like Pip in *Great Expectations*), Dickens gave every one of his ten children nicknames like "Skittles" and "Plorn."

- **EPILEPTIC.** Dickens suffered from epilepsy and made some of his characters—like Oliver Twist's brother—epileptics. Modern doctors are amazed at the medical accuracy of his descriptions of this malady.

- **PRACTICAL JOKER.** Dickens's study had a secret door designed to look like a bookcase. The shelves were full of fake books with witty titles, such as *Noah's Arkitecture* and a nine-volume set titled *Cat's Lives.* One of his favorites was a multi-volume

---

The position paid peanuts, anyway: Charles Schulz was once turned down for a job at Disney.

series called *The Wisdom of Our Ancestors*, dealing with subjects like ignorance, superstition, disease, and instruments of torture, and a companion book titled *The Virtues of Our Ancestors*, which was so narrow that the title had to be printed vertically.

• **EGOMANIAC.** Dickens often referred to himself as "the Sparkler of Albion," favorably comparing himself to Shakespeare's nickname, "the Bard of Avon." (Albion is an archaic name for England.)

• **FAIR-WEATHER FRIEND.** Hans Christian Andersen was Dickens's close friend and mutual influence. Andersen even dedicated his book *Poet's Day Dream* to Dickens in 1853. But this didn't stop Dickens from letting Andersen know when he'd overstayed his welcome at Dickens's home. He printed a sign and left it on Andersen's mirror in the guest room. It read: "Hans Andersen slept in this room for five weeks, which seemed to the family like AGES."

• **MESMERIST.** Dickens was a devotee of mesmerism, a system of healing through hypnotism. He practiced it on his hypochondriac wife and his children, and claimed to have healed several friends and associates.

• **CLIFF-HANGER.** When *The Old Curiosity Shop* was published in serial form in 1841, readers all over Britain and the United States followed the progress of the heroine, Little Nell, with the same fervor that audiences today follow Harry Potter. When the ship carrying the last installment approached the dock in New York, 6,000 impatient fans onshore called out to the sailors, "Does Little Nell die?" (They yelled back that…uh-oh, we're out of room.)

\*     \*     \*

## THE BIG BURRITO

At the 2004 Nevada State Fair, volunteers attempted to set a record for the world's largest burrito. Ingredients: 8,200 tortillas; 2,000 pounds of refried beans; and 1,000 pounds each of sour cream, cheese, and salsa. The finished product was 8,076 feet long, totalling about 8,433,200 calories—enough to feed the average person for $11\frac{1}{2}$ years.

# IT'S A WEIRD, WEIRD CRIME

*In the history of the BRI, we've written about smart crooks, dumb crooks, and even nice crooks. But these crimes were committed by crooks of an entirely different breed.*

## TO TELL THE TOOTH

"A toothless man has been arrested for stealing toothbrushes. According to *O Dia* newspaper, 32-year-old Ednor Rodrigues was filmed taking seven toothbrushes from a supermarket in Ribeirao Preto, Brazil. When he was approached by the police, he tried to deny the robbery—even showing the officers his toothless mouth. He finally admitted to the crime: 'I don't know why I did it. I know it was stupid. I have no teeth, what was I thinking?'"

—*Sunday Mail* [Scotland]

## SCALPED

"Paul J. Goudy, of Lemoyne, Pennsylvania, was sentenced to 23 months probation after pleading guilty to theft by unlawfully taking a man's hairpiece. Last January, Edward Floyd was sitting at a Harrisburg restaurant when Goudy ripped the hairpiece off Floyd. Restaurant witnesses identified Goudy and when questioned by police he admitted that he'd done it on a dare—a friend had offered him $100 to steal the hairpiece. Dauphin County Judge Richard A. Lewis also fined Goudy $500 and ordered him to write a letter of apology to Floyd."

—**United Press International**

## COMPUTERCIDE

"George Doughty of Lafayette, Colorado, won't have any more problems with his computer. He was accused of shooting his Dell laptop four times with a Smith & Wesson revolver in the middle of his Sportsman's Inn Bar and Restaurant. He then allegedly hung the remains of the laptop on the wall 'like a hunting trophy,' said Lt. Rick Bashor of the Lafayette Police Department.

The catacombs beneath the city of Paris contain the bones of more than 3 million bodies.

"Doughty, 48, who owns the establishment, entered the bar from his office and told the two patrons and bartender that he was going to shoot his computer. He then set his laptop on the floor, warned the customers to cover their ears and fired away. Doughty never explained what prompted his actions, but told police that 'it seemed like the right thing to do at the time.'"

—Court TV

## KEEP YOUR EYES ON THE PRIZE, NOT THE PIES

"A 280-lb. thief broke into a Romanian bakery and stole $250, but couldn't resist the sweet temptation. He got stuck trying to exit through a window—after stuffing himself full of pies. The 29-year-old man was still stuck there in the morning when the shop owner, Vasile Mandache, arrived for work. He said, 'I saw all the pie wrappers on the floor, and then saw a pair of stubby, fat legs hanging out the window. I just had to call my friends to come and have a look before we called the police, it was so funny.'"

—Short News

## A PIG'S RANSOM

"'Raw fruit and vegetables—or else the pigs get it!' That's what a Gallatin, Tennessee, woman read in a ransom note after a pair of concrete swine were swiped from her front yard. The foot-tall plaster porkers, one dressed in farmer's overalls and the other in a pink dress, vanished from in front of Mary Romines' trailer. Other pieces of statuary, including concrete chickens and a few other pigs, were disturbed, but not taken. Tacked to the front gate was a note with a specific demand: two ears of corn and one ripe mango.

"Two days after the piggies, worth about $10 each, flew the coop, Romines got another menacing message—a well-done pork chop attached to a note reading, 'Cooked the Pig.' The next night, another note raised the demands—a potato in addition to the corn and mango. Signed 'The Big Bad Wolf' and accompanied by a bag of pork rinds, the note asked Romines if she was scared. 'They think they have me buffaloed, but now I'm mad,' Romines said. 'They may think it's funny, but they're going to be charged with theft.' Police agreed that the perpetrator will be criminally charged. The case remains under investigation."

—Fox News

# THE SAD TALE
# OF CENTRALIA

*On Valentine's Day, 1981, eleven-year-old Todd Domboski was
walking through a field in Centralia, Pennsylvania, when a 150-foot-
deep hole suddenly opened beneath his feet. Noxious fumes crept out
as the boy fell in. He only survived by clinging to some newly
exposed tree roots until his cousin ran over and pulled him
to safety. What was happening here...and why?*

COAL COUNTRY

Eastern Pennsylvania is anthracite coal country. Back at
the turn of the 20th century, miners were digging nearly
300 million tons of coal per year from the region, leaving behind a
vast subterranean network of abandoned mine shafts. In May
1962, while incinerating garbage in an old strip mine pit outside
of Centralia, one of the many exposed coal seams ignited. The fire
followed the seam down into the maze of abandoned mines and
began to spread. And it kept spreading—and burning—for years.

Mine fires in coal country are actually not all that uncommon.
There are currently as many as 45 of them burning in Pennsylva-
nia alone. Unfortunately, there's no good way to put them out.
But that doesn't stop people from trying.

• The most effective method to extinguish such a fire is to strip
mine around the entire perimeter of the blaze. That's an expensive—and in populated areas, impractical—proposition. Essentially,
it means digging an enormous trench, deep enough to get underneath the fires, which are often more than 500 feet below ground.

• An easier (but not much easier) method is to bore holes down
into the old mine shafts, and then pour in tons of wet concrete to
make plugs. Then more holes are drilled and flame-suppressing
foam is pumped into the areas between plugs. It, too, is a very
expensive project, and it doesn't always succeed.

The cheapest way to deal with a mine fire by far is to keep an
eye on it and hope it burns itself out. (One fire near Lehigh,
Pennsylvania, burned from 1850 until the 1930s.) After a 1969

effort to dig out the Centralia fire proved both costly and unsuccessful, they admitted defeat and let the fire take its course. By 1980, the size of the underground blaze was estimated at 350 acres, and large clouds of noxious smoke were billowing out of the ground all over town. The ground temperature under a local gas station was recorded at nearly 1,000°F. Residents of the once-thriving mountain town began to wonder if Centralia was a safe place to live.

When the boy fell in the hole and almost died, the fire beneath Centralia became a national news story. The sinkhole—caused by an effect known as *subsidence*, which occurs when mine shafts collapse, possibly because the support beams are on fire—put the town's 1,600 residents in a fix. Their homes were suddenly worthless. They couldn't sell them and move someplace safer—no one in their right mind would buy them.

The townsfolk were given a choice: a $660-million digging project that might not work, or let the government buy their homes. They voted 345 to 200 in favor of the buyout, and an exodus soon began. By 1991, $42 million had been spent buying out more than 540 Centralia homes and businesses.

**GHOST TOWN**

If you were to visit Centralia today, the first thing you'd notice is that there are more streets than buildings. At first glance, it would seem that someone decided to build a town, but only got as far as paving the roads. If you looked a bit closer, however, you'd notice the remnants of house foundations. Looking still closer, you'd see smoke still seeping out of the ground.

As of 2005, twelve die-hard Centralians reportedly continue to live in the smoldering ghost town. The number has dwindled since a decade ago, when nearly fifty holdouts still called it home. Experts estimate it will take 250 years for the fire to burn itself out.

\*     \*     \*

"Nearly all men can stand adversity, but if you want to test a man's character, give him power."
                                                    —Abraham Lincoln

Time it: A typical spoken sentence in ordinary conversation takes about 21.2 seconds.

# THE DOCTOR IS OUT (OF HIS MIND)

*Got a doctor's appointment soon? Then don't read this. Really.*

## BONEHEADS

In January 2004, Briana Lane suffered serious head injuries in a car crash near Salt Lake City—so serious that doctors had to remove almost half of her skull to treat the bleeding in her brain. Lane was released in February...but without the missing portion of her skull, which remained behind in the hospital freezer. The skull was due to be replaced, but the day before the surgery, the hospital canceled the appointment: they wanted to wait to see if Medicaid would pay for the procedure. In the meantime, all Lane had over her brain was a flap of skin, and she had to wear a helmet to protect it. (She said that every morning she could feel that her brain had drooped to one side during the night.) Lane finally got her skull back in April—*four months* after the initial operation and only, she says, after she called a local TV station and told them the story. "When you think of weird things happening to people," she said afterward, "you don't think of this."

## GLITTERING GLUTEUS

A patient of a hospital in Orange County, Florida, sued the facility in 2005, saying they had wrongly injected cosmetic glitter into his buttocks. The lawsuit claimed that while the patient (who happens to be an undercover policeman) was undergoing sinus surgery in 2000, he was supposed to be injected with pain medication (Demeral), but that one of the shots "felt" wrong. "There was a lot of pain," he said, "and I complained several times that something was wrong in my buttock." Months later, a different doctor removed from the injection site a four-inch mass that contained "green and red sparkling material." All parties agreed that there was, in fact, glitter in the man's buttocks. But the court found that since so much time had elapsed, it could not be determined exactly when and at what facility the glitter had been injected. Amazingly, he lost the suit.

---

At a steady pace of 6 mph, it would take a jogger 173 days to circle the globe.

## BRAIN DECAY

A dentist in Munich, Germany, was sued after deciding to save one of his patients some time—by giving her 14 root canals in one day. The dentist, whose name was not released to the press, fed the woman large glasses of cognac between each drilling during the 12-hour ordeal, telling her it would help ease the pain. Although she probably felt no pain during the operation, she sued because of the enormous pain she suffered for weeks afterward. According to standard dental practices, 14 root canals would normally be performed in several appointments over several weeks. The dentist was ordered to pay her $7,000 in compensation.

## CROUTON-GATE

It's not the doctor that's out of his mind in this story—it's the hospital. In 2004 the Queen's Medical Centre in Nottingham, England, suspended its top brain surgeon, Dr. Terence Hope, because he failed to pay for a bowl of soup and some croutons in the hospital cafeteria. The hospital had a 39-day waiting list for brain surgeries at the time. While outraged patients fumed at the hospital, the British news media had a field day over the fiasco. Hope, who had been with the hospital for 18 years and denied stealing any food, was back on the job five days later. A hospital spokesperson said that they had investigated the alleged soup-and-crouton crime, and conceded that it had been a misunderstanding.

## SPIRITED TREATMENT

A couple in Bengal, India, was arrested in 2005 for treating several people with serious conditions such as appendicitis, gallstones, hernias, and tumors. Kohinoor Bibi and Majid Mandal aren't doctors...so how did they treat their patients? By contacting "ghost doctors." "I don't treat the patients, the ghosts do," said Mandal. "I am only a medium." The couple charged about $60 for the treatments (a lot of money to the local villagers) and amassed a small fortune in their three-month run as healers. Mandal's explanation for the exorbitant cost: "What we earn has to be shared with the ghosts—since they too have families."

# NUDES & PRUDES

*Sometimes it seems like the world can be divided into two kinds of people: those who are offended by public nudity, and those who are offended by people who are offended by public nudity. Here are some of each.*

**N**UDE: In June 2004 a man from Rapid City, Iowa, was robbed by strangers after he answered the door in the nude. The man, whose name was not released by police, claimed he was sleeping in the buff when he was awakened by a knock on his hotel room door. When he answered the door he was tackled by "an undisclosed number of assailants" who hit him on the head and then ran off with his wallet and pants. Police later recovered the man's pants from the hotel parking lot; at last report the wallet was still missing.

**PRUDE:** A court in Karlsruhe, Germany, rejected an appeal from Dr. Peter Niehenke, a 55-year-old sex therapist who was fined $725 for indulging in his "hobby" of jogging nude near his home in Freiburg. Niehenke's defense was that since there's no law specifically banning him from jogging while wearing only socks and running shoes, technically the practice is not illegal. The judge didn't buy it. "The court," he said in his ruling, "does not support the defendant's view that running naked in public is one of his civil rights."

**NUDE:** More nude news from Germany: In December 2004, an 81-year-old German man was robbed of 250 euros (about $300) when two young women asked him to strip naked with them and take a photograph. "After the pensioner had removed his trousers in eager anticipation, the women left in a hurry," taking his pants and his wallet with them, a spokesperson for the Wiesbaden police department told reporters. The man's name was withheld.

**PRUDE:** In January 2005, the Ninth Circuit Court of Appeals ruled that a La Habra, California, town ordinance that required strippers to remain at least two feet away from patrons at all times was legal. The court conceded that while the ordinance did infringe on the strippers' right to free speech, "it did not *entirely*

---

Greek gods of the four winds: Boreus (North), Notus (South), Eurus (East), Zephyrus (West).

ban the performers from conveying an 'erotic message,'" so the two-foot ordinance was constitutional.

**NUDE:** Police in Hillsborough, North Carolina, are on the look-out for a "hairy, big-bellied man with curly black hair" who likes to frequent a fast-food drive-through window in the buff. Police say the man has visited the same Bojangles restaurant several times over the years, but only started going nude in the summer of 2004. Before that he wore "only his underwear…or perhaps shorts that resemble underwear," says Captain Ross Frederick of the Hillsborough Police Department.

**PRUDE:** In December 2004, the city of Villahermosa, Mexico, passed a law banning nudity, even within the confines of a private home. Why the law? Because the city is so hot and humid, many people have taken to walking around nude in their homes, which many find offensive. "When people walk past their windows, you see a lot of things," says city councilwoman Blanca Pulido, who supports the new law. Penalty for being nude in your own home: 36 hours in jail or a $121 fine.

**NUDE:** Police at the Los Angeles International Airport arrested Neil Melly, 31, of Canada, after he stripped naked, climbed over the airport fence, ran across the airfield, and climbed into the wheel well of an airplane as it was backing away from the depar-ture gate. Melly was mad at Qantas Airlines because it refused to sell him a ticket when he tried to pay for it with a credit card receipt instead of an actual credit card. Airport officials say they "will look into improving the fence."

**PRUDE:** In the fall of 2004 the dean of students at Vermont's Bennington College declared war against the college's longtime *un*official policy of being "clothing optional." Why? One student went naked during freshman orientation (when lots of parents were visiting). Dean Robert Graves decided he'd seen enough. "We don't live in a clothing-optional society," he told reporters. Students immediately made plans to protest the ban…in the nude. (But in the spring, after the weather improved.)

---

Siberia gets so cold that boiling water poured from a pan can freeze before it hits the ground.

# FAMOUS DROPOUTS

*Quitters never win...or do they?*

**A**BSENT ANCHORS. Peter Jennings was a poor student in high school and only lasted until 10th grade. Tom Brokaw, the president of the student body in high school, dropped out of the University of Iowa after, as he put it, he "majored in beer and coeds for a couple of years."

**WAYWARD WRITERS.** Their books are required reading in many high schools and universities, but neither Charles Dickens, Joseph Conrad, Herman Melville, George Bernard Shaw, William Faulkner, nor Jack London finished school themselves.

**CLASS-CUTTING COMMANDERS.** U.S. presidents George Washington, Abraham Lincoln, Andrew Jackson, Martin van Buren, and Grover Cleveland all had little or no formal education. British Prime Minister John Major didn't finish high school.

**FORBES-LIST FLUNKIES.** Microsoft's Bill Gates, the richest man in the world, was a college dropout. John D. Rockefeller never finished high school. Neither did Andrew Carnegie, Henry Ford, or Virgin's Richard Branson. Dave Thomas of Wendy's and Ray Kroc of McDonald's also dropped out—but they got jobs in fast food.

**ERRANT ENTERTAINERS.** Robert De Niro, Humphrey Bogart, Sean Connery, Walt Disney, Quentin Tarantino, and Patrick Stewart never finished school. Musical misfits include Frank Sinatra, Elton John, and composers Irving Berlin and George Gershwin. Sonny Bono, who later became a U.S. congressman, dropped out of school in the 10th grade.

**NON-PASSING PIONEERS.** Wilbur and Orville Wright were dropouts. Thomas Edison left school to educate himself, as did Albert Einstein. Einstein did go back to earn a doctorate of physics in 1905, but later offered this warning: "If one studies too zealously, one easily loses his pants."

---

Because he directed the movie *Kundun,* Martin Scorsese is banned from Tibet.

# THE BODY FARM

*Ahh, Tennessee—home to Dollywood, Graceland, the Grand
Ole Opry... and the world's creepiest research facility.*

**P**UTRIFIED FOREST
The Anthropological Research Facility (ARF) of the University of Tennessee lies on three landscaped acres behind the UT Medical Center parking lot. Aside from the razor-wire fence, it looks like a lovely wooded park, complete with people lying on their backs enjoying a pleasant day in the sun. That is, until you smell the foul odor. A second glance tells you these sunbathers are not all on their backs: some are face down in the leaves; some are waist deep in the dirt. Others are encased in concrete or wrapped in plastic garbage bags or locked in car trunks. None of them seems to be enjoying anything. Why? They're all cadavers, planted by scientists from the University of Tennessee for the sole purpose of studying the decomposition of the human body.

Nicknamed "the Body Farm" by the FBI, this research facility develops and provides medical expertise to law enforcement professionals and medical examiners. It helps them pinpoint the exact time of death of a body—a critical part of any criminal investigation involving a cadaver.

## DR. DEATH

ARF (or "BARF," as local critics call it) was founded in 1971 by forensic anthropologist Dr. William Bass. He had been asked to guess the age of a skeleton dug up on a piece of property once owned by a Confederate Army colonel named William Shy. Bass had examined some Civil War–era remains before, but they were mostly dust. Since this skeleton still had pieces of flesh attached to it, his analysis was able to determine that the person was a white male between 24 and 28 years old, who'd been dead about a year. Bass was correct about the race, gender, and age, but way off on the time of death. The skeleton, it turned out, belonged to William Shy himself, who was buried in 1864—107 years earlier. "I realized," Bass later recalled, "there was something here about decomposition we didn't know." He started the facility to help fill in the gaps.

---

Isuzu means "50 bells" in Japanese.

## RIGOR MORTIS 101

The first corpses Bass and his team studied were bodies that had
gone unclaimed at the morgue. At first they had four to five
cadavers a year. Today all cadavers are donated by personal request
and there's a waiting list. ARF researchers currently work with
around 45 bodies a year.

"We go through the FBI reports and come up with the most
common way a perpetrator will bury someone, and use these as our
models," says Dr. Arpad Vass, a senior researcher at the facility.
ARF scientists and graduate students then study the rate of *algor
mortis*—the cooling of the body. The temperature of a corpse drops
approximately 1°F per hour until it matches the temperature of
the air around it—a useful clue for determining time of death.
*Rigor mortis*—the stiffening of the body—generally starts a few
hours after death and moves through the body, disappearing 48
hours later. If a body has been dead longer than three days, they
look for other clues: What bugs have arrived to help with the
decomposition? How old are the fly larvae? Are there beetles?

This process of *insect succession* (which species of insect feed on
a decaying corpse, and in what order), as well as the effects of
weather and climate on decomposition, are all closely monitored
and measured. The scientists use this data to develop methods and
instruments that accurately establish time of death. This expertise
is shared with law enforcement agencies all over the world.

## WHAT'S THAT SMELL?

Dr. Vass's research has shown that a body emits 450 chemicals at
different stages of its decay. Each stage has a unique "bouquet,"
which Vass has given names such as *putrescine* and *cadaverine*.
Using the same aroma scan technology used in the food and wine
industry, one of his students is developing a handheld electronic
"nose" for the FBI that will sniff out the time of death by identifying the presence of these different chemicals in a corpse.

Synthetic putrescine and cadaverine are now used to train
"human remains dogs" (not to be confused with police dogs who
search for escaped criminals). These dogs respond to the specific
scent of death they've been trained to recognize, and they do it
with amazing accuracy: They can tell their trainers whether a lake
is concealing a corpse by sniffing the water's surface for minute

bubbles of gas seeping from a rotting carcass underwater, and they can show police exactly where to dive to retrieve the body. The dogs can detect the faintest scent of a dead body on the ground, even if it was removed from the spot a year earlier.

Another researcher at ARF, Dr. Richard Jantz, has developed a computer program that can determine the gender, race, and height of an unknown skeleton. This software has been invaluable in helping forensic teams identify the victims of ethnic cleansing in Bosnia, Rwanda, and other war crime sites.

## BREAKING IT DOWN

*Warning: the following may require a strong stomach.*

• Rigor mortis sets in just after death. The body stiffens, first at the jaws and neck. After 48 hours, the corpse relaxes and muscles sag.

• During the first 24 hours, the body cools at a rate of about 1°F per hour until it matches the temperature of the air around it. This is called *algor mortis*. Next, blood settles in the part of the body closest to the ground, turning the rest of the body pale.

• After two to three days, *putrefaction* is underway. The skin turns green and the body's enzymes start to eat through cell walls and the liquid inside leaks out. At this stage, fly larvae, or maggots, invade and start to eat the corpse's body fat. The maggots carry with them bacteria that settle in the abdomen, lungs, and skin.

• The bacteria feed on the liquid and release sulfur gas as a waste product. With nowhere to go, the gas causes the corpse to bloat and swell (and sometimes burst). By the end of the third day, the skin changes from green to purple to black. This stage is called *autolysis*, which means "self-digestion."

• Next is *skin slip*. As cells continue to break down, liquid continues to leak. After about a week, it builds up between layers of skin and loosens it, causing skin to start to peel off in large chunks.

• After two weeks, the fluid leaks from the nose and mouth. After three weeks, teeth and nails loosen; internal organs start to rupture.

• After about a month, the bacteria and enzymes have liquified all body tissue until the corpse dissolves and sinks into the ground, leaving only the skeletal remains and what's called a *volatile fatty acid stain*. Sweet dreams...

Handyman hint: Keeping mothballs in your tool chest will help prevent rust.

# VIDEO STINKERS

*Over the years we've recommended dozens of great movies in our "Video Treasures" pages. But there are lots of bad ones out there, too—some so bad that they're actually fun to watch. So here's our compilation of the crème de la crud.*

XANADU (1980) Musical
Review: "Olivia Newton-John is Kira, the daughter of Zeus and a muse who is the inspiration for fine art everywhere. She descends to Earth to come to the aid of a talented artist (Michael Beck) and a former big band clarinetist (Gene Kelly in his final film) and helps them open their dream disco dance club. No, seriously, that's her divine mission." (*Bad Cinema Society*) *Director:* Robert Greenwald.

BABY GENIUSES (1999) *Family*
Review: "Unless you want to see walking, talking toddlers hypnotizing Dom DeLuise into picking his nose, steer clear of this clinker about a power-mad child psychologist who's raising these bright babies in her lab. If these babies are such geniuses, why can't they spark even a single laugh?" (*Leonard Maltin's Movie Guide*) *Stars:* Kathleen Turner, Christopher Lloyd. *Director:* Bob Clark.

THEODORE REX (1995) *Science Fiction*
Review: "Futuristic comedy finds cynical, seasoned cop Katie Coltrane being teamed with Teddy, an eight-foot-tall, three-ton, returned-from-extinction Tyrannosaurus Rex." (*Videohound's Golden Movie Retriever*) *Star:* Whoopi Goldberg. *Director:* Jonathan Betuel.

MOMENT BY MOMENT (1978) *Romance*
Review: "Ever wonder what could possibly make you kill yourself? How about watching a young John Travolta prance around in his underwear for two hours and romance his mom? At least that's our interpretation of his creepy relationship with Lily Tomlin, his domineering 40-year-old look-alike lover. Coincidentally, *Moment* was released the same year as the mass suicide at Jonestown." (*Maxim's 50 Worst Movies of All Time*) *Director:* Jane Wagner.

M&M colors once included violet.

## GYMKATA (1985) Action

**Review:** "Olympic gymnast Kurt Thomas is recruited by the CIA to go fight to the death so they can stick a nuclear missile base in the middle of an Eastern European country. So Kurt has to run through alleys until he finds one that happens to have a horizontal bar set up between two buildings, then he grabs the bar and starts spinning and kicking guys. Apparently the reason this was filmed in Yugoslavia is that the whole country has gymnastics equipment hidden in the rocks and sticking out of buildings, and it gives Kurt a big advantage over the guys with machine guns." (*Joe Bob Briggs' Ultimate B-Movie Guide*) *Director:* Robert Clouse.

## MAD DOG TIME (1996) Drama/Comedy

**Review:** "A gangster boss is released from a mental hospital and returns to a sleazy nightclub to take control of his organization. The way the movie works is two or three characters start out in a scene and recite some dry, hard-boiled dialogue, and then one or two of them gets shot. This happens over and over. The first movie I have seen that does not improve on the sight of a blank screen viewed for the same length of time." (*Roger Ebert*) *Stars:* Richard Dreyfuss, Jeff Goldblum, Diane Lane. *Director:* Larry Bishop.

## THE TERROR OF TINY TOWN (1938) Western

**Review:** "The only singing cowboy movie ever made with a cast made up entirely of midgets. If you've ever seen a singing cowboy western with Roy Rogers, you've seen this one—just shrink the entire cast in half. The story stinks (*Romeo and Juliet* without the gore, good writing, or tragedy) and the acting is pretty awful. Seeing this movie is like a badge of bad movieness." (*Oh, the Humanity: The Worst Films Ever*) *Stars:* Billy Curtis, Yvonne Moray. *Director:* Sam Newfield.

## VIVA KNIEVEL! (1977) Action

**Review:** "Gangsters plan to kill motorcycle stunt rider Evel Knievel in order to use his trailer to smuggle cocaine. In between his stunts, Evel makes the lame walk, causes women to go weak in the knees, cures junkies, reconciles an estranged father and son, and bores cinema audiences." (*Halliwell's Film and Video Guide*) *Stars:* Evel Knievel, Lauren Hutton. *Director:* Gordon Douglas.

**What do you call a fish with no eyes? "Fsh."**

# THE BIRTH OF
# THE NFL, PART I

*On page 103, we told you about the first professional
football player. Here's the story of the NFL—how it went from
a ragtag league of misfits to a multibillion-dollar enterprise.*

## THE FIRST NFL

By the turn of the 20th century, it was clear that professional football was more than a passing fad. Pro teams were popping up in gritty industrial towns in Pennsylvania, New York, Ohio, and Rhode Island. Many were sponsored by steel mills, coal mines, or other businesses to provide a Sunday afternoon diversion on their employees' one day off. These teams usually lost money.

In 1902 David Berry, owner of the Pittsburgh Stars, announced he was forming what he called the "National Football League." It failed miserably, folding within a year.

What went wrong?

• First, only three teams, all from Pennsylvania, joined the new league. Teams from New York and Chicago declined, figuring that fans were more interested in local rivalries.

• Second, pro football's image was at an all-time low. The play was slow, mostly defensive; the players were violent; the games often ended in riots; and the teams were corrupt because big-time gamblers bought out coaches and players.

• The more "refined" games of baseball, golf, and tennis were gaining in stature.

## ADDING DIGNITY

In 1915 Jim Thorpe, the nation's most famous athlete, joined the Canton Bulldogs. In addition to being a gold-medal Olympian and champion baseball player, Thorpe conducted himself with a quiet dignity that people looked up to. His addition to pro football gave it some credibility, but it still didn't have much of a following outside of a team's local community.

After World War I, a new attempt was made to form a national

league. On September 17, 1920, four team owners met in a Hup-
mobile auto dealership in Canton, Ohio, and voted to form what
became known as the American Professional Football Association
(APFA). Over the next six weeks, they persuaded ten other teams
from Ohio, Indiana, Illinois, and New York to join. Jim Thorpe
was appointed president, not because he was an experienced manager (he wasn't), but because his name generated headlines and
again gave the new league credibility.

## IF AT FIRST...

Like its predecessor, the new league was troubled from the start.
They could pay players about $150 per game (not much by today's
standards), and the players still had to supply their own protective
gear. The game itself was still slow; once a team got a touchdown,
they tried to stall for the rest of the game to make it stand. And
few fans showed up: the average game that first 1920 season
attracted only 3,000 fans—less than a tenth the size of a good college football crowd. Three teams—the Cleveland Tigers, the
Detroit Heralds, and the Muncie Flyers—folded after one season;
the rest struggled to survive. There was little indication that these
working-class teams, who played for money, would one day eclipse
the noble college teams, who played for the enjoyment of the sport.

After one year as president of the APFA, Jim Thorpe declined
to run for reelection. Joe Carr, manager of the Columbus Panhan-
dles, was forced into the job. Although Carr had been involved
with football since forming a team in 1904, he only had a fifth-
grade education and showed no interest in running the league. But
the other APFA members felt that as the manager with the most
football experience, Carr was the best candidate, so they waited
for him to leave the room and then elected him president without
his consent. That turned out to be one of the best things that ever
happened to professional football.

## TURNING IT AROUND

If he was going to be president, Carr figured he ought to try to
improve the game's image, so he made some changes.
• In 1921 his office began releasing official weekly standings of
each team in the league so that fans could keep track of how well
their teams were doing.

- He assigned each team a geographic territory, then declared it off limits to all of the other APFA franchises so teams wouldn't drive each other out of business by fighting over the same fans.
- Carr outlawed the practice of hiring college undergraduates to play for pro teams under assumed names. Using ringers was a tempting prospect both for the teams, who needed the talent, and for student athletes, who needed the cash (and had nothing else to do on Sunday afternoons). It drove college coaches crazy.
- In 1922 Carr instituted a standard player's contract (with a reserve clause that gave a player's current team first dibs on him the following season) and capped salaries at $1,200 per game. Both measures helped control costs, which helped strengthen the league.
- The APFA made one other significant change in 1922: they voted to change their name to the National Football League.

## RED GRANGE

Thanks to Carr's reforms, this second NFL looked like it might last a little longer than the first one had, but pro football still needed a lot of help. Mostly, it needed more star players to get fans into the stands. It needed Harold "Red" Grange. He'd become famous playing halfback for the University of Illinois. His uncanny ability to dart and weave his way downfield past his opponents made Grange the best player of his day. Fans called him "the Galloping Ghost."

The newly formed Chicago Bears, coached by George Halas, signed Grange in 1925 for the last two games of the season. The first was against the Chicago Cardinals. Bears-Cardinals games usually attracted 10,000 fans, but with Grange on the field they drew 39,000, by far the largest crowd for a pro game to date. That record fell one week later when 70,000 people turned out to watch Grange and the Bears play the New York Giants. (In a sign of things to come, the following day Grange signed an estimated $125,000 worth of commercial endorsement deals.)

A successful 12-day exhibition tour followed, in which Grange and the Bears played eight teams from eight different cities. (They won the first four but were so exhausted that they lost the last four.) But what mattered most was that pro football was finally on the map. The Bears made an estimated $297,000 in 1925, up from $116,500 the year before; and the New York Giants, who were $40,000 in debt and close to collapse when Grange and the Bears rolled into town, ended the season with $18,000 in the bank. By attracting attention to the struggling Giants, Grange is credited with single-handedly saving the franchise.

## THE STRUGGLE CONTINUES

But Grange couldn't single-handedly save the NFL, which was still in trouble. Sure, the games he played in drew fans, but others were still sparsely attended. To make matters worse, Grange left the Bears and formed his own team after contract negotiations with the Bears broke down (he wanted a one-third ownership stake in the team). The new team was called the New York Yankees, but the NFL denied admission to them because there already was a football team in New York. So Grange formed a new league, the American Football League, which fared about as poorly as the first NFL and folded after a season. But the NFL also had a tough year without Grange as a draw, so they let the Yankees join in 1927. (The football Yankees folded a year later; Grange played the rest of his Hall of Fame career with the Bears.)

So that saved football, right? Wrong. Teams were still losing money and fans were losing interest. The style of play was more defensive than ever, which resulted in low-scoring games being played in cold, empty stadiums—one bad-weather game in New York drew exactly 83 fans.

And then came the Great Depression, which hit hardest against the working-class fan base that was the backbone of the professional leagues. Hardly anyone could afford the 50¢ it cost to see a game, least of all in the smaller cities, where many teams were located. By 1932 the NFL was down to eight teams.

It was time for yet another man to swoop in and save professional football from itself.

*Illegal man downfield—five-yard penalty! Turn to page 401 and read Part II.*

*Turn to page 401 and read Part II.*

\*   \*   \*

"You have to play this game like somebody just hit your mother with a two-by-four."
—Dan Birdwell

# WHAT A DISH!

*BRI writer Kyle Coroneos brought us this article
on his favorite subject (really)—CorningWare.
We found it fascinating. You will, too.*

## SERENDIPITY

In 1952 Donald Stookey, a scientist at the Corning Glass Works Company in Corning, New York, had two lucky accidents in the research lab.

• **Accident #1:** He was heating a piece of glass in a furnace when the temperature controller malfunctioned. It was only supposed to reach 900°C, but instead got much, much hotter. Stookey expected to find a molten lump of glass...but he didn't. The glass was still intact and now had a creamy, white ceramic look to it.

• **Accident #2:** Stookey dropped the hot glass while he was removing it with a pair of tongs. Instead of breaking, it clanged to the floor like a plate of steel.

These two mishaps led Stookey to a new discovery: after molten glass was formed into an object, it could be "cooked" a second time at an even higher temperature to control the crystal growth within the glass, turning it into an extremely hard ceramic. The new material—which he patented as "Pyroceram"—could sustain drastic temperature changes better than glass or metal.

## TAKING AIM

Although Corning already produced a type of glass cookware called Pyrex (the first glass cookware, introduced in 1915), they had a much different vision for Pyroceram: national defense. In fact, Corning had been making glass products for the military since the Civil War. Now it was the Cold War, and the United States and the Soviet Union were were both building and stockpiling nuclear missiles. The military was interested in any new technology that would allow weapons to withstand the rapid temperature changes to which they would be subjected while hurtling though the atmosphere. Pyroceram, it turned out, was the perfect material to use for the missiles' nose cones, which took the brunt of the damage. Corning pitched the idea to defense companies

---

The ancient Romans used stingray stingers to treat toothaches.

such as Hughes Aircraft and Raytheon, and was awarded huge contracts. Over the next 20 years, thousands of nuclear and ballistic missiles with Pyroceram noses were built. In the 1970s, the same technology was adapted to build the heat tiles that now cover NASA's fleet of space shuttles.

## COMING HOME

After winning the contracts, Corning started looking around for other uses for Pyroceram. In 1957 they decided to put it in America's kitchens. CorningWare dishes were an easy sell: they were the only type of cookware that could be used in the oven or the freezer, or put directly from one into the other without cracking. In short, they were the most versatile dishes ever made.

CorningWare's first product line consisted of only three saucepans and a skillet, and sales were modest. But it's estimated that by 1980 there was at least one CorningWare dish in nearly every household in the United States.

## END OF THE LINE

CorningWare had one major drawback: the dishes are so durable that they will last for 1,000 years...which doesn't leave a lot of room for repeat business. After strong sales numbers that lasted into the 1980s, it seemed that everyone who wanted CorningWare already *had* CorningWare, and sales started to plummet.

By 1998 Corning had completely shifted from making home consumer products to developing new glass technology for communications and aerospace. It leased the rights to all of its cooking products to a century-old housewares company called World Kitchen, which kept the CorningWare name, but replaced the Pyroceram with stoneware, a much less durable material. Currently there is no cookware being made of Pyroceram. The original CorningWare dishes are now collectors' items, not because they're rare (millions were made) but because people who have them don't want to give them up.

In 1986 Don Stookey was awarded the National Medal of Technology for his discovery, and 14 years later a CorningWare plate was added to the Millennium Time Capsule. Chances are, when the capsule is opened, the plate will look the same as it did on the day it was made—and still be just as strong.

# UJPORAD

*Uncle John's Page of Random Acronym Definitions.*

**PhD:** An advanced college degree, it stands for *philosophæ Doctor*, which means "doctor of philosophy" in Latin.

**YM Magazine:** The teenage girl publication's name used to stand for "Young Miss," then "Young and Modern." It's currently "Your Magazine."

**ROTC:** Reserve Officer Training Corps, a U.S. armed forces program that recruits and trains college students (on college campuses) to become military officers. ROTC produces 60% of all officers.

**USO:** United Service Organizations, the group that sends comedians and singers to entertain troops stationed overseas.

**Fannie Mae:** Federal National Mortgage Association. Created by Congress in 1938 to loan money to potential home owners.

**DARE:** In the 1980s and '90s, American schoolchildren were taught to say no to drugs in the DARE program, which stood for Drug Abuse Resistance Education.

**Amtrak: America Travel Track:** In operation since 1971, Amtrak is a nationwide passenger train service. Although it's a for-profit corporation, Amtrak is subsidized by the federal government.

*The Man from U.N.C.L.E.:* The secret agency on the 1960s TV show was named United Network Command for Law and Enforcement.

**SWAT:** Special Weapons and Tactics (The term was coined by the 1970s TV cop show *S.W.A.T.*)

**RSVP:** *Répondez s'il vous plaît.* Found on invitations, it's French for "please reply."

**IRA:** Individual Retirement Arrangement (or Irish Republican Army)

**RKO Pictures:** Radio-Keith-Orpheum. This 1930s Hollywood movie studio was the result of a partnership between RCA (Radio Corporation of America) and the Keith-Albee-Orpheum Theatre Company, a chain of New York vaudeville theaters.

# WORD ORIGINS

*More interesting stories about where some words come from.*

**B**ANDANNA
**Meaning:** A large colored handkerchief or neckerchief
**Origin:** "This word derives from a Hindi word *badhnu*, meaning what today is called 'tie-dyeing,' that is, dyeing a cloth but tying sections of it together so that they will not absorb the dye. Hence the spotty or patchy appearance of a genuine large silk bandanna." (From *NTC's Dictionary of Word Origins*, by Adrian Room)

### EASEL
**Meaning:** A wooden frame for holding an artist's work
**Origin:** "Having an easel makes life easier for an artist, and the word's spelling apparently has been influenced by *ease*, but the name of the frame actually comes from the Dutch *ezel*, meaning 'ass' or 'donkey.' The basic idea being that the easel is like a beast of burden." (From *Devious Derivations*, by Hugh Rawson)

### CLAPTRAP
**Meaning:** Nonsense
**Origin:** "Originated in theatrical jargon early the 18th century. It was literally any device or stage action designed to trap claps— that is, applause. Any skilled comic actor knows dozens of bits of business, from slurping his coffee to taking a pratfall, that never fail in getting audience reaction. In the hands of master comedians, such trickery can be high art; in lesser hands it's simply... claptrap." (From *Dictionary of Word and Phrase Origins*, *Volume III*, by William and Mary Morris)

### NICE
**Meaning:** Pleasant, agreeable, kind, satisfactory
**Origin:** "*Nice* is one of the more celebrated examples of an English word changing its meaning out of all recognition over the centuries—in this case, from 'stupid' to 'pleasant.' Its ultimate source was Latin *nescius*, 'ignorant.' This passed into English via the French *nice* with minimal change of meaning, but from then on a

---

The word "mafia" was intentionally left out of the *Godfather* movies.

slow transformation took place, from 'foolish' to 'shy,' to 'fastidious,' to 'refined' to 'pleasant' or 'agreeable' (first recorded in the 18th century)." (From *Dictionary of Word Origins*, by John Ayto)

## JOURNEYMAN
**Meaning:** An experienced and competent but undistinguished worker
**Origin:** "From the Old French *jornee*, meaning 'day.' In Medieval times, a journeyman was a competent craftsman who was qualified to work for a day's wages. He was more skilled than an apprentice but not as skilled as a master craftsman." (From *Once Upon a Word*, by Rob Kyff)

## SAWBUCK
**Meaning:** A $10 bill
**Origin:** "Originally a sawbuck referred to a movable frame (or sawhorse) used to support wood while it is being sawed, probably a borrowing from the Dutch *zaagbok*, literally 'saw-trestle.'

"Also originally, a $10 bill had the Roman numeral X (10) printed on it. Most U.S. paper currency had values in Roman numerals; even in the early 19th century bills were called 'Vs,' 'Xs,' 'Cs,' and so forth. The 'X' started being called a sawbuck because of the resemblance of the X to the crossed legs of the sawhorse. The popularity of 'sawbuck' was strengthened by the introduction of the word buck for 'a dollar,' which arose slightly later." (From *Jesse's Word of the Day*, by Jesse Sheidlower)

## LIBEL
**Meaning:** A published defamation of a person's character
**Origin:** "Libel comes from the Latin *libellus*, 'little book'—and it refers to what one Roman did when he wanted to defame another. He issued a little book setting forth the other fellow's alleged misdeeds. These 'little books' could also be posters or broadsides designed to be read by the public at large and passed from hand to hand." (From *Dictionary of Word and Phrase Origins, Volume II*, by William and Mary Morris)

# GOOD DOG!

*Can a dog be a hero? These people sure think so.*

**G**OOD DOG: Woodie, a collie mix
**WHAT HE DID:** In 1980 Rae Anne Knitter and her fiancé, Ray Thomas, were hiking on a nature trail in Ohio. Knitter had Woodie on a leash. At one point, Thomas climbed up to the edge of a shale cliff to take a photograph. A few moments later Woodie began pulling on his leash so frantically that he eventually broke free. He ran to the edge of the cliff, glanced down... and promptly leapt off. When Knitter reached the top, she looked down and saw both her fiancé and her dog lying in a stream 80 feet below. Woodie was nudging Thomas's head (he was unconscious), holding it out of the water until paramedics arrived. Woodie broke both hips, but recovered. So did Thomas.

**GOOD DOG:** Weela, a 16-month-old American pit bull terrier
**WHAT SHE DID:** One day in 1993, 11-year-old Gary Watkins was playing in his backyard when Weela uncharacteristically charged the boy and knocked him over—just in time to put her body in between Gary and a rattlesnake. Weela received two bites to her face, but recovered. Good thing, too, because not long after that, the Tijuana River flooded their town—and over the next two months, Weela helped rescue 29 dogs, 13 horses, a cat, and 30 people from the floodwaters. For her feats of bravery, she was named the 1993 Ken-L Ration's Dog Hero of the Year.

**GOOD DOG:** Major, a boxer
**WHAT HE DID:** In July 2005, a black bear approached three children playing badminton in the front yard of Bill and Dawn Rusko near Ligonier, Pennsylvania. Major got between the kids and the bear, and when the bear kept coming, Major attacked the animal. He jumped up and bit it in the face, and finally drove it back into the woods. Unfortunately, Major chased the bear and disappeared. (Okay—happy ending: Bill Lusko and his children spent the next two days searching the woods for Major...and found him. He reportedly ate two bowls of pork chops before curling up for a nap with the kids.)

# BAD DOG!

*Can a dog be a pain? These people sure think so.*

**B**AD DOG: Shep, a seven-year-old collie
**WHAT HE DID:** In 2005 Arnold Luscombe of Devon, England, was driving down the road with Shep in the passenger seat when he had to stop for a flock of sheep. As he got out to clear the road, Shep jumped into the driver's seat...and knocked the car into gear. Luscombe turned around just in time to see his Saab going over a 40-foot embankment. It crash-landed in a creek below. Luscombe scrambled down to the car, where, he told BBC News, "Shep was sitting behind the wheel quite unconcerned." Luscombe had the car winched out of the creek and said that Shep was no longer allowed in the driver's seat.

**BAD DOG:** Shadow, a collie
**WHAT HE DID:** Gordon Husband, 66, was walking Shadow near the River Wye in Hampton Bishop, England. He threw a stick into some brush for the dog, and the dog promptly returned with a live hand grenade in its mouth. (The site was near an abandoned army base.) Husband gently took the grenade from Shadow's mouth and called police. A bomb unit came and exploded the device. "Shadow is always coming back from the river with stuff," the relieved owner said, "but usually just rubber balls."

**BAD DOG:** Harvey, a three-year-old bulldog
**WHAT HE DID:** Harvey is the portly pet of British TV star Johnny Vaughan, host of BBC's *Johnny Vaughan Tonight*. In 2003 dog and master were returning from the veterinarian in the star's Maserati sports car when Vaughan stopped the car to let the dog out for a pit stop. But as he exited the running vehicle, Harvey bounded over the gearshift, accidentally pushing it into drive. "Then," said Vaughan, "the little critter jumped into the footwell and pressed the accelerator." The $100,000 car shot down the road and crashed into a parked van. Damage: $17,600. (The insurance company refused to pay for it.) "I was too shocked to be angry," Vaughan said. "I just couldn't believe my dog had crashed my car."

# LOST IN TRANSLATION

*BRI member Christine Degueron sent us these actual instructions for her Nikota Multi-Purpose Rotary Drill. Our guess: the translator needed a few more years of school (or a few less beers).*

**1. Putting on Jumper:** Do not carry far clothes or decoration. They can be mangled by mobile parts. If working in the open air, the rubber gloves and skid-proof footwear are recommendable. Bind your plait shed together or carry a hair net.

**2. Keeping Your Body in Stability:** Stand on steadily. Keep your body in balance at any time. Don't climb the ladder not fastened against the wall. Don't work standing on chair or similar matter.

**3. Keeping Site Clean:** The disordering working site has the potential of hidden danger.

**4. Extension Cable Line:** The extension cable line with the unqualified and undamaged indication can be used. When you purchase the extension cable line, it is necessary to consult with the related attentions.

**5. You Are Always Attentive:** Observe its work. Advance rationally. Do not use the tool if you are unknown the work. Do not let other persons operate the machine, hold it of its field or work away.

**6. Ensure Workpiece in Stability:** Use chip devices or a screw cane in order to hold the workpiece.

**7. Little Pressure:** You do not use in the use of the multifunctional tools to high pressure; bit it and disks ability broken. Use only clean and sharp accessories parts.

**8. No Overload for Tool:** They work better and more certainly in the indicated achievement area.

**9. Control Its Devices on Damages:** Control your device before each utilize or damages. Device or connection line damages should show, the device may be used no longer until these were removed regular. All parts correctly must be mounted in order to guarantee the flawless business of the device.

---

Tolstoy's *War and Peace* was originally titled *All's Well That Ends Well.*

# YOU WANT FRIES WITH THAT?

*A few tidbits from the BRI's french fry files.*

## ORIGIN

So who was the first person to slice a potato into strips and fry them in oil? Nobody knows for sure. France claims a Frenchman was first. Belgians claim they invented it. Still others credit Thomas Jefferson with the achievement in 1802. The most likely answer: they all invented a version of the french fry. People were eager to experiment with this versatile vegetable, so chefs from all over probably sliced and fried them. What is known, however, is that American soldiers returning from France (or possibly Belgium) after World War I started making fries in their homes, just like the ones they were served overseas.

## FRY-BRARY

The first literary mention of "chips" (the English term for fries) came in Charles Dickens's *A Tale of Two Cities* (1859), in which the author referred to "husky chips of potatoes, fried with some reluctant drops of oil." The french fry made its literary debut in 1894 in O. Henry's *Rolling Stones*: "Our countries are great friends. We have given you Lafayette and French fried potatoes."

## CAPITAL OFFENSE

Is it "French" fries or "french" fries? Answer: according to most dictionaries, the initial "f" is usually uncapitalized. Why? In this case, "french" doesn't refer to France—it refers to the way the potato is sliced in long strips, or "frenched."

## COMPU-TATERS

When the McDonald brothers opened their first restaurant in 1940, the featured food was hot dogs (hamburgers weren't added to the menu until a few years later). But french-fried potatoes were there from the beginning, and McDonald's knew even then that a superior fry would mean return business. Their biggest challenge

---

When the Statue of Liberty was restored, her steel framework was coated with Teflon.

was making the quality of the fries consistent, which is difficult when the cooking process consists of dropping raw potato strips into a boiling cauldron of oil. Some came out too crisp; others too limp. So McDonald's spent millions of dollars to turn fry cooking into an exact science. They even opened a research lab in 1957 solely dedicated to the problem. They created a "potato computer"—a machine that could monitor the temperature of the oil and alert the cook when the batch was done. The potato computer is still going strong today. And McDonald's is still testing different oils, sugars, and thicknesses in the ongoing quest for the perfect fry.

## SACRED FRIES

In fact, McDonald's relentless pursuit of the perfect fry got the company in trouble in 2001. Two Hindus and a non-Hindu vegetarian brought a class-action suit against the fast-food giant, claiming that McDonald's "intentionally failed to publicly disclose its use of beef tallow in the cooking process under the guise of 'natural flavor.'" McDonald's lost and was forced to pay a $10 million settlement to various vegetarian organizations and retract an earlier statement that claimed its fries were suitable for vegetarians.

## PUBLIC ENEMY #1

During the tense times leading up to the 2003 war in Iraq, American legislators protested France's opposition to the conflict by insisting that *french* fries be changed to *freedom* fries in Congressional cafeterias. "We are at a very serious moment, dealing with very serious issues," countered French Embassy spokeswoman Nathalie Loisau, "and we are not focusing on the name you give to potatoes." Ironically, the lawmaker who first proposed the patriotic name change has since changed his tune. Congressman Walter Jones (R-NC) is now a staunch anti-war advocate. And once again, french fries are on the menu in the Congressional cafeteria.

## BRANDED

A bumbling crook named Colin Wilson stormed into a Leeds, England, fast-food restaurant and demanded all of the money from the cash register. Because the would-be thief had no gun (he was threatening them with a wooden table leg), the manager decided to fight back. He pulled the fry basket from the vat of hot grease and whacked it across Wilson's face. Screaming in pain, Wilson ran out of the restaurant and went to a nearby hospital, where he was arrested after the nurse called police to inform them that they had "a patient with an outline of a chip basket burned into his forehead."

## FRENCH FRY MADNESS
Don't come between Gregg Luttman and his french fries—especially on New Year's Day. Allegedly sporting a huge hangover, Luttman pulled into the drive-through line of a Pennsylvania Burger King and went berserk when he was informed that they were out of fries. According to the police report, he made "an obscene gesture at the drive-through clerk, berated Burger King workers, and nearly hit an employee with his truck." After officers arrived and got him into the back of a squad car, he kicked out the back window. He was fined $150 and given two years' probation.

## POTATOHEAD
Mindy Marland, a bartender at the Checkered Flag Bar & Grill in Wallcott, Iowa, was working one night in 2005 when she saw a waitress carrying a plate of food to a table. On the plate she saw an extremely long french fry. "I was intrigued by it and took it off the plate," she said. After measuring it out at a whopping eight inches, Marland decided to auction it on eBay. Bids started at $1—the winning bid was $197.50.

## WACKO-JACKO
According to Rudy Provencio, who worked for Michael Jackson from 2001 to 2003, the pop star refers to money as "french fries."

\*　　\*　　\*

## AT&D'OH!
In 2002, AT&T introduced a new junk e-mail filter for its Internet service subscribers. A few weeks later, AT&T began receiving angry phone calls from customers upset about an unannounced rate increase. AT&T didn't understand—they'd sent a rate hike notice via e-mail to all its customers. What happened: AT&T's e-mail filter blocked AT&T's messages, assuming it was spam.

# FAMOUS LASTS

*All good (and bad) things come to an end someday.*

**THE LAST MARRIED POPE.** Adrian II was already married when he became pope in 867. He refused to give up his wife and adopt a life of celibacy.

**SPRECHEN SIE ENGLISCH?** The last king of England who couldn't speak English (there were several) was George I, prince of Hanover, Germany. During his 13-year reign (1714–1727), he never learned to speak or write English.

**THE LAST PRESIDENTIAL SLAVE OWNER.** When he married Julia Dent in 1848, Ulysses S. Grant inherited a slave from her family. He freed the man, William Jones, on March 29, 1859.

**ALL THAT GLITTERS IS NOT GOLD.** The last year Olympic gold medals were actually made of gold: 1912.

**GOOD-BYE, MODEL T.** The last Model T Ford rolled off the production line in Detroit, Michigan, on May 27, 1927. More than 15 million Model Ts had been built, more than any other type of car of its time.

**THE LAST SILENT MOVIE.** The last full-length silent movie released in the United States was *The Poor Millionaire*, starring Richard Talmadge and Constance Howard, which hit theaters on April 7, 1930.

**THE LAST MAN ON THE MOON.** U.S. astronaut Capt. Eugene A. Cernan of *Apollo 17* was the last person to set foot on the Moon, on December 14, 1972. His last words while on the lunar surface: "Let's get this mother out of here."

**THE KING'S LAST LP.** The last studio album recorded and released by Elvis Presley was *Moody Blue*. Released July 28, 1977, it went to #3 on the charts. Elvis died less than a month later on August 16. He was 42.

# THE LEADED GAS CONSPIRACY

*It happens all the time. A product comes out and is found to be harmful, but they keep making it anyway. Here's the story of one of the most harmful products of all.*

**KNOCK KNOCK**

In the early days of the automobile industry, gasoline motors were highly prone to engine knock, caused by low-octane fuel igniting too early in the engine's cylinders. It sounded like a sharp tapping or rattling, and that wasn't far off—the motor was rattling itself apart. At the same time, horsepower was lost because the fuel wasn't being burned efficiently, all of which made for a lot of very noisy and very sluggish automobiles. With thousands of new cars entering the road each year, something had to be done.

Luckily, there was an easy solution: grain alcohol. Internal combustion engines ran great on it, but it was too expensive to be the standard motor fuel by itself. Testing conducted for General Motors by Charles Kettering's Dayton Engineering Laboratories Company (DELCO) showed that alcohol raised the octane of gasoline—allowing for higher engine compression and eliminating knock. By 1921 a blend of 30 percent alcohol to 70 percent gasoline was the fuel of choice among most automotive engineers.

But later that year an engineer named Thomas Midgley, the DELCO engineer assigned to solve the problem, found a cheaper way to eliminate engine knock. While working under contract for General Motors, he added a small amount of tetraethyl lead to gasoline and discovered that it also did the trick. Even better, lead was much less expensive than grain alcohol. But Midgely's cost-cutting solution would come at a very high price.

**HAZARDOUS MATERIAL**

Lead is a neurotoxin that collects in the blood and bones of humans and damages the central nervous system. Overexposure can cause convulsions, blindness, hallucinations, and cancer—as well as coma and death. Its dangers have been known since at least 100 B.C., when Greek physicians described lead poisoning and noted the danger posed to workers by fumes from lead smelting operations. In Midgley's time, health risks associated with lead-based paint were so well documented that in 1920 the League of Nations proposed banning its use. But despite all the risks associated with lead, and ignoring the proven effectiveness of cleaner-burning alcohol/gasoline blends, in 1923 General Motors, DuPont, and Standard Oil formed the Ethyl Gasoline Company to produce and sell gas with a tetraethyl lead additive.

## LET THE BATTLE BEGIN

Almost immediately, workers in leaded gasoline plants started showing signs of lead poisoning. By 1924 at least 15 workers had died from exposure before better ventilation was added to factories. The scientific community called for the banning of lead, labor unions called for safer working conditions, and the New York Board of Health banned sales of leaded gas in 1924. The Ethyl Company found itself at the center of a public health debate—and it was ready to fight.

When the U.S. Public Health Service held hearings on the matter the following year, Midgley testified: "So far as science knows at the present time, tetraethyl lead is the only material available that can bring about these [anti-knock] results."

Midgely was lying: science knew about alcohol blends. Midgley himself owned several patents on alcohol blends, and three years earlier he'd claimed that "alcohol is unquestionably the fuel of the future." Now he was saying lead was perfectly safe—pouring leaded gas over his hands and sniffing its fumes to prove his point. But Midgely left out another fact: he was suffering from lead poisoning and had been forced to take time off to recuperate in 1923.

## INCONCLUSIVE

In the end, the Public Health Service recommended that a committee be formed to study the effects of leaded gas. Their report: "Owing to the incompleteness of the data, it is impossible to say definitely whether exposure to lead dust increases in garages where tetraethyl lead is used."

The Ethyl Company declared itself vindicated, and leaded gas was back on sale in 1926.

Exxon spent over $100 million on market research before changing its name from Esso.

## IT'S A CONSPIRACY!

If Midgely and Ethyl knew that lead was so harmful compared to the alternatives, why did they try to cover it up? Money. Because adding lead to gasoline was cheaper than adding alcohol, as long as Ethyl had control over the lead additive business, Ethyl controlled the entire gas industry...and would fight tooth and nail to keep it that way.

✔ Car dealers warned their customers about lead's dangers until 1927—when GM ordered their dealers to promote it.

✔ The following year the Lead Industries Association was formed to counter the negative publicity. The Ethyl Company—along with its parent companies, GM, DuPont, and Standard Oil—hired scientists willing to claim that lead couldn't be conclusively tied to illness.

✔ The Ethyl Company refused to sell to distributors who also carried alcohol blends.

✔ Because it was a national company, Ethyl was able to undercut the price of any independent filling station that tried to buck the system. During the Great Depression, people sought out the cheapest gas they could find—Ethyl made sure it was theirs.

Henry Ford called alcohol the "fuel of the future" (as had Midgely years before) and continued to make carburetors that would run on either gas or gas/alcohol blends until 1929. But by 1936 it no longer mattered: leaded gasoline accounted for 90 percent of the fuel sold in the United States, most of that produced by Ethyl.

## CLEANING UP

In the 1950s, a geochemist from the California Institute of Technology named Clair Patterson (who was not on the Ethyl Company's payroll) hypothesized that atmospheric lead levels had increased drastically since leaded gas was introduced in 1923. His proof came from ice core samples taken from glaciers in Greenland. In areas where more snow falls than melts every year, ice builds up in layers that can be counted and studied (much like a tree's growth rings). By counting back through 40 years of annual snowfall and measuring the amount of lead in each layer, Patterson was able to show in a 1965 study that the high levels of atmospheric lead found in industrialized countries were a result of leaded gasoline use. Patterson's findings led to the Clean Air Act of 1970. A provision in the act required automakers to install catalytic converters in all new cars. Catalytic converters, it just so happened, are fouled and rendered useless by lead deposits.

The oil industry still continued to resist. With the infrastructure still in place to make—and profit from—leaded gas, they tried to sell as much of it as they could before it was phased out. For years industry "experts" insisted that precatalytic converter motors would be harmed by unleaded gas—which has since proven not to be the case.

Finally, in 1986, leaded gasoline was removed from American gas pumps for good, though it continues to be sold throughout the developing world, and was common in Eastern Europe until the European Union banned it in 2000. Today, alcohol blends are increasingly being used to boost octane and to meet improved emissions standards. Lead is being replaced by the very additive it replaced in the 1920s—alcohol.

### THE WORLD'S MOST DANGEROUS MAN?

Leaded gas wasn't Midgley's only contribution to the modern world. After curing engine knock with tetraethyl lead, he turned his attention toward the development of a non-toxic, non-flammable refrigerant gas for use in refrigerator and air conditioner compressors. In 1928 he came up with *chlorofluorocarbons*, or CFCs—the chemical whose use is credited with creating the hole in the ozone layer. These two technological advances have led some to note that Thomas Midgley may have had a bigger impact on the environment than any other single organism in the history of the Earth.

**What goes around…**Midgley contracted polio in middle age and suffered partial paralysis. He died in 1944 when he was accidentally strangled by a contraption he had built to help himself in and out of bed.

\*       \*       \*

"Men and nations behave wisely once they have exhausted all other alternatives."

—Abba Eban

---

*Oberammergaueralpenkräuterdelikatessenfrühstückskäse* is a type of cheese.

# YOU CALL THAT ART?

*Ever been in a gallery or museum and seen something that made you wonder, "Is this really art?" So have we. Is it art just because someone says it is? You be the judge.*

**ARTIST:** Mark McGowan

**THIS IS ART?** This London-based artist has a reputation for odd endeavors, such as pushing a nut with his nose to Prime Minister Tony Blair's office as a protest against the high cost of school tuition, and rolling on the ground for seven kilometers while singing "We Wish You a Merry Christmas" to highlight the work of office cleaners. McGowan's latest project, however, has grabbed the most attention: in early 2005, he went to Scotland and took pictures of himself using keys to scratch the paint off other people's cars. So far, the 39-year-old artist has admitted to vandalizing 47 cars in the greater Glasgow area. He plans to display the photos in local Glasgow galleries. Surprisingly, police have received no complaints...yet.

**ARTIST'S STATEMENT:** "I do feel guilty, but if I don't do it, someone else will. They should feel glad that they've been involved in the creative process."

**ARTIST:** James Robert Ford

**THIS IS ART?** Ford's piece, entitled *Bogey Ball,* was two years in the making. He displayed it in four different London galleries, but was unable to attract a buyer. It now rests on a shelf in his apartment, waiting for someone willing to shell out the asking price of £10,000 (about $18,000). What is it? A golf ball–sized ball of Ford's dried snot. (He's been collecting it since 2003.)

**ARTIST'S STATEMENT:** "It's a physical record of all the different places I have been and people I've met. And it will be hard to let go, but at the same time, it's hard not to have any money."

**ARTIST:** Damien Hirst

**THIS IS ART?** Critics call Hirst, a conceptual artist from Leeds, England, "Mr. Death." Why? He sliced two dead cows in half and placed the pieces in four large clear plastic vats filled with

---

When a sumo wrestler retires, his "topknot" (his hair) is removed in a special ceremony.

formaldehyde. The "artwork"—*Mother and Child, Divided*—earned him the 1995 Turner Prize, one of the art world's most prestigious awards.

**ARTIST'S STATEMENT:** "I want to make people feel like burgers. I chose a cow because it's banal. Nothing. Doesn't mean anything. What is the difference between a cow and a burger? Not a lot. I want people to look at cows and feel 'Oh my god,' so then in turn, it makes them feel like burgers."

**THE ARTIST:** Lee Mingwei

**THIS IS ART?** The Taiwanese artist cooked a meal and then picked a stranger at random to eat it with.

**ARTIST'S STATEMENT:** "When people ask me, Is it art? I ask them, What is an apple? Usually they give a descriptive answer—it's a fruit, it's red, etc. Then I ask, when do you really know it's an apple? And most people say, when I eat it. That's when you know it's art, when you experience it with your senses, with your memory, when you own the work. That would be a better way to decide it's art—or maybe you don't have to decide at all."

**THE ARTIST:** Carlos Capelán

**THE WORK:** "Only You"

**THIS IS ART?** This Uruguayan artist attempted to recreate fractal patterns…using his toenail clippings. The pieces were displayed at a London gallery in 2004.

**ARTIST STATEMENT:** My work "playfully explores issues of self, ego and identity."

\*     \*     \*

## IM TLKing

*Shorthand expressions for Internet chat rooms and text-messaging:*

**GAL:** Get a life

**J2LUK:** Just to let you know

**IMHO:** In my humble opinion

**RUOK:** Are you okay?

**H&K:** Hugs and kisses

**OTOH:** On the other hand

**BCNU:** Be seeing you

**BFN:** Bye for now

---

It's human nature that when two people greet, their eyes widen and their eyebrows lift.

# WHAT A DOLL

*For every Barbie or G.I. Joe that's created, there are hundreds*
*of toy ideas that die a quick death. Here are a few of them.*

EMERALD THE ENCHANTING WITCH (1972)
Amsco Toys made this doll to capitalize on two popular
fads: Barbie dolls and witches (but cute ones, like Samantha
on TV's *Bewitched* or *Sabrina the Teenage Witch* in comic books).
Like Barbie, Emerald was posable and came with lots of outfits.
But unlike Barbie (or Samantha or Sabrina), Emerald had laven-
der skin, lime green hair, and hollow black eye cavities with flashing green lights in them. Little girls apparently didn't like the doll.
According to reports, it was "too scary."

## LEGGY (1971)
With the advent of the miniskirt in the late 1960s, showing a lot
of leg suddenly became a fashion trend. That was the idea behind
Hasbro's aptly named Leggy. The doll was 10 inches tall—and
seven of the ten inches were Leggy's legs. Result: huge legs, a tiny
torso, and a mutant-looking doll that quickly bombed.

## THE LOVE BOAT (1981)
After Mego Toys turned down the chance to make *Star Wars* toys
(they missed out on $1 billion in sales that went to rival Kenner
Toys), the company started snapping up the rights to characters
from every TV series and movie they were offered. Result: dolls
and action figures that probably weren't very good ideas. *The Love
Boat*, for example, was a very popular television show, but it aired
at 10 p.m., wasn't action-oriented, and had mostly love- and sex-
related plotlines that didn't interest children. Nevertheless, Mego
released four-inch figures of Captain Stubing, Doc, Gopher, Isaac
the bartender, Julie, and Vicki, and a two-foot-long replica of the
cruise ship. They sold so poorly that Mego decided not to release
another line of toys, even though they were already manufactured:
action figures based on the TV show *Dallas*.

## M*A*S*H (1982)
Another Mego Toys release of a show kids didn't watch. Over its

long run, M*A*S*H evolved from a broad comedy with elements of drama into a drama with traces of comedy. Had Mego released these dolls in the early 1970s when M*A*S*H was more appealing to kids, they might have sold. But they waited until 1982 to unveil their versions of the gang from the 4077th (including two different Klinger dolls—one in military uniform and one in drag). The dolls bombed, although the 8-inch Hot Lips Houlihan doll (modeled after actress Loretta Swit) reportedly sold well among teenage boys, and, according to *Toymania* magazine, the Father Mulcahy figure was the first action figure to depict a member of the clergy.

## DOZZZY (1986)

In the 1980s, toy shelves were crowded with dolls that talked, walked, drank, and peed. And then there was Dozzzy. Dozzzy slept...and that was all it did. Its eyes were permanently closed and it came dressed in pajamas.

## GROWING UP SKIPPER (1975)

In the late 1960s, Mattel introduced a series of friends and family for Barbie, including Barbie's teenage sister, Skipper. But could Skipper stay a teenager forever? Apparently not. In 1975 Mattel released Growing Up Skipper, a doll that could instantly change from adolescent to adult and back again. With the pull of an arm, Skipper grew an inch taller, her waist got smaller, and her bustline expanded. Another arm pump returned Skipper to her more modest, less curvy dimensions. Mattel discontinued the doll in 1976, giving in to protests from feminist groups and concerned parents who didn't think little girls should be playing with such an overtly sexual doll.

\*     \*     \*

### GOOD FOR HER...BUT FOR US?

Sue McIlwraith, a supermarket worker from West Bromwich, England, passed her driving test on the 20th attempt. From 1996 to 2003, she took more than 300 lessons, which cost her £7,000 (about $12,000). "To be honest," said Mrs McIlwraith, "when it comes to driving I'm not the sharpest knife in the drawer."

# JUST PLANE WEIRD

*These days, no one makes jokes on a plane, least of all the pilot. Here's the harrowing tale of a practical joke that almost went horribly wrong.*

## CRASH COURSE

In 1947 an American Airlines pilot named Charles Sisto was in command of a propeller-driven DC-4 aircraft carrying 49 passengers from Dallas to Los Angeles. Along with Sisto were his copilot, Melvin Logan, and John Beck, a DC-3 pilot who was learning how to operate the more sophisticated DC-4. While cruising along at 8,000 feet, Captain Sisto invited Beck to take the controls. As Beck was settling into the captain's chair, Sisto thought he'd have a little fun at the rookie's expense—he fastened the gust lock, a device that locks up both the rudder and the elevator and is supposed to be used only on the ground.

Beck was obviously confused when the DC-4 started climbing...and climbing...and kept climbing, no matter what he did. Beck tried everything he could think of, but he couldn't level the plane out. Finally, suppressing his laughter, Captain Sisto decided that the joke had gone on long enough and unlocked the gust lock. Bad idea: while trying to correct the plane's altitude, Beck had left the controls set to an extreme position. Once the gust lock was off, the airplane went straight into a nose dive.

The sudden lurch threw Sisto and Beck, who were not strapped in, out of their seats. They hit the ceiling—which happened to be where the propeller controls were located—and shut off three of the four engines. This actually turned out to be a good thing, because shutting off the propellers slowed the plane's descent and allowed copilot Logan, who *was* strapped in, to level the plane just 350 feet from the ground. They made an emergency landing in El Paso, Texas.

Many of the passengers were injured, but none seriously. At first, the three pilots claimed that the autopilot had failed, but after a lengthy investigation, Sisto finally confessed to his ill-conceived practical joke.

He was fired.

---

**No strings attached?** Female Marines serving during WWII were called Marinettes.

# OOPS!

*More tales of outrageous blunders to let us know that someone's screwing up even worse than we are. So go ahead and feel superior for a few minutes.*

## OFF-FENCE-SIVE MANEUVER

"A Shinnston, West Virginia, woman called for help on her cell phone Wednesday after a camel sat on top of her while she was painting a fence. Firefighters and the camel's owner helped move the animal off the woman, who was having trouble breathing, according to ambulance driver Brent Hicks. 'There is no protocol on something like this,' he said. The names of the woman and the camel's owner were not released."

—*Houston Chronicle*

## NICE SMOKING JACKET

"Israel's finance minister, Benjamin Netanyahu, was really fired up during a radio interview conducted outside the cabinet room on Sunday. 'Can't you smell the smoke?' the Army Radio reporter suddenly asked.

"'What do you mean?' Netanyahu shot back.

"'Minister, your cigar is on fire. The one inside your suit jacket. You are burning up!' the reporter replied urgently.

"At this point, Housing Minister Isaac Herzog came to the rescue. 'Throw it on the floor, Bibi.' Herzog cried. Emergency over, the reporter asked Netanyahu why he had put the cigar in his jacket pocket.

"'Smoking is forbidden here,' Netanyahu said. But why a lit cigar? 'I didn't know it was lit.'"

—**Reuters**

## REAL TOUGH LOVE

"A Watauga, Texas, woman identified only as 'Lori,' told *Fort Worth Star-Telegram* reporters that she recently phoned 911 after coming home to find her daughters fighting. The 911 dispatcher, Mike Forbess, responded to the mother's plea for help by saying: 'OK. Do you want us to come over to shoot her?'

---

**Your government at work: It is illegal to swim on dry land in Santa Ana, California.**

"After Forbess' comment, the woman fell silent for about five seconds and then asked, 'Excuse me?'

"Forbess, a dispatcher for five years, told her he was joking and apologized. But it was too late. (Forbess immediately told his supervisor what happened and was severely reprimanded.)"

—Associated Press

## DON'T DRINK THE...

"Aliso Viejo, California, officials fell prey to an Internet prank that warns about 'the dangers of dihydrogen monoxide,' otherwise known as $H_2O$ or... water. The City Council was about to vote on a law banning the use of foam containers made with the substance. Officials said a paralegal was the victim of a spoof Web site identifying it as an 'odorless, colorless chemical' that can cause death if inhaled."

—USA Today

## FAILING GRADE

"In March 2004, the University of California, Davis, issued an apology to 6,000 students who received an e-mail indicating they were awarded a prestigious Regents Scholarship. It was a mistake. Within three hours a second e-mail was issued congratulating those same students on being admitted to UC Davis, but without the scholarship. Only 800 students were actually selected to receive the Regents Scholarship."

—UC News Service

## HOUSE IT GOING?

"Former *Baywatch* star Carmen Electra has discovered she's living in the wrong house—the one she thought she'd bought is next door. The actress, who purchased the Los Angeles property with her husband, David Navarro, admits she didn't realize she'd put in a bid on the wrong home until she moved in. She says, 'I got the houses confused. The day we moved in, I walked in the living room and I said, "Honey, this isn't the house!" I was a little disappointed because I thought the pool was somewhere else, but now I've gotten used to it.'"

—World Entertainment News

---

Don't look now, but the average person loses about 1,600 eyelashes per year.

# WHY ASK WHY?

*Sometimes the answer is irrelevant—it's the question that counts.*

If money doesn't grow on trees, why do banks have branches?

What disease did cured ham have?

Why do we say we "slept like a baby" when babies wake up every hour and a half?

Why do alarm clocks "go off" when they start making noise?

Instead of "All things in moderation," shouldn't it be "Some things in moderation"?

Why do we yell "Heads up!" when we should be yelling "Heads down!"

Why is it so hard to remember how to spell "mnemonic"?

Why is it called quicksand when it sucks you down very, very slowly?

When French people swear, do they say, "Pardon my English"?

Why is it called the Department of the Interior when they are in charge of everything outdoors?

Why are they called marbles if they're made out of glass?

If everyone lost five pounds at the same time, would it throw the Earth out of its orbit?

What color hair do bald men put on their driver's license?

How do you know when it's time to tune your bagpipes?

If practice makes perfect, and nobody's perfect, then why practice?

How do you throw away a garbage can?

Why do we put our suits in a garment bag and our garments in a suitcase?

When two airplanes almost collide, why is it a "near miss"? Shouldn't it be a "near hit"?

How can something be both "new" and "improved"?

Why do we shut up, but quiet down?

How did the "Keep Off the Grass" sign get there in the first place?

---

But can it fetch? The Philippine cloud rat barks like a dog.

# MODERN MALADIES

*Modern technology—it's made life a lot easier for all of us.*
*But with every silver lining...there also comes a cloud.*

CARPAL TUNNEL SYNDROME
The *carpal tunnel* is a small space in the wrist—about the diameter of your index finger—surrounded by the carpal bones on the top and the transverse carpal ligament on the bottom. That space is filled with tendons, arteries, lymphatic vessels, and the median nerve. In a healthy wrist, all those parts fit perfectly and glide by each other easily. But when the wrist is used for repetitive motion over long periods of time, one or more of those tendons may become inflamed, which can cause friction with the other parts, including the nerve. Result: a tingling, numb sensation on the thumb side of the hand, and/or pain in the wrist. With the advent of the computer age and people sitting at a keyboard for hours at a time, carpal tunnel syndrome has become increasingly common. According to the U.S. National Center for Health Statistics, carpal tunnel syndrome now results in more work days lost than any other work-related injury.

## BACKPACK SYNDROME

In the 1990s, backpacks became the schoolbook bag of choice for students of all ages in the United States. Studies done at that time reported a growing number of complaints about back pain from school-age children—and said it was related to the backpack trend. They found two problems: 1) The number of books students are required to have by schools had increased. Many packs weighed 20 pounds or more—a lot for a twelve-year-old; and 2) Kids were wearing the packs incorrectly. Kids considered it uncool to wear the packs with both straps—they chose to wear them over one shoulder, instead. This led to shoulder pain and, after prolonged misuse, could even cause curvature of the spine, an especially harmful condition for still-developing kids.

## CELL PHONE SYNDROMES

• **Cell phone elbow:** Since the late 1990s, more and more worker's compensation claims have been filed for *epicondylitis*: painful inflam-

---

S'not a joke: The Maori of New Zealand believe that God sneezed life into humans.

mation of the muscles and soft tissues around the bone projections on either side of the elbow. How did people get the condition? According to doctors, from overuse of their cell phones. Cells allow people to be on the phone almost anywhere—in cars, restaurants, bars, and even outdoors—so overuse has become common. And, as most people have experienced, holding a phone to your ear for a prolonged period of time makes your elbow sore. (Note: It used to be called "tennis elbow.")

• **Increased allergies:** In 2003 Dr. Hajime Kimata of Unitika Hospital in Kyoto, Japan, studied 52 allergy sufferers—half of them were talking on their cell phones; the other half were not. Discovery: cell phone radiation increases allergy symptoms. "When we did blood tests we found that the mobile phones had raised the levels of antigens in the blood, which provoke allergic reactions such as eczema, hay fever, and asthma." Kitama said he thinks that microwaves emitted by cell phones are responsible for the increased antigens.

## ORTHOREXIA NERVOSA

Colorado-based physician Dr. Steven Bratman coined this term in 1996 for a new type of eating disorder: an unhealthy obsession with eating too well. (*Orthorexia* means "correct appetite.") At the time, he says, he had the condition himself; he was so obsessed with eating healthy food that he ate only vegetables that he pulled from the ground himself. He then realized that he had a dangerous eating disorder, not unlike anorexia nervosa ("loss of appetite"). Some of the symptoms: thinking about healthy food for more than three hours a day, planning tomorrow's menu today, continually limiting the number of types of foods you eat, and feeling critical of others who don't eat as well as you do. "Eating for pleasure is part of life," Bratman says. "Any move to give that up should be seen as a very dramatic and radical change."

\*     \*     \*

### LOONEY ANIMAL LAWS

• Goldfish may ride Seattle city buses, provided they lie still.

• In Kentucky, it's illegal to walk behind a mule without speaking to it.

# BRI SURVIVAL GUIDE

*We're not paranoid, but we do have quite a few survival books
here at the BRI...because, well, you just never know. Here
is a selection of advice from these guides. (Uncle John's
disclaimer: We're bathroomologists, not survivalists.)*

U SING COMMON SENSE
Rule #1 for any catastrophe: *Stay calm.* Easier said than
done? Not really. If your car careens off a cliff, you may
think that you'll scream all the way down. But many people who
have survived near-catastrophes report quite the opposite: time
slows down and the mind clicks into a serene clarity of purpose.
Still, a clear mind will do you little good without any knowledge
of what to do next. So here is some of that knowledge.

## TORNADO

People who live in Tornado Alley are probably well-versed in what
to do, but what about someone who's just passing through?

• First, be aware when you're in a tornado-prone area. Tornado
Alley extends from the Deep South in the United States up
through the Plains states (Texas, Oklahoma, Kansas, Nebraska,
South Dakota, and North Dakota), into the Southwest, and as far
north as Canada, which has the second-most tornadoes in the
world (the U.S. has the most). And the violent thunderstorms
that spawn twisters can happen in any month of the year.

• Watch the skies—if they quickly become unusually dark, find
shelter and tune in to a weather report. *Tornado watch* means that
the conditions are ripe for a twister. Stay off the roads and stay
glued to the weather. *Tornado warning* means that one has been
spotted. Seek shelter immediately.

• If possible, learn where the safest place is *before* a storm comes,
but if you don't know, here's what to look for. First choice: a storm
shelter specifically designed to withstand tornadoes. They're usually underground and have strong, locking doors on top that won't
get ripped off by a twister. Second choice: a basement. Hide under
a heavy table to protect yourself from flying debris, and keep as far

---

**A three-month-old baby pelican weighs more than its mother.**

away from any outside walls as possible. Crouching under stairwells is also a good option. No basement? Then find a room on the first floor that doesn't touch any outside walls and stay away from windows. A bathroom is best. Hide in the bathtub with a mattress over your head. (Plumbing pipes are often buried in the ground, so a tub may be the only thing left where a house used to be.) A hall closet is also a good shelter. Wrap yourself up in heavy blankets or quilts. Don't go upstairs—tornadoes are known for ripping off roofs.

• If you're outside, your biggest danger isn't the tornado—it's flying debris. Stay low. Find a ditch and lie face down. Wind speeds around a tornado can reach upwards of 200 mph, but at ground level (or below) they're usually much slower. Keep in mind: if there are heavy rains, be wary of flash floods.

• Don't hide in a car, which can be picked up and thrown, or under a highway overpass, which can leave you vulnerable to flying debris.

• An eerie calm can occur just before and after a tornado strikes, so don't think it's over just because the wind dies down. Danger remains until the sky is clear.

## FALLING OFF A BRIDGE

• If you're forced to jump from a bridge into water, try to aim for the deepest part of the water, usually near the center. Avoid piers or pylons, as debris tends to collect around them.

• While in the air, keep your body as vertical as possible. Point your toes downward and protect your crotch with your hands. Also clench your buttocks to keep water from rushing in and causing internal damage.

• Once you're in the water, fan out your arms and legs to slow your descent.

• If there were other people or objects on the bridge that may be falling down behind you, swim away as quickly as you can.

## FOREST FIRE

• Nearly all forest fire casualties occur because the victims ignored orders to evacuate. So don't tempt fate—if you're told to leave, go.

• A common misconception is that forest fires only travel uphill. They actually travel *fastest* when going uphill, but will go wherever the wind takes them. Your best bet is to travel in the direction where the sky is the lightest. If you have a car, use it. But if you're stuck in a car that won't move, your best chance is to stay inside it with the windows tightly shut and the vents closed. Fires travel fast, so the car may shield you from the heat long enough to survive. There is a risk that the gas tank will explode, but a car still gives you more of a chance to survive than being out in the open.

• If a fire is looming down on you, find a lake, pond, or river, and swim to the deepest part. Submerge yourself and be very careful when you come up for air. The heat from the fire can severely burn your face. A hat or a jacket can be used to shield your head when you surface, but don't stay up for too long or your shield may catch fire. (By the way, don't drink the water—the ash and fumes will make it toxic.)

**Real-Life Example:** The 1910 Idaho forest fire was massive— more than a million acres burned and 86 people died. One group of survivors was a forest ranger named Edward Pulaski and his team. When the fire raged down on them, they made for a nearby mine…and did everything right. "The mine timbers at the mouth of the tunnel caught fire," Pulaski later recounted, "so I stood up at the entrance and hung wet blankets over the opening, trying to keep the flames back by filling my hat with water, which fortunately was in the mine, and throwing it on the burning timbers." The tactic worked: although the smoke made them lose consciousness, the barrier of wet blankets kept them alive long enough for the fire to move on.

## HOUSE FIRE

"So strong is the fear of fire," writes Anthony Greenbank in *The Book of Survival*, "that the unprepared victim relies completely on his blind instinct of self-preservation. Often this instinct is wrong and means exhaustion, asphyxiation, or cremation.…Heat can be kept at bay long enough for escape, but you must keep your cool and deal with first things first."

• Indoor fires can spread very fast (unless they are very small and can be easily put out), so don't waste precious seconds looking for valuables. Get everyone out of the house as soon as possible.

Are you average? A typical adult American male is 5'10" tall. A typical female is 5'4".

- Do not try to put out a stove fire with water; this will make it spread. The best way is to smother it with a non-flammable object, such as a wet blanket.

- Wherever possible, keep all doors and windows shut. This will slow the spread of the fire.

- If you need to open a closed door, be very careful. Use a piece of clothing to touch the doorknob and slowly open the door, using it as a heat shield. If you've determined that it is safe to enter the room, do it quickly and close the door. If you have to break down a door, your foot is far more effective than your shoulder. Aim your kicks right next to the doorknob.

- Once outside, get a safe distance from the fire and call 911.

- Smoke detectors save lives. Be sure there are enough for your entire house and that they all work properly.

## DOG ATTACK

- Do not approach a strange, aggressive dog—you might get bitten and, even worse, you could end up with rabies. Telltale signs of a rabid dog: foaming at the mouth, glazed eyes, and staggering.

- If a dog is charging at you, running away will make you vulnerable. Only run if you're sure you can get to a fence, tree, or a doorway well before the dog gets to you.

- If there's no escape, prepare yourself for the attack. Two defense plans: 1) Hit the dog hard, directly on its nose to deter it; 2) Hold your forearm out in front of you. When the dog goes for it, jam it down his throat and keep pushing. Use your other arm to flip the dog over. This will incapacitate him.

- If there is more than one dog, crouch into the smallest ball you possibly can, shielding your head and hands.

- After the attack, go immediately to a hospital to be vaccinated for rabies. Also, get as detailed a description of the dog(s) as you can.

*For more about how to survive in this*
*dangerous world, go to page 393.*

# SENATE SCUFFLES

*The U.S. Senate is supposed to be a temple of decorum where political leaders can debate the great issues of the day with dignity and mutual respect, but...*

## HOT FOOTE

In 1850 the issue of slavery had turned the Senate into a hotbed of emotion. Vice President Millard Fillmore worried publicly that "a slight attack, even an insinuation often provokes a more severe retort, which brings out a more disorderly reply, each Senator feeling a justification in the previous aggression." He promised, in his role as president of the Senate, to act at the first hint of disorder to prevent any conflict from getting out of hand.

Two weeks later, his worst fears came true when Missouri Senator Thomas Hart Benton got into a nasty argument with Mississippi Senator Henry Foote over a simple point of order. Benton, a bull of a man, charged up the aisle at Foote; the diminutive Foote drew a pistol. "Let him fire!" Benton yelled. "Stand out of the way and let the assassin fire!" Fortunately, he didn't—a disaster was avoided when the Senate quickly adopted a motion to adjourn.

## PAIN BY CANE

On May 22, 1856, South Carolina's Senator Andrew Butler was ridiculed on the Senate floor by anti-slavery advocate Charles Sumner of Massachusetts during a debate over whether Kansas should be admitted to the Union as a slave or free state. During his speech, entitled "The Crime Against Kansas," Sumner accused Butler of leading the effort to spread slavery to Kansas, for Butler, he said, had taken "a mistress, who, though ugly to others, is always lovely to him...I mean, the harlot, Slavery."

Butler's response is not recorded, but by all accounts Sumner concluded his speech and the day's session continued. Meanwhile in the House of Representatives, Butler's cousin, Congressman Preston Brooks, was preparing his own response to what he considered a grievous slander against a kinsman and fellow Southerner. Moments after the Senate adjourned for the day, Butler grabbed a cane and strode into the Senate chamber. Sumner was sitting at

---

Poll result: Only 9% of Americans know George Washington was a Revolutionary War general.

his desk putting stamps on copies of his speech to send to constituents. Slamming his metal-tipped cane onto the unsuspecting Sumner's head, Brooks proceeded to beat the helpless man viciously. Then he turned on his heels and walked out.

To their partisans each man became an instant hero. The stunned and bloodied Sumner was carried away by friends. It took him months to recover from his wounds, but he returned to the Senate and served another 18 years. As for Brooks, he survived a Senate censure vote and was even re-elected to office, but died six months later at the age of 37.

## DEATH BY DUEL

In 1859 Senator David Broderick of California, a power broker in the Democratic Party's anti-slavery faction, was challenged to a duel by political enemy and pro-slavery activist California Chief Justice David Terry. They met at dawn at Lake Merced, south of San Francisco. Broderick had the first shot, but when his gun misfired, Terry calmly put his bullet through Broderick's chest. Broderick now has the unique distinction of being the only U.S. senator to be killed in a duel while in office. Terry was tried for murder and acquitted, and three years later he joined the Confederate Army. In 1889 Terry himself was gunned down by the Supreme Court Justice Stephen Fields' bodyguard after Terry confronted Field in a train station restaurant and slapped him.

## SCORE ONE FOR THE SENATOR

Over the years many senators have been attacked by disgruntled constituents, but only once has a senator been the one to start the fight. In 1917 an anti-war protester named Alexander Bannwart and two other men confronted Massachusetts Senator Henry Cabot Lodge in his office. They wanted to urge Senator Lodge to vote "no" on the upcoming resolution to enter World War I. Bannwart and Lodge argued. The words "coward" and "liar" were spoken. Suddenly the 67-year-old senator decked the 36-year-old pacifist and laid him out cold. The protester was arrested, but Lodge said he was too busy to press charges. Two days later, Lodge voted with the majority of his fellow senators to go to war. Bannwart caught the patriotic fever gripping the nation and, announcing he'd changed his mind, enlisted in the army.

As late as 1967, women were banned from running marathons without a chaperone.

# TONGUE TWISTERS

*Try to say these three times fast. And pay no attention to the person banging on the bathroom door, wondering what's going on in there.*

Who washed Washington's white woolens when Washington's washerwoman went west?

Lesser leather never weathered wetter weather better.

Shave a cedar shingle thin.

Which wristwatches are Swiss wristwatches?

A thin little boy picked six thick thistle sticks.

Flee from fog to fight flu fast!

The bootblack bought the black boot back.

We surely shall see the sun shine soon.

Miss Smith's fish sauce shop seldom sells shellfish.

Which wicked witch wished which wicked wish?

I slit the sheet, the sheet I slit, and on the slitted sheet I sit.

Give papa a cup of proper coffee in a copper coffee cup.

Imagine an imaginary menagerie manager managing an imaginary menagerie.

The epitome of femininity.

Fred fed Ted bread, and Ted fed Fred bread.

Many an anemone sees an enemy.

Any noise annoys an oyster but a noisy noise annoys an oyster most.

**Number one cause of burglar alarm activation in the U.S.: Owner error. (Burglaries are 7th.)**

# TWO-TIMING

*We recently read a newspaper story about an identical twin who switched places with his brother so that the brother could escape from prison. That got us wondering—how often does this happen? Answer: More often than you might think.*

TWINS: Bernic Lee and Breon Alston-Currie, 19, of Durham, North Carolina

BACKGROUND: In May 2002, both brothers were being held at the Durham County jail. Bernic Lee was awaiting trial for murder, and Breon was being held on an unrelated robbery charge.

TWO-TIMING: On the day that Breon was scheduled for release, the jail's computer crashed. The guards, working from a handwritten list of inmates to be released, went to Bernic Lee's cell and asked him if he was Breon. Bernic Lee said yes. His face matched the photo on the release form (they're twins, remember) and he gave the right home address, but he didn't know Breon's Social Security number. No problem. It's not uncommon for inmates to not know their own Social Security numbers, so the jailers released him anyway.

WHAT HAPPENED: Bernic Lee spent about seven hours on the outside, then turned himself back in. He later pled guilty to second-degree murder and was sentenced to 9 to 12 years in prison. County officials never figured out whether Breon played any part in the snafu. "I have no information to believe that," says the jail's director, Lt. Col. George Naylor. "I have no information not to believe it, either."

TWINS: Carey and David Moore, 27

BACKGROUND: Both brothers were serving time in the Nebraska State Penitentiary in October 1984.

TWO-TIMING: One afternoon they met up in a conference room in the prison and switched clothes when nobody was look-ing. Afterward Carey, posing as David, was released into the prison yard. David, posing as Carey, was escorted back to Carey's cell. The ruse was exposed when Carey reported for David's kitchen duty. The kitchen supervisor realized that "David" wasn't really David and reported the incident to the guards.

**WHAT HAPPENED:** When confronted, the twins admitted the switch. It's doubtful that it was anything more than a prank, though, and even less likely that the brothers would have kept it up much longer—David was serving 4 to 6 years for burglary; Carey was awaiting execution on death row.

**TWINS:** Two 18-year-old twins living in Sweden in December 2004 (Their names were not released to the public.)

**BACKGROUND:** One of the brothers was serving a 10-month sentence in the Kronoberg jail for assault and robbery. Then one day the other brother came to visit. The two were indistinguishable, except for a birthmark on the incarcerated twin's body.

**TWO-TIMING:** The brothers were allowed a 45-minute, *unsupervised* visit. Guess what happened! They switched clothes and the one without a birthmark used an ink pen to make a fake one. When the visit ended, the brother who was serving time walked out of the jail and disappeared.

**WHAT HAPPENED:** For all we know, the innocent twin might have served the entire 10-month sentence for his brother, were it not for one thing: that night, he panicked at the thought of having to spend a night in jail, called for a guard, and confessed the deception. As of late December, the guilty brother was still loose, and the "innocent" one, temporarily out on bail, was facing the prospect of doing some time of his own. "He thinks he's going to walk," Warden Lars Aake Pettersson told reporters. "But that's probably not going to happen."

**TWINS:** Tony and Terry Litton, 19, of Cardiff, Wales

**BACKGROUND:** Tony was about a year into a two-year sentence for burglary when Terry came to visit him at the Cardiff prison in March 1990.

**TWO-TIMING:** Somehow, the brothers managed to strip down to their underwear and switch clothes in the middle of a bustling visitors room without attracting the notice of the guards. When the visit was up, Terry went back to Tony's cell and Tony walked out of the prison with the rest of the visitors.

A word of advice to identical twins: if you and your sibling

---

Last "witch" burned at the stake in North America: Josefina Arista (Mexico, 1956).

plan to trade places, don't have your names tattooed to the backs of your necks. Tony and Terry did; when an inmate noticed that Tony's now read "Terry," he alerted a guard. The twins' dad, Ken Litton, couldn't figure out why they pulled the stunt, especially since Tony was about to come up for parole anyway. "This time they've gone too far," he told reporters. "The police won't see the funny side of it."

**WHAT HAPPENED:** Tony was caught three days later and returned to jail to serve out his *full* sentence (no parole this time), plus extra time for the escape. Terry served some time of his own for helping him. (No word on whether they were allowed to visit each other in prison.)

**TWINS:** Ronald and Donald Anderson, 43, of Oxnard, California

**BACKGROUND:** In July 1993, "Ronald" checked himself into the county jail and began serving a six-month sentence for assaulting his estranged wife. Four days later he was arrested again, for assaulting his wife a second time. But how could he have done it if he was still in jail?

**TWO-TIMING:** Police checked the fingerprints of the man who'd checked himself into jail as Ronald; sure enough, it was Donald. When asked why he was serving his brother's sentence for him, Donald explained that he was better suited for jail time than Ronald was.

Donald was speaking from experience—it was the *third* time he'd gone to jail for his brother. Years earlier he had served a two-month jail sentence for Ronald in Philadelphia, and when he moved to California he did time in the Ventura County Jail for traffic tickets that Ronald had run up using Donald's driver's license. In the 1970s, Donald even shipped off to Korea for Ronald after Ronald joined the Army, and then decided he didn't want to go.

**WHAT HAPPENED:** For the second assault on his wife, Ronald was convicted of spousal battery, attempted murder, and robbery (he stole his wife's purse) and given the maximum sentence of 14 years in prison. He is now serving time for both of his convictions. Donald got off scot-free—apparently it's not a crime in Oxnard to do someone else's time. Today he lives in an apartment across the street from the jail. "If I could take my twin's place now, I would do it," he says.

# STREET NUMBER NUMEROLOGY

*Playing with numerology is kind of like reading your horoscope: even if you don't believe in it, it's fun to see what it says. So here's a way you can have fun with your street address.*

## BY THE NUMBERS

B Numerology is the study of the mystical relationship between numbers, physical objects, and living things. Here's how it works: start by taking a number that's associated with you—your street address, for example—and add the digits together. Then repeat the process until you end up with a single digit. If you live at 762 Outhouse Lane, add the digits together to get 7+6+2 = 15. Then add the 1 and the 5 together to get 6. For numerology purposes, your address is a "6." *Note:* If you live in an apartment, use your apartment number only. Now, calculate *your* numerology address number and then look below to see how it applies to you.

## ADDRESSING THE SITUATION

*1* Because it's the first number, 1 is considered very powerful. It symbolizes independence, ambition, and new beginnings. A 1 address is said to be good for artists, the self-employed, and anyone else who has a home office and expects to do a lot of work there. It's also good for people with strong egos.

*2* This is a romantic number; 2 addresses are good for young couples (*two* people). Do you live alone in a 2 address? You may feel lonely or depressed; the lack of a second person can be draining. These houses are good places for visitors, parties, and other social gatherings.

*3* Represents creativity, teamwork, and good fortune; 3 addresses are best for artists and people who think differently. This house is upbeat and full of energy, but be warned: it's also unfocused, so it may not be the best place to set up your home office. Religious people may find it hard to live here, too, as it may be difficult to concentrate on prayer.

---

Average American household size in 1900: 4.76 people. In 2000: 2.62.

4 Because 4 is the first number that can be created by multiplying numbers other than 1 and itself, it is a very special number. It's very solid because the simplest three-dimensional object, a *tetrahedron*, has four sides. (Picture a pyramid with three sides plus a fourth side serving as the base.) A 4 address is very well grounded, which makes it a good place for young families, career-oriented people, and people who place great importance on budgeting and spending money wisely. Artists, writers, and other creative people may find this house too rigid and confining.

5 This number represents freedom, adventure, intelligence, and unconventional thought. A 5 address can be pretty chaotic, though; if you're single you may find it easy to attract friends and significant others into your home and heart, but difficult to keep them there. This is a good place to think creatively, but a bad place for narrow-minded or irresponsible people.

6 This is the most nurturing number of all; as such it's considered a good address for just about anyone, but especially for families with teenagers (or grown-ups who act like teenagers). The Bathroom Readers' Institute, by the way, is a 6 address.

7 Commonly thought of as a lucky number, 7 is also considered a very spiritual number. It's very conducive to contemplation, study, and prayer, so a 7 address is a good place for students, religious people, and single people. Although if you're lighthearted or superficial, or tend to "act on a whim" a lot, this may not be the best place for you to live.

8 Because a figure eight is two loops created by a single line, this number has very strong karma—what goes around comes around. So if you work hard in an 8 address house, you will be more than rewarded for your effort, but conversely, if you lead a lazy, corrupt, or immoral life in this house, expect to get what's coming to you.

9 This number inspires creativity, change, and growth. It's better for single people than families, though, because a 9 address encourages involvement in community groups and social work. But either way, it's a good number to live in.

# GETTING PERSONAL

*Everybody likes to sneak a peek at the personal ads once in a while. Even when they're serious, they're fascinating. And when they're strange, they're irresistible.*

## WOMEN SEEKING MEN

**Pussycat, serious, 28,** seeks ugly man with middle-class lifestyle.

**Lady Guinevere**/Elizabeth Taylor/ Barbara Walters seeks Huckleberry Finn/Richard Dreyfus/Picasso, or any combination of the above.

**Recent widow** who has just buried fourth husband is looking for someone to round out a six-unit plot. Dizziness, fainting, shortness of breath not a problem.

**Winning smile:** Active grandmother with original teeth seeks dedicated flosser to share corn on the cob and caramel candy.

**IF U CN RD THS AD** u cn hav a dat w/me. Bored, attractive secretary late 30s seeks macho executive-type, late 40s, unattached male for long coffee breaks and other diversions. Send resume.

**Write in 25 words or less** why you want to date me.

**Stop Fission!** Naturally radiant lady with hot core will bring you to a controlled meltdown. Absolutely no nukes.

## MEN SEEKING WOMEN

**Ordinary man, 30,** would like to meet ordinary woman.

**Menelaus, Conqueror of Troy** wishes to meet the beautiful maiden he ravished many lifetimes ago.

**Love-starved SWM** seeking a trophy wife with upper-class looks and attitude to take to my next high school reunion.

**Fat, flatulent, over 40,** cigar-smoking redneck seeks sexy woman with big hair to cook, clean, and pick up unemployment checks.

**White male, 50, but looks 49,** seeks a person who is female and breathing.

**DWM, 45,** and uglier than a bucket of rattlesnakes. I chew tobacco, but I take my hat off at the dinner table. If you can bake an apple pie and kiss this ugly face, I want to hear from you.

**DWM, 55, tall, fit, successful** Blah, Blah, Blah; seeking appealing, romantic, Blah, Blah, Blah.

---

**Smart guy: Albert Einstein never memorized his home phone number.**

# MY OTHER VEHICLE IS IN ORBIT

*We keep thinking that we've seen every clever bumper
sticker that exists, but every year readers send us
new ones. Have you seen the one that says...*

I'm Still Hot. It
Just Comes in Flashes.

MY OTHER VEHICLE
IS IN ORBIT.

Remember: It's pillage
*first,* then burn.

It's my cat's world. I'm just
here to open cans.

**Just keep staring—
I may do a trick.**

Whenever I feel blue, I
start breathing again.

Coffee makes it possible to
get out of bed; chocolate
makes it worth it.

My dog is smarter than
your honor student.

PHYSICALLY *PFFFFFT!*

If all else fails, stop
using all else.

Don't Drink and Derive.
Alcohol and Calculus Don't Mix.

**What would Scooby do?**

BOTTOMLESS PIT OF
WANTS AND NEEDS

I'm so old that "getting
lucky" means finding my
car in the parking lot.

Buckle up—it makes it
harder for the aliens to
snatch you from your car.

*a PBS mind trapped
in an MTV world*

Welcome to Middle Earth.
Now go home.

Officer, will this bumper sticker saying
**SUPPORT LAW
ENFORCEMENT**
save me from getting a ticket?

The only difference between a
rut and a grave is the depth.

Dangerously under-medicated.

**If I Had a Life, I Wouldn't
Need a Bumper Sticker.**

# THE KING'S JEWELS

*Elvis Presley—he was such a huge star that even if you're not a big fan, you're probably familiar with his songs. Here's a look at the stories behind some of his biggest hits.*

## "ARE YOU LONESOME TONIGHT?"

If you like this song, thank Colonel Tom Parker's wife. Without her influence Elvis would never have heard of it, let alone recorded it. Written in the 1920s by two songwriters named Roy Turk and Lou Handman, it had been sung by Al Jolson (and other artists) and then languished for more than 20 years before the Blue Barron Orchestra recorded it in 1950. Their big band version only went to #19 on the charts, but Mrs. Parker loved it, and she persuaded the colonel to have Elvis record an updated version. In 1960, the King's "Are You Lonesome Tonight?" opened at #35 on the pop charts, making it the first American single to break into the top 40 its first week. The next week it went to #2, and the following week it hit #1 and stayed there for five weeks.

## "HOUND DOG"

Believe it or not, when Elvis was first booked to play Las Vegas in 1956, his act bombed. The King was popular with teenagers, not with their parents—and that's who went to casinos. So his month-long engagement at the New Frontier Hotel was cut to two weeks, freeing up time for Elvis to take in some of the other acts in town. One of the groups he saw was Freddie Bell and the Bellboys; one of the songs they sang was "Hound Dog," a slow song by Willie Mae "Big Mama" Thornton that hit #1 on the R&B charts in 1953.

Freddie Bell sang it comically as if it were a novelty song, even adding his own lyrics, including "You ain't never caught a rabbit and you ain't no friend of mine." Elvis saw the band perform several times and laughed out loud every time they sang "Hound Dog." When he started performing the song live, RCA Records encouraged him to record it. Elvis resisted at first—"Hound Dog" was a *novelty song*, after all—but he put his own stamp on it by speeding it up and singing it like a rock-and-roll song, which is exactly what it became. "Hound Dog" spent 28 weeks on the pop

**Why was Elvis's popular 1956 song "Paralyzed" never released as a single? RCA Victor...**

charts, including eleven weeks at #1.

## "LOVE ME TENDER"

In 1956 Elvis went to Hollywood to film *The Reno Brothers*, his first movie. He was hoping he wouldn't have to sing in it—he wanted people to see him as a serious actor, not a singer who made movies—but Twentieth Century Fox (and Colonel Tom Parker) soon put a stop to that, hiring an accomplished songwriter named Ken Darby to write four songs for the movie. For one of them, Darby took a shortcut: he took an old folk song called "Aura Lee" and wrote new lyrics. He must not have liked "Love Me Tender" very much—rather than take credit for it, he listed his wife, Vera Matson, as the author even though she had nothing to do with it.

Fox was impressed: they even renamed the movie *Love Me Tender* to cash in on what they thought was a surefire hit. Their judgment, not Darby's, proved correct: *Love Me Tender* was the second-highest-grossing film of 1956, and the single knocked "Hound Dog" to #2 on the *Billboard* pop chart, making Elvis the first-ever artist to push his own song out of the #1 spot.

## "JAILHOUSE ROCK"

For Elvis's third movie, MGM hired the team of Jerry Leiber and Mike Stoller to write the title song, which, thanks to the popularity of "Love Me Tender," would also serve as the title of the film. (Leiber and Stoller were also the guys who wrote "Hound Dog" for Big Mama Thornton.) They spent a couple of months trying to come up with songs, but when they flew to New York to report on their progress, they still had nothing. One of the record company execs, a bear of a man named Jean Aberbach, came to their hotel room and asked to hear the title song. Informed that they still hadn't written it, he shoved a couch in front of the door, sat down on it, and told them they weren't leaving until the song was done.

Leiber and Stoller started scanning the film script for ideas. Maybe it was the scene that called for a big production number in a prison block; maybe it was the big guy sitting on the couch. In any event, four hours later they had finished not just "Jailhouse Rock" but three other songs as well. (Aberbach let them out of the hotel room.) "Jailhouse Rock" spent 27 weeks on the *Billboard* charts, including seven weeks at #1.

# THE 12 DAYS
# OF MYTHMAS

*Secret codes and urban legends—Uncle
John's idea of a perfect combination!*

## SECRET TEACHINGS

There's been a story going around for years that the song
"The Twelve Days of Christmas," which seems like a nonsense song, actually contains coded teachings of Catholicism. It
was written, the story says, during England's anti-Catholic era,
after King Henry VIII split with the Catholic Church and founded
the Anglican Church in the 1500s. The open practice of Catholicism actually did become illegal in England, and remained illegal
until the Emancipation Act of 1829. During that era one could be
imprisoned or even executed for being a Catholic. To avoid such
punishment and to preserve the faith, the story continues, some
clever Jesuit priests wrote the song, with each day's "gifts" representing the Catechism—the essential teachings of the Church.

## THE HIDDEN SYMBOLS

• The "true love" that is giving the gifts, the story says, is God.

• The "partridge in a pear tree" represents Jesus Christ.

• Two turtle doves: the Old and New Testaments.

• Three French hens: the Holy Trinity; or the three Virtues:
Faith, Hope and Charity.

• Four calling birds: the four Gospels (Matthew, Mark, Luke, and
John).

• Five golden rings: the first five books of the Old Testament,
known as the Pentateuch.

• Six geese a-laying: the six days of creation.

• Seven swans a-swimming: the seven sacraments.

• Eight maids a-milking: the eight Beatitudes.

• Nine ladies dancing: the nine fruits of the Holy Spirit.

- Ten lords a-leaping: the Ten Commandments.

- Eleven pipers piping: the eleven "good" apostles (Judas Iscariot, who betrayed Jesus, isn't included).

- Twelve drummers drumming: the 12 points of doctrine of the Apostle's Creed.

## URBAN LEGEND?

The story has been widely spread, especially on the Internet, and is taken by many to be fact. The only problem: there's no historical evidence to support it. And there's a lot of logic to refute it:

- All the "hidden" teachings except one wouldn't have to be hidden at all—they are common to both religions. There would be no reason a Catholic would hide the Old and New Testaments behind "two turtle doves"—since Anglicans follow the two testaments, as well. The same is true of all the other gifts except for the sacraments: Catholics have seven; Anglicans just two.

- If the song was written to secretly teach religious tenets, why would it be a Christmas song, which would be sung only at Christmas? How would they teach the Catechism for the rest of the year?

- What some people believe happened is that through the years, the song was mixed up with another more openly religious song about the twelve days of Christmas. "The New Dial," also known as "In Those Twelve Days," dates to at least 1625, and is remarkably similar to "The Twelve Days of Christmas." It has one verse for each day, and in some cases the exact same subject matter: two for the two testaments, three for the Holy Trinity, and so on.

- Many people still believe that the song is a secret Catholic code. One of their arguments: there's no solid proof that the song *isn't* the secret teaching device they believe it to be—so we really can't know for sure. That's what legends are made of. Either way—it's still a nice song and kids all over the world love it.

*       *       *

**So when *are* the twelve days of Christmas?** They're after Christmas, not before. They start on Christmas Day and end with the Feast of Epiphany, which is traditionally celebrated on January 6.

# FORGOTTEN HISTORY: SHAYS' REBELLION

*"A little rebellion now and then is a good thing," wrote Thomas Jefferson in 1787. But the American Revolution was long over—so what was he referring to? Shays' Rebellion.*

**B**ACKGROUND
After winning the revolution against the British in 1783, the victorious American soldier-citizens went home with optimism for a bright future. Almost immediately, though, things began to get grim. The lack of centralized federal power bred local governments that ruled with dictatorial corruption. A postwar economic depression hit hard. Boston merchants, in debt to foreign suppliers, demanded immediate payment from debtors. Farmers in western Massachusetts discovered that much of their state- and bank-issued currency was now worth much less than its face value. Many were sent to debtors' prison and saw their land, livestock, and belongings sold for pennies on the dollar.

## PROTEST
A 39-year-old farmer and former captain in the Revolutionary War, Daniel Shays, became the leader for a group of increasingly desperate farmers. At first, they peacefully petitioned the government against the political forces that seemed to unfairly target farmers and working people. Disproportionate property taxes, poll taxes that made voting unaffordable, harsh debt laws, unsympathetic judges, the high cost of pressing (and defending) lawsuits, and the lack of a stable currency left people at the mercy of banks and merchants to define how much their property was "really" worth.

When it became clear that their protests were being ignored, the desperate farmers' tactics escalated. They began by raiding jailhouses to free imprisoned debtors. Wearing their old Continental Army uniforms (with a sprig of hemlock tucked into their hats), the self-named "Regulators" occupied the Northampton courthouse on August 29, 1786, making it impossible for the court to

---

Deadliest epidemic ever: The Black Death, claiming 75,000,000 victims from 1347 to 1351.

imprison debtors or seize their property. Inspired by this act of insurrection, other farmers occupied courthouses in Concord, Taunton, Great Barrington, and Worcester. In late September, Captain Shays led a band of 1,500 followers to occupy the Springfield Courthouse to prevent the Supreme Judicial Court from doing business.

## REVOLT

Shays and his men swore they weren't leading an insurgency, but rather were continuing the 1776 revolt against tyranny. "I earnestly stepped forth in defense of this country," wrote one member of the group in an open letter to the public, "and liberty is still the object I have in view."

In response, Governor James Bowdoin of Massachusetts, funded by contributions from large Boston merchants, hired 4,400 militiamen under the command of General Benjamin Lincoln to put down the revolt. When Shays heard of Lincoln's attempt to capture the Worcester debtors' court in January of 1787, he led 2,000 volunteers in an assault on the Federal Arsenal in Springfield, hoping to capture the armory and beef up their firepower. They believed that their neighbors and fellow veterans would join them, as had happened in previous raids. Instead, to shouts of "Murder!" a much smaller force of mercenaries fired cannons into the crowd, killing four men and injuring 20, and repelling Shays's "Regulators."

In the meantime, General Lincoln marched his men through a nighttime snowstorm from Worcester to Springfield, and took the Regulators completely by surprise, forcing them to surrender.

## PARDON ME

Offered a general amnesty, most of Shays's men took it. Shays escaped to Vermont, but he was tried for treason in absentia, along with six other leaders.

But what to do with them? Samuel Adams, former Revolutionary agitator and now back in his role as an affluent businessman, argued for execution. "Rebellion against a king may be pardoned or lightly punished," he wrote, "but the man who dares to rebel against the laws of a republic ought to suffer death."

Thomas Jefferson was one of the few who disagreed. "A little rebellion now and then is a good thing," he wrote from Europe. "It is a medicine necessary for the sound health of government. God forbid that we should ever be twenty years without such a rebellion." General Lincoln, who had successfully subdued the rebellion, also advocated clemency.

Nevertheless, seven of the leaders were sentenced to death. Two were hanged. Others were publicly marched to the gallows before being informed that they had been reprieved by Massachusetts's new governor, John Hancock.

## DEFENDER OF LIBERTY

Shays himself avoided that drama. He applied for amnesty from the safety of Vermont and permanently relocated to New York. The government eventually pardoned him for his part in the rebellion that bears his name. He retired on a veteran's pension for his service in the Revolutionary War. Daniel Shays died in 1825, maintaining to the end that his fight in Massachusetts was for the same principles he defended in 1776.

\* \* \*

## PRIZE FIGHT

In February 2005, *Los Angeles Times* film critic Patrick Goldstein wrote about how the major movie studios had initially rejected many of the films that were nominated for that year's Academy Awards. Instead, said Goldstein, they chose "to bankroll hundreds of sequels, including a follow-up to *Deuce Bigalow: Male Gigolo.*"

Rob Schneider, the star of the *Deuce Bigalow* movies, responded by taking out full-page ads in *Variety* calling Goldstein unqualified to attack his movie—he'd never won any awards, particularly a Pulitzer Prize, "because they haven't invented a category for Best Third-Rate, Unfunny Pompous Reporter."

In August 2005, in his review of *Deuce Bigalow: European Gigolo, Chicago Sun-Times* critic Roger Ebert noted the Schneider-Goldstein feud and said, "As chance would have it, I have won the Pulitzer Prize, and so I am qualified. Mr. Schneider, your movie sucks."

# SPELLING TEST

*Think you know how to spell pretty well? Take this quize and find oat. Guess witch of these commonly misspelled words is spelled correctly. (Answers on page 519.)*

1. **a)** Milenium **b)** Millenium **c)** Millennium

2. **a)** Dumbell **b)** Dumbbell **c)** Dumbel

3. **a)** Seperete **b)** Seperate **c)** Separate

4. **a)** Necesary **b)** Neccesary **c)** Necessary

5. **a)** Minniscule **b)** Miniscule **c)** Minuscule

6. **a)** Accommodate **b)** Acommodate **c)** Accomodate

7. **a)** Liason **b)** Liaison **c)** Liaision

8. **a)** Harras **b)** Harrass **c)** Harass

9. **a)** Occurrence **b)** Ocurence **c)** Occurence

10. **a)** Embarrass **b)** Embarass **c)** Embaras

11. **a)** Indipendent **b)** Independant **c)** Independent

12. **a)** Questionaire **b)** Questionairre **c)** Questionnaire

13. **a)** Brocolli **b)** Broccoli **c)** Broccolli

14. **a)** Recomend **b)** Recommend **c)** Reccommend

15. **a)** Sincerelly **b)** Sincerly **c)** Sincerely

16. **a)** Kindergarten **b)** Kindegarten **c)** Kindergarden

17. **a)** Supercede **b)** Superseed **c)** Supersede

18. **a)** Grammar **b)** Gramar **c)** Grammer

19. **a)** Refered **b)** Referred **c)** Reffered

20. **a)** Immence **b)** Immense **c)** Imense

# FAKE NEWS

*The mark of a truly good phony news story:*
*People in high places fall for it.*

**K** ENNY ROGERS: ROASTED
The Web site Zug.com reported that a book signing by
country music star Kenny Rogers had disintegrated into
a riot in which 19 people were injured. According to the report,
Rogers had refused to sign a female fan's unspecified body part;
the fan turned violent and incited the crowd. Zug linked to a
report on the Web site of WTF-TV, based in Hazelton, the location of the riot. MSNBC, ABC, and the Associated Press all
carried the story. But they failed to verify all of the facts: WTF-TV
isn't real (WTF is Internet shorthand for "What the f***?"),
Hazelton isn't real, and there was no riot. Kenny Rogers hadn't
even written a book. Zug and WTF's sites both even had dis-
claimers telling readers the whole thing was a prank. Zug's intent:
to point out that the news media often rushes to report stories
without verifying their accuracy.

## WE REFUSE TO RETRACT

In 2004, the Chinese newspaper *Beijing Evening News* reported
that the United States Congress had threatened to move out of
Washington, D.C., unless a new, modernized Capitol building
with a retractable roof was built. *Evening News* writer Huang Ke
had copied, nearly word for word, the entire story from its source:
*The Onion*. (Ke didn't know that *The Onion* is a satirical newspaper.) The *Evening News* refused to admit fault, until the story was
proven to be untrue. A few days later the paper apologized, but
blamed *The Onion* for the error, writing "Some American newspapers frequently fabricate offbeat news to trick people into noticing
them with the aim of making money."

## HOOSIER DADDY

In 2003 the *Hoosier Gazette* ran an item on its Web site about an
Indiana University study that found that 100 percent of parents
irreversibly lose 12 to 20 IQ points upon the birth of their first
child. That, according to lead researcher Hosung Lee, is why every

parent thinks their kid is the world's funniest, smartest, and cutest. Newspapers in England, Russia, and the Netherlands ran the report, and it was the lead story on Keith Olbermann's MSNBC talk show. The only problem: the *Hoosier Gazette* is a comic newspaper; the story and study were hoaxes. The next day, Olbermann apologized on air, saying, "So there's no survey showing that parenthood will cost you at least 12 IQ points. But did you hear about the one showing how many IQ points newscasters lose when they see a story they really want to run?"

## IN OTHER NEWS: THE PRESIDENT IS NOT A NINJA

In 2002 two teenagers started the "Fake CNN News Generator" Web site to prank their friends with phony news stories that looked like they came from CNN. Without the teens' knowledge, word of mouth took over: after the site was mentioned on a morning radio show, two million visitors a day suddenly started generating "Fake CNN News" stories...and spreading them. Newspapers and TV stations ran dozens of stories they thought had originated with the real CNN, among them that rock star Dave Matthews had died of a drug overdose and that the Olsen twins had decided to attend Miami University. (Matthews and Miami U. both had to issue public denials.) Most angered, though, was CNN. Only a week after the Fake CNN News Generator was inadvertently made public, the cable news channel sent a threatening "cease and desist" letter and shut the impostor down.

## TERRORISTS WANT TO INTERRUPT YOUR DINNER

In late 2002 Dan Nichols, a detective in Branch County, Michigan, read an article entitled "Al-Qaida Allegedly Engaging in Telemarketing." Nichols had been leading an investigation of scams that targeted the elderly, and he jumped on the story, using it as the basis for a press release. He warned the public that buying magazines, time shares, or long-distance service over the phone could be funding terrorist cells. Local and national news picked up the story...which was bogus. Nichols had read it in *The Onion*.

Unaware that it was satire, Nichols says he got to the article via a link on the Michigan Attorney General's Web site. (The AG's office denies linking to *The Onion*—they're aware it's fake.) "I enjoy a good joke," Nichols said, "I just hate it when it's on me."

# EDITED FOR SENSITIVITY

*In the weeks after 9/11, the entertainment industry scrambled to remove any images of the World Trade Center or casual references to terrorism from new movies, music, or television. Here are a few examples.*

In September 2001, Jackie Chan was supposed to start filming *Nosebleed*, in which he was to play a World Trade Center window washer who uncovers a terrorist plot to blow up the towers. It was going to be filmed on location. It was scrapped entirely.

• Images of the World Trade Center were digitally removed from the background of episodes of *Law and Order*, *Friends*, and *The Sopranos*. (Interestingly, the 2003 miniseries *Angels in America* was shot after 9/11, but since it takes place in the 1980s, the towers were digitally reinserted for historical accuracy.)

• The first trailer for *Spider-Man* showed a group of criminals thwarted when Spidey traps them in a web and hangs their entangled car between the two WTC towers. After 9/11, the trailer was immediately removed from circulation, as were posters that showed a reflection of the Twin Towers in Spider-Man's eye.

• *Party Music*, an album by the rap group The Coup, was delayed a month until October 2001 in order to redesign the cover. The original version pictured two members of the group holding a detonator in front of the World Trade Center, engulfed in flames.

• In the original ending of *Men in Black II*, the World Trade Center towers split open and release a cloud of UFOs into the air, setting off a huge urban battle. After 9/11, a new sequence was produced.

• Microsoft deleted the World Trade Center from the New York skyline for its popular virtual pilot video game, Flight Simulator.

• The Arnold Schwarzenegger action movie *Collateral Damage* was originally supposed to hit movie theaters in October 2001, but was delayed until February 2002. The plot: a firefighter travels to South America in pursuit of the terrorists that killed his family.

• Producers of the 2002 film version of H. G. Wells's novel *The*

Mississippi did not ratify the 13th Amendment (which outlawed slavery) until 1995.

*Time Machine* cut a scene in which meteors rain down on New York City and cause mass destruction.

• The comedy *Big Trouble*, which climaxes with a nuclear bomb that threatens to explode a passenger airplane, was delayed from September 2001 to April 2002.

• The scheduled November 2001 opening of the Broadway musical *Assassins*, about the men and women who had tried to kill American presidents, was postponed.

• Release of the crime drama *Heist* was moved a month forward to November 2001 because of a scene in which Gene Hackman's character outsmarts airport security and brings a bomb on a plane.

• Although it had already been released in early 2001, the rock band Jimmy Eat World changed the name of their album *Bleed American* to *Jimmy Eat World* after 9/11. The original title seemed lurid in light of terrorist attacks on American citizens.

\*     \*     \*

## SPACED-OUT SPORTS

"The trouble with officials is they just don't care who wins."
—Tommy Canterbury, basketball coach

"I have a God-given talent. I got it from my dad."
—Julian Winfield, Missouri basketball player

"Ninety percent of putts that are short don't go in."
—Yogi Berra

"It was a once-in-a-lifetime catch that only happens every so often."
—Randy Moss

"I might just fade into bolivian."
—Mike Tyson

"No comment."
—Michael Jordan, on being named one of the NBA's most reporter-friendly players

# TICK TOCK TIMELINE

*What better way to tell the history of clocks than with a timeline?*

P RE-HISTORY
Early humans had no way to keep accurate time, but did
they need to? Following the sun's path across the sky told
them when it was morning, midday, afternoon, and night—
enough to gauge when their prey (or predators) were out. Clocks
wouldn't become necessary until the advent of civilization, when
humans stopped roaming the plains and started building cities.

• **1500 B.C.** The world's first timepiece, the sundial, appears in
Egypt. Using a pole, or *gnomon*, to cast the sun's shadow, a clock is
etched into the dial face to give a somewhat accurate reading of
the time of day, but only if it's sunny out. (The day is divided into
12 two-hour segments.) The sundial spreads first to Greece and
then to the rest of the civilized world, where it will be the common (and only) timekeeping device for more than a millennium.

• **400 B.C.** The earliest version of a mechanical clock, the *clepsy-
dra*, or water clock, appears in Greece. It measures time by dripping
water at a constant rate from one bucket, through a small hole,
into a second bucket. The receiving bucket has marks along its side
corresponding to the time of day. While not as accurate as a sundial, it could at least tell rudimentary time at night or on cloudy
days.

• **250 B.C.** In Greece, a mechanical bird is attached to the clep-
sydra. It whistles when the water reaches a predetermined level,
creating the world's first alarm clock.

• **A.D. 980** The Saxon king Alfred the Great measures time with
specially made candles that are designed to burn at a constant
rate. It's not very reliable.

• **1300s** Sandglasses, also known as hourglasses, are used in cold
climates (where water freezes). One problem is that the coarse
grains of sand gradually wear away the center hole and shorten the
time it takes for the sand to pour through, which throws off the
accuracy. On ships, a 28-second sandglass is used to gauge speed:

It takes 14 seconds for water at the top of Venezuela's Angel Falls to reach the bottom.

A wooden log is attached to a rope and then thrown overboard. The speed at which the rope, which is knotted about every 47 feet, runs out gives us the nautical term *knots*.

• **Late 1300s** The word "clock" first enters the English language. It comes from the medieval Latin *clocca*, meaning "bell." Linguists believe it is an onomatopoeic word, resembling the sound a bell makes when it clangs (which is used to alert townsfolk as to the time). The word won't be used in its modern form until the late Middle Ages, when large clocks begin to replace the bells in bell-towers (such as Big Ben in London).

• **1400s** European scientists begin work on a fully mechanical clock, which spawns the *verge and foliot* system, a T-shaped device driven by lead weights that move one hand around a clock face. A toothed wheel is turned by the main gear, which is designed to turn, then stop, then turn again, at regular intervals. The ticking clock has arrived.

• **1450** The spring-driven clock makes its debut. The weights are replaced by springs, but the technology is still in its early stages. Result: as the spring unwinds, the clock slows down.

• **1504** Peter Henlein of Germany creates the first portable—but not very accurate—timepiece that can be carried in a pocket.

• **1577** The minute hand is invented by Jost Burgi. He adds it to a clock that he is making for Tycho Brahe, an astronomer who needs a more accurate clock for stargazing (so he can better predict the movement of the planets and stars). Minute hands won't be common on clocks until more than a century later.

• **1602** Like Brahe, Galileo Galilei needs an accurate timekeeping device for his astronomical work. After noticing that a pendulum swings at a constant rate, he draws up plans for a pendulum clock, but never builds one.

• **1657** Dutch clockmaker Christiaan Huygens markets the first pendulum clock, claiming it will "keep equaller time than any now made." The pendulum replaces the foliot of earlier clocks. The toothed wheel is still there, momentarily preventing the gears from advancing, but it is now the regular swing of the pendulum that determines the rate at which the wheel advances.

- **1650s** French mathematician Blaise Pascal combines a piece of string and a pocket watch to create the first wristwatch, an idea that will take more than a hundred years to catch on.

- **1680s** The second hand begins appearing on a few specially made clocks, but also won't be commonplace for another century.

- **1714** English Parliament offers a cash prize of £20,000 to anyone who can solve "the problem of the longitude." Without accurate sea clocks, ship captains can only guess how far east or west they've traveled. Sandglasses can only tell them their speed; pendulum clocks are accurate, but only work on level ground; spring-driven clocks still don't keep good enough time. Over the course of a monthlong sea voyage, even slightly inaccurate timekeeping can result in a ship going hundreds of miles off course.

- **1761** After nearly 40 years of experimenting, Englishman John Harrison answers Parliament's challenge by inventing a clock that works at sea. Improved steel manufacturing allows him to utilize springs that are far superior to those used in earlier clocks. Harrison, a skilled metallurgist, uses some metals that expand and others that contract—important because of the extreme changes in temperature that chronometers are likely to encounter at sea. Harrison's clock loses only five seconds in six weeks. It not only makes sea travel much more safe and reliable, it makes him rich.

- **1783** Benjamin Hanks, a Connecticut goldsmith (and a former Revolutionary War drummer) patents the first self-winding clock.

- **1787** The mechanical alarm clock is invented by Levi Hutchins of New Hampshire, but the alarm can only go off at 4 a.m.

- **1845** The U.S. Naval Observatory in Washington, D.C., begins dropping a *time ball* at noon each day. This allows ships on the Potomac River to set their chronometers precisely before heading out to sea. Other harbors around the world soon begin the practice. The final year the Naval Observatory will use its time ball is 1936. The ball won't be dropped again until midnight, December 31, 2000, to mark the new millennium.

- **1875** A popular song by Henry Work begins with the lyrics "Oh, my grandfather's clock…" From now on pendulum clocks will become more commonly known as grandfather clocks.

---

Pithy fact: The white membrane in citrus fruits is also called the "rag."

- **1876** Seth Thomas Jr. of New York City patents the first mechanical alarm clock that can be set to go off at any time.

- **1886** The R.W. Sears Watch Company (later changed to Sears Roebuck) begins manufacturing the first mass-produced wrist-watches.

- **1905** A German clockmaker named Hans Wilsdorf sees three things wrong with wristwatches: they're not very accurate, not very reliable, and not very fashionable. He tinkers with existing watches and starts the process of correcting all three problems. With his brother-in-law he starts the Wilsdorf & Davies Watch Company in England. In 1908 they change the name to Rolex.

- **1923** British watch repairer John Harwood creates the self-winding wristwatch. It is much smaller than older watches, which required an exterior knob, or crown, to wind the watch, and also allowed dirt to get in the gears. Rolex adopts the technology and perfects it in 1931 with its "Perpetual Rotor," a mechanism now seen as "the basis for self-winding movements."

- **1926** The Rolex Oyster is released, the world's first waterproof timepiece (not counting the hourglass).

- **1927** A Bell Laboratories scientist named Warren Marrison creates the first quartz clock, accurate to within two thousandths of a second per day. The technology will soon be used in wristwatches.

- **1945** The idea of creating atomic clocks is presented by American physicist Isador Rabi. He suggests using a method called *atomic-beam magnetic resonance.* Simply put, this means finding an atom that continually vibrates at a constant, measurable frequency. Four years later, after finding the hydrogen atom too unstable for the task, the National Bureau of Standards creates the world's first atomic clock, using ammonia.

- **1957** The Hamilton Watch Company unveils the first electric watch. It uses the same balance-wheel mechanism that has been in clocks for centuries, but now a battery powers it instead of a spring, eliminating the need to wind the watch.

- **1960** Using quartz technology, Bulova markets the first digital watch.

- **2000** Keeping time is more important than ever in modern society. Between watches, clocks, cars, cell phones, microwave ovens, radios, and DVD players, and computers, more than a billion new timepieces enter the world each year.

- **Into the Future…** Scientists are finding that even atomic clocks may not be the most accurate way to keep time, at least with the method we're using now. Here's the technical lowdown from the Science Museum in London:

> Errors in the timekeeping of atomic clocks are mainly a result of the fact that the atoms are moving. If the atoms are made to move more slowly, accuracy increases. *Caesium fountains* are still in their experimental phase but have already achieved accuracies of one second in 15 million years. It is thought that by taking one into space, they may be made ten times better. An even more advanced type of clock is the *trapped ion machine*, which may eventually reach an accuracy of one second in 10 billion years.

But even with all the advances that have been—and will be—made in timekeeping, we may never be able to create a clock that is accurate enough to ensure that everyone will show up to a meeting on time.

*       *       *

## FUTURE TENSE

In spring 2005, MIT engineering student Amal Dorai set out to prove that time travel is possible. But instead of testing scientific theories (traveling at light speed, going through a black hole), he invited time travelers of the future to a "Time Traveler Convention" at MIT at 10 p.m., on May 7, 2005. People from the future would be aware of such a congregation, he said, and if time travel was really possible, they'd show up. Nobody showed up. So that proves time travel doesn't exist, right? Not necessarily. Dorai's theories: Perhaps there's a cataclysmic event in the near future, in which humanity will be wiped out; or perhaps the people of the future are too dumb to figure out time travel; or maybe future humans find present humans boring and decided not to come.

# KID STUFF

*Just because you're young doesn't mean you can't make a difference. Here are a few of the remarkable kids featured in Elizabeth Rusch's book,* Generation Fix.

**ZACHARY EBERS** of St. Louis, Missouri, was 14 when he thought up Breakfast Bonanza, a program that helps feed kids in school breakfast programs over the summer. He collected 5,000 boxes of cereal to give to food banks and pantries.

**DUSTIN HILL,** 14, didn't let his battle with cancer stop him from getting fresh fruit and vegetables to hungry people in Portland, Oregon. He founded PlanIt Kids, a group that tends his organic garden and gathers produce from U-Pick farms to feed the poor.

**LACY JONES, KATE KLINKERMAN,** and **BARBARA BROWN,** ages 16, 15, and 15, started Don't Be Crude, an oil-recycling program in rural Texas, as a 4-H project. Since then, their program has kept more than 30,000 gallons of used oil and herbicides out of the ground in their community.

**ANN LAI** of Beachwood, Ohio, was 16 when she invented a microsensor that measures sulfur dioxide emissions. $SO_2$ is the most damaging chemical in acid rain, so Ann's sensor has the potential to be used to monitor factory smokestacks everywhere.

**APRIL MATHEWS** and **KERRI STEPHEN,** both 14, started a support program for homeless kids in Woodbridge, Virginia, after April's family lost their home. It's called AfterShare Kids.

**KRISTEL ROSE PAÇANA FRITZ** was shocked that many kids who'd lost their hair from cancer didn't have wigs to cover their heads. So she talked dozens of high schoolers in San Jose, California, into donating their hair to Locks of Love, a program that provides wigs to kids and others with medical hair loss.

**CHARLIE KING JR.** and **DAVON KING** felt that police in Eastpointe, Michigan, were unfairly stopping African-American kids from riding their bikes in the predominantly white Detroit suburb. So they sued...and the judge agreed. They won the suit.

---

Fleas jump at 140 times the force of gravity—20 times that of a space shuttle during launch.

# LOONEY LAWS

*Believe it or not, these laws are real.*

A train conductor in Illinois may not collect fares without wearing his conductor hat.

It's against the law to slap a man on the back in Georgia.

In Fort Madison, Iowa, the fire department is legally required to practice for fifteen minutes before going to a fire.

In Warren, Idaho, puppets must wear distinctly American clothes.

It is illegal to mispronounce the word "Joliet," but only in Joliet, Illinois.

By law, restaurants in Kansas may not serve ice cream on cherry pie.

It's against the law to yell "Oh boy!" in Jonesboro, Georgia.

New Hampshire law says that when two cars meet at an intersection, each must wait for the other to pass.

If you're in a meat market in Los Angeles, *do not* poke the turkey to see how tender it is.

Minnesota forbids women from impersonating Santa Claus.

Unrestrained giggling on the street is illegal in Helena, Montana.

It's illegal to draw funny faces on window shades in Garfield County, Montana.

Newark, New Jersey, forbids the sale of ice after 6 p.m. without a prescription.

In South Foster, Rhode Island, any dentist who extracts the wrong tooth must have a similar tooth pulled by the village blacksmith.

Any map that does not prominently display the city of Lima, Ohio, is illegal to sell in Lima, Ohio.

In Portland, Maine, it's illegal to tickle a girl under the chin with a feather duster.

In Seattle it's illegal to carry a concealed weapon that exceeds six feet in length.

A dead juror may not serve on a jury in Oregon.

---

**Know your rhinos:** African rhinos have two horns; Indian and Javan rhinos have one.

# THE DEATH RAY!

*We see a lot of crazy contraptions in science fiction
movies. But real scientists—some crazier than
others—have actually tried to build them.*

**M**ACHINE: Death Ray
**WHAT IT DOES:** Vaporize enemy planes
**SCIENTIST:** Nikola Tesla (1856–1943)
Tesla was one of the greatest inventors of all time. His genius is
the reason we use alternating current (AC) to power electric
appliances. He invented the first radio, radar, radio-controlled
ships, and the speedometer. He also invented the "Tesla Coil,"
familiar from *Frankenstein* movies for its arcing bolts of electricity,
but still used today for sending radio and TV signals over long
distances.

In 1943 the 87-year-old Tesla contacted the U.S. War Department and offered to sell them his secret "teleforce" weapon, a cosmic ray gun that would shoot a narrow stream of accelerated atoms
at enemy airplanes up to 250 miles away...and melt them. The
War Department thought Tesla was crazy and declined the offer.
Tesla then offered the weapon to several European nations, but
before any could take him up on it, he passed away.

Tesla was said to have stored a compact prototype of the "death
ray" in a trunk in the basement of his hotel. After his death a
Russian spy purportedly raided his room and stole a safe containing the plans for the device, along with the prototype.

In 1943 Tesla was thought to be a lunatic, but 40 years later,
President Ronald Reagan successfully pitched the same basic idea
to Congress and called it "Star Wars."

**MACHINE:** Orgone Energy Accumulator
**WHAT IT DOES:** Collects energy to use as a power source
**SCIENTIST:** Wilhelm Reich (1897–1957)
Reich was famous for his pioneering studies in sex and psychology.
In 1939 he became convinced that an endless supply of invisible
"life force" energy, which he called *orgone*, surrounded the Earth in
vast moving currents. He invented a special box, or "accumulator,"

to trap the orgone.

Reich's orgone accumulator was a six-sided box built of alternating layers of organic and metallic materials. The organic layers attracted the Earth's orgone and the metallic layers radiated the energy toward the center of the box. Patients would sit inside the box and absorb the orgone into their skin and lungs, which was supposed to improve the flow of life energy and release any energy blocks that might be making the patient ill.

Reich used the orgone accumulator as part of a controversial cancer therapy and opened several clinics to deliver it. But the FDA charged him with violating the Food, Drug, and Cosmetic Act by making false and misleading claims to the public. A judge ordered that every orgone accumulator be destroyed and Reich thrown in jail, where he died of heart failure in 1957.

Since his death, Reich's followers have looked for a way to turn orgone into usable power, but without success. The problem, they say, is that Reich ordered his research papers to be sealed for 50 years, because he felt the world wasn't ready for his advanced ideas. His papers are to be unsealed in 2007. Perhaps then we'll find out if there's any truth to the orgone business.

**MACHINE:** Anti-Gravity Flying Saucer
**WHAT IT DOES:** Flies by repelling gravity
**SCIENTIST:** Thomas Townsend Brown (1905–1985)
Brown was an American physicist best known for his attempts to use gravitational fields as a means of propulsion. In the 1920s, he found that when he charged a capacitor to a high voltage, it moved toward its positive pole, creating an "ion wind." He claimed that this effect proved a link between electrical charge and gravitational mass, and could be harnessed to create flight. In 1953 Brown demonstrated his "electrogravitic" propulsion for the U.S. Army at Pearl Harbor by flying a pair of metal disks around a 50-foot course. Energized by 150,000 volts, the disks, which were three feet in diameter, purportedly reached speeds of several hundred miles per hour. According to Brown, the military immediately classified the project and no more was heard about it. But throughout the 1950s, Brown's work was cited as a possible explanation for how UFOs might be able to fly.

**MACHINE:** Project Habbakuk
**WHAT IT DOES:** Unsinkable aircraft carrier made of ice
**SCIENTIST:** Geoffrey Pyke (1894–1948)

In 1943 Pyke, a science advisor to the British military, made a radical proposal: build unsinkable aircraft carriers out of ice to protect Atlantic convoys against attacks from German U-boats. The scale of these floating landing strips would be immense: 2,000 feet long with a 50-foot-thick hull and a displacement of 2 million tons. And since they were to be made out of ice, the vessels would have been virtually unsinkable, but easy to repair if damaged by torpedoes. A 1,000-ton prototype was being built on Patricia Lake in Alberta, but the project was abandoned when the British were informed that it would cost $70 million and take 8,000 people working for eight months to build it. The refrigeration units were turned off and the hull sank to the bottom of the lake, where it melted.

**MACHINE:** Newman Motor/Generator
**WHAT IT DOES:** Produces an almost endless supply of energy
**SCIENTIST:** Joseph Newman (1936–)

Accepted laws of physics say that you can't get more energy out of a generator than you put into it. Newman, a self-taught scientist from Louisiana, thinks otherwise. He's patented a generator that he claims operates at over 100 percent efficiency, effectively generating more energy than it uses. If his machine works as he describes it, that would mean all powered machines—cars, boats, home appliances, airplanes—could run forever on a single fuel charge.

Unfortunately, Newman has been unable to convince the scientific community that his generator works. The National Bureau of Standards tested his machine and found that his generator only delivered 33 percent to 67 percent of the energy put into it. Another test by engineers from Mississippi State University had the generator working at 70 percent efficiency. Have these reversals sent Newman back to the drawing board? Not at all. He continues to tinker with his generator, raising money for future work by auctioning off scale models of it.

---

**See for yourself:** No matter which way his head points, Mickey Mouse's ears face forward.

# THE CURSE OF THE CURSING STONE

*A flood. A fire. A recession. A livestock disease and a crummy soccer team. Could it all be the work of a rock with a curse chiseled into it? Some folks in England think so.*

## THE BAD LANDS

In the late 1500s, the border between England and Scotland was in dispute, and neither kingdom was able to maintain law and order in the region. The area became known as the "Bad Lands." Local criminals—notorious for pillaging nearby villages, murdering their inhabitants, and making off with their livestock—were called "reivers" (*reive* meant "to rob" in Old English).

In 1525 the archbishop of Glasgow decided he'd had enough. He sat down and composed a long curse against the reivers and ordered it read from the pulpit of every church. "I curse their head and all the hairs on their head," the curse began, "I curse their face, their brain, their mouth, their nose, their tongue, their teeth, their forehead," and on and on for more than 1,000 words, making it one of the longest curses in recorded history.

The curse had no effect—the Bad Lands stayed bad until 1603, when Queen Elizabeth I of England died and her cousin, King James VI of Scotland, was crowned King James I of England. Now that the same king ruled both Scotland and England, the border dispute became moot and law and order were restored.

## THE CURSING STONE

The archbishop's curse made news again in the late 1990s, when the city of Carlisle, England, nine miles south of the Scottish border, commissioned a local artist named Gordon Young to create something special for the city's millennium celebration.

The city wanted the artwork to reflect the local history, so Young, who claims reiver ancestry, carved 383 words of the archbishop's curse into a 14-ton granite boulder. Then, despite the objections of local religious groups who feared the stone would bring bad luck, the city council placed the "cursing stone" in an underground walkway connecting Carlisle Castle with a nearby museum, right in the center of the city. Cost: $19,000.

## BETTER LATE THAN NEVER

Do curses, like wine, improve with age? The Archbishop's curse didn't work back in 1525, but shortly after the boulder was installed, downtown Carlisle was hit by its worst flood in 100 years, followed by an outbreak of foot-and-mouth disease, a severe economic downturn, and a major fire. And Carlisle United, the local soccer team, played so poorly that it was thrown out of its league.

After five years of what seemed like unrelenting bad luck, in early 2005 City Councillor Jim Tootle accused the stone of causing "disasters reaching biblical proportions." He introduced a motion to destroy the stone—or at least move it outside city limits. "Most people treat it as a joke," Tootle said, "but when they start to sit down and think, there might well be something in it. Something is coming from this stone." Estimated cost of removing the stone: $10,000.

But the 52 councillors voted to keep the stone where it was; it's there today if you want to see it. Gordon Young, who's also a rabid Carlisle United fan, denies the stone has caused the city's misfortunes and says he's relieved by the decision. "It's a powerful work of art but it's certainly not part of the occult," he says. "If I thought my sculpture would have affected one Carlisle United result, I would have smashed it myself years ago."

Two months later, Carlisle's unemployment rate went up.

## THE CURSE

So how powerful is the curse? Here it is in its entirety—read it and decide for yourself. (If your luck starts to turn, feel free to rip these pages out of the book along the dotted line.)

I curse their head and all the hairs of their head; I curse their face, their brain, their mouth, their nose, their tongue, their teeth, their forehead, their shoulders, their breast, their heart, their stomach, their back, their womb, their arms, their legs, their hands, their feet, and every part of their body, from the top of their head to the soles of their feet, before and behind, within and without.

I curse them going and I curse them riding; I curse them standing and I curse them sitting; I curse them eating and I curse them drinking; I curse them rising, and I curse them lying; I curse them at home, I curse them away from home; I curse them within the house, I curse them outside of the house; I curse their wives, their children, and their servants who participate in their deeds. I curse their crops, their cattle, their wool, their sheep, their horses, their swine, their geese, their hens, and all their livestock. I curse their halls, their chambers, their kitchens, their stanchions, their barns, their cowsheds, their barnyards, their cabbage patches, their plows, their harrows, and the goods and houses that are necessary for their sustenance and welfare.

May all the malevolent wishes and curses ever known, since the beginning of the world, to this hour, light on them. May the malediction of God, that fell upon Lucifer and all his fellows, that cast them from the high Heaven to the deep hell, light upon them.

May the fire and the sword that stopped Adam from the gates of Paradise, stop them from the glory of Heaven, until they forebear, and make amends.

May the evil that fell upon cursed C

*Hmm. We don't why, but our typesetter seems to have met with a mysterious end.*

\*　　\*　　\*

## AND NOW...A HUMOR BRAKE

One day an auto mechanic was working under a car and some brake fluid accidentally dripped into his mouth. "Wow," he thought to himself. "That stuff tastes good!" The next day he told a friend about his amazing discovery. "It's really good," he said. "I think I'll have a little more today." His friend was concerned but didn't say anything. The next day the mechanic told his friend he'd drunk an entire cup full of the brake fluid. "It's great stuff!" A few days later he was up to a bottle a day. And now his friend was really worried.

"Don't you know brake fluid is toxic? It's very bad for you," said the friend. "You'd better stop drinking it."

"Hey, no problem," he said. "I can stop any time."

In the movie *Twister,* the sound of the tornado was created by slowing down a camel's moan.

# HERE COMES THE SPAMMOBILE!

*You've heard of the Oscar Mayer Wienermobile; maybe you've even seen it in person. Here are a few more vehicles to watch for while Uncle John finalizes his design for the Pot Rod.*

## THE ZIPPO CAR

**Looks Like:** A 1940s-era black sedan, with the passenger compartment ripped out and replaced by two giant Zippo lighters, with their tops flipped open and neon flames sticking out.

**Details:** Zippo founder George G. Blaisdell had the first Zippo Car built onto a Chrysler Saratoga New Yorker in 1947. It cost him $25,000, which was a lot of money back then. But Blaisdell didn't have much to show for it—the car was so heavy that the tires blew out regularly. Rebuilding it onto a Ford truck chassis would have solved the problem, but the redesign made the car several inches taller than government regulations allowed. The estimate for fixing *that* problem was $40,000, so Blaisdell abandoned the project. Apparently he never even picked it back up from the Ford dealership that was hired to do the work. The dealership eventually went out of business; no one knows what happened to the car, but it probably ended up at the wrecking yard. A replica of the original car was built in 1996 (hopefully with better tires).

## THE ECKRICH FUNHOUSE

**Looks Like:** Eckrich makes sausages, and it's not easy being a sausage company in search of a promotional vehicle. Why? If you go with the obvious, a sausage shape, you'll just remind people of the competition—the Oscar Mayer Wienermobile. Having missed the wiener boat, Eckrich settled for a cartoon-looking house.

**Details:** They call it the Funhouse (it has windows with flower boxes filled with daisies that squirt water at unsuspecting passersby). There's nothing particularly sausagey at all about it, except maybe that most people eat their sausages at home. But, hey—Eckrich had to come up with *something.*

How about you? The average American driver spends 55 minutes a day in the car.

## THE MEOW MIX MOBILE

**Looks Like:** A van converted into a crouching cat that looks like it's about to pounce. The cat comes complete with a motorized tongue that licks "whisker to whisker" 20 times a minute.

**Details:** A lot of promotional vehicles raise money for charity; Clawde the Red Lobster (an ad-mobile for the Red Lobster restaurant chain) supports the Special Olympics, for example. But the Meow Mix Mobile has a charity all its own: Meows on Wheels. "As the Meow Mix Mobile travels around the country, it will be delivering Meow Mix brand cat food to people who have difficulty purchasing it themselves," the company's Web site says. "If you know any cat owners who are homebound, elderly or disabled, or for any reason have difficulty getting to the store to purchase food for their cats, we want to hear from you."

## THE SPAMMOBILE

**Looks Like:** A blue bus with big Spam decals on each side that are supposed to make it look like a big can of Spam. What it really looks like is a city bus covered with Spam ads.

**Details:** The "Spambassadors" who drive the Spammobile crisscross the United States handing out free spample-sized Spamburgers (patties of Spam Lite, Less Sodium Spam, Smoked-Flavored Spam, Oven Roasted Turkey Spam, and regular Spam on tiny hamburger buns) to the public. Mmmmmm!

## OTHER VEHICLES

• **The Lifesavers Pep-O-Mint Car:** One of the coolest vehicles of all, the 1918 Pep-O-Mint car looked just like a roll of Lifesavers on four of those old-fashioned wooden spoked wheels. The driver sat right in the middle of the roll; the O in Pep-O-Mint served as the left and right-side windows.

• **The Hershey's Kissmobile:** Looks like three big foil-wrapped Kisses (Regular, Almond, and Hugs) sitting on a giant Hershey's bar. The driver sits in the regular Hershey's Kiss (it has a curvy, kiss-shaped windshield); the other two kisses hold free samples.

• **The Mr. Peanut Hot Rod:** A motor home remade into a peanut-shaped race car, complete with a giant engine block sticking out of the "hood" and a giant Mr. Peanut sitting in the faux driver's seat. Why a hot rod? Mr. Peanut is "the Official Snack of NASCAR."

# UJI! HANABATA!

*When people from different cultures meet, they often develop a unique "bridge" language, or "pidgin," to communicate. Drawing from European, Asian, and native languages, Hawaiian pidgin is a tasty stew of words and expressions that you'll seldom hear on the mainland. Some examples:*

**Howzit?** Aloha!

**Whas da haps?** What's up? What's happening?

**Whadascoops?** Another word for *Whas da haps?*

**Leddahs** (Pronounced "LEH duhs")**:** See you later.

**Bakatare** ("Bah kah TAH ray")**:** Crazy

**Weed:** With

**Cockaroach:** A verb that means to sneak or steal. It can also mean stingy or cheap.

**Hanabata:** Boogers; snot

**Go holoholo:** Go out

**Moemoe** ("Moe ay MOE ay")**:** Go to sleep.

**Uji!** ("OOH gee!")**:** Eew! Yucky!

**Skebei** ("Skeh BAY")**:** Dirty old man

**Make ass:** Make a mess; make a fool of yourself

**Cool head main ting:** It's not a big deal. Also: Minors! ("MY nuhs")

**Stink eye:** The evil eye—a dirty look

**Okole:** Butt; rear end

**Grind:** To eat

**Grinds:** Food

**Ete:** A nerd

**I owe you money o' wot?** Stop staring at me!

**Usedtato** ("USED tah toe")**:** Used to

**Lepo:** A loser. It can also mean "filthy."

**Junk:** Crummy, bad

**Junks:** Junk, stuff

**Stuffs:** Stuff, junk

**Mines:** Mine

**Pressure out:** Freak out

**Chicken skin:** Goosebumps Also: Stand-up hairs

---

**Generally speaking, an egg is warmer at its broad end than at its narrow end.**

# SCOTLAND'S DISH

*Back in the 1950s, the BRI's future food historian, Jeff*
*Cheek, took a trip to Scotland while on one of his clandestine*
*missions with the CIA. (He won't tell us why he was there.)*
*But he did write this story of haggis for us—the origin, the*
*tradition, and the elusive hunt for a wee, tiny beastie.*

## WASTE NOT, WANT NOT

Scotland has given the world many gifts: plaid, golf, the poetry of Robert Burns, and Scotch whisky. They have also offered us their national dish—*haggis*—but there are few takers...once they find out what haggis is made of. It is the offal (the waste parts) of a slaughtered sheep, minced and then boiled in the sheep's stomach. The dish and name most likely came from the Vikings—the Swedes have a similar dish, *hagga*, but they use choice cuts of meat to make it. The frugal Scottish farmers, however, wasted nothing, so instead of discarding the lungs, heart, and liver, they used these along with homegrown oats to make haggis. And the Scots have revered it for centuries.

In his "Address to a Haggis," 18th-century poet Robert Burns called the dish "the Great Chieftain of the Pudding Race." And it has become a Scottish tradition to serve haggis on Burns Night, January 25, to celebrate the poet's birthday. Loyal Scotsmen are also supposed to eat haggis on November 30, St. Andrew's Day, to honor Scotland's patron saint.

## DOWN THE HATCH

Another tradition may explain the dish's lasting popularity: you don't eat the haggis by itself—it must be served with "neeps, tatties, and a dram." Translation: turnips, mashed potatoes, and Scotch whisky. (Possible rationale: everything tastes better if you wash it down with whisky.)

As you might imagine, most non-Scots (and many natives) are quick to reject a dish of innards, so many of the restaurants in Scotland prepare a more palatable version of haggis for their squeamish visitors: it's cooked in pots instead of stomachs and uses choice cuts of meat instead of the awful offal.

---

The world record for haggis hurling is held by Alan Pettigrew: 180'10".

## HAGGIS HUNTING

Now *you* know where haggis comes from, but gullible tourists are told a different tale by the Scots: The haggis is actually a "wee beastie" that lives in the bogs and glens of Scotland. It's easy to recognize these little creatures—their legs are shorter on one side than the other. Why? From scurrying sideways up the steep Scottish hills, of course. It's very difficult to find a haggis, as they only come out at night. And they have very sensitive ears.

"So if ye go huntin' for the haggis, don't wear anything under ye kilt. The sounda ye underwear rubbin' against ye plaid will send 'em divin' for cover, laddie! And another thing: before ye go, ye've gotta drink lots and lotsa Scotch to mask ye human odor. Them haggis have very sensitive noses, too, ye know!"

Result: Scores of happy, half-naked, inebriated tourists wandering around the countryside after midnight, drinking whisky and swearing that they just saw a real, live haggis...but it got away. "If ye com' back next year," you'll be told, "perhaps ye'll catch one of them wee, tiny beasties."

Here is a recipe for traditional haggis.

**Ingredients:**

- 1 pound sheep liver
- 1 large onion, chopped
- 2 pounds dry oatmeal
- 1 sheep stomach, scraped and cleaned

- 1 pound suet, chopped
- 3 cups meat stock
- ½ teaspoon each cayenne pepper, salt, and black pepper

**Preparation:** Boil liver and onion until liver is done. Mince together. Lightly brown oatmeal in a hot skillet, stirring constantly to prevent burning. Mix all ingredients. Fill stomach with mixture, pressing to remove the air. Sew stomach securely, then prick several times with needle so it won't burst. Slow boil for four hours. Serve with "neeps, tatties, and a dram."

**Something to chew on while waiting for the haggis to cook:** A Scottish chef, John Paul McLachlan, created the world's most expensive haggis for Burns Night in 2005. He marinated Scottish beef in Balvenie cask 191, a 50-year-old Scotch (only 83 bottles exist), and then boiled it in a sheep's stomach. Cost: $5,500.

# HOLLYWOOD LISTS

*If you love movies…and you love lists, then this page is for you. (Everyone else please turn the page. Thank you.)*

### 5 Actors Who Played Elvis
1. David Keith
2. Michael St. Gerard
3. Kurt Russell
4. Bruce Campbell
5. Jonathan Rhys-Meyers

### 5 Movie Code Names (used during filming to fool prying eyes)
1. "Radiator Blues" (*Harry Potter and the Prisoner of Azkaban*)
2. "A Boy's Life" (*E.T.*)
3. "Blue Harvest" (*Return of the Jedi*)
4. "The Burly Man" (*Matrix Reloaded*)
5. "Watch the Skies" (*Close Encounters of the Third Kind*)

### 5 Harley-Davidson Owners
1. Goldie Hawn
2. Olivia Newton-John
3. Barbra Streisand
4. Liz Taylor
5. Cher

### 8 Films with One-Letter Titles
1. A (Germany, 1969)
2. E (Canada, 1981)
3. G (U.K., 1974)
4. I (Sweden, 1966)
5. M (U.S., 1951)
6. W (U.S., 1974)
7. X (Germany, 1928)
8. Z (U.S., 1983)

### 6 Left-handed Actresses
1. Julia Roberts
2. Angelina Jolie
3. Shirley MacLaine
4. Nicole Kidman
5. Greta Garbo
6. Sarah Jessica-Parker

### 7 Directors Who Never Won a "Best Director" Oscar
1. Martin Scorsese
2. Ridley Scott
3. Stanley Kubrick
4. Alfred Hitchcock
5. Cecil B. DeMille
6. Orson Welles
7. David Lynch

### 5 "Colorful" Actors
1. Redd *Fox*
2. Tom *Green*
3. Betty *White*
4. Jennifer *Grey*
5. Jack *Black*

### 8 Stars with Two First Names
1. Raul Julia
2. Kevin James
3. Tom Arnold
4. Meg Ryan
5. Bruce Willis
6. Jason Alexander
7. Larry David
8. John Wayne

### 7 Stars Who Started on Soap Operas
1. Meg Ryan (*As the World Turns*)
2. Ricky Martin (*General Hospital*)
3. Demi Moore (*General Hospital*)
4. Tommy Lee Jones (*One Life to Live*)
5. Tobey Maguire (*General Hospital*)
6. Marisa Tomei (*As the World Turns*)
7. Teri Hatcher (*Capitol*)

Kermit the Frog was awarded an honorary doctorate from Southampton College in 1996.

# POOR RICH PEOPLE

*Want to be rich? You're not alone. A 2003 Gallup poll found that*
*while only 2% of Americans describe themselves as rich, 51%*
*say that it's their life's goal. But beware: wealth isn't all*
*it's cracked up to be. Take it from those who know.*

"I have made millions, but they have brought me no happiness."
—John D. Rockefeller

"Your fortune is rolling up, rolling up like an avalanche. You must keep up with it! You must distribute it faster than it grows! If you do not, it will crush you and your children and your children's children."
—Frederick Gates,
*Rockefeller's financial advisor*

"I am the most miserable man on Earth."
—John Jacob Astor

"The care of $200 million is enough to kill anyone. There's no pleasure in it."
—William H. Vanderbilt

"If I had my life to live over again, I'd be a $30-a-week librarian."
—Andrew Carnegie

"I was happier when doing a mechanic's job."
—Henry Ford

"There is always the question. You wonder if people like you for you—or the inevitable disturbing question: 'Are they after something?'"
—Mary Lea Johnson,
*Johnson & Johnson heiress*

"I have a problem with too much money. I can't reinvest it fast enough, and because I reinvest it, more money comes in. Yes, the rich do get richer."
—Robert Kiyosaki, *investor*

"A great fortune is a great slavery."
—Seneca,
*Roman philosopher*

"I don't care whether I win or lose, and when you can't enjoy winning at poker, there's no fun left in anything."
—John MacKay,
*"Comstock Silver King"*

"I'm not a paranoid deranged millionaire. G*d*mm*t, I'm a billionaire!"
—Howard Hughes

---

**Worth the wait:** A Vermont maple tree isn't tapped for syrup until it is at least 40 years old.

"I never feel sorry for poor boys. It is the children of wealth who deserve sympathy; too often they are starved for incentive to create success for themselves."
—James Cash Penney, *founder of JC Penney*

"It's a terribly hard job to spend a billion dollars and get your money's worth."
—George M. Humphrey, *U.S. Secretary of Treasury*

"Golden shackles are far worse than iron ones."
—Mahatma Gandhi

"In some ways, a millionaire just can't win. If he spends too freely, he is criticized for being extravagant and ostentatious. If, on the other hand, he lives quietly and thriftily, the same people will call him a miser."
—J. Paul Getty, *billionaire*

"Success is a lousy teacher. It seduces smart people into thinking they can't lose."
—Bill Gates

"Of the billionaires I have known, money just brings out the basic traits in them. If they were jerks before they had money, they are simply jerks with a billion dollars."
—Warren Buffett

"Money doesn't always bring happiness. People with $10 million are no happier than people with $9 million."
—Hobart Brown, *artist*

"There's no reason to be the richest man in the cemetery: you can't do any business from there."
—Colonel Harland Sanders

"I'd like to live as a poor man, but with lots of money."
—Pablo Picasso

\*     \*     \*

## MAKING MONEY THE ONASSIS WAY

Wealth was such a burden for Aristotle Onassis that he never wore an overcoat. Why? Because if he wore a coat, he'd have to leave a big tip for the coat check girl (she'd expect it). And his coat would have to be expensive (rich people are expected to wear fine clothes). And since his coat was expensive, he'd have to insure it (someone might steal it). "Without a topcoat," said Onassis, "I save twenty thousand dollars a year."

In Saudi Arabia, a woman may divorce her husband if he doesn't supply her with coffee.

# INFAMOUS WEAPONS

*We couldn't find Uncle John's old Fart Bazooka, but*
*we managed to find some other famous weapons.*

## JOHN WILKES BOOTH'S GUN

The gun that Booth used to assassinate President Abraham Lincoln now resides in the basement museum of Ford's Theatre, in Washington, D.C. The gun is a single-shot flintlock, made by Philadelphia gunsmith Henry Derringer. It's tiny—just six inches total in length with a 2½" barrel—but it's powerful, firing a .44-caliber bullet. The gun was found on the floor of the theater box where Lincoln sat. Also in the museum is the knife with which Booth stabbed one of Lincoln's companions, Major Henry Rathbone, in the arm before Booth jumped from the box to escape.

What about the bullet that killed one of the most revered figures in American history? You can see that, too. It was removed during a post-mortem autopsy and was kept by the U.S. War Department until 1940, when it went to the Department of the Interior. It can be viewed today at the National Museum of Health and Medicine in Washington, D.C.

## THE SARAJEVO PISTOL

On June 28, 1914, Gavrilo Princip shot and killed the heir to the Austro-Hungarian throne, Archduke Franz Ferdinand, and his wife, Sophie, in Sarajevo, Bosnia. The assassinations caused a chain reaction of events which, within less than five weeks, led to the start of World War I. The gun was a Browning semiautomatic pistol, model M1910, serial #19074.

Princip, just 19, was a member of the Serbian nationalist group called the Black Hand. He fired seven shots into the royal couple's car from five feet away, then attempted to shoot himself, but was stopped by passersby and quickly arrested. Princip died in prison of tuberculosis in 1918 (the disease was one reason he took the mission). After his trial, the pistol was presented to Father Anton Puntigam, the Jesuit priest who had given the archduke and duchess their last rites. He hoped to place it in a museum, but when he died in 1926 the gun was lost...for almost 80 years.

---

The yokohama, a Japanese bird, has tail feathers 12 feet long.

In 2004 a Jesuit community house in Austria made a startling announcement: they had found the gun (verified by its serial number). They donated it to the Vienna Museum of Military History in time for the 90th anniversary of the assassination that started a war that would eventually kill 8.5 million people. Also in the museum are the car in which the couple were riding, the bloodied pillow cover on which the archduke rested his head while dying, and petals from a rose that was attached to Sophie's belt.

## THE MUSSOLINI MACHINE GUN

On April 28, 1945, Italian dictator Benito Mussolini and his mistress, Claretta Petacci, were captured while trying to flee into Switzerland. They were executed by an Italian communist named Valter Audisio, who shot the pair with a French-made MAS (Manufacture d'Armes de St. Etienne) 7.65mm submachine gun.

The gun disappeared until 1973, when Audisio died. He'd kept it in Italy until 1957, when, during a resurgence of Mussolini's popularity, he secretly gave it to the communist Albanian government for safekeeping. With Audisio's death, the Albanians proudly displayed the gun "on behalf of the Italian people." Its home is now Albania's National Historical Museum. Audisio once wrote that the only reason he used the machine gun was that the two pistols he tried to use had jammed. He also said that he had no orders to shoot Petacci—but she wouldn't let go of Il Duce.

## LEE HARVEY OSWALD'S GUNS

The gun that Lee Harvey Oswald allegedly used to assassinate President John F. Kennedy is a Mannlicher-Carcano .38 bolt-action rifle, 40 inches long, and weighs eight pounds. He bought it through a mail-order company for $12.78. Something with as much historical significance as Oswald's rifle would become the property of the people of the United States, right? Wrong. Murder weapons are normally returned to the families of their owners, and Oswald's gun was no exception—it was returned to Oswald's widow. The National Archives purchased the rifle from Marina Oswald. The Archives also has the .38 Special Smith & Wesson Victory revolver that Oswald had with him that day and used (allegedly) to kill Officer J. D. Tippett before being arrested. Two days later, Oswald was shot and killed by Jack Ruby.

A lantern in the tomb of Buddhist Kobo Daishi has been burning for over 1,100 years.

## JACK RUBY'S GUN

Ruby was a Dallas strip-club owner and small-time mobster who killed the alleged killer of the president. Just why he did it remains a mystery. But on November 24, 1963, in the basement of the Dallas jail—which at the time was crowded with police officers, reporters, and cameramen—Ruby walked right up to Oswald and shot him once in the side. The gun he used was a .38-caliber Colt Cobra revolver that he bought at Ray's Hardware and Sporting Goods (on the advice of Dallas police detective Joe Cody).

The gun was returned to Ruby's family, where it promptly became tangled in a legal battle over Ruby's estate between the lawyer who was appointed executor and Ruby's brother, Earl. It wouldn't be resolved until 1991, when a judge found for Earl Ruby, who immediately put the gun up for auction and it sold to a collector named A. V. Pugliese. Price: $220,000. In 1992 a friend of Pugliese's brought it to Washington, D.C., and offered to show it to Speaker of the House Thomas Foley. The gun was seized by police and almost destroyed, per D.C.'s strict gun-control laws, but lawyers were able to get it back. On November 24, 1993, the 30th anniversary of the shooting, Pugliese had Earl Ruby fire 100 shots with the gun and offered the spent shells for sale. Price: $2,500 each. (They only sold a few.)

## SADAAM HUSSEIN'S PISTOL

When former Iraqi president Sadaam Hussein was captured in a "spider hole" in Iraq in December 2003, he had several weapons with him. One was a pistol. Major General Raymond Odierno reported that Hussein was holding the loaded pistol in his lap when he was captured, but didn't make a move to use it. The Army had the pistol mounted and, in a private meeting, the Special Forces soldiers who took part in the capture presented it to President George W. Bush.

When news of the war souvenir broke in May 2004, reporters asked President Bush if he planned to give the pistol to the next Iraqi president. No, he said, it "is now the property of the American government." The gun is kept in a small study off the Oval Office, and, according to one White House visitor who later spoke to *Time* magazine, the president "really liked showing it off. He was really proud of it."

# HALFTIME

*More than 30 years after the first Super Bowl broadcast,
the halftime show is no longer just something to fill TV
airtime while the football players rest—it's now a
spectacle unto itself. Here are some highlights.*

**H**UT HUT HUT!
**1967:** Marching bands from the universities of Arizona
and Michigan perform.

**1970:** The NFL experiments with big-name celebrity halftime entertainers. Their first big star: Carol Channing.

**1972:** "A Salute to Louis Armstrong," with Ella Fitzgerald, Al Hirt, the U.S. Marine Corps Drill Team…and Carol Channing. Armstrong had died the previous summer. Songs included "High Society" and "Hello, Dolly."

**1976:** Up With People, a "clean-cut" troupe of young dancers and singers, kicks off the yearlong American bicentennial celebration with a collection of patriotic songs called "200 Years and Just a Baby." Up With People returned in 1980 ("Salute to the Big Band Era"), in 1982 ("Salute to the '60s"), and in 1986 ("The Beat of the Future," ironically, their last Super Bowl appearance).

**1988:** Chubby Checker sings "The Super Bowl Twist" while the Rockettes dance on a giant grand piano–shaped stage. The rest of the field is filled with 88 grand pianos. The occasion: it's 1988.

**1990:** "A Salute to New Orleans and Snoopy's 40th Birthday," combines New Orleans musicians (clarinetist Pete Fountain, Cajun fiddler Doug Kershaw, and blues singer Irma Thomas) with 400 dancers, a 500-voice choir, marching bands from three Louisiana colleges, and actors dressed up like characters from the *Peanuts* comic strip.

**1992:** To promote the upcoming Winter Olympics (to be broadcast, like the 1992 Super Bowl, on CBS), Brian Boitano and Dorothy Hamill figure skate while Gloria Estefan sings a song called "Pump It Up, Frosty."

A can of foot powder was once elected mayor of Picoaza, Ecuador.

**1993:** Michael Jackson sings "Heal the World," accompanied by a choir of 3,500 children.

**1995:** Disney produces the halftime show, which they use to promote a new Indiana Jones–themed ride at Disneyland with an Indiana Jones–themed show, featuring Patti LaBelle, Tony Bennett, Arturo Sandoval, Miami Sound Machine, and 1,000 dancers.

**1998:** "A Salute to Motown's 40th Anniversary" concludes with Boyz II Men, Smokey Robinson, Martha Reeves, the Temptations, and Queen Latifah all singing "Dancing in the Streets" together.

**2003:** Shania Twain performs "Man! I Feel Like a Woman" but is accused of lip-synching.

**2004:** Justin Timberlake and Janet Jackson play Timberlake's hit "Rock Your Body." Jackson's "wardrobe malfunction" introduces a new phrase into the lexicon.

**2005:** Paul McCartney sings "Drive My Car," "Get Back," "Live and Let Die," and "Hey Jude" (without lip-synching or exposing himself).

## OTHER HALFTIME PERFORMERS OVER THE YEARS

- Clint Black
- James Brown
- Woody Herman
- Helen O'Connell
- U.S. Air Force Band
- New Kids on the Block
- Diana Ross
- Aerosmith
- P. Diddy
- Tanya Tucker
- ZZ Top
- Stevie Wonder
- Phil Collins
- Travis Tritt
- The Blues Brothers
- The Judds
- No Doubt
- Enrique Iglesias
- Toni Braxton
- Christina Aguilera
- U2
- Britney Spears
- 'NSYNC
- Mary J. Blige
- Big Bad Voodoo Daddy
- U.S. Marine Corps Drill Team
- Sting
- Nelly
- Kid Rock

**Heads up!** 94% of Americans say they would stop to pick up a quarter lying in the street.

# IRONIC, ISN'T IT?

*More tales of irony to help you*
*keep things in perspective.*

## UNLUCKY STRIKE

"A six-year-old racehorse named Rain, Hail or Shine died in its paddock in Wellington, New Zealand, after being struck by lightning. 'I've never heard of it happening before,' said his trainer, Ralph Manning. 'But it must have hit us pretty hard. The electric fencing had melted against the wall.' Waterhouse, a horse which shared the paddock with Rain, Hail or Shine, was unscathed and celebrated its good fortune by running second at a race later that day."

—**CBS Sports**

## THERE GOES THE JUDGE

"In March 2003, U.S. Supreme Court Justice Antonin Scalia accepted an award by the Cleveland City Club for his contributions to freedom of speech, which Scalia said he would be glad to accept at the club's meeting…provided no television or radio coverage was allowed."

—**CNN**

## TO PROTECT AND WIN

"A group of policemen from a division that fights illegal gambling in Sao Paulo, Brazil, was caught using illegal gambling machines after witnesses turned them in. The police were gambling at a local bar during work hours."

—*Lawyers Weekly* (Australia)

## HIS CAREER IS SHOT

"Todd the Human Cannonball has been fired—because he is terrified of flying. It's not the gun that shoots him 40 feet above the circus ring at 60 mph that scares him; it's airplanes.

"When Todd Christian, 26, a lifelong daredevil, injured his knee while performing the stunt, his employers, the Cottle and Austen Circus, decided to send him for safety training at a space center in Brazil. But Christian refused to go.

"'I know it sounds silly because I'm a human cannonball, but if I'm on a plane for a long time, I panic,' he said. The cannonball's refusal left circus owners only one option: they fired him."

—*The Times* (U.K.)

## SUFFERING SUFFRAGETTES

"Kansas State Senator Kay O'Connor, who once said that giving women the vote was a symptom of weakness in the American family, now wants to be Kansas' top elections official. Senator O'Connor, 63, announced that she is seeking the GOP nomination for secretary of state next year. In 2001 she received national attention for her remarks about the 19th Amendment to the U.S. Constitution, ratified in 1920, which gave women the right to vote. 'The 19th Amendment is a symptom of something I don't approve of,' she said at the time. 'I believe the man should be the head of the family. The woman should be the heart of the family.'"

—**Yahoo! News / AP**

## WORKFARCE DEVELOPMENT

"In October 2003, the Indiana Department of Workforce Development, whose mission is to help unemployed Indiana residents (including those who have lost jobs because their work was contracted overseas), awarded a $15 million computer services contract to Tata American International Corp. Tata was to hire 65 programmers to work on the agency's information software. Two weeks later, state officials canceled the contract after realizing that Tata is a subsidiary of a Bangalore, India, company and that the 65 programmers were being brought in from India."

—*Computerworld*

## INTELLIGENCE

"The CIA convened a panel of scientists in January 2003 to discuss potential terrorist uses of life-science research. The panel concluded that, despite the risks, openness in scientific study was absolutely crucial. Two weeks later the CIA said the panel's conclusions on openness was classified."

—*Federation of American Scientists News*

# WORD GAMES

*Time to test your critical thinking skills.*
*(Answers are on page 517.)*

### 1. By the Numbers
Each number below represents a letter in a common word.

**1234567890**

- **1234:** carries heredity
- **456:** period of time
- **567:** "I smell a _ _ _."
- **890:** charged particle
= _ _ _ _ _ _ _ _ _ _

### 2. Sum Fun
Both 11+2 and 12+1 equal 13, but they have something else in common. What? (Remember: it's a *word* game.)

### 3. Painful Words
He starts and ends two painful words. One comes from too little love; the other comes from too much noise.

What are the words?

### 4. Looking Back
What do "subcontinental" and "uncomplimentary" have in common?

### 5. Magic Words
What do these three words have in common?

polish, job, and herb

### 6. Branching Out
Find the tree names hidden in each of these sentences.

- So then I begged Ma: "Please, please help me!"

- "Whoa, Kramer, nice entrance," mused Jerry.

- That rec room is a nightmare in pastel, Mom!

- "Eve, I believe we're made of carbon," said Adam.

- Mozart excites me, but Chopin eludes me.

- Our very own doubting Thomas penned a winner!

- From the pit he yelled, "I, Jacob, am booming!"

### 7. Another Magic Word
Written in full, this word describes a place that does not exist at all. Yet if you add one space inside the word, it instantly comes right to you.

What is this magic word?

### 8. Weighty Riddle
Forward I am very heavy, backward I am not.

What am I?

# CANADIANS ON CANADA

*Some quotes from the Great White North.*

"Canada is a country whose main exports are hockey players and cold fronts. Our main import is acid rain."
— **Pierre Trudeau**

"I have to spend so much time explaining to Americans that I am not English and to Englishmen that I am not American that I have little time left to be Canadian."
— **Laurence J. Peter**

"Canada is the essence of not being: not English; not American. And a subtle flavour— we're more like...celery."
— **Mike Myers**

"We'll explain the appeal of curling to you if you explain the appeal of the National Rifle Association to us."
— **Andy Barrie, radio host**

"Canadians don't have a very big political lever. We're nice guys."
— **Paul Henderson, athlete**

"Maybe you live somewhere that doesn't have snow in April; if so, I hope you appreciate it."
— **Spider Robinson, author**

"Canadians are the people who learned to live without the bold accents of the natural ego-trippers of other lands."
— **Marshall McLuhan**

"Hockey captures the essence of Canadian experience. In a land so inescapably and inhospitably cold, hockey is the chance of life, and an affirmation that despite the deathly chill of winter we are alive."
— **Stephen Leacock**

"The great themes of Canadian history are as follows: keeping the Americans out, the French in, and trying to get the Natives to somehow disappear."
— **Will Ferguson**

"There's something romantic about being Canadian. We're a relatively unpopulated, somewhat civilized, clean, and resourceful country."
— **k. d. lang**

"I speak English and French, not Klingon. I drink Labatt's, not Romulan Ale...My name is William Shatner and I AM CANADIAN!"
— **William Shatner**

---

The clothespin, the circular saw, and the metal-tipped pen were all invented by Shakers.

# FIRE 101

*Burning question: Did you ever wonder how fire
works? We did. Here's what we found.*

**HOT TOPIC**

The scientific definition of fire is "a rapid, persistent chemical reaction that releases heat and light, especially the exothermic combination of a combustible substance with oxygen." That chemical reaction is called *oxidation*, which happens when oxygen atoms in the atmosphere combine with atoms "borrowed" from other elements, in this case, from fuel. (Another form of oxidation: rust—it's just a lot slower.) For fire to occur, three ingredients must be present:

• **An oxidizing agent.** Can come from a pure oxygen source (like a welding tank) or, more commonly, the air. All that's needed is an atmosphere of at least 16 percent oxygen; normal air is about 21 percent.

• **Fuel.** Can be anything from a solid (wood, plastic, or wax), to a liquid (gasoline or alcohol), or a gas (propane).

• **A heat or ignition source.** Could be lightning, friction (as when striking a match), focused light, or a chemical reaction.

### YOU'RE FIRED

For oxidation to take place, the fuel must be heated to a certain temperature, known as the *ignition temperature*. It's different for different substances: paper's ignition temperature, for example, is 451°F. When a fuel reaches its ignition temperature, a chemical reaction occurs that begins to decompose it into flammable gases known as *volatiles*. Some solids, like wood, go directly from solid to gas, while others, like wax, go from solid to liquid and then to gas. This depends on the chemical makeup of the fuel. In either case, the volatiles then violently interact with the oxygen in the atmosphere—that's called *combustion*.

Using a candle as an example, when you apply a burning match (the ignition source) to the wax on the wick (the fuel), the wax will heat to a certain temperature (the ignition temperature). It will begin to evaporate and release gases (the volatiles), which then react with the oxygen in the air (combustion). Result: fire.

The heat from the fire will then cause the wax to keep melting and moving down the wick, evaporating, igniting, and burning away. Because the fire then produces its own heat—a necessary ingredient—it's called a *persistent* chemical reaction.

## EXTINGUISHED

You already know how to put out a candle—but do you know why it goes out? When you blow out a candle, the wax has cooled below its ignition temperature. If it didn't go out, you didn't lower the temperature enough—or for long enough. Try pressing the wick between your thumb and finger. The fire will go out because you removed the fuel source by stopping the wax from climbing up the wick. Or put a glass over the candle, taking away the oxygen.

With larger fires, it's usually difficult to take away the fuel, so fire extinguishers work by eliminating either the oxygen, the heat, or both. *Water extinguishers* work by cooling the fuel; *dry powder extinguishers* work by smothering the fire, thereby taking away the oxygen; *foam extinguishers* both smother and cool the fuel; and *carbon dioxide extinguishers* displace the oxygen in the air while simultaneously cooling it.

## MORE FACTS

• Spontaneous combustion occurs when a fuel reaches its ignition temperature without the aid of an outside ignition source. This can happen because some substances naturally react with oxygen in the air, but most often it's from *spontaneous heating,* a slow buildup of heat. A cause of many house fires is the spontaneous heating of oily rags. If there is insufficient ventilation—like in the back of a garage—the heat can build up enough for fire to occur.

• Hot fact: You can't have fire without oxygen, right? Wrong. All that's necessary is an *oxidizing agent,* meaning an element that easily takes electrons from other atoms. Oxygen is the most common agent, which is why the reaction is called "oxidation." *Fluorine,* however, is the strongest known oxidizer—much stronger than oxygen. Used in the production of atomic bombs and rocket fuel, fluorine can cause substances like steel or glass to instantly burst into flame. And those flames are virtually impossible to put out.

# UNPLANNED WORLD RECORDS

*More people who made it into the* Guinness Book of World Records *and probably wish they hadn't.*

## WORST STUDENT DRIVER

On August 3, 1970, Miriam Hargrave, 62, of Yorkshire, England, finally passed her driving test...on her 40th attempt. After so much effort, did she start driving right away? Nope. Hargrave had spent so much money on her driving lessons—$720 was a lot of money in 1970—that she couldn't afford to buy a car.

## OLDEST SURGERY PATIENT

James Henry Brett Jr. was 111 years and 105 days old when he had hip surgery in Houston in November 1960. He died four months later (from old age, not from the surgery).

## SHORTEST MARRIAGE

On September 11, 1976, 39-year-old Robert Neiderhiser dropped dead at the altar just after he and his fiancée, Naomi Nicely, were pronounced man and wife at a Presbyterian church in Greensburg, Pennsylvania.

## SLOWEST-SELLING PUBLISHED BOOK

In 1716 the Oxford University Press printed 500 copies of a book titled *Translation of the New Testament from Coptic into Latin*, by David Wilkins. It took 191 years to sell them all.

## FARTHEST-FLYING HUMAN PROJECTILE (involuntary)

On December 6, 1917, a ship loaded with munitions exploded in the harbor at Halifax, Nova Scotia, killing more than 1,900 people. It was the largest man-made explosion of the pre-nuclear age. One man, William Becker, was lucky: He was in a rowboat about 300 feet away from the ship when it exploded, propelling him 1,600 yards—the length of 16 football fields—across the harbor. He swam to safety and lived until 1969.

# UNCLE JOHN'S
# STALL OF FAME

*More examples of people and bathrooms
making beautiful music together.*

**H**onoree: Paul Moghadan, who owns the Chevron gas station in West Covina, California, 20 miles east of L.A.
**Notable Achievement:** Created the best gas station restroom in America, perhaps in the world
**True Story:** When Moghadan started at Chevron in 1966, they told him that keeping the gas station bathroom clean and well stocked should be his highest priority. He took the message to heart…and when the time came for him to remodel his restroom in 1992, he had his brother, an architectural designer, come up with something special.

Moghadan's brother delivered. If you ever have to make a pit stop in West Covina, be sure to stop at the Chevron: you'll see silver columns, marble counters, stone tile, and even a chandelier. The job cost $5,000 more than a typical remodel, but Moghadan says he averages 20 compliments a day and business at the gas station is booming. People even bring their relatives in to see the bathroom. "It's the best restroom I've ever seen," said Jose Montes, who lives in town. "You feel like you're rich when you're in there."

**Honoree:** Archaeologists working for English Heritage, an organization that renovates old castles and other important historic sites
**Notable Achievement:** Finding England's most important bathroom
**True Story:** In May 2005, the archaeologists were restoring Bolsover Castle in northern England when they unsealed an outbuilding that had been blocked off for more than a century. Inside was a large room, thought to have been the bathroom, and a smaller room that was used to heat the bathwater. What makes them so sure the rooms were once used for bathing? A small hole in the wall that connects the two rooms is very similar to one in a nearby well house; they think the holes were used to run a lead pipe from the well house to the bathroom.

The castle was once the home of Sir William Cavendish (1593–1676), who was exiled to Paris at the end of the English Civil War. It was in Paris that Cavendish picked up the habit of regular bathing, which hadn't been common in England since the fall of the Roman Empire a thousand years before. Historians have long credited him for starting a "bathing room" fad when he returned home from exile, but it's only now that they've found the bathing room that started it all.

**Honoree:** Michael Zinman, a businessman, book collector, and supporter of the University of Pennsylvania in Philadelphia
**Notable Achievement:** Donating money to help pay for the Van Pelt Library's men's rooms…and not being shy about it
**True Story:** If you're ever in the library and need to make a standing pit stop, you'll notice a silver plaque posted at eye level above the urinal. It reads: "The relief you are now experiencing is made possible by a gift from Michael Zinman." The plaques were installed above each urinal at Zinman's request. "I have a warped sense of what the world is like, and I am poking barbed gentle fun at society," Zinman said. (The library also has a plaque next to the spot where President Gerald Ford once got stuck in the elevator.)

**Honoree:** The city of Hampton, Virginia
**Notable Achievement:** Creating new life with old toilets
**True Story:** In 2000 the city began a program to collect old toilets, sinks, and other porcelain fixtures that could be used to rebuild oyster beds in the nearby Back River that have been damaged by pollution and disease. The city collected fixtures for about two years, then smashed them into pieces about the size of oyster shells (baby oysters like to attach themselves to mature oyster shells) and built an artificial reef in the Back River.

In 2004 scientists examined the reefs to see if the oysters were putting the toilets to good use. Sure enough, they were—in samples taken from the reefs, just as many baby oysters had attached themselves to the toilet shards as had attached themselves to real oyster shells. "Really, anything that's made into the size of a shell, is hard, and doesn't float, oysters will find it and grow there just fine," says Jim Wesson, the director of oyster restoration at the Virginia Marine Resources Commission.

The Pentagon was built with twice as many bathrooms as needed (because of segregation).

# THE TALLEST MAN IN THE WORLD

*You may think being the tallest guy in the room is a great thing.*
*Here's the story of a man who probably wouldn't agree.*

**TALL TALE**

On February 22, 1918, Addie Wadlow gave birth to an 8½-pound baby boy in the town of Alton, Illinois. She and her husband, Harold, named him Robert.

The boy was normal-sized at birth, but he didn't stay that way for long: by the time he was six months old, he weighed 30 pounds (twice as much as a typical six-month-old weighs). By 18 months, he weighed 62 pounds. In the first two years of Robert's life, his parents—and apparently even his doctors—didn't think there was anything particularly odd about the rapid growth. They just thought he was a naturally big kid who was growing earlier than most kids. Sooner or later, they figured, his growth would slow down and his peers would catch up.

**BIG KID**

That notion could not have lasted long. By the time Robert was five years old, he stood 5'4" tall, just seven inches shorter than his father, and wore clothing made for a 17-year-old. He passed his father in height before he turned eight, and by nine Robert could carry his dad up the stairs of the family home.

What was it that caused Robert to grow at such an astonishing rate? Ironically, it was caused by one of the smallest organs in the human body: the pituitary gland, a pea-sized organ located in the center of the skull, just beneath the brain. Robert's pituitary gland was producing too much growth hormone. Today pituitary abnormalities can be treated with surgery and hormone therapy, but in the early 1920s things were different. When Robert was 11, a doctor told the family that attempting such surgery would probably kill the boy, so the Wadlows gave up on that idea and focused on giving their son as normal a childhood as possible.

## THE BIG TIME

As a young boy, Robert naturally turned heads wherever he went.
(He once terrified a department store Santa when he ran after
him to tell him what he wanted for Christmas.) But he remained
virtually unknown outside the small community of Alton until
1927, when he visited St. Louis with his father and caught the eye
of some newspaper reporters. The reporters measured and weighed
the third-grader (he was 6'2½" and 180 pounds) and published
several photos in the *Globe-Democrat*.

The pictures were picked up by the Associated Press and published in newspapers all over the country, and Robert became one
of the most famous kids in the United States. Visitors began
trekking to Alton in the hopes of catching a glimpse of the world's
biggest little boy. People would park their cars outside his elementary school just to watch him walk home from school. When he
passed their car they'd drive down a few hundred feet, park the
car, and watch Robert walk by again. Some people followed him
all the way home.

## SMALL WORLD

From his earliest memories, Robert towered over his peers—he
never knew people his own age who were his size. By the start of
his teenage years he'd grown taller than all of the adults he knew.
By his mid-teens, Robert entered a new phase of his life: he literally began to outgrow the world around him. Until then his hobbies
had included photography and playing the guitar, but his hands
grew so large that operating a camera or playing his favorite
instrument became impossible.

By his 16th birthday, Robert stood more than 7'10" tall and
weighed 370 pounds, making him the tallest person in the United
States. Even the largest-sized clothing didn't fit him anymore;
from now on everything he wore would have to be tailor-made,
using three times as much cloth as normal-sized clothing. His
shoes had to be made by hand, too (the machinery that mass-
produced footwear was designed to make shoes only up to about a
size 15, and Robert's feet would one day top out at size 37). And
because Robert's feet never stopped growing, he had to order his
shoes a few sizes too large so they would still fit by the time they
arrived.

---

Columbus's ship, the *Santa Maria*, weighed less than the *Titanic's* rudder.

## TAKING ITS TOLL

Robert's rapid, uncontrollable growth was more of a handicap than you might think: he needed to take long walks and participate in other regular exercise to keep up the muscle strength that supported his enormous frame. But his rapidly growing bones couldn't get all the calcium they needed, so they were weak and prone to injury. He didn't have much sensation in his feet, either, which made walking more difficult. As Robert got older his body became increasingly frail and unsteady; falls became more dangerous. By his late teens he was walking with a cane.

When Robert entered college in 1936 at the age of 18, he was 8'3½" tall and less than an inch away from becoming the tallest human in recorded history. Rather than walk to school as he had in high school, he now had to take a cab. Too large to sit upright in a normal-sized car, he had to crouch on his hands and knees across the backseat. When he arrived at school, he shoved one leg backward out the door, then the other, and backed his way out of the cab.

## IF THE SHOE FITS

College proved to be too much of an ordeal for Robert. He could not sit at a normal desk. Fountain pens and notebooks were tiny and unwieldy in his hands, making note-taking during lectures almost impossible. He had trouble working the microscope in his biology class and drawing diagrams of the organisms he was studying in his lab notebook. Even going up and down stairs was a challenge—Robert's 18-inch-long feet were too big to fit on the steps. And because he didn't fit in—literally—with the other students, he was frequently lonely.

Robert finished his first year of college but didn't return for a second. Instead, he decided to open a shoe store. To do that he needed money, of course, and he knew how to get it: in the past he and his dad had made occasional promotional tours for the International Shoe Company. Now that Robert was finished with school, he talked his dad into quitting his job and traveling with him full-time until he had enough money to open his own shoe store in Alton.

By now Robert was so large that travel by train or airplane was pretty much out of the question—sure, if the railroad or the airline agreed to remove a row or two of seats, there might be room enough for Robert to sit, but he could no longer squeeze himself into the tiny train and plane bathrooms. So he and his dad bought a car that was big enough to seat seven people, ripped out the middle row of seats, and hit the road—Dad did the driving, and Robert sat in the back (he was too tall to drive).

In the summer months, Robert made appearances in northern states; in the winter Robert and his dad headed south. They would stay out for a few weeks at a time, typically visiting two towns every day. Robert drew huge crowds wherever he went, and it soon proved to be impractical to greet so many people inside the shoe stores. So they began working with an advance man who arranged for either a large truck or a platform to be set up outside each store.

Most of the people who came to see Robert were polite, but he had to put up with the same old jokes ("How's the weather up there?") at every stop, and some people even pinched his legs through his trousers or kicked him in the shins to see if he was walking on stilts. Robert took it in stride—but if the pincher or kicker was wearing a hat (and nearly everyone did in the 1930s), he playfully retaliated by grabbing it and putting it someplace high where the person couldn't easily get it back.

## GENTLE GIANT

In all, Robert and his dad visited more than 800 towns in 41 different states between 1937 and 1940, traveling more than 300,000 miles in the process. On July 4, 1940, they were scheduled to ride in a parade in Manistee, Michigan. Robert wasn't feeling well, but he decided to go ahead with the parade anyway.

The parade lasted more than two hours, and in that time Robert's condition deteriorated until he could barely hold his head up. By the time he made it back to the hotel he had a fever of 101°F. The hotel doctor looked Robert over and found the source of the problem: an infected blister on Robert's ankle, caused by a poor-fitting metal brace. The brace had been fitted a few weeks earlier to strengthen his ankle. (By his early 20s, Robert had very little feeling left in his feet; if he had noticed the blister at all, he didn't realize how serious it was.) When doctors couldn't find a hospital nearby that was equipped to handle a patient as large as

Robert—he was too big to fit in a hospital bed—they decided it would be better to treat him right there in the hotel room.

Over the next several days, the infection worsened and Robert's condition deteriorated. Had it happened just a few years later, Robert could have been treated with penicillin and might have made a full recovery. But penicillin had not yet come into widespread use, and once an infection got established there was little that could be done to stop it. At 1:30 a.m. on the morning of July 15, Robert passed away in his sleep. At the time of his death he was 8'11", making him a full seven inches taller than the previous record holder, an Irishman who died in 1877.

He never did get to open his own shoe store.

Robert's body was returned to Alton, where it was buried in a 10'9"-long, 1,000-pound casket, carried by 12 pallbearers and eight assistants. The big man got a big send-off as every business in Alton shut down on the day of the funeral. More than 40,000 people filed past the casket before it was laid to rest.

## LEGACY

If you're lucky enough to find a shoe store that Robert Wadlow visited on one of his publicity tours, it might still have a pair of his shoes on display—he left a pair at every stop. And, if you visit Alton, Illinois, you can see his lifesize bronze statue, erected in 1985. The town museum has a display of some of Robert's personal possessions.

During his lifetime Robert resisted being exploited for his size, and he feared that his remains might be exploited, too. So before he died, Robert asked his father to do everything he could to prevent his body from being abused after his death. Accordingly, Harold Wadlow refused to allow a postmortem exam, and he had his son buried under eight inches of reinforced concrete to protect against grave robbers. The family also destroyed Robert's clothing and most of his oversized personal possessions, to prevent them from being displayed in freak shows.

"We treated Robert after death just as he would have wanted us to," biographer Frederic Fadner quotes Harold Wadlow saying in his book *The Gentleman Giant.* "I am sure that he died with complete confidence in us. We could not and did not betray that confidence after he was gone."

Whoa! An alligator can run as fast as a horse.

# ICE CREAM TOILETS

*Communication can be difficult…even in your native language.*
*Here are actual signs posted across America and England.*

*In a dry cleaner:*
We do not tear your clothing with machinery. We do it carefully by hand.

*At a convention:*
For anyone who has children and doesn't know it, there is a day care center on the first floor.

*At a camera store:*
One Hour Photos Ready In 20 Minutes

*At a clothing store:*
Men's wool suits—$10. They won't last an hour.

*At a health clinic:*
We Unblock Your Constipation With Our Fingers

*At a post office:*
This Door Is Not To Be Used As An Exit Or An Entrance

*At a church:*
No Trespassing Without Permission

*At a basketball court:*
Anyone Caught Hanging from the Rim Will Be Suspended

*At a golf course:*
All Persons Caught Collecting Balls On This Course Will Be Prosecuted And Have Their Balls Removed

*In a bookstore:*
Rare, Out-of-Print, And Non-Existent Books

*In a pizza parlor:*
Open 24 Hours Except 2 a.m. to 8 a.m.

*At a campsite:*
Ice Cream Toilets

*At a drugstore:*
Why be cheated elsewhere when you can come here?

*At a general store:*
We Buy Junk and Sell Antiques

*At a department store:*
Our bikinis are exciting— They are Simply the Tops

*In a pharmacy:*
We Dispense With Accuracy

*At a tire shop:*
My boss told me to put something on the sign

---

**A single day's trash from New York City would fill the Empire State Building.**

# WARHOLISMS

*Andy Warhol was more than just one of America's most famous artists. He created "Popism" and became America's high priest of pop culture. Here are some of his cynical observations about the world he worshipped.*

"If you want to know all about Andy Warhol, just look at the surface of my paintings and films, and there I am. There's nothing behind it."

"I asked 10 or 15 people for suggestions and finally one friend asked the right question, 'What do you love most?' That's how I started painting money."

"During the 1960s, I think, people forgot what emotions were supposed to be. And I don't think they've ever remembered."

"It's the movies that have really been running things in America ever since they were invented. They show you what to do, how to do it, when to do it, how to feel about it, and how to look how you feel about it."

"My idea of a good photo is one that's in focus and of a famous person."

"I love Hollywood. Everybody's plastic, but I love plastic."

"I'm afraid that if you look at a thing long enough, it loses all of its meaning."

"When I got my first TV set, I stopped caring so much about having close relationships."

"I met someone who said wasn't it great that we're going to have a movie star for president, that it was so Pop. And when you think about it like that, it *is* great. It's so American."

"I never think that people die. They just go to department stores."

"It would be very glamorous to be reincarnated as a great big ring on Liz Taylor's finger."

"Isn't life just a series of images that change as they repeat themselves?"

"I always thought my tombstone should be blank. No epitaph, no name. Well, actually, I'd like it to say 'figment.'"

"I'm bored with that line. My new line is, 'Everybody will be famous *in* 15 minutes.'"

# PARTY GAMES

*Some fun and challenging ways for you
and your friends to pass the time.*

## UN-THUMB HEROES

**What you need:**
1 roll of Scotch tape
1 roll of wrapping paper
1 pair of scissors
1 pair of shoes with laces
A pad of paper and pencils

**How to play:**
**1.** Have the players help each other tape one of their fingers to their thumb.
**2.** Now see if they can accomplish different tasks without using their thumbs: tying shoes, wrapping a gift, writing their names.
**3.** First to finish wins.

## APPLE BEAR

**How to play:**
**1.** The first player says a word that begins with A.
**2.** The next player repeats the A word, then thinks of a word beginning with B... and so on.
**3.** Each player has to say all of the previous words before thinking up a new one.
**4.** If someone goofs, start over.
**5.** If everyone can make it through the entire alphabet, everybody wins!

## SNIFF TEST

**What you need:**
1 four-inch square of tissue paper
2 breath mints (optional)

**How to play:**
**1.** Two players stand nose to nose.
**2.** One keeps the tissue stuck to his nostrils by sniffing in.
**3.** The other tries to capture the tissue by sniffing it away.
**4.** After 30 seconds, whoever has the tissue wins.

## WRITE WRONG WAY

**What you need:**
Paper and pencil
4 thumbtacks

**How to play:**
**1.** Each player writes his or her name on a piece of paper.
**2.** Tack a piece of paper to the wall.
**3.** Take a pen and stand on your right leg facing the paper.
**4.** Swing your left leg in a circle, clockwise, while writing your name on the paper.
**5.** The winner is the player with the closest match to his or her original signature.

---

**Hot fact:** In 1994, scientists discovered a volcano near the South Pole under 1.2 miles of ice.

# PAIN IN THE...

*Now it can be told: An embarrassing product designed
for...ahem...southern comfort has a secret history.*

# BACKGROUND

Although it's designed only to treat hemorrhoids, Preparation H has long been rumored to have other uses. And celebrities and beauty experts aren't afraid to talk about them.

• In *Beauty: The New Basics*, makeup expert Rona Berg advocates using it to reduce water retention under the eyes.

• Beauty pageant contestants reportedly use Preparation H to temporarily eliminate cellulite.

• Conan O'Brien admitted on his talk show in 1999 that his makeup artist uses it to reduce the puffiness around his eyes.

• Peter Lamas, a makeup artist for the Victoria's Secret catalog, uses Preparation H to eliminate blemishes.

• Professional bodybuilders use it to make muscles look bigger by removing excess water.

• Actress Sandra Bullock uses it to fight wrinkles.

• Other rumored uses: relieving the pain of dry or cracked skin; healing bed sores and surgical scars; soothing chicken pox; and giving skin a healthy glow.

Sound crazy? Not really. Preparation H cures hemorrhoids, which are just swollen tissue. Applied as directed, the ointment reduces swelling and relieves pain. And that's precisely what it does in all those other rumored uses. So if all of this were true, Preparation H would be a wonder drug. It's even inexpensive. But don't go down to the neighborhood pharmacy to pick up a case just yet.

## BACKSTORY

Part of the legend is true: the health and beauty secrets of Preparation H have been known since the 1960s. Americans discovered how it made scars and puffiness disappear, and they passed the word along to friends, who passed it along, and so on. By the early

1990s, the rumors had reached Wyeth Consumer Care—the company that manufactures Preparation H. They were delighted; all these other purported uses could be a gold mine. Wyeth recognized that if Preparation H were marketed as a cosmetic aid or pain reliever, it could eliminate the embarrassment of buying the product. They could sell tons more.

But in order to sell Preparation H for anything other than its listed use (as a hemorrhoid medication), they would need FDA approval. To prove Preparation H was effective at healing scars and eyebags would require millions of dollars of research and government red tape that could last years. Wyeth ultimately decided it just wasn't worth it.

But they were stuck. Once Wyeth knew about the rumor, legally they couldn't boast of the medication's alternate uses. Besides, they'd be opening themselves up to lawsuits. So in 1995 they reformulated Preparation H. The chemical responsible for the skin and tissue healing, biodyne, a yeast derivative, was replaced with phenylephrine HCI, a compound that restricts blood vessels, which limits its effectiveness to treating only hemorrhoids. The newer formula is also without shark oil, which supposedly made the old Preparation H an excellent fish bait.

## HINDSIGHT

So the golden age of Preparation H is over, right? Nope. The FDA has jurisdiction over only American drugs. Original-formula Preparation H, with biodyne and shark oil, is still available in Canada (and can be shipped to neighboring countries). The stuff you buy in the United States cures only hemorrhoids—it's completely useless to rub on your baggy eyes. So if all those movie stars and makeup experts are using Preparation H, they're probably getting it from Canada. In fact, used non-hemorrhoidally, the new formula might actually hurt you: phenylephrine has been shown to dangerously raise blood pressure.

\*　　\*　　\*

"I don't think necessity is the mother of invention. Invention, in my opinion, arises directly from idleness, possibly also from laziness."

—Agatha Christie

# Q & A:
# ASK THE EXPERTS

*More questions, with answers from the nation's top trivia experts*

## AH CHEW

Q: *Why does pepper make us sneeze?*

A: "*Piperine*, a chemical in pepper, is the culprit. It provides the biting sensation that accompanies the aroma to the mouth when tasted. Since piperine bites the tongue, it obviously also bites the delicate membranes of the nose. Our table pepper, though, tends to be ground finely. When pepper particles are drawn into the nose, our body has the good sense to try to expel them, just as it would try to expel any other dust particles…by sneezing." (From *What Are Hyenas Laughing At, Anyway?* by David Feldman)

## GOT QUESTION?

Q: *Why is milk white?*

A: "Since cows eat grass all day, it would make more sense if milk were green, right? But milk is full of *casein*—a protein rich in calcium—which is white. Milk also contains cream, which has fat, which is also white. That's why low-fat and skim milks are not as white as whole milk." (From *Why Do Donuts Have Holes?* by Don Voorhees)

## TONGUE TWISTERS?

Q: *Why do people sometimes stick out their tongues when they're concentrating on a hard job?*

A: "When you need to concentrate on something—say, a word problem—you are using the part of the brain also used for processing motor input. Ever see people slow down when they're thinking of something difficult while walking? It's caused by the two activities fighting for the same bit of brain to process them. By biting your lip or sticking your tongue out, you're keeping your head rigid and suspending motor activity, and hence, minimizing interference." (From *The Last Word 2* by the *New Scientist* magazine)

---

"It has yet to be proven that intelligence has any survival value." —Arthur C. Clarke

# BIG, STARRING HARRISON FORD

*Some roles are so closely associated with a specific actor that it's hard to imagine he or she wasn't the first choice. But it happens all the time. Can you imagine, for example...*

**F**RED ASTAIRE AS WILLY WONKA (*Willy Wonka & the Chocolate Factory*, 1971) Astaire lobbied hard to get the lead in the film version of Roald Dahl's novel, but was too old (he was 70). Joel Grey was also considered, but was too short (5' 5"). Then they offered it to Gene Wilder, who only agreed to do it if he could perform a somersault in his first scene.

**MARILYN MANSON AS WILLY WONKA** (*Charlie and the Chocolate Factory*, 2005) When Warner Bros. announced they were remaking the film, Manson really wanted the lead role. And director Tim Burton thought the controversial music star could pull it off, too. But citing "scheduling conflicts," Manson ultimately withdrew his name. Other stars considered: Nicolas Cage, Christopher Walken, Steve Martin, Robin Williams, and Michael Keaton. In the end, Burton chose his friend Johnny Depp, who says he based part of his Wonka character on...Marilyn Manson.

**MEL GIBSON AS ROMAN MAXIMUS** (*Gladiator*, 2000) Director Ridley Scott's first choice for the lead was Gibson, who had proven he could carry an epic in *Braveheart* (1995). But by 2000, Gibson was in his late 40s. "I'm getting a bit old for this, don't you think?" he asked. So Scott went with his second choice, Russell Crowe, and it turned out to be a good one: Crowe won the Oscar for Best Actor and the film won Best Picture.

**DANIEL DAY-LEWIS AS ARAGORN** (*The Fellowship of the Ring*, 2001) From the beginning, Peter Jackson envisioned Day-Lewis starring in the *Lord of the Rings* trilogy, so he offered him the part. But at the same time, Martin Scorsese handpicked Day-Lewis to play Bill, the villain in *Gangs of New York* (2002). He read both scripts and decided that Bill was a more interesting character, so he went with *Gangs*. The Aragorn role then went to Stuart Townsend, who was fired soon after filming began because Jackson thought he was "too young." At the last minute, Viggo Mortensen was brought in.

**GEORGE CLOONEY AS JACK LOPATE** (*Sideways*, 2004) Clooney really wanted the part of the washed-up actor in Alexander Payne's hit film about two men who travel through California's wine country. Payne liked Clooney, but thought he was too famous to be believable as a washed-up actor. So Payne went out and found a real washed-up actor, Thomas Hayden Church.

**CARY GRANT AS GEORGE BAILEY** (*It's a Wonderful Life*, 1946) This Christmas classic may have never been made without Cary Grant. Why? He urged his studio, RKO Radio Pictures, to purchase the film rights to a short story called "The Greatest Gift of All." (The author had been trying to sell it, but no studio wanted it until Grant showed interest.) RKO screenwriters were unable to turn the dark story into one that Grant liked, so he dropped the project. A few years later, director Frank Capra got ahold of the script and rewrote it for James Stewart.

**HARRISON FORD AS JOSH BASKIN** (*Big*, 1988) Steven Spielberg was set to direct *Big* and wanted Ford to play the 13-year-old boy. But Spielberg dropped out, fearing that his presence would take the spotlight from his sister Anne, who cowrote the script. Penny Marshall was offered the director's chair and wanted Tom Hanks, but he was busy making *Dragnet*. Robert De Niro was asked to star, but he demanded too much money ($6 million). They courted Jeff Bridges, but he turned it down. By that time, Hanks was available. (Debra Winger was set to play his love interest, but she got pregnant. So she suggested Elizabeth Perkins, who got the part.)

**RICHARD GERE AS JOHN MCCLANE** (*Die Hard*, 1988) Bruce Willis was actually the fifth choice to play the role. It was first offered to Richard Gere, one of the biggest box office draws of the 1980s. But Gere turned it down. Why? At the time he was exploring Buddhism, and *Die Hard* was too violent for him. He took a hiatus from making movies and worked on human rights causes until 1990's *Pretty Woman*.

# VANISHED!

*Hey—this stuff was really important. Where'd it all go?*

## CARD CATALOGS

From the late 1800s, libraries kept records of all the books they owned on 3 x 5" cards, filed in large wooden bureaus with card-sized drawers. Every book had at least three cards: one each for title, author, and subject (and sometimes more than one subject). As libraries grew, so did the card catalogs. By 1980, the Library of Congress had 60 million in their catalog; the New York Public Library had 8,973 drawers full. Card catalogs were filling up entire rooms and hallways. The solution: computers. In 1981 a branch of the Chicago Public Library became the first in America with a computerized index. Over the next 15 years, more than 95 percent of American libraries adopted electronic indexing systems. Endless scrolling of pages on a computer screen replaced endless riffling through giant drawers of cards. Most libraries even offer their indexes on the Internet. (Ironically, libraries now have multiple computers on their premises, which in some cases take up almost as much room as the card catalogs did.)

## TONSILLECTOMIES

Tonsils are small glands that protect the respiratory tract from disease. Children get lots of colds and infections every year and for most of the 20th century doctors believed that tonsils only worked so many times before they became useless organs that actually served as a place for infections to fester. So tonsils were routinely taken out, usually if strep throat was contracted. A tonsillectomy required anesthesia and a night in the hospital, but afterward the sore throat made eating anything other than ice cream difficult, which sweetened the deal for the child. So why don't they perform tonsillectomies anymore? It turns out the conventional medical wisdom was wrong: tonsils don't wear out. In fact, they don't really do much at all. A 1963 British medical study found that children whose tonsils were removed were no less prone to infections than children who still had their tonsils. In other words, an operation millions of children had undergone was completely useless.

---

In Germany, Humpty-Dumpty is *Humpelken Pumpelken*. In Denmark, he's *Lille-Trille*.

## TELEGRAMS

Samuel Morse invented the telegraph in 1837. Electrical currents sent in a system of pulses and patterns (Morse code) were translated into words, forming messages, or "telegrams." It was the first means of instant long-distance communication, decades before the telephone. It caught on fast. Western Union had a coast-to-coast network of electrical telegraph lines in place by 1861. Messages would be sent from one telegraph office to another, then printed or written out, and hand-delivered to the intended recipient. They lasted well into the 20th century, even after the birth of the telephone, but faded in the late 1940s as phone service improved and long- distance calls became cheaper. Western Union is still around, but they've switched their business to wiring money.

## MENDING

Up until the 1950s, many mothers spent their evenings patching worn knees on pants, fixing shirt collars, and mending holes in dresses. Nothing was beyond fixing if money could be saved by not having to buy something new. Even socks were saved. The hole was stretched over a "darning egg" and a series of stitches filled the gap. But as women increasingly worked outside the home from the 1960s on, working mothers didn't want to spend what little extra time they had mending holes in socks. At the same time, mass-produced clothing was becoming less expensive and more disposable. Today, rips in pants seldom get patched and holes in socks rarely get darned. The old garments just get thrown away.

## UNANSWERED PHONES

For the first several decades of widespread phone usage, if nobody was around to answer the phone, the call was gone forever. Couldn't get out of the bathtub? Gone. Couldn't get the front door open in time? Gone. How many businesses missed an important sale? How many teenagers missed a big date? In 1960 Phonetel introduced Ansofone, America's first practical telephone answering machine—a heavy, clunky tape recorder with two reels: one to play outgoing messages and one to record incoming messages. Simpler phone jacks and cheaper technology made the next generation of answering machines popular in the 1970s. Now computerized "voice mail" has outpaced answering machines in sales since the late 1980s.

The first answering machines weighed about 10 pounds.

# DUBIOUS ACHIEVERS

*Some awards we all hope not to get some day.*

**M**OST MUGGABLE. Reiner Hamer of Öberhausen, Germany, was in the restroom of a nightclub when three men robbed him of his wallet. Hamer immediately borrowed a friend's cell phone, went outside to call the police...and got mugged again. Three different men held him up: the first took the phone; the second, his watch; the third, his cigarettes. Minutes later he was assaulted yet again, this time losing his jacket to a gang of five more muggers.

**BIGGEST BEANEATERS.** British supermarket giant Tesco did a survey in 2004 to find out which British town bought the most cans of baked beans per household. The winner: West Bromwich. "So loved are beans in West Bromwich," said Tesco spokeswoman Florinda Deiana, "that local shoppers buy an average 11 cans each week." In recognition, Tesco dubbed the town "the Windy City."

**BEST NOSE-DRINKER.** China's *Star Daily* newspaper reported on a man with a curious talent: Jin Guolong of Henan, China, can hold the rim of a glass up to his nose and "drink" through his nostrils. According to the report, Jin can nose-drink a full glass of orange juice in seconds.

**COOLEST CLIMBER.** In 2004, 35-year-old Paul McKelvey walked 100 miles from Liverpool to the top of Mount Snowden (3,560 feet)...with an 84-pound refrigerator strapped to his back. The ex–Royal Marine completed the trip in four days. And though it may have been a dubious achievement, he did it for a good cause: he raised money for a children's hospice called Zoe's Place.

**BIGGEST WINDBAG.** On May 25, 2005, lawyer Nicholas Stadlen finished his opening statement in defense of the collapsed Bank of Credit and Commerce International (BCCI). In doing so, he broke the record for the longest speech in British legal history: 119 days. The newspaper *The Mirror* noted the event with the headline: "I Rest My Face."

---

Number one cause of accidental death in the U.S.: car accidents, followed by falls.

# UNCLE JOHN CLEANS YOUR KITCHEN

*Spending your precious "reading room" time learning kitchen cleaning tricks may seem like a waste. But if it makes your chores pass more quickly, that frees up more time for the reading room, doesn't it?*

• A fun (and better) way to clean a blender: partially fill it with hot tap water, add a little soap, let it run for 10 seconds.

• You can remove minor scratches from glassware by "polishing" it with toothpaste.

• Smelly garbage disposal? Throw half a lemon down the drain and grind it up; the acid will kill the odor and replace it with the lemon's fresh scent.

• To clean chrome, use a damp sponge and baking soda. To remove rust from chrome, wrap your finger in aluminum foil and rub the chrome until the rust is gone, then wipe with a damp cloth.

• Denture cleaning tablets (Efferdent or a similar brand) can clean a smelly thermos. Fill it with warm water, drop in three denture tablets, let it sit for an hour, and then rinse.

• Eliminate coffee or tea stains in mugs by filling them with an equal mixture of table salt and vinegar.

• To clean a cutting board, sprinkle it with salt, then rub it with a slice of lemon.

• Washing an especially greasy load of dishes in the sink? Adding vinegar to the dish water will help cut the grease.

• Is grease making the drain in your kitchen sink sluggish? Pour in a cup of baking soda, followed by a cup of table salt, and then a quart of boiling water. You should notice an improvement right away.

• Does your microwave smell like fish? Pour a teaspoon of vanilla extract into a glass measuring cup and microwave on high for a minute.

• You know that an open box of baking soda absorbs bad odors in the fridge; a small bowl of vanilla extract will give it a nice scent.

• You can kill the germs in a damp sponge by putting it in the microwave for 30 seconds. As soon as you see steam, the germs are dead.

---

**In Bram Stoker's original novel, Dracula had a mustache.**

# THE SAD FATE OF MURDEROUS MARY

*Here's a look at one of the most bizarre
episodes in American circus history.*

## BIG DAY

On September 12, 1916, the Sparks World Famous Shows circus rolled into the town of Kingsport, Tennessee. In the days before television and radio, life could get pretty dull in small towns and the day the circus came to town was an event. The entire circus—performers, animals, everything—paraded through the middle of town to where the tents were going to be set up.

The animals in the Sparks circus included five elephants. "Mighty Mary," the largest of the five, was the star of the entire circus: she was featured on posters and billed as "the Largest Living Land Animal on Earth." Their parade through town went off without a hitch and so did the 2 p.m. matinee show. But a trip to a local watering hole later that day ended in tragedy.

## KIDS, DON'T TRY THIS AT HOME

A few days earlier, the circus had passed through St. Paul, Virginia, where a drifter named Walter "Red" Eldridge signed on as an assistant to the elephant trainer and continued with them to Kingsport.

It was Eldridge's job to make sure the elephants were fed and watered, and when the matinee performance ended, he and the other assistants climbed atop their charges and set off for a watering hole about a half-mile away. Eldridge was riding Mary, who led the rest of the elephants in single file. The procession drew a small crowd of townspeople, who followed closely behind.

According to witnesses, when Mary stopped to nibble on a watermelon rind that was lying in the street, Eldridge prodded her with his "elephant stick," a wooden stick with a metal hook at one end, to get her moving again. Mary ignored him and kept eating, so Eldridge whacked her really hard on the head.

The cruel blow was the last mistake Eldridge would ever make. Mary flew into a rage, grabbing Eldridge with her trunk and throwing him against a wooden stand. Then, while he was lying motionless on the ground, she walked over and stomped his head with her foot.

## MURDEROUS MARY

Terrified spectators ran for their lives as circus workers tried to calm Mary down. Today, if a mistreated elephant lashed out at an abusive handler, much of the public would sympathize with the elephant. That wasn't the case in 1916. According to newspaper reports, when Mary calmed down, the crowd returned, this time shouting, "Kill the elephant! Kill the elephant!"

Word of the death quickly spread beyond the town. Local newspapers covered the story extensively, giving Mary the nickname "Murderous Mary," and reported rumors that she had killed as many as 15 men in the past. *Fifteen* men was certainly an exaggeration, but had Mary killed before? In those days when an elephant killed someone, it was common for the circus to change the animal's name and quietly sell it to another circus. It's possible that this had been done with Mary. Almost a century after the fact, no one knows for sure.

## WHAT TO DO?

Given all the publicity, even if Charlie Sparks, the owner of the circus, had wanted to sell Mary to another show, it was doubtful he'd have been able to. Besides, Mary was the star of the show, the thing that people came to see more than anything else. Sparks wanted to keep Mary...if he could.

The summer touring season was nearly over; soon the circus would shut down for the winter. With any luck, by the following summer the furor would have died down. But if Sparks had hopes of keeping Mary with the circus until then, he quickly came to realize that it was impossible: Already the mayors of two upcoming stops, Johnson City and Rogersville, Tennessee, had sent word that if Mary was still with the circus it would not be allowed inside the city limits. As news of Eldridge's death continued to spread, it was likely that other towns would drop out, too. There were even rumors that the governor of Tennessee was preparing to order Mary destroyed, and that a mob of vigilantes armed with a Civil War cannon was on its way to do the job itself.

Russian bricklayers have been known to mix vodka into their mortar to keep it from freezing.

Sparks had bills to pay, a payroll to meet, and animals to feed. To do this he needed money; to get money he needed to put on his circus. He considered his options…and realized he didn't have any. Mary would have to be put down. What's more, she'd have to be put down in a very public way, so that people would be satisfied that she really *was* dead, not just lying low until the heat was off.

## HOW TO DO IT

Shooting Mary was too risky—a crowd would likely be on hand to witness the execution, and there was a danger that someone might be hit by rifle fire, or that Mary would go on a rampage if the first shot failed to kill her. Tearing Mary in half by tying her to two locomotives and sending them off in opposite directions was rejected as cruel and inhumane.

No doubt with an eye on publicity, Sparks decided that a public hanging was the best way to put Mary down. The nearby town of Erwin had a railroad yard with a 100-ton "derrick car" (a railroad car with a crane on it) that was used to load and unload lumber. It was strong enough to do the job, so Sparks had the circus make an unscheduled stop in Erwin the following day.

## THE MAIN EVENT

On the afternoon of September 13, the Sparks circus put on a matinee performance in Erwin. Mary was not part of the show— she was chained to a stake in the ground behind the big top and, according to eyewitnesses, was nervously swaying back and forth while the show went on without her.

When the matinee ended the *real* show began. A mob of as many as 3,000 people crowded into the railroad yard to witness the spectacle; throngs of people climbed atop locomotives and boxcars to get a better view. A little after 4 p.m., Mary and the other elephants were marched single file into the railroad yard and alongside the derrick car that would serve as the gallows. Mary was chained to the railroad track to keep her from escaping. Then the other elephants, who were there to keep Mary calm, were led away so that they wouldn't witness what was about to happen. As they walked away, Mary became visibly upset and once again started swaying back and forth. A circus worker placed a chain around Mary's neck, looped it through a steel ring to form a noose, and attached it to the derrick arm.

## A GRUESOME END

When the signal was given, the derrick operator pulled a lever and the derrick arm began to rise. As it did the chain began to tighten around Mary's neck. Her head was raised, her front feet lifted off the ground, and then the rear legs followed, until she was dangling in midair about six feet off the ground.

Suddenly there was a loud SNAP! and Mary crashed to the ground. The chain had snapped, and now Mary was loose. Terrified that she was about to go on a rampage, the crowd tried to run for it. But Mary didn't move—she just sat there, stunned, on her hindquarters. She had apparently broken her hip in the fall.

After a few minutes a circus worker climbed onto Mary's back and attached a heavier chain around her neck. The derrick arm was raised again and Mary was lifted off the ground. This time the chain held—a few minutes later she was dead. Later that day, her body was lowered into a hole that had been dug alongside the railroad track and buried. The exact location of her grave has since been forgotten.

## MEMORY OF AN ELEPHANT

In one sense, when Charlie Sparks had Mary killed he successfully put the unfortunate incident of Red Eldridge's death behind him. Johnson City and Rogersville lifted their bans, and the circus was permitted to perform. Life returned to normal.

In another sense, however, the story of Murderous Mary has never died. While Mary was being hanged, an unknown photographer in the crowd snapped a single picture of the big elephant dangling from her noose in midair. The photo still survives; if you look you can probably find a copy of it on the Internet.

Have you ever heard of Sparks World Famous Shows? Neither has anyone else—the small circus folded years ago and today only circus buffs remember it. What *has* survived is the infamous photograph of Mary hanging by the neck from the railroad derrick. It has achieved more fame than the Sparks circus ever did.

What about Erwin, Tennessee? To this day its greatest claim to fame is that it is "the town that hung the elephant," and Murderous Mary is (still) its most famous citizen. The townspeople have even been blamed for the incident, though the only reason it happened in Erwin was because that's where the railroad yard was. "It made people from Erwin look like a bunch of bloodthirsty rednecks," Hilda Padgett of the Unicoi County Historical Society told the Associated Press in 1999. Kingsport, the town where Red Eldridge actually died, emerged with its reputation unscathed.

## GONE...BUT NOT FORGOTTEN

If you ever happen to find yourself in Erwin, the railroad yard where Mary was killed is still there. Today it's owned by the CSX Corporation, one of the country's largest railroads. But you won't find any monuments, plaques, or other reminders that this is the place where Murderous Mary met her maker—embarrassed city fathers have squelched every attempt to create a memorial. "They want to keep it quiet, but it's part of our history," says Ruth Pieper, an Erwin resident who is working to get a memorial built on the site. "And if it's told correctly, people will understand and hopefully won't blame Erwin anymore."

\*　　\*　　\*

### A LOVE STORY

A tree toad loved a she-toad
who lived up in a tree.

He was a two-toed tree toad,
but a three-toed toad was she.

The two-toed tree toad tried to win
the three-toed she-toad's heart,

For the two-toed tree toad loved the
ground the three-toed tree toad trod.

The two-toed tree toad tried in
vain to sate her every whim.

From her tree toad bower
with her three-toed power,
the she-toad vetoed him.

---

More people are allergic to cow's milk than to any other food.

# FINGER LICKIN' QUIZ

*Here's another chance to test your pop culture IQ. Okay, so it's not an intelligence test…but it's fun. Do you know which products or brands spawned these advertising slogans? Answers on page 519.*

**1.** "Don't hate me because I'm beautiful."

**2.** "The quicker picker upper."

**3.** "Have it your way."

**4.** "Just do it."

**5.** "It's like having a borgasmord!"

**6.** "It's not nice to fool Mother Nature."

**7.** "Mother, please. I'd rather do it myself."

**8.** "I'd rather fight than switch."

**9.** "When you got it, flaunt it."

**10.** "Mama Mia, that's a spicy meat-a-ball!"

**11.** "They're magically delicious."

**12.** "When you care enough to send the very best."

**13.** "Strong enough for a man, but made for a woman."

**14.** "Finger lickin' good."

**15.** "You've come a long way, baby!"

**16.** "We bring good things to life."

**17.** "Double your pleasure, double your fun."

**18.** "We drive excitement."

**19.** "Less filling. Tastes great."

**20.** "How do you spell relief?"

**21.** "Betcha can't eat just one."

**22.** "Sometimes you feel like a nut; sometimes you don't."

**23.** "Ancient Chinese secret, huh?"

**24.** "Help! I've fallen and I can't get up!"

**25.** "Stronger than dirt."

**26.** "It's the real thing."

**27.** "No more tears."

**28.** "Nothin' says lovin' like something from the oven."

**29.** "Because life is not a spectator sport."

---

**Remember this tomorrow: An average person will forget 80% of what they learned today.**

# WORD ORIGINS

*A few more interesting stories about where words come from.*

## HOPSCOTCH

**Meaning:** A children's game of hopping into and over squares drawn on the ground

**Origin:** "The word *scotch* here has nothing to do with the inhabitants of Scotland. It's a 15th-century word for a 'cut, incision, scratch, or score on the ground,' which is how the boxes were drawn before kids got their hands on chalk. Schoolchildren have been playing *scotch-hoppers* since at least 1677." (From *Devious Derivations*, by Hugh Rawson)

## AGONY

**Meaning:** Extreme suffering

**Origin:** "This word originally was the Greek *agonia*, meaning 'contest,' especially any athletic contest. Since at least one party—the loser—in an athletic contest usually suffers some pain or anguish, the word gradually came to mean what it does today." (From *Dictionary of Word and Phrase Origins, Volume III*, by William and Mary Morris)

## CENT

**Meaning:** A monetary unit equal to one hundredth of a dollar

**Origin:** "Why are *pennies* called *cents* in America? As part of the trend to de-English our language at the time of the Revolution, Governor Morris proposed the word *cent*—one hundredth of a dollar—to replace the British word *penny*. The attempt was not entirely successful, since *penny* is still widely used on this side of the Atlantic." (From *Dictionary of Word and Phrase Origins, Volume II*, by William and Mary Morris)

## INVEST

**Meaning:** Put money into a financial plan with the expectation of a profit; devote one's time to an undertaking

**Origin:** "The etymological notion underlying *invest* is of 'putting

---

**Now you know:** The liquid inside a Magic-8 ball is a mix of water, antifreeze, and blue dye.

on clothes.' It comes from Latin *investire*, a compound verb formed from the prefix *in-*, and *vestis*, 'clothes.' It retained that original literal sense 'clothe' in English for several centuries, but now survives only in its metaphorical descendant. Its financial sense, first recorded in the early 17th century, is thought to have originated from the idea of dressing one's capital up in different clothes by putting it into a particular business, stock, etc." (From *Dictionary of Word Origins*, by John Ayto)

## BANG
**Meaning:** A sharp, loud noise or a hairstyle
**Origin:** "'Bangs,' the hair style, comes from the same root as 'bang,' the sound of a gun or slamming door. It comes from an Old Norse word, *banga*, meaning 'to hammer.' In English, 'bang' first meant 'to strike violently,' but gradually came to be used for any violent movement, especially one which caused a loud noise. It continued to evolve, which brings us at last to modern haircuts. 'Bangs' are so-called because they are created by cutting the hair 'bang-off'—abruptly and straight across the forehead." (From *The Word Detective*, by Evan Morris)

## HOAX
**Meaning:** An act meant to trick or dupe someone
**Origin:** "Believed to be a contraction of the word *hocus* from the term *hocus pocus*, which first appeared in the early 17th century. It may be derived from the name of a conjuror in the time of King James known as 'The Kings Majesties most excellent Hocus Pocus.' Before every trick he would call out the nonsense phrase, *Hocus pocus, tontus talontus, vade celeriter jubeo*. This phrase was itself probably an imitation (or mockery) of the Latin *hoc est corpus* ('this is my body'), used by Catholic priests performing the act of transubstantiation. (From *The Museum of Hoaxes*, by Alex Boese.)

\*     \*     \*

**A Groaner.** Two cows are standing next to each other in a field. Daisy says to Dolly, "I was artificially inseminated this morning." "I don't believe you," says Dolly. "It's true. No bull," says Daisy.

---

Gardeners' claim: Roses cut in the afternoon will last longer than ones cut in the morning.

# THE CURSE OF THE LITTLE RASCALS

*When Robert Blake was arrested in 2002 and charged with the murder of his wife, a lot of people began to look back and wonder if the kids who starred in the* Our Gang *films were under some kind of cloud.*

## BACKGROUND

According to *Our Gang* producer Hal Roach, 176 kids played in the 221 *Our Gang* films made between 1922 and 1944. Only a few of these became major stars in the series.

It's not unusual for child stars to have a difficult time as they move into adulthood, and if anything life in the 1920s, '30s, and '40s was even tougher. Children who worked on the series typically started out earning less than $100 a week, and they never earned residuals—when the *Our Gang* films made their way to television in the early 1950s, the kids didn't get a penny. Result: when their fame ended, they didn't have money to fall back on like child stars do today.

When you consider how many kids cycled through the *Our Gang* series, it stands to reason that quite a few of them would have problems later in life. Even so, the number of kids who suffered misfortune over the years is startling. You can't help but wonder: Are the Little Rascals cursed?

## LOSS OF INNOCENCE

• **Carl "Alfalfa" Switzer:** Like many of the Little Rascals, Switzer had trouble finding movie roles as he grew older. He landed bit parts in films like *It's a Wonderful Life* and *The Defiant Ones,* supporting himself at such odd jobs as bartender, dog trainer, and hunting guide between acting gigs. He was shot to death in 1959 following an argument over $50. He was 31. (Carl's older brother, Harold, also appeared in the *Our Gang* series; in April 1967 he murdered his girlfriend and then killed himself. He was 42.)

• **William "Buckwheat" Thomas:** When his career in front of the camera ended, Thomas became a film technician with the

Technicolor Corporation. In October 1980, a neighbor who hadn't seen Thomas in several days entered his home and found him dead in his bed. Cause of death: heart attack. Thomas was 49.

• **Robert "Wheezer" Hutchins:** A cadet in the Army Air Corps, Hutchins was killed in 1945 while trying to land his plane during a training exercise. He died a few days shy of his 20th birthday.

• **Matthew "Stymie" Beard:** A high school dropout, Beard fought a heroin addiction for more than 20 years and was frequently in and out of prison. He beat the habit in the 1970s, but passed away in 1981, at age 56. Cause of death: pneumonia, following a stroke.

• **"Darla" Hood Granson:** Contracted hepatitis while in the hospital for minor surgery and died in 1979 at the age of 47.

• **Norman "Chubby" Chaney:** Chaney's weight was due to a glandular problem; by the time he was 17 he weighed more than 300 pounds. In 1935 he had surgery to treat his condition; that dropped his weight down to 130 pounds, but he never regained his health. He passed away in 1936 at the age of 18.

• **"Scotty" Beckett:** Scotty was the kid who wore a cap turned to the side of his head. A classic case of a troubled former child star, Beckett slid into alcohol and drug abuse when his acting career petered out. He had two failed marriages, a history of violence, and numerous run-ins with the law. In 1968 he checked into a Hollywood nursing home after someone beat him up; two days later he was dead. Investigators found a bottle of pills and a suicide note by his bed, but the coroner never ruled on whether it was the beating or the barbiturates that killed him. He was 38.

• **William "Froggy" Laughlin:** Rear-ended and killed by a truck while delivering newspapers on his motor scooter in 1948. He was 16.

• **Richard "Mickey" Daniels:** Long estranged from his wife and children, Daniels died alone in a San Diego hotel room in 1970. Cause of death: cirrhosis of the liver. Years passed before his remains were identified and claimed by his family. Daniels was 55 when he died; he is buried in an unmarked grave.

• **Bobby Blake:** (He used his real name, Mickey Gubitosi, in the *Our Gang* films until 1942.) If you're charged with murdering your wife and you beat the rap, does that count as *being* cursed or *beat-*

---

Mark Twain called the accordion a "stomach Steinway."

*ing* the curse? In the 1990s, Blake took up with a woman named Bonnie Lee Bakley. He didn't know it at the time, but she was a celebrity-obsessed con artist who wanted to have a baby with a Hollywood star. Blake took the bait, and in 2000 Bakley gave birth to Blake's daughter. Five months later they were married.

On May 4, 2001, Bakley was shot in the head and killed while sitting in her car outside a restaurant where she and Blake had just eaten dinner. In April 2002, Blake was arrested and charged with Bakley's murder; in March 2005, a jury found him not guilty. He beat the rap, but the media continues to doubt his innocence. Blake says that as a result of the ordeal, he's now destitute.

## OTHER RASCALS' FATES

• **Robert "Bonedust" Young.** Fell asleep while smoking in bed in 1951; he died in the ensuing fire at the age of 33.

• **Jay "Pinky" Smith (aka the freckle-faced kid).** Stabbed to death in 2002 by a homeless man he'd befriended, who then dumped Smith's body in the desert outside of Las Vegas. He was 87.

• **"Dorothy" Dandridge.** Committed suicide in 1965 after losing all of her money in a phony investment scheme. She was 41.

• **Kendall "Breezy Brisbane" McComas.** Committed suicide in 1981, two weeks before being forced into retirement as an electrical engineer. He was 64.

• **Darwood "Waldo" Kaye.** Waldo was the rich kid with glasses who competed with Spanky and Alfalfa for Darla's affections. In 2002 he was struck and killed by a hit-and-run driver while walking on the sidewalk. He was 72.

• **Pete the Pup:** The first dog to play Pete was poisoned by an unknown assailant in 1930.

## VOICE OF REASON?

Hal Roach, who outlived many of his child stars and died in 1992 at the age of 100, never believed that the kids were cursed. "Naturally, some got into trouble or had bad luck," he told an interviewer in 1973. "They're the ones that made the headlines. But if you took 176 other kids and followed them through their lives, I believe you would find the same percentage of them having trouble in later life."

---

Six standard eight-post Legos can be combined in 102,981,500 different ways.

# FICTIONAL VACATION

*On page 96, we told you how you can visit the* Field of Dreams *baseball diamond. Here are some other tourist attractions based on fictional places.*

• Tourists can take a *Sopranos* tour in suburban New Jersey. Stops include Satriale's Pork Store, the place where Livia Soprano is "buried," and the Bada Bing nightclub. The tour includes cannolis and a meeting with actor Joe Gannascoli, who plays Vito on the show.

• Sam Spade, the detective in Dashiell Hammett's *The Maltese Falcon*, kept his office in the Hunter-Dulin Building at 111 Sutter Street, San Francisco. The building is real; the office is fictional.

• *Gunsmoke* was filmed in California, but set in Dodge City, Kansas. Since the 1960s, about 100,000 people a year visit the real Dodge City to see replicas of buildings from the show.

• The house used for exterior shots of *The Brady Bunch* is at 11222 Dilling Street, North Hollywood, California. The current residents installed an iron fence to keep out fans hoping to catch a glimpse of the Bradys.

• *The Wizard of Oz* takes place in Kansas, but neither the book nor the movie say *where* in Kansas. So the town of Liberal decided that it was *there*, and in 1981 opened a museum they call Dorothy's House—an old farmhouse that kind of looks like the one in the 1939 movie.

• The 1990s TV series *Northern Exposure* took place in the fictional town of Cicely, Alaska, but was filmed in the real town of Roslyn, Washington. The Roslyn Museum houses artifacts and memorabilia from the show.

• People still visit Fort Hays, Kansas, setting of the 1990 movie *Dances with Wolves*. Only problem: the movie was filmed in South Dakota.

• *Twin Peaks* was filmed in Snoqualmie, Washington, and North Bend, Washington. You can visit the show's Mar-T Cafe in North Bend, where they sell cherry pie, "a damn fine cup of coffee," and official Log Lady logs.

- What do **The Breakfast Club, Ferris Bueller's Day Off**, and **Sixteen Candles** have in common? All were written by John Hughes and all take place in Shermer, Illinois. It's a fictional place, based on Hughes's hometown of Northbrook, Illinois. Landmarks from the movie, however, are real. Fans can see the "Save Ferris" water tower and the high school used in *The Breakfast Club*.

- Visiting New York? Take the *Seinfeld* tour. It's led by Kenny Kramer, who inspired Michael Richards's Kramer character on the show. Stops include: the Soup Nazi's restaurant, Monk's Diner (Tom's Restaurant in real life), and the building used to film exterior shots of the office where Elaine worked. It's a great way to spend Festivus.

- Bedrock City in Custer, South Dakota, is a re-creation of the town of Bedrock from **The Flintstones**. It includes the Flintstone and Rubble homes, the main street (with a bank being held up by a caveman), and Mt. Rockmore, a mini Mt. Rushmore (with Fred, Barney, and Dino instead of presidents).

- **Little House on the Prairie** (the books and the TV show) is based on author Laura Ingalls Wilder's life, growing up in the 1860s near Wayside, Kansas. People who visit Wayside can see modern replicas of the show's schoolhouse, post office, and the Ingalls's cabin.

- Fans of **Gone With the Wind** can't visit Tara—it's fictional. But they can visit the Road to Tara Museum in Clayton County, Georgia. Highlights include replicas of some costumes used in the 1939 movie, such as Scarlett's drapery dress, two seats from the Atlanta movie theater where stars of the movie saw the film's premiere, and a copy of the novel autographed by the author, Margaret Mitchell.

- Andy Griffith was born in Mt. Airy, North Carolina, which became the model for Mayberry on **The Andy Griffith Show**. Every September, Mt. Airy holds "Mayberry Days" (cast members attend). There's a statue of Andy and Opie and replicas of Floyd's Barber Shop, the jail, and Andy's house. But don't look for the fishing hole seen in the opening credits—that's in Beverly Hills.

# SPY HUNT: GRAY DECEIVER, PART II

*Here's the second part of our intriguing tale of espionage, money, and politics. (Part I is on page 110.)*

## TO TELL THE TRUTH

The map of dead drops (places where spies and their handlers exchange money and secret documents) that the FBI found in CIA agent Brian Kelley's home was pretty incriminating, but it wasn't enough to secure a conviction, so the Bureau decided to trick Kelley into taking a lie detector test. They arranged for him to be transferred to a "new assignment," debriefing a non-existent Soviet defector. To be approved for the new assignment, Kelley's CIA superiors explained to him, he had to take a polygraph test.

The results of the test stunned even the seasoned FBI mole hunters—Kelley passed with flying colors. There wasn't a flicker of a guilty response anywhere on the test. Fooling a lie detector test so thoroughly takes a lot of skill. This guy was *good*.

## KNOCK KNOCK

Next, they set up a "false flag" operation: an FBI agent masquerading as an SVR agent knocked on Kelley's door and warned him that he was about to be arrested for spying and needed to leave the country. The agent then handed Kelley a written escape plan and told him to be at a nearby subway station the following evening. Then the man disappeared into the night...and the FBI waited to see what Kelley would do. If he made a run for the subway station, that would in effect be an acknowledgement that he was indeed a spy—people who aren't spying for the SVR don't need help fleeing the country.

The next morning Kelley went to work as usual and reported the incident to the CIA. He even gave an accurate description of the "SVR agent" to a sketch artist. Once again the FBI was astonished by Kelley's skill under pressure. Somehow he must have detected that the SVR guy was a fake and was not taken in by the trick. He was so cool and collected that the investigators gave him

---

"Bubble gum" flavor originally was a combination of wintergreen, vanilla, and cinnamon.

a new nickname—the "Iceman."

## IN YOUR FACE

The FBI still lacked enough evidence to get a conviction and was running out of options. They made a last-ditch attempt at tricking Kelley into incriminating himself. On August 18, 1999, he was called into a meeting at CIA headquarters and confronted by two FBI agents who told him that they knew everything about his spying, even his SVR code name, KARAT. Kelley professed astonishment and denied everything, so the FBI agents pulled out Kelley's handwritten map. "Explain this!" one of them said.

"Where did you get my jogging map?" Kelley asked.

The interview did not go as the FBI had hoped. Kelley didn't crack—he even offered to answer questions without his lawyer present and to take another polygraph test. The agents turned him down: if Kelley could fake one lie detector test, he could fake two.

After questioning him for more than seven hours, the agents gave up. Kelley was stripped of his CIA badge and security clearances, placed on paid administrative leave, and escorted out of CIA headquarters. But he wasn't arrested or charged with spying—there still wasn't enough evidence. He spent the next 18 months on leave while the FBI built a case against him. The mole hunters confronted his daughter, also a CIA employee, and told her that her father was a spy. She claimed to know nothing about her father's spying. Neither did Kelley's other children when they were confronted, nor did his colleagues and close friends when they were interviewed. No one had suspected a thing. Kelley was that good.

## SHOPPING

By the spring of 2000 the FBI had compiled a 70-page report recommending that the Justice Department charge Kelley with espionage, which is punishable by death.

While the Justice Department considered the matter, the FBI expanded its search for evidence against Kelley to the former Soviet Union. They tracked down a retired KGB officer who they thought might have some knowledge of the case and lured him to the United States for a "business meeting." Then, when the officer arrived in the United States, the FBI made its pitch—it was will-

Q: What was the first record album to go gold in the U.S.? A: *Oklahoma!* in 1958.

ing to pay him a fortune in cash if he would reveal the identity of the mole. The ex-KGB officer made a counteroffer: he had the mole's entire case file in his possession and was willing to sell it outright to the FBI. He added that the file even contained a tape recording of a 1986 telephone conversation of the mole talking to his Russian handlers, so there was no question that the FBI would have the evidence it needed to win a conviction.

## VOICE RECOGNITION

The FBI eventually agreed to buy the file for $7 million. It also agreed to help the KGB officer and his family to relocate to the United States under assumed names. The money changed hands, and in November 2000 the file slipped out of Russia and arrived at FBI headquarters. There was enough material in it to fill a small suitcase—hundreds of documents, dozens of computer disks, a cassette tape, and an envelope with the words "Don't Open This" written on it.

The FBI was convinced it finally had the evidence it needed to convict Brian Kelley on spying charges and to put him to death. All the agents had to do was read the files, listen to the recorded conversation on the tape, and build their case. They put the cassette in a tape recorder, pushed PLAY, and waited to hear Kelley's voice. Their long campaign to bring him to justice was at an end.

## AN UNEXPECTED DEVELOPMENT

Or was it? It quickly became obvious that the voice the FBI heard talking to the KGB agent wasn't Brian Kelley's. Once again, the FBI agents were in awe of Kelley's abilities as a spy. Even when talking to his KGB handlers, he had had the good sense to protect his identity by having an intermediary—a "cut out," as they're known—make his call for him.

One of the FBI agents, Michael Waguespack, recognized the voice, but couldn't place it. Meanwhile another agent, Bob King, had started reading through some of the spy's correspondence with his Russian handlers and had come across an unusual expression that sounded familiar: in two different places, the spy quoted World War II General George S. Patton telling his troops, "Let's get this over with so we can kick the $#%@ out of the purple-pissing Japanese." Bob King remembered his supervisor in the Russian analytical unit, an agent named Robert Hanssen, repeatedly using the same quote in conversation.

Huh?

"I think that's Bob Hanssen," he told the other agents. Waguespack knew Hanssen, too, and he went back to listen to the tape again. Sure enough—the voice was Robert Hanssen's.

## OFF THE HOOK

It took a minute for the mole hunters to realize it (and probably longer than that for them to admit it), but they had been on the trail of the wrong man, an employee of the wrong intelligence agency, for more than three years.

Brian Kelley wasn't a master spy at all—he was an innocent man. The searches and electronic surveillance hadn't found anything because there wasn't anything to find. He passed the polygraph test because he was telling the truth. He reported the "false flag" sting to his superiors because he had nothing to hide. His jogging map really was a jogging map. The "dry cleaning" at Niagara Falls? He was there on official CIA business and the mole hunters tailing him happened to lose him in traffic. Shopping at the same mall as the SVR? A coincidence—everybody shops somewhere.

With his time in the Air Force and the CIA, Kelley had served his country with honor and distinction for 38 years; yet all he had to show for it was a 70-page FBI report to the Department of Justice recommending that he be tried for espionage and executed.

## BAD LUCK, GOOD LUCK

What are the odds that a retiring KGB officer would have taken Robert Hanssen's file with him when he retired, and that the FBI would have been successful in tracking him down? Or that they would have been willing to cough up $7 million for the file? To this day, Kelley, his family, and his friends all wonder what would have become of him had the FBI been unable to get (or unwilling to pay for) Hanssen's KGB file.

*Now that the FBI had Hanssen's file, how would*
*they catch this elusive master of espionage?*
*Part III of the story is on page 459.*

---

Some air fresheners contain numbing agents, which anesthetize the nose.

# ANGELS & HONEY TRAPS

*Here's some more spy lingo to practice before
you make your next brush pass.*

- **Confidential:** The classification for secret documents whose disclosure would result in "damage" to U.S. national security. If disclosure would result in "*serious* damage," it's classified **Secret**. If disclosure would result in "*exceptionally grave* damage," it's **Top Secret**.

- **Angel:** Member of an enemy intelligence service.

- **Talent spotter:** Someone on the lookout for foreign nationals who might be recruited as spies.

- **Nightcrawler:** A talent spotter who hangs out in bars, strip clubs, or other seedy places looking for military or government employees who can be plied with booze, drugs, sex, or blackmailed into becoming spies.

- **The Firm:** The CIA; also known as the Company.

- **Blowback:** False information that is planted in the foreign news media in the hope that it will *blow back* and be reported as legitimate news in the United States.

- **Honey trap:** Using sex to entrap an existing spy or to blackmail someone into becoming a spy.

- **Brush pass/contact pass:** Passing information to or from a spy as you brush past him on the street or in a crowd.

- **Walk in:** Someone who becomes a spy by walking into a foreign embassy or similar post and volunteering his services.

- **Raven:** A male agent who uses sex to entrap females into becoming spies—a spy gigolo.

- **Blind date:** When an intelligence officer meets with his spy at a time and place of the spy's choosing. Blind dates are dangerous because the spy could be setting a trap.

- **Turn:** To cause an agent to become a double agent, i.e., betray her own spy agency and begin working for another.

- **Re-doubled agent:** A double agent who's been caught and forced to feed misleading information to the enemy.

---

**Pigbird:** A baby pelican eats about 150 pounds of fish in its first three months.

# BOOMERANG!

*Okay, let's throw this history of the boomerang*
*out there and see where it goes...OW!*

**GET BACK**
It ranks right up there with the kangaroo and the koala as being a quintessential Australian icon: the simple and fascinating device known as the boomerang. Believed by aviation experts to be the earliest heavier-than-air flying device made by humans, it has been part of Australian Aboriginal culture for thousands of years. Its invention may very well have been an accident.

Archaeological evidence suggests that Australian Aboriginals used "throwing sticks" for hunting at least as early as 15,000 years ago. They were long, thin, bladelike weapons specifically designed to fly as far and as *straight* as possible. So how did they end up with one that returned to the thrower? One theory is that some ancient hunter made a throwing stick that was shorter and lighter than usual and from a piece of wood with a pronounced curve in it, features that caused it to fly in a circular path back toward the point of origin. That made it relatively useless as a weapon, being difficult to throw accurately and too light to do serious damage to an animal. So why are they still around? Probably because they were simply fun to throw and catch. Whatever the reason, the boomerang was invented in southeastern Australia at least 10,000 years ago, and over the centuries became an integral part of aboriginal cultures throughout the southern part of the continent.

## EARLY AEROSPACE ENGINEERS
What makes a boomerang return to its thrower? The laws of aerodynamics—applied sideways. A boomerang, with its V-shape, is basically two small wings joined together. They are shaped like airplane wings, with one flat side and one curved side. On an airplane the curved side is the top of the wing. As it moves through the air, the laws of aerodynamics cause air pressure to build up on the flat side, creating *lift* that pushes up on the bottom of the wing. The faster the wing moves through the air, the more lift it generates.

---

**Can ewe believe this? The first dice were made from sheep ankle bones.**

Because a boomerang spins like a propeller while it flies forward, at any given moment one of the two wings is moving in the direction of the flight. That means it's moving through the air faster than the other wing and, therefore, creating more lift. Since a boomerang is thrown to fly vertically, rather than horizontally like an airplane, the lift pushes it to the side rather than up. It keeps pushing as it continues to fly, sending it on a curved trajectory which—if you know how to throw it correctly—will send it all the way back to you.

## BOOMERANG FACTS

• Throwing sticks weren't unique to Australia—ancient examples have been found all around the world. Several were even discovered in the tomb of King Tut. Evidence shows, however, that only in Australia was one developed that actually returned to the thrower.

• There were more than 500 languages spoken by different tribal groups in Australia when Europeans arrived, and there were many different names for the returning throwing stick. *Boomerang* comes from a word in the Dharuk language of the Turuwal people, from the area around what is now Sydney.

• Joe Timbery, an Aboriginal designer, thrower, and boomerang champion, was world-renowned among boomerang fans. In 1954 he even demonstrated his skills for Queen Elizabeth. Among his feats that day: having 10 boomerangs in the air simultaneously, and catching every one.

• In the 1960s boomerangs found their way into the world of competitive sports. Every two years, international teams compete for the Boomerang World Cup. (2004 winner: Germany.)

• Manual Schultz of Switzerland holds the world record for the longest throw with a full return: 780 feet.

• In 1993 John Gorski of Avon, Ohio, threw a boomerang that caught a thermal updraft—and flew up to an elevation of 600 feet. It stayed aloft for 17 minutes...before Gorski caught it again.

• Traditional warning to new boomerangers: "Remember—you are the target!"

# BRUSHSTROKES

*Painters don't always paint with paints;
sometimes they paint with words.*

"When I judge art, I put my painting next to a God-made object, like a tree or flower. If it clashes, it is not art."
—Marc Chagall

"Painting is the grandchild of nature. It is related to God."
—Rembrandt

"There was a reviewer who wrote that my pictures didn't have any beginning or any end. He didn't mean it as a compliment, but it was."
—Jackson Pollock

"Painting is stronger than I am. It can make me do whatever it wants."
—Pablo Picasso

"Painting is one thing but art is another. You can teach an elephant to paint, but you can't teach it to be an artist."
—Warren Criswell

"I paint because I need to. I paint whatever passes through my head without any other consideration."
—Frida Kahlo

"I shut my eyes in order to see."
—Paul Gauguin

"People discuss my art and pretend to understand as if it were necessary to understand, when it's simply necessary to love."
—Claude Monet

"I paint for myself. I don't know how to do anything else, anyway."
—Francis Bacon

"Literature expresses itself by abstractions, whereas painting, by means of drawing and color, gives concrete shape to sensations and perceptions."
—Paul Cézanne

"I hate flowers—I paint them because they're cheaper than models and they don't move."
—Georgia O'Keeffe

"Drawing is like making an expressive gesture with the advantage of permanence."
—Henri Matisse

"Only when he no longer knows what he is doing does the painter do good things."
—Edgar Degas

"The pain passes, but the beauty remains."
—Pierre-Auguste Renoir

Take our word for it: It takes a Twinkie about 45 seconds to explode in the microwave.

# ANIMALS IN THE NEWS

*Some news stories that will make you go wild.*

**P**ET PROJECT
"A Chinese man pretending to be a hunchback tried to smuggle his pet turtle on to a plane. Wu, who is in his 60s, strapped the turtle to his back before boarding the plane to Chongqing. He got through security but was then stopped by a guard who thought his hump looked odd. A quick search uncovered an eight-inch diameter turtle weighing about 11 pounds. Wu, who was flying home after eight years in Guangzhou, said he knew he wasn't allowed to take live animals on board but was very attached to his turtle. Finally, he changed planes and checked the pet as baggage."

**—Ananova**

### JUST THE FAX
"A kitten picked the wrong place to relieve herself when she peed on a fax machine, sparking a fire in her Japanese owner's house. Investigators concluded that the blaze was caused by a spark generated when the cat urine soaked the machine's electrical printing mechanism. The fire damaged the kitchen and living room before it was put out by the homeowner, who was treated for mild smoke inhalation, said Masahito Oyabu, a fireman at the Nagata fire station in central Kobe. 'If you have a cat or a dog,' added Oyabu, 'be careful where they urinate.'"

**—Reuters**

### RUN AWAY!
"Firemen in the eastern Ukrainian city of Donetsk fled a burning sauna in panic after mistaking a three-meter boa constrictor for a fire hose, the Itar-Tass news agency reported. The reptile, named Yasha by its owner, had succumbed to smoke and lost consciousness on the floor before the emergency workers arrived to tackle the blaze. A member of the startled fire crew eventually heeded pleas by the sauna staff to save the snake and dragged it to safety."

**—Mail & Guardian (U.K.)**

---

In Ventura County, California, it's illegal for cats or dogs to mate without a permit.

## BIRDIE

"Two storks in Germany are in something of a muddle, having stolen a mass of golf balls from a course, and filled their nest with them. The pair of bird-brains have now built *two* nests in the middle of the green in order to house their expanding collection. It is thought that they are collecting the balls because they think the little white spheres are eggs, and are trying to hatch them. Bird expert Georg Fiedler said their choice of location is nothing short of a 'biological sensation,' because usually storks nest exclusively in trees and buildings. 'Between 1894 and 1997,' he said, 'only 16 stork couples have ever been reported to have had their nests on the ground.'"

—*New Telegraph* (U.K.)

## WEIRDY WOODPECKER

"Car owners in Sullivan, New York, are covering their mirrors in an attempt to outsmart a territorial woodpecker who apparently believes his reflection is an enemy. Tim Taylor, owner of Thruway Auto Glass, said he replaced 30 smashed mirrors last year and 18 this year, all from cars of people who live in this area east of Syracuse. 'People come in pretty mad. One guy's been here three times already because he keeps forgetting to cover the mirrors,' Taylor said. Anne Miller has had two mirrors on her Pontiac Grand Prix smashed and watched the bird attack her neighbor's Malibu. 'I told him to shoo,' she said. 'But instead of flying off, he walked across the windshield and did the passenger mirror. I was flabbergasted.'"

—*The Post-Standard*

\* \* \*

## AS THE WORM TURNS

Most Canadians are probably unaware of it, but according to scientists, there are virtually no native earthworms in Canada. There once were, but the last ice age, during which nearly all of Canada was covered by ice sheets and which ended approximately 14,000 years ago, wiped them out. They never recovered. When Europeans settled Canada, the soils of imported plants and the hooves of animals carried European earthworms, which, with no competition, soon took over the country's soil.

---

More blonde hair dye is sold in Dallas, Texas, than any other U.S. city. (Insert blonde joke here.)

# HAIR IN CANADA...

*Hair's the news from Canada.*
*(Remember: you heard it hair first.)*

**M**ONSTER HAIR
Nine people from Teslin, Yukon Territory, reported seeing "a large hairy man" in July 2005. Chucka Choumant and Trent Smarch, two men who saw the creature, said it was more than nine feet tall and completely covered in hair. They believed it to be the legendary Sasquatch and pointed to some evidence it left behind: a tuft of reddish-brown hair they found in some branches. The hair was sent to a conservation officer in Whitehorse where, they hoped, DNA testing would determine just what the creature was. The results came back a few weeks later. It was bison hair.

**PROTEST HAIR**
Two Saskatchewan ranchers were upset when the United States banned Canadian cattle imports after the mad cow scare in 2003. Early in 2004, Jay Fitzpatrick and Miles Anderson decided to show their displeasure by refusing to cut their hair until the ban was lifted. They expected it to last only a few months, but a year later the ban was still on. The protest attracted national attention and caused some unforeseen problems: "I squeal like a little girl pulling that comb through my hair," Fitzpatrick said. When the ban was rescinded in July 2005, the two men finally got haircuts. And they turned the barber visit into a charity event: dozens of locals turned up to watch their long locks get clipped—and raised more than $3,000 for the local curling rink.

**FARM HAIR**
In January 2005, Dr. Margaret Gruber, an agricultural researcher for the Canadian government, announced a new project: growing hairy canola plants. She hoped that they would help control flea beetles, which now cause an estimated $150 million in damage to Canadian canola crops annually. The beetles, she said, "don't like hair to get in their way." Canola naturally has small hairs, but the researchers are going to spend the next three years making them even hairier.

## VIOLENT HAIR

In 2004 a 26-year-old Winnipeg man got his hair cut and dyed in a salon in a local mall. He didn't like it. He returned the following day and demanded his money back. The store offered to recolor his hair, and the man accepted—but he didn't like it that time, either. "There was nothing you could do to make him happy," the colorist told the *Winnipeg Sun*. "First it was too ashy. Then it was too gold, then it wasn't gold enough." The man then threatened the salon employee, and security guards were called. Suddenly, a witness said, "It became like professional wrestling." The man punched one of the guards in the face and kicked another, then proceeded to trash the store. Police finally subdued the man and charged him with assault, saying it was the city's first known case of "hair rage."

## BODY HAIR

Every February people from all over Canada—and many from around the world—flock to the annual Yukon Sourdough Rendezvous in Whitehorse. The festival celebrates the rugged lifestyle of the people in the far, frozen north. One of the most popular events at the festival is the "Women's Hairy Leg Contest." Contestants compete in three different leg-hair categories: the densest hair, the longest hair, and the most horrific hair. The winners are chosen by a local barber. Their prize: each receives a gold-plated razor.

## HILL HAIR

People who visit the town of Hairy Hill, Alberta, often ask how the town got its name. The answer can be found in the University of Alberta's Folklore and History Collection (in a document entitled "How Hairy Hill Got Its Name"): When the first settlers arrived in the late 1800s, they were puzzled by one aspect of the place they'd chosen as the site of their new homes. "Everywhere they looked they saw large mats of hair covering the ground." They didn't figure it out until the next spring, when they saw hundreds of buffalo "roaming lazily along the slopes of the hill." It turned out that the hill was a regular spring feeding ground for the bison—and every spring they shed their heavy winter coats. And that is how Hairy Hill got its name.

---

In a microwave, water molecules vibrate at the rate of 5 billion times per second.

# FIRST-CLASS MAIL

*Way back in the 20th century, people used to correspond through the real mail—using real paper and everything. Here are some hilarious old letters we recently found.*

To: A. J. Child and Son, Mail Order House
123 Washington Ave,
St. Louis, Missouri

Gentlemen:
   Your advertisement states that you can furnish everything. My need is simple. I would ask you to rush by express one corpse. Make it as fresh as possible.

                                    Respectfully yours,
                                    Dr. J. Dollison

*And the response...*

Dr. J.Dollison
Eugene, Oregon

Dear Dr. Dollison,
   There are a number of our customers that we would like to annihilate and deliver to you in the form you have requested. Also, we have a useless employee that we have time and again asked to pick up papers under the elevator. If we are successful, shall advise you further. In the mean time cannot fill your order for a corpse.

                        A. J. Child and Son
                        Mail Order House

**During WWII, Disney created over 1,000 military insignias for the armed services.**

Dr. J. J. Newman
New Orleans, La.

Sir:
I am on to you and your kind. Yesterday my children had some dental work done on their teeth by you. Then you gave them some candy to eat. Candy makes more cavities as everyone knows. first you fill their cavities, then you fill my children full of candy to make more cavities to make more work for yourself. This could go on infinitely if I did not discover your scheme. I will not pay you for either the work done on James and Mary, nor for the candy you gave them.

Not as ever,
Mrs. A. Kern

*From a Chinese clerk applying for a post in England...*

Dear Sir,
I am Wang. It is for my personal benefit that I write for a position in your honourable house. I have a flexible brain. My education was impressed upon me in the Peking University. I can frive a type-writer with good noise and myh English is great. My references are of good and should you hope to see me they eill be read by you with great pleasure.

My last job has left itself from me for the good reason that the large man is dead.

It was on account of no fault of mine.

So honorable sirs what about it? It I can be of big use to you I Will arrive on some date that you should guess.

Yours faithfully,
WANG

In England, drunk driving became illegal in 1872.

Marshall Field Co.
State Street
Chicago, Ill.

Gentlemen:
   Where do you get that stuff about
"the customer is always right"? I think
you are all wrong. Now if I am right
about you being wrong, then the customer is not always right.
   I am a customer of your store so (Let
me quote from the classics) ib so
facto, I am right by your own admission. Then if I am right, you are
wrong, and if I am wrong, you are
liars.
   Go sit on a tack.

                          Yours truly,
                          B. Boone

Copy to:
My Attorney

---

Mme. Ara Hats
88 E. 57th Street
New York, New York

Dear Mme:
   I wear the front of my hat backwards
because the front part back makes the back
front more becominger. Is it a mistake?
                          Julia P.

---

The world's first known vending machine dispensed holy water. (Egypt, A.D. 100)

# "I KNOW SOMEONE WHO LOOKS JUST LIKE YOU"

*Uncle John has news for you: you may have a twin brother
or sister that you know nothing about. Sound crazy? It
sounded crazy to these folks, too…but it was true.*

## JENNY FINDS MARGARET

Jenny Mitchell, 57, of Windsor, England, had always known she was adopted, but she knew nothing of her birth mother. In 1997 she decided to see what she could find out, so she sent away for a copy of her birth certificate. She noticed that the time of birth—4:00 p.m.—was written down next to the date of birth.

In some countries it's common for the hospital to note the time of birth, but as Mitchell learned, in Great Britain they only note the time of birth when they need to distinguish between one multiple birth and another. "It took a while for the penny to drop," she told England's *Sunday Mirror*. "And then my head started reeling. I couldn't believe it. I was a twin!"

In Great Britain adoption records are kept secret, so when Mitchell started looking for her sister she got nowhere…until she hired a detective who was an expert at tracking down long-lost relatives. He found Mitchell's sister, Margaret Williams, living in Cardiff, Wales. Williams was stunned. Her first inkling that she had an identical twin was when the detective called her one morning in 1998. "I asked him to break the news to Margaret," Mitchell says. "I was frightened she might not want to know me. But when we got talking it was as if we'd talked all our lives."

## BRENT AND GEORGE FIND EACH OTHER

In 1971 Laura Cain, a 20-year-old college sophomore, became pregnant by her boyfriend, Randy Holmes, and nine months later gave birth to fraternal twins. The stress of caring for twins was difficult for them, so they placed the babies in foster care while they put their lives in order. A few months later they got married, and went to the foster care agency and got their twin sons, George and Marcus, back. Or at least that's what they thought, for 20

---

The chemical process that turns bread into toast is called the Maillard reaction.

years, until September, 1991, when a kid named Brent Tremblay happened to enroll at Carleton University in Ottawa. One afternoon Brent was sitting in a student lounge when a girl walked up to him and said, "Hi, George!" When Brent told her his name wasn't George, she gave him a funny look and walked off. A few days later it happened again; but this time the girl went and got her friend George—George Holmes—to show him the guy who looked like him. "It was like looking into a mirror," George says. "It was incredible."

George and Brent looked alike, shared many of the same interests, and even had similar mannerisms. Their friends insisted that they had to be identical twins, but how could they be? Brent was adopted, and George lived with his biological parents. And he *already* had a twin brother—Marcus. Still, the resemblance was so uncanny that even they began to wonder.

In August 1993, all three boys and Laura Cain had their DNA tested. The results confirmed that George and Brent are, indeed, identical twins, and that Laura Cain is their birth mother. (Laura is certain the doctor who delivered them told her they were *fraternal* twins, which is why she wasn't troubled by the fact that George and Marcus didn't look alike.)

So who is Marcus really? An investigation revealed that Brent and George were placed in the same foster home with a third newborn—Marcus—who'd been born to a different mother five days earlier. When Laura and Randy went to get their twins back, the foster home accidentally gave them the wrong kid. Marcus went home with George; Brent was left behind at the foster home and was later put up for adoption. How could such a mixup happen? Ottawa's Children's Aid Society looked into the matter, but after 20 years they were unable to come up with anything. By then the woman who ran the foster home was in her 80s and suffering from Alzheimer's. They'll never know how it happened.

## LINDA FINDS IAN

Linda Sloan knew she was adopted: she lived in a children's home until she was adopted by a family in Clackmannanshire, Scotland. But that's *all* she knew—and probably would have been all she'd *ever* know, had she not bumped into one of her adoptive mother's relatives while vacationing in Spain in 1997. That relative put her in touch with another family member who had worked in the children's home where Linda spent her early years. And that family member remembered that Linda had a twin brother.

Linda spent the next two years searching for her brother, and came up with nothing. Finally in 1999, she contacted the "Helpline" column of her local newspaper, the *Scottish Daily Record*, and asked for their assistance. After two years of searching on her own, how long did it take the paper to find her brother? Two days. Then the telephone rang and "a voice asked if I was the L. Sloan in the *Daily Record*," Linda recounted. "I said I was, and he said, 'Well, I'm your brother.' "

The caller—Ian McLuckie—filled Linda in on their life story. He'd been raised by their birth mother, who had given birth to twins following a wartime affair with an American G.I. Two kids turned out to be too much for the single mom, so she put Linda up for adoption and kept Ian. She never gave Ian even a hint that he had a twin sister out there somewhere. "I can't get my head round the fact that after 54 years, I have a sister," Ian says. "It has all been so amazing."

## WENDY FINDS JOHN

When she was a kid growing up in the town of Cheltenham, England, Wendy Brooks, 62, had no idea that she was adopted, let alone a twin. Then, when she was about 10 years old, her cousin blurted it out during an argument. She immediately confronted her adopted mother, Annie Finch, who admitted the truth and told Wendy how she'd been adopted. Ten years earlier, Finch explained, she had caught a woman abandoning a twin boy and girl on her doorstep. Finch could only afford to take one child, and she wanted a girl, so she took Wendy. The birth mother left with her son, and Finch never learned what happened to them.

Wendy married an American when she was 15 and moved to Oklahoma two years later. She thought about her brother all the time, but it wasn't until she was in her mid-50s that she became obsessed with tracking him down. The search dragged on for six long years. Finally, in 2001 she tracked down John Bennett, a poultry farmer living in Suffolk, England, and told him she was his twin. Bennett, who had been raised in an orphanage, knew nothing of his birth mother and was relieved to finally know something about his past. "I haven't come off the ceiling since it started," he told England's *Guardian* newspaper. "I didn't know I had a twin, though I always had a feeling that *something* was out there."

## THE ROSEENS FIND BRYANNA

In 2001 Randy and Jane Roseen were in the process of adopting an orphaned baby girl from the People's Republic of China. They sent a care package to the foster home, and with it they included a small disposable camera. When Randy flew to China to get the girl, whom they named Cyanna, the camera was included with her belongings from the foster home.

When the Roseens had the film in the camera developed, a few photos showed Cyanna lying in her crib with another baby that looked just like her. The babies weren't officially listed as twins in the foster home's records because they'd been found separately—Cyanna had been abandoned at a hospital, and the other baby had been found on the doorstep of a government building. But they looked so much alike that the foster home assumed they were twins and put them together in the same crib. Had they been officially recognized as twins, Chinese adoption policy would have required that the two girls be adopted together. But they weren't, so they were split up.

The Roseens decided to adopt the second child. Officials at China's Center of Adoption Affairs were skeptical that the babies were really twins, but when they saw the photographs the resemblance was so striking that they ordered DNA tests. The tests confirmed that the girls were a genetic match. And not a moment too soon: the other girl was about to be adopted by another family. Months of paperwork and red tape followed, but by April 2002 everything was in order and the second baby, whom they named Bryanna, was delivered into their arms. "It's like a thousand miracles," Randy says. "Every time something went wrong, someone would step in."

\*    \*    \*

"Every parting gives a foretaste of death, every reunion a hint of resurrection."
—Arthur Schopenhauer

---

In 1965 a U.S. Navy bomber accidentally dropped a "practice" bomb on a store in Florida.

# BAD GRANNY

*Why, Grandma, what big teeth you've got!*

## GRANNY'S GOT A GUN

"A bored granny has been given a suspended prison sentence after staging a fake bank robbery as a practical joke. The 80-year-old, identified only as 'Elfriede,' threatened a cashier at a bank in Austria with a toy pistol and hissed, 'This is a stickup.' Then she started to laugh. 'My heart stopped for a second,' the terrified bank employee said later. 'But when she started laughing, I realized that it was just a joke.'

"When the pensioner told the court that she'd done it 'for a laugh,' the judge warned her that she wouldn't be let off so lightly if she does it again within the next three years.

"Elfriede replied, 'If I live that long. But thanks.'"

—Ananova

## BLACK MARKET BABA

"Russian police have arrested a gun-smuggling granny who kept mobsters supplied with everything from artillery to assault rifles.

"The newspaper *Komsomolskaya Pravda* said Tuesday that 'Baba Nina' (Grandma Nina) and her eight-person gang had been bringing in weapons from the Baltics for more than a year. The report described the woman as a Robin Hoodish figure who supported a large number of relatives and a handicapped son while she and her husband lived in a modest apartment with only a black-and-white TV. But it added that the pensioner ran her gang with 'an iron hand' and knew most of the mobsters in the region.

"Disguising herself as one of the millions of 'shuttle traders'—small-time entrepreneurs who buy goods cheap abroad, then sell them at a profit back home—Baba Nina flew to Lithuania twice a month, returning with black-market weapons hidden in her bags among cheap T-shirts and trousers. On the telephone, she spoke in code to gang members, calling machine guns 'big trousers' and handguns 'small trousers.' The newspaper said she is now in jail, but has settled in nicely. 'Other prisoners pay her respect.'"

—Associated Press

In the weightlessness of space, an astronaut's heart actually shrinks.

## GANJA GRANNY

"Meet Molly Williams. The 78-year-old West Virginia woman may have the distinction of being America's oldest pot dealer. She was nabbed last week on felony drug charges after state police investigators executed a search warrant on the woman's home and discovered two pounds of marijuana (divided for distribution in plastic baggies) stashed in a grocery bag at the 'bottom of a deep freeze.' Williams's boyfriend, 72-year-old Jack White, told cops that the pot was his old lady's. She now faces 15 years in prison."

—**The Smoking Gun**

## ORGAN-IZED CRIME

"The boy thought his grandmother was taking him to Disneyland, but Russian police say she had other plans: to sell her grandson so his organs could be used for transplants. Police in Ryazan, 125 miles southeast of Moscow, said Saturday that they arrested a woman after they were tipped that she was trying to sell her grandson to a man who was going to take him to the West. There his organs were to be removed and sold, a Ryazan police officer said. After a surveillance operation, police moved in to arrest the woman, who was being aided in the scheme by the boy's uncle. They expected to get about $70,000. When asked how he could sell his nephew, the uncle replied: 'My mother said that it is none of my business, he is her grandson.'"

—*Washington Post*

## GRANDMADAM

"Lindenwold, New Jersey, police made a surprising discovery when they busted the alleged madam of a prostitution ring. The woman running the show was an 80-year-old grandmother.

"Authorities arrested Vera Tursi last month during a sting operation to crack down on prostitution rings posing as legal escort services. Tursi admitted her role in the business, saying she took it over a few years ago from her daughter, who had died. Tursi said she needed money to subsidize her Social Security checks.

"Undercover police first began to wonder about the age of their suspect when they called the escort service as part of their sting operation. They said she seemed to have difficulty breathing."

—**CNN**

# APOUJRAD

*Another Page of Uncle John's Random Acronym Definitions.*

**ISBN:** International Standard Book Number. Every published book has a unique 10- or 13-digit number to identify it to librarians and book sellers. (It's listed on the bar code.)

**NASCAR:** National Association for Stock Car Racing.

**SRO:** If all the seats at a play or concert are sold out, the venue might let you stand in the back of the hall. That's called Standing Room Only.

**Gestapo:** Germany's state police in World War II, it's an abbreviation of *Geheime Staatspolizei*, which means "secret state police."

**XXX and OOO:** Added at the end of a letter, the Xs symbolize kisses; the Os mean hugs. It probably originated in the Middle Ages, when illiterate people would sign an X for their name and then kiss the paper as a sign of good faith.

**A.M. and P.M.:** *Ante Meridiem*, Latin for "before midday." P.M. means *Post Meridiem*, or "after midday."

**B.C.:** Before Christ. Describes years before the modern era of history. B.C. has fallen out of favor in academic circles and has been replaced by the politically correct **B.C.E.**, or "Before Common Era."

**A.D.:** *Anno Domini*, Latin for "in the year of our Lord," used to denote time after the life of Christ. The politically correct term now used is **C.E.**, or "Common Era."

**MiG:** The name of the Cold War–era Soviet fighter jet is short for Mikoyan-Gurevich, the name of the manufacturer.

**C-SPAN:** It stands for Cable Satellite Public Affairs Network. (C-SPAN broadcasts mostly Congress and Senate sessions.)

**VIN:** Vehicle Identification Number. It's a 17-digit code used to identify cars.

**3M:** The consumer goods company (they make Post-Its and Scotch-Guard) used to be called Minnesota Mining and Manufacturing Company—three Ms became 3M.

# LEMONS

*Just about everyone has owned an unreliable car. Uncle John's was a 1979 Triumph Spitfire that caught fire one time when he drove it home from the mechanic. But that piece of junk was nothing compared to these losers.*

## THE STUTZ BLACKHAWK (1972–87)

From 1911 through the early 1930s, the Stutz Motor Car company was one of the most exclusive automakers in the United States, but by 1935 it was bankrupt. In the late 1960s, an investment banker named James O'Donnell resurrected the Blackhawk name and began converting Pontiac Grand Prixs into ultra-luxury two-door coupes. It had running boards, fake chrome exhaust pipes along both sides of the car, and a spare tire sunk into the trunk lid. Leather luggage that matched the leather seats came standard; mink carpets and a mink-lined trunk were optional. The company also offered to build limousines, convertibles, and four-door sedans based on the same design. The Blackhawk debuted at $23,000 in 1972 and nearly doubled in price to $43,000 for 1973, when the average new car cost about $5,000.

**Fatal Flaw:** The Blackhawk looked like a pimp-mobile designed by Liberace and was probably the ugliest ultra-luxury car ever made. Besides, how many people were dumb enough to pay Rolls Royce prices for a Pontiac Grand Prix, even if the trunk was lined with mink? Elvis Presley was: he bought the first production model (and later bought four more). Evel Knievel bought a Blackhawk; so did Robert Goulet, Dean Martin, and Sammy Davis, Jr. With its goofy looks and customers like these, the Blackhawk was doomed to be ridiculed as a plaything of celebrities with more money than taste. Still, O'Donnell managed to build more than 500 cars before finally going out of business in 1987.

## THE CHRYSLER TC MASERATI (1989–91)

In the mid-1980s, Chrysler was looking for a car that would help improve its stodgy image. So it bought part of the Italian auto manufacturer Maserati. The two companies then worked on a joint venture: the turbocharged TC Maserati convertible.

**Fatal Flaws:** Timing was one problem—Chrysler announced the car in 1986, but production snafus kept it off the market for nearly three years, during which time many potential customers bought other cars. Image was another problem—the TC was touted as something new and different, but it was built on Chrysler's K-car platform and was virtually indistinguishable from a regular Chrysler LeBaron convertible, even though it was hand-assembled in Milan and cost a lot more. About the only difference was that the TC had a faulty engine that blew its oil seals when it over-heated. And it did that a lot, warping the poorly designed cylinder heads that were one of Maserati's few contributions to the car. Faulty oil pressure gauges kept the problem from being detected until the engine had already been destroyed. Even if the engine hadn't been such a dud, customers balked at the idea of paying Maserati prices for a car that looked just like a LeBaron. Chrysler sold only about 7,300 of the cars before it pulled the plug in 1991.

## THE JAGUAR XJ40 (1986–94)

Jaguar began designing a replacement for its aging four-door XJ6 sedan way back in 1972, but the financial troubles of parent company British Leyland kept it from coming to market for 14 long years. Finally in 1986, the XJ40 hit the showroom floor. It was billed as the most advanced car in the world, complete with electronic self-leveling suspension, a dashboard computer that detected and diagnosed mechanical faults, and nearly two miles of wiring to support these and numerous other fancy electronic gadgets.

**Fatal Flaw:** The fault detection system was supposed to alert owners to mechanical problems before they became serious (and expensive), but the system was the faultiest equipment of all. After a few trips to the dealership to service problems that turned out to be nothing, most owners ignored the system even when it detected *real* faults. Result: repair costs went up instead of down. The XJ40 was supposed to address Jaguar's notorious reputation for unreliability, but all it did was make it worse. It wasn't until Ford bought Jaguar in 1990 that the company's image began to improve.

## THE ALFA ROMEO ALFASUD (1972–83)

In the late 1960s, Alfa Romeo announced that instead of building its new mini car, the Alfasud, in Milan, where it had always built its cars, it was shifting production southward to Naples (*sud* is Italian for "south"). And they would manufacture Alfasuds at a rate of 1,000 cars a day, faster than the company had ever made cars before.

**Fatal Flaw:** Alfa Romeos didn't have a great reputation for quality to begin with, and when production moved south things got much worse. Few workers in Naples had ever built cars before, and they had trouble keeping up with the fast production pace. Even worse, they were building the cars using poor-quality recycled steel from the Soviet Union and sabotaged components made in Milan by workers upset about losing jobs to the south. Door handles and other plastic pieces broke off in owners' hands as the metal rusted away around them; engines self-destructed if they were driven too hard. Alfasuds rotted away so quickly that few are still on the road today. But amazingly, the cheap little car stayed in production until 1983 and is actually considered a sales *success*.

## THE ASTON MARTIN LAGONDA (1976–89)

The auto company famous for making James Bond's sports cars was close to going under in the mid-1970s when the makers decided that building a four-door sedan—the company's first—would be a good way to raise cash. Aston Martin didn't have the money to engineer the new model from scratch, so the company just extended the chassis of one of its two-door sports cars and built a big sedan onto it. The Lagonda sold for nearly $50,000 when it was introduced in 1976; a decade later it sold for nearly $150,000. For a time it was marketed as the "World's Most Expensive Sedan."

**Fatal Flaws:** The Lagonda was emblematic of everything that was wrong with automotive design in the 1970s. It was ugly—it had a long, pointy snout that was as angular as a piece of paper folded in half. And it was unreliable—the "futuristic" red LED instrument panels failed so often that they were eventually replaced with little cathode ray TV screens, which failed even more often. The wiring was buggy, the pop-up headlights didn't pop up, the handling was squishy, and the paint job was so bad that the car became known as a rust bucket. That was a lot to put up with in the "World's Most Expensive Sedan," and although the company spent 15 years and untold millions of dollars trying to work out all the bugs, the Lagonda never did catch on with Aston Martin purists. Only about 600 Lagondas had been manufactured by the time the company ended production in 1989.

---

Fungus humongous: The rare mushroom *oxyporus nobilissimus* grows to 3 feet in height.

# CARNEGIE'S WISDOM

*American industrialist Andrew Carnegie (1835–1919) was known for both his ruthless business practices and his generous philanthropy. (He's the man behind Carnegie Hall.)*

"As I grow older, I pay less attention to what men say. I just watch what they do."

"No man can become rich without himself enriching others."

"He that cannot reason is a fool. He that will not is a bigot. He that dare not is a slave."

"The 'morality of compromise' sounds contradictory. Compromise is usually a sign of weakness. Strong men don't compromise, it is said, and principles should never be compromised. I shall argue that strong men, conversely, know *when* to compromise and that all principles can be compromised to serve a greater principle."

"All honor's wounds are self-inflicted."

"Pioneering doesn't pay."

"Think of yourself as on the threshold of unparalleled success. A whole, clear, glorious life lies before you. Achieve! Achieve!"

"There is little success where there is little laughter."

"You cannot push anyone up the ladder unless he is willing to climb."

"People who are unable to motivate themselves must be content with mediocrity, no matter how impressive their other talents."

"The first man gets the oyster, the second man gets the shell."

"Any fool can criticize, condemn, and complain—and most fools do."

"Be more concerned with your character than with your reputation. Your character is what you really are while your reputation is merely what others think you are."

"One of the most tragic things I know about human nature is that all of us tend to put off living. We are all dreaming of some magical rose garden over the horizon—instead of enjoying the roses blooming outside our windows today."

# AMAZING GRACE

*It's one of the most famous hymns in history—so famous that even
if you're not religious you probably know the first stanza by heart.
Here's the story that once was lost, but now is found.*

## THE WRETCH

On May 10, 1748, John Newton, a sailor in the English
slave trade, was heading home to England when his ship
ran into a severe storm in the North Atlantic. So much seawater
poured into the cabin that it seemed the ship was about to sink;
Newton pumped water for nine hours straight and then, as his
energy finally gave out, he shouted, "Lord have mercy on us!"

Not long afterward, the weather began to clear and the bat-
tered ship was able to limp into port. Newton had never been a
religious man—in addition to working in the slave trade, he was a
gambler, a heavy drinker, and he cursed such a blue streak that
even other slave traders were shocked by the foulness of his language. "Not content with common oaths and imprecations, I daily
invented new ones," he recalled in his memoirs many years later.
But his deliverance from the storm changed him.

## A NEW MAN

Convinced that his prayers had been answered in his moment of
need, Newton became an Evangelical Christian and gave up gambling, drinking, and swearing on the spot. Seven years later, when
an illness forced him to give up the seafaring life, he returned to
England and worked for several years as the surveyor of tides in
Liverpool. There he met many of the most prominent Christians
of the day, including John Wesley, the founder of Methodism.
Inspired by their example, he became a minister in the Church of
England and was assigned to a church in the village of Olney, west
of London.

It was in Olney that Newton met William Cowper (pronounced "Cooper"), one of the most popular poets of the 18th
century. Cowper, too, was a religious man, and he helped Newton
organize a weekly prayer meeting in the village. The two men set
a goal of writing a new hymn for every prayer meeting and took

---

**It takes an hour and a half to cremate an average adult.**

turns doing it, each man writing one every other week.

In December 1772 Newton composed a hymn, which he titled "Faith's Review and Expectation," better known today by the first two words of the first stanza:

*Amazing grace! How sweet the sound*
*That saved a wretch like me!*
*I once was lost, but now am found,*
*Was blind, but now I see.*

## AMAZING FACTS

• Newton wrote the words to the original seven stanzas; over the years other contributors have added their own words to the hymn.

• No one knows who composed the melody; the hymn was sung to a number of other tunes before the current one became popular.

• In the more than 200 years since "Amazing Grace" was written, it has gone on to become arguably the most popular hymn of all time. It has become an anthem for all sorts of people struggling against injustice, even if they aren't Christians. Both sides sang it during the American Civil War; both sides sang it during the civil rights movement of the 1960s, too. Cherokee Indians sang it on the Trail of Tears in the late 1830s.

• To date, "Amazing Grace" has been recorded more than 1,000 times; it is so popular with contemporary black recording artists that it is commonly mistaken to be an old Negro spiritual.

## MYTH-UNDERSTOOD

It's common for people to assume, when they learn that the author of this hymn of redemption was not a black man, but rather a former *slave trader*, that the song is addressing the issue of slavery. When Newton converted to Christianity, he must have left the slave trade and then written "Amazing Grace" to atone for his deeds, the logic goes. He's a "wretch" because he was a former slaver, and he "once was blind but now can see" because after he embraced religion he was finally able to see slavery for the evil that it was. There are even tales that when Newton experienced his religious conversion in 1748, he turned his ship around, sailed back to Africa, and set his slaves free.

## STILL BLIND

Nothing could be further from the truth. Newton may have grown quickly as a composer of hymns—he composed 280, many of which are still sung today—but his spiritual growth took longer. After converting to Christianity, Newton returned to slave trading and spent the next five years buying slaves on the African coast and transporting them in bondage to British colonies in North America and the Caribbean. He worked his way up to captain of his own slave ship in the process, all the while devoting his free time to study and prayer.

According to historian Adam Hochschild, Newton and another Evangelical Christian slave ship captain once visited one another each evening for nearly a month. "A strange scene to imagine," he writes in his book, *Bury the Chains*, "the two captains in their tri-cornered hats pacing the deck, earnestly talking of God and sin through the night, while slaves lie in shackles below them."

## BETTER LATE THAN NEVER

Between 1764 and 1788 Newton wrote several books and delivered thousands of sermons, many of which were published and survive to this day. In them he frequently condemns adultery, usury, blasphemy, dishonesty, the size of the English national debt, and just about every kind of sin one can imagine. Except slavery—he doesn't condemn that even once.

It wasn't until 1788, when an anti-slavery movement was sweeping England, that Newton finally turned against slavery, condemning it in a pamphlet titled "Thoughts upon the African Slave Trade." In it, Newton makes a "confession, which comes too late," adding that "it will always be a subject of humiliating reflection to me, that I was once an active instrument in a business at which my heart now shudders."

Newton is often credited with devoting the remainder of his life to ending slavery, but that isn't true either. He published his pamphlet in 1788 and testified against slavery in Parliament the following year, but after that he dropped the subject. Though he lived until 1807 (the year that slavery was abolished throughout the British empire) and continued delivering sermons at a prodigious rate, he rarely mentioned slavery again. And he never wrote an anti-slavery hymn.

# THE POLITICALLY CORRECT QUIZ #2

*Here are more real-life examples of "politically correct"*
*and "incorrect" behavior. How sensitive are you?*
*The "correct" answers are on page 515*

**1.** What computer term was banned by the Los Angeles County purchasing department in 2003?

**a)** Hard drive (too suggestive)

**b)** Floppy disc (too suggestive)

**c)** Master/Slave drives (an offensive term that "violates the region's cultural diversity")

**2.** What longtime Paris strip club came under fire in 2004 for having an offensive name?

**a)** The Ugly American (Open since 1967)

**b)** Crazy Horse Paris (Open since 1951)

**c)** Tres Chicks (Open since 1972)

**3.** In February 2005, Kraft Foods Inc. agreed to stop making which candy, on grounds that some people were offended by it?

**a)** Galtoids—pink "curiously strong mints for women" that came in a metal tin shaped like a woman's purse ("Sexist, stereotypical and demeaning to women.")

**b)** Pimp-O-Mints—inspired by the hit TV show *Pimp My Ride* (The term pimp is "racist and offensive.")

**c)** Road Kill Gummi Candy, similar to Gummi bears except the candy snakes, chickens, and squirrels were flattened and covered with tread marks (Encourages children to be cruel to animals.)

**4.** In 2005 Mercedes-Benz began offering which of the following options on its entire line of luxury cars?

**a)** "Leather free." Fabric and fake leather are offered as substitutes.

**b)** "Wood free." Sustainable bamboo is offered as a substitute for endangered rain forest hardwoods.

**c)** "Fragrance free." The new car smell is removed for asthmatics and allergy sufferers who find it irritating.

**5.** The organization that regulates sumo wrestling in Japan has rejected which of the following reforms:

**a)** Bouts with American professional wrestlers—it's an insult to the art of sumo.

**b)** "Sumo pants" for young boys who are too shy to wear the traditional *mawashi* garment, which leaves them feeling next to naked. The move was proposed to reverse the declining number of boys who take up the sport.

**c)** Instant replays ("Too western.")

**6.** In 2005 Great Britain's BBC TV network ruled that which of the following pieces of footage should not have been shown on the *TV's Greatest Moments* comedy show:

**a)** Narcolepsy sufferers nodding off in the middle of a narcolepsy self-help group. ("Insensitive.")

**b)** Prince Charles slipping on an icy sidewalk and falling on his bum. ("Disrespectful to the royal family and the future king.")

**c)** A drunken vicar passing out while trying to deliver a sermon. ("Offensive to the faithful.")

**7.** In June 2004 the State of New Jersey's Civil Rights Division ruled that bars and taverns can no longer engage in which of the following "discriminatory" business practices:

**a)** Buy one, get one free (favors heavy drinkers over moderates)

**b)** Ladies' night (favors women over men)

**c)** Unisex restrooms (favors men over women)

**8.** Sweden's IKEA furniture company recently agreed to change its furniture assembly instructions. From now on they'll show:

**a)** More non-Swedes—people of color—in the diagrams that show people how to put their furniture together.

**b)** More women assembling furniture.

**c)** More middle- and low-income people assembling furniture.

---

**Food for thought:** A diet of only dry food is called *xerophagy*.

# POLICE SQUAD

*Having a badge doesn't make cops any less flawed than*
*the rest of us. Sometimes they do boneheaded things.*
*Here are some examples from the news.*

**M** AKE IT SO
"One of the police chiefs in charge of national policy on
firearms has said he would like a gun for officers which
can 'temporarily switch people's brains off.' Ian Arundale, assistant
chief constable of West Mercia and head of the Association of
Chief Police Officers' firearms unit, said a 'phaser' would be an
ideal type of less-lethal weapon. 'What we would like in the future
is a *Star Trek*–style phaser that, perfectly safely, temporarily switches someone's brain off so that officers can move in,' he told *Jane's
Police Review Magazine.* 'We know we're not going to get that,
probably not in my lifetime anyway, but we will look at anything
that takes us in that direction.'"
**—The Guardian (U.K.)**

**OFF THE CUFF**
"French Justice Minister Dominique Perben criticized prison
guards who handcuffed an inmate to her hospital bed while she
gave birth on New Year's Day. 'It should not happen again,' Perben told RMC radio. 'Things should be handled differently, it's
absurd.' The Paris-based International Prison Observatory said the
prisoner had been handcuffed—despite vociferous protests from
medical staff—after she had refused to allow a member of the
prison escort to attend the birth."
**—Reuters**

**NAKED CITY**
"A suspended Illinois State Police trooper was arrested yesterday
in Lake County and charged with two counts of official misconduct. Police say Officer Jeremy Dozier spotted a parked car behind
a hotel in Gurnee and ordered the vehicle's occupants, a 17-year-
old woman and a 20-year-old man, to get out of the car. Authorities allege the trooper then told the couple to undress and run
around a nearby construction site. Dozier was also charged with

In India, milk is sold in frozen blocks; in Denmark, it's sold in dehydrated sheets.

official misconduct earlier over accusations that he forced another young couple to strip to their underwear during a traffic stop."

—Associated Press

## CHIEF SLEAZY

"Police in the U.S. were shocked when they raided a brothel, only to discover that their chief was one of its customers. Police Chief James Leason has been suspended without pay after allegedly being caught in the bust in New Jersey. The top cop apparently did not know his officers had the brothel under surveillance. He was arrested as he left the building after engaging in various sex acts with one of the two female employees, authorities said. Leason, 56, was charged with promoting prostitution and misconduct in office. He faces up to 15 years in prison if convicted."

—*Sydney Morning Herald*

## PRIORITIES

"Chicago police detective Janice Govern was scheduled for a dismissal hearing based on a 2001 incident in which, allegedly, she nonchalantly continued to shop in a Dominick's store even after a customer told her that the bank branch inside the store was being held up. According to a witness, she told the fellow customer to call 911 but that she resumed shopping and in fact was waiting in a checkout line when uniformed officers arrived at the store."

—*Chicago Sun-Times*

## DIAPERED AND DANGEROUS!

"Police in the town of Puerto Progreso, in the Mexican state of Yucatán, arrested a one-year-old baby on the charge that it was an accomplice to a robbery at a supermarket. The baby's father, Roger Segundo, 28, had hidden six bottles of vodka in the baby's stroller and attempted to leave without paying for them. A police spokesperson said: 'The policeman who got there first thought it was the right thing to do to list the baby as an accomplice, because the bottles were in his stroller.' He said the baby was turned over to its mother in the morning when other officers realized the 'accomplice' was a baby."

—**Mexico.com**

# JUST PLANE AMAZING

*How two American bombers piggybacked
their way into German legend.*

L OOK OUT...BELOW
On New Year's Eve, 1944, one of the most remarkable
events in the history of aviation took place in northern Germany. The end of World War II was near; Allied planes were
pounding German cities with continuous bombing runs. U.S. Air
Force Captain Glenn Rojohn was piloting one of those planes, a
B17 Flying Fortress. The 22-year-old, already on his 22nd mission,
and his squadron were heading back to England after a bombing
raid on Hamburg. After crossing the German coastline, the group
of 37 bombers was suddenly attacked by German fighter planes.
"They were having a field day with us," Rojohn said later. "We
lost plane after plane." Only 25 of those planes would make it
home from the mission, and Rojohn's wasn't one of them.

When the bomber in front of his was hit and went down in
flames, Rojohn instinctively gunned forward to fill the gap. Keeping formation was paramount to defense. But then he felt a terrible impact. The plane had been hit, and not by German bullets. It
was a collision with another bomber...from below. Not only that,
the two planes were now stuck together. The lower plane's upper
gun turret had punctured the top plane's belly, and the top plane's
lower turret had punctured the lower plane's roof. The planes were
almost perfectly aligned, nose to nose and tail to tail, according to
Rojohn's copilot, 2nd Lt. William Leek Jr., like two "breeding
dragonflies."

## PIGGYBACK BOMBERS

What caused the planes to collide? It could have been the fact
that the formation was flying into an 80-knot headwind, and all
the planes were bouncing up and down. Or it could have been
that the pilot and copilot of the lower bomber, 1st Lt. William G.
MacNab and 2nd Lt. Nelson B. Vaughn, had been disabled by

---

**Sore feet? Sea urchins walk on their teeth.**

enemy fire and lost control of the aircraft. (Both men were seen slumped over in their seats after the collision and neither survived, so the cause of the collision remains unknown.)

Staff Sgt. Edward L. Woodall Jr., the gunner in the lower plane's bottom gun turret, did survive. "At the time of impact," he said, "we lost all power." The lower gun turret, or "ball" turret, was a small, rotatable compartment on the belly of the plane. Without power, Woodall had to rotate the turret with a hand crank to get it to the "exit" position so he could crawl up into the plane's fuselage. When he finally did, he was surprised to see his counterpart from the other plane above his head. Staff Sgt. Joseph Russo was in the ball turret from the upper plane. He wasn't badly injured, but neither he nor his crewmates could get his turret to the exit position. There was no way to get him out. Realizing that he wasn't going to have a chance to bail out of the plane, Russo began reciting Hail Marys, probably unaware that his radio mike was on and that his voice could be heard by the entire crew.

## BAILOUT

Rojohn cut his engines to prevent them from exploding. Then, using the three functioning engines of the pilotless craft below for power, Rojohn and Leeks muscled the two planes into turning south toward the German coast. With their feet on the instrument panel and holding the controls with all their might, the two pilots fought to keep the planes from going into a spiral. Rojohn then ordered his men to bail out, and one by one the top turret gunner, radio operator, navigator, waist gunner, tail gunner, and bombardier parachuted out of the rear exit of the plane. Russo, the ball-turret gunner, was still stuck. "I could hear him saying his Hail Marys over the intercom," Leek said. "I felt that I was somehow invading his right to be alone. This was the hardest part of the ride for me."

They crossed the coast at 10,000 feet and were going down fast. Rojohn ordered his copilot to bail out. Leek knew that Rojohn wouldn't be able to keep the plane from going into a spiral or have time to bail out by himself, so he disobeyed orders. "I knew one man left in the wreck could not have survived," he said, "so I stayed to go along for the ride."

At 12:47 p.m., a German anti-aircraft commander on the island of Wangerooge, off the German coast, wrote in his diary:

---

Ptuey to you too: Masai tribesmen spit on each other in greeting.

"Two fortresses collided in a formation in the NE. The planes flew hooked together. The two planes were unable to fight anymore. The crash could be awaited so I stopped the firing at them." Bewildered German civilians wondered if the Americans had a strange new double-deckered bomber, as Rojohn and Leek screamed over the island and then over the north German countryside. "The ground came up faster and faster," Leek said. "Praying was allowed. We gave it one last effort and slammed into the ground."

## SUDDEN IMPACT

When they hit ground, the lower plane exploded, sending the upper plane up, forward, and back to Earth. The Flying Fortress slid across the ground until its left wing hit a building and the plane came to a halt. Neither pilot could believe it: not only were they both alive, they were barely hurt. They climbed out of the wreck and looked at the plane in shock. "All that was left," Rojohn said, "was the nose, the cockpit, and the seats we were sitting on." The rest of the plane had disintegrated.

Two of the men who jumped from Rojohn's plane didn't survive, and the unfortunate Russo was believed to have been killed on impact. But four of the jumpers did survive, as well as four who had evacuated from the lower plane. Ten of the two planes' sixteen crewmembers were saved by Rojohn and Leek's determination. All ten were taken prisoner (one was interrogated by the Germans for two weeks about the new "secret weapon"), and all were released at war's end five months later.

## AFTERMATH

After the war, Captain Rojohn went home to Pennsylvania, got married, and had two children, but through the years he searched military and Social Security records to find his copilot. In 1986 his efforts finally paid off when he got the phone number of Leek's mother in Washington state. When he called her, she said that her son, who had moved to California, happened to be in town for a visit and was standing right there. In 1987 the two pilots met for the first time in 43 years. The details of their conversation remained private; William Leek died a year later.

In 1994 the flight came back into Rojohn's life when a German author sent him a book about the history of Wangerooge during the war years, including an entire chapter on the piggyback flight. Little did Rojohn know that it was part of northern German legend, and that some people even celebrated it every New Year's Eve. The author was looking for survivors of the flight, hoping they could come to the 50th anniversary celebration.

Rojohn received the letter too late for the anniversary, but he contacted the author and, in 1996, he and his wife, Janie, visited the island of Wangerooge and then went to the pasture on the German mainland where Rojohn and Leek had crash-landed 52 years earlier. They were interviewed by reporters from all over Germany, and a TV station even organized a reenactment of the flight. "They flew me out over the North Sea to where I had the midair collision," he said. "Then they flew me over the exact route. It was a very emotional time. When we landed on the island, they told me to look up. I saw that they had hoisted the American flag for me. I can't tell you how that made me feel."

## POSTSCRIPT

In 1997 Gordon Hildebrand, 70, of Wasco, Oregon, saw an article in *World War II* magazine about the piggyback flight. Hildebrand had grown up next door to the family of William MacNab, the pilot of the *other* plane. MacNab was just 19 when the crash occurred, and his parents had never found out how their son had died. They were only told that their son was missing in action. MacNab's parents were long dead, but Hildebrand called MacNab's siblings, who, after 53 years, finally learned their brother's fate.

The MacNab family contacted Rojohn. They invited him to Oregon, where he was welcomed as a hero, even serving as the grand marshal of Wasco's Memorial Day parade. "It was almost like Bill came home," Hildebrand said. Ann Phillips, one of MacNab's surviving sisters, told the *Pittsburgh Post Gazette*, "I'll never forget Glenn Rojohn. He was an answer to a prayer. He brought me closure after all those years waiting for news." In 1999 Hildebrand and two of MacNab's cousins flew to Pennsylvania to attend a regular luncheon held for Air Force veterans. They gave Rojohn a plaque that read: "You have filled a void in our lives with your presence and become a member of our family and a friend forever." Glenn H. Rojohn died on August 9, 2003, at the age of 81. He was the last survivor of the flight.

# THE ROBOTS ARE COMING!

*In preparation for the inevitable day when robots rise up and take over the world, you may want to familiarize yourself with these recent advancements in robot technology.*

## CLONEBOTS

Scientists at Cornell University have built a small robot that can make copies of itself. The robot is made of several 10-centimeter-wide modules, each of which is fitted with electromagnets (so they can be attached to other modules) and a computerized replication program. Using the program, the robot can take single modules—the same ones of which it is made—and stack them, constructing a clone of itself. Scientists hope to use the technology to make self-repairing robots.

## POOBOTS

Experts at the University of the West of England in Bristol have developed a robot that creates its own power supply: it attracts flies, then eats them, then turns them into electricity. But there's a catch. The "EcoBot II" uses a reserve of human excrement to attract the flies. The robot digests the bugs in eight fuel cells. It uses the bacteria from the excrement to break down the sugars in the flies, releasing electrons that create an electric current. The scientists' goal is to eventually make the EcoBot II predatory, finding and devouring flies on its own whenever it senses that its energy reserves are low. Until then, however, it has to be manually fed fistfuls of dead flies to supplement those attracted by the poop.

## JOCKBOTS

In May 2005, teams of scholars from colleges around the world met at the Georgia Institute of Technology for the RoboCup U.S. Open, a series of five robotic competitions. The aim of the contest was to develop a team of robots that by the year 2050 will be technologically advanced enough to play soccer against a human team. Among the events: five-inch-tall robots play soccer with a golf ball; robot dogs play soccer; and teams of humans play soccer against robots while riding Segway power scooters.

## JOCKEYBOTS

The most popular spectator sport in the United Arab Emirates is camel racing. The traditional choice for camel jockeys has always been children—they're small and lightweight. Until now. When human rights groups actively started to condemn the practice as a form of slavery, U.A.E. Interior Minister Sheikh Khalifa bin Zayed al-Nahayan found an alternative: he hired several private high-tech labs to create a generation of *robot* jockeys. The tiny, human-looking robots are smaller and lighter than child jockeys and respond to commands via a remote control system mounted on the camel.

## BALLBOTS

The University of Uppsala, Sweden, has developed a new security system and burglar deterrent: a ten-pound robot in the shape of a 20-inch black ball. Equipped with radar and infrared sensors, when it senses an intruder, it follows one of many preprogrammed courses of action: it can dial the police, sound an alarm, repeatedly take the burglar's picture, or pursue the thief at up to 20 mph—faster than a human being. It even gives chase over water, mud, and ice.

## DOCBOT

A robot used at the University of California–San Francisco Medical Center for delivering medicine to patients' rooms ran amok in June 2005. Rather than going to the hospital pharmacy to pick up medications as programmed, Waldo the Robot sped past the pharmacy at a high speed and zoomed wildly into the hospital's cancer ward. Waldo barged into an examination room where a doctor was administering radiation treatment to a cancer patient and then he finally stopped…for good. He suddenly wouldn't move, leave the room, or respond to commands. The patient, however, ran out of the room, screaming in terror.

\* \* \*

"It's not so much how busy you are, but why you are busy. The bee is praised; the mosquito is swatted."
— Marie O'Conner

Arnold Schwarzenegger holds a degree in marketing and business administration.

# LET'S DO A STUDY!

*If you're worried that the really important things in life aren't being researched by our scientists...keep worrying.*

In 2004 researchers at Odeon Cinemas determined that celebrities making appearances at awards shows and movie premieres expose an average of 59 percent of their skin. That's up from 39 percent in 1994. After scanning thousands of celebrity photographs and videos, they also determined that the least skin-flaunting decade was the 1970s, when stars showed off just 7 percent. If the trend continues at this rate, the researchers say, movie stars will be 75 percent naked by 2010. (Woo hoo!)

• Thirty medical students at University College of London studied Gollum, a character in the *Lord of the Rings* trilogy, and determined that his split personality, spiteful behavior, wild mood swings, and extreme paranoia indicate a presence of schizophrenia and/or multiple personality disorder. In addition, his bulging eyes and slight, skeletal body suggest a thyroid problem.

• Why has the redheaded, baby-faced Belgian comic-book sleuth Tintin seemed to remain the same age over the course of 50 years? According to Claude Cyr of Sherbrooke University in Quebec, it's not because the authors chose to keep him that way. Cyr studied 23 comics and found that Tintin lost consciousness nearly 50 times, concluding that this string of accidents delayed Tintin's physical growth as well as the onset of adolescence.

• Researchers at the University of Hungary in Budapest analyzed videos of sporting events at which the "Wave" was being performed. They noted it almost always moves clockwise around the stadium, travels at a speed of about 40 feet per second, and that the average width of a wave is 15 rows of seats.

• In 2005 Children's Hospital in Boston announced that according to their research, eating a lot of fast food leads to obesity. Doctors observed 3,000 young people in a cardiac health study and discovered that the kids who ate burgers and fries more than twice a week gained an average of 10 pounds more than those who ate fast food less than once a week.

---

**Too much information? The human body produces about 7 miles of hair per year.**

# THE CURSE
# OF THE ICEMAN

*In Uncle John's Ultimate Bathroom Reader, we told you about the 5,300-year-old "Iceman" that was found in the Austrian Alps in 1991. Now it seems he's cursed the people who disturbed his resting place. Is it possible? Read on and decide for yourself...if you dare.*

## BACKGROUND

In September 1991, some people hiking high in the Tyrolean Alps along the Austrian/Italian border found a body sticking out of a melting glacier. It turned out to be the world's oldest fully preserved human, and the first ever found with "everyday clothing and equipment," including a copper axe, a dagger, and a bow with arrows. Because the body was found in a small protective basin that would have provided shelter from bad weather, archaeologists initially assumed that he got caught in a freak storm, sought shelter in the basin, and then froze to death.

In the years that followed the discovery, scientists subjected the remains to countless medical and diagnostic tests to see what they could learn about it. When they ran a CAT scan (a procedure similar to an X-ray), they made a startling discovery: the Iceman had a flint arrowhead lodged in his shoulder. Then, when the scientists reexamined a surviving fragment of the Iceman's coat, they noticed a tear in the coat that matched the arrowhead's location in his shoulder. DNA tests on the Iceman's knife and from one of his arrows revealed traces of blood from three different humans. He also had fresh, deep cuts on his hands, wrists, and chest.

Based on this evidence, the scientists came up with a new theory on how the Iceman died: he wasn't killed by the weather, he was shot in the back during a fight.

## CURSED?

It stands to reason that the Iceman—also called Oetzi, or Ötzi, because he was discovered in the Ötztal Alps—would be mad at the people who killed him. But is he also angry at the people who, 5,300 years later, disturbed his resting place? In the 14 years since

---

his body was discovered, several people associated with the discovery have died. Consider what happened to these people:

- **Helmut Simon,** 67, the man who, along with his wife Erika, first stumbled on the Iceman while hiking through the Tyrolean Alps in 1991. In October 2004, Simon returned to the Alps for his first visit since finding the body. On October 15, he went on another hike, in what seemed to be good weather, but was caught in a freak blizzard. Several days later his frozen body was found at the bottom of a 300-foot cliff. "We only get one or two deaths a year from people caught in bad weather," a spokesperson for the Austrian mountain rescue service told reporters after Simon's body was recovered. "For this to happen to the man who discovered the Iceman, and for his life to be claimed in the same way as that of his discovery, has caused a lot of people to take seriously the question of whether there really is a curse on those who moved the body."

- **Dr. Rainer Henn,** 64, head of the forensic team that removed the Iceman from the glacier and transported the body to a laboratory in Innsbruck, Austria. Henn died in a car accident in 1992 while on his way to give a lecture on Oetzi.

- **Kurt Fritz,** 52, the climbing guide who led Dr. Henn to the place where the Iceman was discovered. In 1993 Fritz was killed in an avalanche. And he was the *only* one killed—the other members of his climbing party were spared.

- **Rainer Hoelzl,** 47, the Austrian television journalist who was granted permission to film the Iceman's removal from the glacier. Not long afterward Hoelzl was diagnosed with a brain tumor; he died in 2004.

- **Dieter Warnecke,** 45, wasn't directly associated with the Iceman, but he was the leader of the search team that found Helmut Simon's body. Warnecke dropped dead of a heart attack within an hour of Simon's funeral.

- **Konrad Spindler,** the Innsbruck University archaeologist who headed the Iceman investigation team, was asked if he believed in the curse. "It is all media hype," he answered. "The next thing the media will be saying is that I am next on the list." He was. Five months later, Spindler died of complications from multiple sclerosis.

---

**Makes sense: Venice is the most frequently flooded city on Earth.**

## FINAL THOUGHT

Even if the Iceman does have a beef with the people who disturbed his rest and poked and prodded his mummified remains, he doesn't seem to mind visitors. When Oetzi was moved to the South Tyrol Museum of Archaeology in Bolzano, Italy, the local tourist trade shot up by an estimated 4 million euros per year. If anything, the "curse" has helped business, not hurt it.

Today tens of thousands of people visit the museum and file past the Iceman's refrigerated chamber for a quick peek. And as far as anyone can tell, he hasn't bothered any of them.

\*  \*  \*

## UNCLE JOHN'S STALL OF SHAME

**Honoree:** Bob Apple, a city councilman and bar owner in Spokane, Washington

**Dubious Achievement:** Removing the toilet paper from the restrooms of his bar

**True Story:** In August 2005, citing cost-cutting measures, patrons at Bob Apple's Comet restaurant who needed to use the facilities were told to "check out a roll" from the bartender, leaving their driver's license as collateral. Councilman Apple blamed his customers' "continuous thefts of toilet paper products" as the reason for the rash move.

Concerned citizens didn't take the new rule sitting down. Doug Clark, a columnist for the *Spokesman-Review* and patron of the Comet, went to a local Costco and bought a bundle of bathroom tissue. "We're talking 45 rolls of two-ply," he wrote. "Five hundred sheets per roll. That's 45,000 total squares—enough quality wipeage to handle a Comet crowd even on chili dog night."

He wrapped the bundle in a red, white, and blue ribbon, marched down to city hall, and put the rolls on Apple's desk. Clark also gave the councilman a card that was signed with: "Here's hoping everything comes out all right in the end."

That helped convince Apple to change the rule—that and the fact that the Washington Health Department threatened to shut down the Comet if he didn't restock his stalls.

# HIPPOS IN THE NEWS

*Take a walk on the wild side—with hippos.*

## THE TORTOISE AND THE HIPPO

In January 2005 a dehydrated baby hippo was found on the coast of Kenya by wildlife rangers. Flooding caused by the Indian Ocean tsunamis of 2004 had separated it from its mother. The one-year-old calf, nicknamed "Owen" by the rangers, was taken to a wildlife sanctuary—where he quickly befriended a 100-year-old male tortoise named "Mzee." Park officials said the baby hippo had adopted the tortoise as its mother and that the two "had become inseparable." Park manager Paula Kahumbu said, "Owen follows Mzee around and licks his face."

## HIPP-O BEHAVE, BABY!

Zookeepers at the Berlin Zoo announced in 2005 that Europe's oldest hippo needed medication...contraceptive medication. The 53-year-old hippo, Bullette, had already birthed 20 calves in her life and had been observed "energetically mating" with her long-time mate, Ede. The zookeepers were afraid that having another calf could kill Bullette, so they started giving the 6,000-pound hippo "bread-roll size" birth-control pills. They also said it was very uncommon for a hippo of such an age to still show any interest in sex.

## HUNGRY HUNGRY HIPPO

In 1998 Thailand's *Pattaya Mail* newspaper reported that a "circus dwarf" named Od had died in a bizarre hippo-related accident. The longtime performer apparently bounced sideways off a trampoline and landed right in the mouth of a yawning hippopotamus. Hilda the Hippo, the story said, instinctively swallowed, and the unfortunate Od came to an odd end. The 1,000-plus spectators on hand thought it was part of the act and applauded wildly...until they realized that a tragedy had occurred.

**Note:** It never happened. The story *did* appear in the Thai newspaper, just as it has in many other newspapers around the world since at least 1994, but it has been exposed as an urban legend.

---

Cool fact: NASA astronaut underwear is lined with tubes of water to prevent overheating.

# OOPS!

*More tales of outrageous blunders.*

## RECIPE FOR DISASTER

"The April 2004 issue of *Southern Living* magazine had an unusually explosive feature: the icebox dinner roll. Step one of the recipe called for boiling one cup of water and a half-cup of shortening over high heat for five minutes. Obviously they hadn't tested it themselves. The result was a bubbling concoction of melted fat that erupted on stovetops, injuring at least five *Southern Living* readers, including one who needed treatment for burns. John Olson, a food scientist at rival *Cook's Illustrated* magazine, who tried the recipe, calls the mixture 'like napalm.' The magazine issued the first product recall in its nearly 40-year history, asking distributors to yank copies of the issue from newsstands."

**—Wall Street Journal**

## FINGER FOOD

"A woman from Saransk, Russia, almost lost her hand after putting it into a tank filled with piranhas. She was trying to clean the tank when the carnivorous fish attacked her in a feeding frenzy during which they stripped the flesh from two fingers. The predators only let go when the woman smashed them against the side of the tank. She thought the tank, which belonged to her son, contained goldfish. A neighbor said: 'She had no idea the pet fish in the tank were predators.'"

**—FemaleFirst**

## HOW DO YOU SPELL PRESIDANTIAL?

"The White House went all-out to showcase the advantages of President Bush's ambitious financial agenda this week, but in the end the 'challenges' proved too much. The word 'challenges'—a main theme of a two-day White House economic conference that ended on Thursday—was misspelled on a large television monitor that stood in front of Bush during a panel discussion. 'Financial Challanges for Today and Tomorrow,' the message proclaimed in dark blue capital letters against a bright yellow background."

**—Reuters**

---

Safety first: A Japanese company has invented training wheels for high heels.

## THE EYES HAVE IT

"Sunshine Coast great-grandmother Terry Horder got the fright of her life when she accidentally stuck her eyes shut with super glue. The 78-year-old was defrosting the fridge when her eyes started watering and she reached for a bottle of allergy eye drops. But instead of grabbing the medicated drops she got Loctite 401. Her husband of 57 years, Joe Horder, said his normally outspoken wife was suddenly very quiet. 'Normally you can't shut her up but she went very silent and I just heard this little voice say, "Dad, I think I've glued my eyes shut,"' Mr. Horder said. Mr. Horder called Triple-0 (Australia's 911) and paramedics soon arrived to take her to Caloundra Hospital's emergency ward.

"'They soaked my eyes for around five minutes and then pried the lashes apart, which wasn't pleasant. But about 10 minutes later I was good as new,' she said."

—*Queensland* [Australia] *Newspapers*

## ON THE WRONG TRACK

"Trains on a busy German route were delayed for hours after a train driver pulled the emergency brake fearing that a man next to the tracks was trying to kill himself. Authorities then closed the track, causing a chain reaction that delayed 11 trains for 4.5 hours. Police said the 70-year-old man was spotted as he leaned over the track near Cologne, but it turned out he was just trying to reach some blackberries."

—*USA Today*

## BRAINS NOT INCLUDED

"The state government's computer networks shut down for 16 hours in a power failure earlier this week. Computers froze for an entire business day. Result: Many offices had to close and court-ordered child support payments were delayed to 516,000 children. The shutdown could have been prevented if officials had heeded a warning that the computers needed replacement batteries."

—*Atlanta Journal-Constitution*

\*     \*     \*

**Chinese proverb:** "Don't laugh at age. Pray to reach it."

---

Artist Salvador Dalí once designed a telephone shaped like a lobster.

# WHAT A DOLL

*The people who came up with these dolls must have*
*been as empty-headed as the dolls themselves.*

N EEDIES (2005)
Manufactured by Codependent Designs, which says Need-
ies are "like rain on a sunshiny day." They're depressed,
emotionally fragile…and needy. Dannie, Mossie, and Brettie
require constant hugging and squeezing, which they reward by
dishing out flattering compliments. Stop hugging them and they
cry. And if you're hugging another Needie doll (which they can
sense via an electronic hookup) they'll bad-mouth the other doll.
The company says these dolls are inspired by "codependent, high-
maintenance relationships."

### C.B. McHAUL (1977)
In the late 1970s, American pop culture had a brief obsession with
truck drivers. There were the *Smokey and the Bandit* films and the
hit song "Convoy," about truckers communicating via another
1970s fad, the CB radio. Trying to cash in on the fad, Mego Toys
released a line of eight truck driver dolls (the main character was
C. B. McHaul, an obvious ripoff of C. W. McCall, who'd recorded
the hit song "Convoy"). When the dolls flopped they were
McHauled to the dump.

### TYSON (1999)
Tyson was a 13-inch doll that looked a lot like Barbie's boyfriend,
Ken. But where Ken was available in different skin colors, Tyson
came in only one version: African-American. That wasn't the only
difference: Tyson was muscular, anatomically correct, and homosexual. According to manufacturer Totem International, Tyson was
"the world's first Black gay doll." Totem was promptly sued by
boxer Mike Tyson and model Tyson Beckford, both of whom are
African-American and bald—but not homosexual—and feared
people might think the doll was based on them. So Totem took
the doll off the market, right? Nope. Both lawsuits were withdrawn
and the doll was released in 1999. (And it's still available.)

# CANOE PLANTS

*Hawaii has some of the most lush, beautiful vegetation in the world.*
*Visitors assume that all those plants are native to the islands...but*
*they're wrong. Almost all of them come from somewhere else.*

## SURVIVOR: SOUTH PACIFIC

If you were about to climb into a canoe and set out across the Pacific Ocean to find a new home, what items would you bring to ensure that 1) you didn't starve or die of thirst as you spent weeks (or months) on the sea; and 2) when you finally landed on some unknown island, you'd have everything you needed to begin a new life? And what if you could only bring plants? Your food, clothing, and shelter would have to come from the seeds, roots, cuttings, and small plants you packed in your canoe. Could you do it?

The ancient Polynesians could...and did. Thousands of years ago, at a time when European sailors were unable to navigate beyond sight of shore, the Polynesians explored more than 12 million square miles of Pacific Ocean—an area larger than Canada, Mexico, and the United States combined. They travelled in 90-foot-long double-hulled canoes that could hold as many as 100 people on the large open platform that was built between the two canoes. And they brought their natural world with them.

Voyaging as far as 2,500 miles in a single stretch, the Polynesians populated the islands scattered across the South Pacific: Samoa, Fiji, Tahiti, Tonga, New Zealand, Easter Island, and the Hawaiian Islands, among many others. Because they never knew what they would find when they landed on a new island, they took what they'd need once they got there. And what they needed was the plants that they relied upon for survival and comfort.

## SPREADING THE SEEDS

Around 1,700 years ago, they brought to the Hawaiian Islands many of the plants that seem so natural to the islands today, such as the coconut palm and Hawaiian bamboo. Because the Polynesians had no written language, archaeologists have studied oral tradition and scientific evidence to figure out just which plants they brought. They've come up with a list of about 32, known today as the "canoe plants."

One was the *kamani* tree, which grows up to 60 feet tall. The Polynesians used its wood to build canoes and huts, the oil from the seeds was used to make lamp oil, and the tree's small orange blossoms were used for floral leis. They also brought the *maia* or banana tree with them. In addition to providing food, its large leaves were used for roofing, the peels were made into poultices to treat wounds, and the tree trunks were used as rollers to push heavy canoes into the sea. *Ko*, now called sugarcane, was used as a medicine and food, and the leaves were used as thatching for huts.

The *Niu*, or coconut palm, was one of the most useful of all. The coconuts contain food and as much as a quart of fresh water each—important during long canoe trips. Each tree provides lumber or shade, and as many as 100 coconuts a year for 75 years (which, in times of drought, may be the only source of fresh water). The palm fronds were woven into hats, baskets, mats, and other useful items.

## BRANCHING OUT

Some of the other canoe plants that Polynesian's brought with them when they made Hawaii their home:

- **Awapuhi kuahiwi:** the fragrant leaves were used as a spice and also to treat tooth and stomach aches. Known as "shampoo ginger," it contains a natural soap still used in herbal shampoos today.

- **Ipu:** a gourd with a hard shell that was used to make bowls, storage containers, and drums.

- **Kalo (also called taro):** roots were used to make the starchy Polynesian staple *poi*; juice from the stems to make red dye.

- **Awa:** its sedative properties were used to make the intoxicating drink (*kava*).

- **Ohe:** (Hawaiian bamboo) used to build houses, furniture, bridges, ladders, fishing poles, and irrigation troughs. And young shoots can be eaten.

- **The Kukui tree:** it can reach 60 feet and is used for lumber, and it produces candlenuts, which are edible and contain an oil used to fuel torches. The bark and flowers are medicinal.

Top five Internet-using countries: Sweden, Denmark, U.S., Norway, and Australia.

- **Ohiaai trees:** (mountain apple) they bear a sweet oval-shaped fruit, and the bark and leaves had medicinal uses.

- **Pia, uala, and uhi:** three tubers that were cooked and eaten like potatoes. The uala was especially helpful because it grew well in poor soil and drought conditions—and was used as fish bait.

- **The olona tree:** inner bark was woven into cloth, ropes, and fishing nets.

- **Olena:** roots were ground into powder for a spice (today it's used to give curry its yellow color). Also used as a medicine and fabric dye

- **The kou tree:** an evergreen that grows up to 40 feet tall, it provided timber, and the flowers were used to make leis.

- **The hau tree:** soft wood was used to make the canoes' buoyant outriggers; bark fibers were were braided into rope.

- **The ulu tree:** (breadfruit) light wood was used for drums, canoes, and utensils. Sap was used to treat cuts, or as a glue; even as chewing gum.

- **The milo tree:** its sap had no flavor, making the wood perfect for food containers.

- **Ape ("ah-pay"):** its huge, heart-shaped leaves were used medicinally, mostly for fever.

- **The wauke tree:** bark was pounded into sturdy white cloth known as *tapa*. Dyed brown, red, yellow, and orange (with dyes made from other plants), it was used to make clothing.

- **Ki:** considered the most sacred of all Hawaiian plants, it was planted around homes to keep evil spirits away. The leaves were used to wrap food, thatch huts, and make sandals and hula skirts. The root was used to make *okolehao*, an alcoholic beverage similar to brandy.

## ALOHA

If you're lucky enough to visit the Hawaiian Islands, make sure you get to the Hana Maui Botanical Gardens on Maui or the National Tropical Botanical Garden on Kauai (Uncle John loved it). They have specimens of nearly all the canoe plants, which may give you a better idea of just how much the Polynesians influenced the islands' flora. And you can even see some of the rare native plants (the ones that the canoe plants have now nearly wiped out).

# SUCK WIND, GOOFY FOOT!

*More Hawaiian pidgin words and expressions to impress the Haoles with.*

**Brah:** Brother, bro

**Huhu:** Upset. *No huhu* means "Don't get upset."

**Haah?** What? Could you repeat that?

**Garans** ("GAY runs"): For certain; guaranteed

**Buddahead** (derogatory): A Japanese person (from Japan)

**Kotonk:** A Japanese American

**Make** ("MAHK ay"): Dead

**Shibai** ("She BUY"): B.S.

**Bukbuk:** A Filipino. Also known as a *Manong.*

**Like beef?** "You wanna fight?"

**Li dat:** Like that

**Ehu:** ("EEwho"): A native Hawaiian with red hair

**Kukae** ("Koo KAI"): dog doo

**Funny kine:** Odd or unusual

**Ahanakokolele!** ("Ah ha na ko ko LEH leh!"): You should be ashamed of yourself!

**Kay den:** Okay then

**Geev um!** Go for it!

**Haole** ("HOW lee"): A Caucasian

**Haolefied:** A Hawaiian who begins to act like a Caucasian has become "haolefied."

**Brok da mout:** Taste's good.

**Haad rub:** A hard time.

**No shame!** Don't be shy (nothing to be ashamed of)

**Goofy foot:** A surfing term for someone who surfs with his right foot forward instead of his left, which is more common.

**Go benjo:** Go pee.

**Fut:** Fart

**Futless:** Confused, frustrated

**Suck wind!** Go take a flying leap!

**Suck rocks!** Suck wind!

**Da kine:** Any object you can't remember the name of.

---

The first *Encyclopedia Britannica,* published in 1771, was only 3 volumes long.

# BRI SURVIVAL GUIDE

*On page 251 we shared some of the survival tips we've collected from the books in our BRI library. Here are a few more.*

## EARTHQUAKE

• If you live in an area that's prone to earthquakes, you can earthquake-proof your home by fastening all large bookshelves securely to the walls. This is especially important in bedrooms where any large piece of furniture may fall on a bed.

• If you feel your house shaking heavily, crouch under the heaviest table you can find—the closer to the center of the house, the better. Interior doorways may also protect you if there's no other option, but keep away from windows.

• The danger isn't over just because the shaking has stopped—get outside immediately. The quake may have weakened the foundation, and an aftershock—which can happen at any time—could cause the house to collapse. If you have time and know how to do it, shut off the main gas valve to protect your home from fire. (Afterward, don't turn it back on yourself; have the gas company do it.) Don't light any matches, lighters, camp stoves, or flares after an earthquake.

• If you're outside when a quake hits, find open ground. Stay away from buildings and power lines. Assume any downed line is active, whether it's sparking or not.

## PLANE CRASH

In a 2005 *Time* magazine article entitled "How to Get Out Alive," Amanda Ripley writes:

> We tend to assume that plane crashes are binary: you live or you die, and you have very little choice in the matter. But in all serious plane accidents from 1983 to 2000, over half the passengers lived... And some survived because of their individual traits or behavior.

The key is to know beforehand what the escape routes are and then to not hesitate when the time comes to flee—but not to panic, either. Here are some things to keep in mind:

• Put down the magazine and listen to the flight attendant's safety

How do you know if a vanilla bean has just been harvested? It has no flavor or scent.

instructions, especially about emergency exits. You may think you've heard it all before, but different planes have different escape methods. Numerous studies have shown that people with a mental plan of escape are much more likely to make it out alive.

- Plane crashes almost always start with a sudden movement, so keep your seat belt fastened at all times and only move throughout the cabin when absolutely necessary.
- Many who survive the initial crash are killed by fire because they hesitate to get out or try to collect their belongings first. Leave your carry-on items behind and *get off the plane.*
- Once you've escaped, get a safe distance from the plane but stay close enough for rescuers to find you.
- If the plane crashes in water, don't inflate your life vest until you are safely out of the plane.
- Finally, think twice before you grumble because you can only afford to fly coach—sitting in the rear of the cabin is your best chance of surviving a plane crash.

**Real-Life Example:** On March 27, 1977, a Pan Am 747 was preparing for takeoff when a Dutch KLM jet mistakenly tried to land on the same runway, causing a horrendous collision and slicing off the top of the 747. One Pan Am passenger, 70-year-old Floy Heck, froze in her seat and had no clue what to do next. But her husband, Paul, who'd survived a house fire as a boy, had been studying the escape routes and calmly urged his wife to get up quickly and follow him. As they made their way to the nearest exit, Floy noticed that several passengers were just sitting there, dazed. Sixty seconds later, the plane was engulfed in flames. Only 61 of the 396 Pan Am passengers—including the Hecks—survived. A total of 583 people on both planes were killed, making it the worst civil aviation accident in history.

## CAR CRASH INTO WATER

- To decrease the risk of the car going into the water in the first place, never park facing water; always try to park parallel to it. If you do have to park facing water, use the parking brake.
- When you hit the water, try to roll down a window. Although this will make the car sink faster, it will give you an escape route. If you don't get a chance to open a window (or can't because

they're electric), then wait before you try the door. Opening it too soon will cause an onrush of water that could potentially injure you. Let the car fill up with water until it's almost full, then the pressure outside will be equal to the pressure inside and the door should open easily. If neither the doors nor windows will open, try kicking the center of the windshield.

• If you can't escape, turn on all the lights to increase your chances of being spotted from the surface. Look for a small air pocket to help you breathe.

## CAR CRASH OFF A CLIFF

• If you have time, move out from behind the steering wheel, which could crush you on impact. A quick mover may be able to fasten the other seatbelt before the car hits anything. However, if your car has an airbag, stay put.

• Clasp your arms around your body so they don't dangle.

• Keep your eyes closed to protect them from glass.

• Cars don't automatically explode like they do in the movies, but that is certainly a risk, so after impact quickly get yourself and any other survivors a safe distance from the car.

## SNAKEBITE

A lot of misinformation has been spread about what to do after getting bitten by a poisonous snake. Actually, the wrong treatment can potentially be more harmful to the victim than not treating it at all. Not only that, it can put the rescuer in danger, as well.

**What Not to Do**
• Don't try to suck the venom out—it can enter your bloodstream and poison you.

• Don't put any ice on the wound—it will make it more difficult to remove the venom.

• Don't cut around the wound—it may cause infection.

**What to Do**
• Carry a snakebite kit in your first-aid kit when you're out hiking, or keep one at home if poisonous snakes live in your area. The kit has a suction device and instructions on how to use it.

• Unless you are 100 percent certain that the bite didn't come from a poisonous snake, assume the snake was poisonous and get to a hospital as soon as possible.

- If you don't have a snakebite kit, wash the affected area with water (and soap if you have some).
- Immobilize the bite; keep it below the heart to decrease blood flow. Wrap a bandage or cloth between the heart and the bite, no more than four inches away from the bite. Be careful not to tie it too tight—cutting off the blood flow could damage an artery or limb. You should be able to fit one finger between skin and bandage. Loosen the bandage for about 30 seconds every five minutes.
- Try to get a good look at the snake so you can describe it to the doctor. Take special note of the head: most poisonous snakes have triangular heads that resemble a shovel. If possible, capture or kill the snake and bring it with you to the hospital.

## STREET ATTACK

- When walking at night, stay in well-lit areas and travel with friends whenever possible.
- If you feel that someone is following you with ill intentions, speed up and listen carefully for the footsteps of your pursuer. If he speeds up too, start running and shouting as loudly as you can, drawing as much attention to yourself as possible.
- If you're accosted, try to determine the attacker's intent. If it's a simple robbery, calmly give them what they want—especially if they have a weapon. None of your possessions are worth your life. Without making too much eye contact, try to note as many details as you can about their appearance, voice, and mannerisms.
- If the attacker intends to cause you bodily harm and doesn't have a gun, then try one of these weapons:
- Pepper spray. A good idea if you live in a potentially dangerous area.
- Keys. Bunch them in your hand with the ends sticking out between your fingers. A successful strike to the neck, eye, or groin could end the attack right away.
- Your foot. Go for the groin—it will give you a longer reach than your assailant, especially because you'll be leaning back when kicking.
- Other weapons: comb (drag it underneath the nose); umbrella (for puncturing); makeup (blow powder in the assailant's face to

blind him); also nail files, pens, or anything with a point.

Any of these will usually give you one chance to escape. So make your move and get away as fast as possible—and as loudly as possible. The best thing to yell is, "Call the police! I'm being attacked!" And yell it over and over.

## MOB

At any sporting events, concerts, or other public gathering there's always the possibility that a mob mentality will break out and people will get trampled. Keeping calm can save your life in this situation.

• Know where the nearest exit is. Try to make a habit of looking for possible escape routes whenever you enter a new place. (This isn't paranoia, it's common sense.) At the first sign of trouble, start heading for the exit.

• If you find yourself trapped in a mob, the most important thing is to stay on your feet and move with the crowd. Stopping for even a second may cause you to lose your footing and get trampled.

• Take a deep breath and tense up your shoulders, biceps, and chest muscles. Bunch your arms up against your stomach to make yourself as solid as possible.

• If you have a small child, carry him or her in front of you. If at all possible, don't let the child walk.

• Keep quiet for two reasons: 1) You'll call less attention to yourself, which could save you from pepper spray, flying fists, or bullets; and 2) It can be hard to see through a mob, so keeping quiet may allow you to hear escape instructions from police or venue officials.

## BEING TIED UP

Although this rarely occurs outside the movies, it does happen. If it happens to you, here's a neat magician's trick (Houdini used it) that may help you escape:

• While your captor is tying you up, make yourself as large as possible by inhaling and pushing your chest out. Flex any muscles that are being tied up, but do it as subtly as possible so as not to raise suspicion. When your captor leaves, relax. You'll get at least a half an inch of slack in the ropes, which should be more than enough for you to wiggle your way to freedom.

# DUMB CROOKS

*More proof that crime doesn't pay.*

**B**URNING TO GET RID OF THEM
"A 46-year-old man allegedly set his own home on fire in order to get two visitors to leave. Dean Craig was charged with felony arson after splashing rubbing alcohol on the floor of the two-story home in Aurora Township, Illinois, and using a lighter to ignite the fire, the Kane County Sheriff's office said. Craig allegedly had asked two visitors to leave, but when they refused, he threatened to light his house on fire. When police arrived at Craig's home, it was engulfed in flames."

—**Associated Press**

### BOOK 'EM

"The Boone County Sheriff's Office arrested Robert White, 29, of Florence, Kentucky, after he allegedly borrowed more than $600 worth of books, CDs, and DVDs from the Boone County Public Library and sold them at the flea markets in Walton, Kentucky, and Cincinnati, Ohio. Detectives said White also sold $20,000 worth of material from eleven other libraries in Ohio and Kentucky. How did they catch him? He used his real name when applying for a library card."

—**ChannelCincinnati.com**

### CHECK IT OUT

"A Canyon, Texas, man walked into a store one morning and paid for his purchase with a check. The clerk took the required information from the man's driver's license, plus his phone number. After completing the transaction, he put the check in the register.

"An hour later the check casher was back, this time with a knife. He proceeded to rob the store and make his escape. But he had made no attempt to alter his appearance, and the clerk had no trouble remembering him. When Randall County Sheriff's deputies arrived on the scene, not only was the victim able to furnish a good physical description, he also handed over the check with the man's complete identification information."

—*Wanted! Dumb or Alive*

# FUNNY BUSINESS

*And we don't mean "ha-ha" funny.*

## SPEED FILLS (THE COFFERS)

In 2004 the city of Coopertown, Tennessee, realized they had a law-enforcement problem: the cops were costing the city too much money. The *Robertson County Times* reported that the police department cost about $125,000 to run, but that they had given out only $17,000 worth of traffic tickets. To take care of the problem, the city lowered speed limits and had the cops start handing out more tickets. In the first six months of 2005, the revenue from court fines jumped to more than $155,000—a 700 percent increase over all of 2003. "Our police department," said Mayor David Crosby, "will be self-sufficient from now on."

## MY FRIEND BILL

In May 2005, the government watchdog group Public Citizen found an odd provision in the 700-page Senate energy bill: it provided federal loan guarantees to "coal-gasification" plants in any "western states" situated at an elevation above 4,000 feet. Public Citizen looked to see how many companies fit that description and found only one: Medicine Bow Fuel & Power of Medicine Bow, Wyoming. That company was formed by DKRW, a Houston-based energy company—started and run by former executives of Enron. If the bill passed, the provision would give the company hundreds of millions of taxpayer dollars in loans—money they wouldn't have to pay back if the company failed.

After Public Citizen issued a statement about the questionable provision, the Senate Energy and Natural Resources Committee denied that it was written with DKRW in mind. The proposal was written for another project, they said, that hadn't been publicly announced yet...and was a secret.

## HUMBLE STUDENTS

While four University of Memphis basketball players were playing in a big Saturday-night game for the school in 2004, the campus apartment they all shared was broken into and burglarized.

---

Sounds fishy: In 1992, a 352-pound tuna sold at an auction in Japan for $69,273.

According to the police report (which got into the hands of the local press), the stolen items included: $2,500 in diamond earrings, $4,000 in custom-made shirts, $6,000 worth of shoes, and eight mink coats worth $40,000. Two days later a university spokesman said the report was wrong—the mink coats were only worth $28,800 and didn't actually belong to the students, who were all on scholarships. (It is forbidden for colleges to pay athletes.)

## GREASING THE WHEELS

In June 2005 documents leaked to the *New York Times* showed that Philip Cooney, chief of staff to the White House Council on Environmental Quality, had altered several scientific reports on global warming. His changes, such as adding the words "significant and fundamental" before the word "uncertainties," softened the reports' findings. Richard Piltz, the former government official who leaked the documents (he had resigned in disgust three months earlier), said that Cooney had made the changes to create "an enhanced sense of scientific uncertainty" about the implications of climate change.

Cooney has no scientific training in his background; he's a lawyer. His last job before President Bush appointed him to the White House: he was a lobbyist at the American Petroleum Institute. Two days after the *Times* revealed Cooney's pseudo-scientific editing work, he resigned from his position. The White House said it was unrelated to the leaks.

**Final Funny Note:** The day after Cooney resigned from the White House, he got a new job...at ExxonMobil.

## AND ON A GOOD NOTE...

In December 2004, after an 18-month battle, Internet software company PeopleSoft was taken over by rival Oracle. Oracle immediately announced that 5,000 PeopleSoft employees would be laid off. In April 2005, David Duffield, PeopleSoft's co-founder and former CEO (he quit when the company was taken over) started a fund called "Safety Net." It offered as much as $10,000 in tax-free grants to any of his former employees who were in financial troubles because of the merger. He started the fund with $10 million of his own money.

# THE BIRTH OF THE NFL, PART II

*Professional football was in trouble...until*
*George Preston Marshall rode into town.*

## ACTION ATTRACTION

Let's face it: Americans prefer watching sports that have the potential for a lot of scoring. That's why professional football was still on the fringe in the 1930s. Most games featured one, maybe two touchdowns, and field goals were rarely attempted because the goalposts were at the back of the end zone. Result: many games ended in ties. College football fared better because the intense rivalries added drama, and the players were younger, faster, and played "for the love of the game." With the exception of a few standouts, pro players, on the other hand, were seen as washed-up wannabes at best, or cheating thugs at worst. But was it the players' fault—or the rules and business practices of the NFL?

## THE MARSHALL PLAN

George Preston Marshall, a wealthy football fan, blamed it on the inherent faults of the game. Pro football needed excitement, and he made it his mission to add some—no matter what the purists thought. In 1932, using the small fortune he made from a laundromat chain, Marshall bought part ownership of the tottering Boston Braves. With him he brought a list of changes and set to work lobbying the other NFL owners to approve them.

• Marshall liked to watch the players throw the ball, which rarely happened because of so many restrictions on the forward pass. In 1933 he persuaded the other teams to remove them.

• He thought the ball would be easier to throw if it was smaller and pointier, so the following year he got the NFL to reduce the size of a regulation ball by about 1½" at the fattest part.

• At Marshall's insistence, the NFL moved the goalposts from the rear of the end zone to the goal line. That made field goals and extra-point kicks more likely to succeed, which increased scoring and reduced tie games.

• Another innovation Marshall pushed through was moving the ball 10 yards in from the sideline whenever play went out of bounds. That sped up the pace of the game; teams no longer had to waste an entire down (or two) getting it back to the center of the field.

• Marshall was also the driving force behind splitting the league into eastern and western divisions. That added drama to the season by creating two races for divisional titles, followed by a championship game to decide the league's best team.

• In 1936 Marshall helped implement the NFL's first college draft system, which evened out league play by giving the worst teams in the league the first shot at the best new players.

### IT'S A HIT

Marshall's changes worked. Pro football became more fun to watch, which put more paying customers in the stands, making the sport more commercially viable. The average attendance at an NFL game—about 5,000 people in the early 1930s—rose to nearly 20,000 by 1939.

But the NFL still lacked the national attention it craved. That came thanks to a championship game in 1940. Marshall was once again in the middle of it all—but this time he lived to regret it.

The Chicago Bears were up against the Washington Redskins, who Marshall had relocated from Boston after he bought the team. Two weeks earlier, the Redskins had finished the regular season by beating the Bears 7–3 after a Bears receiver dropped a pass in the fourth quarter. Chicago wanted an interference call; the refs didn't make it, so the Bears went home losers. However, they knew that revenge was waiting for them in the upcoming championship game against those same Redskins.

It didn't help matters when Marshall, who had a reputation as a loudmouth (and a bigot—he was one of the last NFL owners to integrate his team), attacked the Bears after the game. "They can't take defeat," he told reporters. "They are a first-half club. They are quitters—the world's greatest crybabies."

Marshall's attack got the public interested in the rematch, which, by coincidence, would also be the first pro football game

---

ever broadcast nationally over network radio. For millions of people living in cities with no pro football franchise, the broadcast would serve as their introduction to the NFL. (It was also the last NFL game in which a player—Bears end Dick Plasman—would play without a helmet.) If the game proved to be interesting to the folks listening at home, they'd probably tune in again during the 1941 season. The future of the entire league, not just the Bears and the Redskins, was riding on the game.

The Bears heard Marshall's "crybaby" taunts and came out fighting. Under the leadership of their coach and owner, George Halas, the Bears slaughtered the Redskins 73–0, still the most lopsided defeat in the history of the NFL. More than 36,000 people witnessed the carnage at Washington's Griffith Stadium, including a record 150 sportswriters from all over the country.

George Preston Marshall, the man credited with saving the league in the 1930s by reinventing the game, would also be remembered for the worst loss ever.

## ON THE AIR

Thanks to that one championship game, pro football was more popular then ever in 1941, but it still wasn't the draw that baseball—or even college football—was. Radio helped to spread its appeal, but it was television that solidified it.

TV was a brand-new medium in the late 1940s and NFL owners didn't care about it—few people owned televisions. By 1950, however, there were an estimated four million TV sets in the United States, reaching some 30 million viewers. At first the NFL was against broadcasting its games, afraid that people would stay home and watch TV for free instead of paying to come to the stadium. What happened in California that year proved them right. The Los Angeles Rams decided to televise their entire season. Result: attendance at Rams games dropped by nearly half from 205,000 in 1949 to 110,000 in 1950. The Rams got the message. The following year they televised only away games, and attendance at home games shot up to 234,000. By the end of 1951, most teams were broadcasting their away games, but *only* away games. If fans wanted to see a home game, they had to watch it in person.

Football and television seemed made for each other. Advancing the ball ten yards to gain a first down gave the game a lot of drama between touchdowns, and the short breaks between plays left plenty of time for analysis and commentary by experts. Even people who were new to football could learn about the game by listening to the announcers.

Pro football's fan base began to soar, and spending Sunday afternoon watching football quickly became an American institution. By 1954 an estimated 34 percent of the Sunday afternoon viewing audience was tuned to the NFL. Thanks to television, pro football was finally beginning to eclipse college football as the most-watched, most-important form of the sport. The National Football League—which for so long had been on the brink of failing—was now truly a "national" league. And it was here to stay.

\*　　\*　　\*

### ...ONE MORE THING: THE AFL

In 1959 Lamar Hunt, son of Texas oilman H. L. Hunt, applied to the NFL for an expansion franchise...and was turned down. So Hunt and several other spurned suitors formed the American Football League, which was the seventh or eighth league by that name (all the others had collapsed). The NFL responded to this challenge the same way it had all the others—it ignored the AFL and waited for it to die on its own.

Seven years later the AFL was still in business in spite of the fact that CBS, which broadcast NFL games, refused to give AFL scores in its news broadcasts and *Sports Illustrated* printed only black-and-white photos instead of the color shots it used with the NFL. So in 1966 the two leagues agreed that their champion teams would meet in the first AFL-NFL World Championship Game on January 15, 1967. In 1970 the two leagues merged.

"AFL-NFL World Championship Game" was a pretty clunky name, and Lamar Hunt wanted something better. One day he saw his daughter bouncing a rubber ball and asked her what it was. "A Super Ball," she told him. "Super Bowl" started out as a nickname, but by the third inter-league championship game, played on January 12, 1969, the name was official. Today the Super Bowl is one of the biggest events of the television year, with 40 percent of U.S. homes tuning in to watch the game.

# HUT 1...HUT 2...HIKE!

*Football: A mindless game of men with helmets running into each other?
Or a complex ballet of strategy mixed with speed and brute force?*

"Football isn't a game but a religion, a metaphysical island of fundamental truth in a highly verbalized, disguised society, a throwback of 30,000 generations of anthropological time."
—**Arnold Mandell**

"Let's face it, you have to have a slightly recessive gene that has a little something to do with the brain to go out on the football field and beat your head against other human beings on a daily basis."
—**Tim Green**

"The NFL, like life, is full of idiots."
—**Randy Cross**

"Football isn't a contact sport, it's a collision sport. Dancing is a contact sport."
—**Duffy Daugherty**

"Most football teams are temperamental. That's 90% temper and 10% mental."
—**Doug Plank**

"Pro football is like nuclear warfare. There are no winners, only survivors."
—**Frank Gifford**

"I'd catch a punt naked, in the snow, in Buffalo, for a chance to play in the NFL."
—**Steve Henderson**

"Baseball is what we were. Football is what we have become."
—**Mary McGrory**

"If my mother put on a helmet and shoulder pads and a uniform that wasn't the same as the one I was wearing, I'd run over her if she was in my way. And I love my mother."
—**Bo Jackson**

"I like to believe my best hits border on felonious assault."
—**Jack Tatum**

"The pads don't keep you from getting hurt. They just keep you from getting killed."
—**Chad Bratzke**

"You're kind of numb after 50 shots to the head."
—**Jim Harbaugh**

"Football is a game of clichés, and I believe in every one of them."
—**Vince Lombardi**

---

**A working ballerina goes through an average of three pairs of ballet slippers a week.**

# 13 NAMES FOR A 12-INCH SANDWICH

*They're all basically the same: a long roll filled with layers of meat, cheese, tomatoes, lettuce, and condiments. But what you call them depends on who you ask and where they're from.*

## HOAGIE

**Ingredients:** Italian ham, prosciutto, salami, provolone cheese, lettuce, tomatoes, and onions on a long roll, with oregano-vinegar dressing

**Origin:** During World War I, Italian immigrants who worked in the shipyards at Philadelphia's Hog Island would eat these long sandwiches for lunch. A common meal in Italy, native Philadelphians took to them, first calling the sandwich a "hoggie" in reference to Hog Island, then later "hoagie." It became the official sandwich of Philadelphia in 1992, beating out the cheesesteak.

## ZEP

**Ingredients:** The same as a hoagie

**Origin:** The name is short for "zeppelin" (because it's zeppelin-shaped). True zeps are found only within the city limits of Norristown, Pennsylvania, a small town 20 miles outside of Philadelphia. This sandwich also started with Italian immigrants.

## HERO

**Ingredients:** Pork and other meats, provolone cheese, usually with roasted peppers, vinegar, olive oil, and lettuce served on crusty Italian bread

**Origin:** It was also introduced to locals by Italian immigrants, but "hero" was the New York City name coined sometime late in the 19th century. According to legend, New Yorkers named it a "hero" because "it took a true hero to finish one in a single sitting."

## GRINDER

**Ingredients:** Similar to a hoagie or a hero, but usually toasted

---

By English law, the phrase "time immemorial" means history before the reign of Richard I.

Origin: Italian immigrants set up sandwich shops near the East Coast shipyards during World War II. Their main customers were "rivet grinders," the men who ground rivets on warships, and the term passed along to the sandwiches. Today, this term is especially popular in Michigan and the upper Midwest.

## SUBMARINE (OR SUB)

Ingredients: Boiled ham, hard salami, cheeses, lettuce, tomatoes, onion, maybe some garlic and oregano on Italian bread

Origin: This New Jersey sandwich was named by Dominic Conti, an Italian grocery store owner from the city of Paterson. In 1927 Conti went to see the *Holland I*, a submarine on display in Jersey's Westside Park. The sub reminded Conti of the biggest sandwich he sold in his store, so he borrowed the name.

## ITALIAN

Ingredients: The same as a submarine

Origin: The only difference between this and the New York sandwiches is geography; it's found mainly in the Midwest and upper New England.

## ROCKET, TORPEDO, and BOMBER

Ingredients: Similar to a hoagie or a submarine

Origin: These are other working-class names for working-class sandwiches. Like the grinder, they were named for the immigrant workers who built the rockets, torpedoes, and bombers during World War II. Also, many WWII-era bombers were erected using a new technique called "Sandwich Construction."

## CUBAN

Ingredients: Roast pork, ham, cheese, and a pickle on Cuban bread, grilled in a press until the contents are warmed by their own steam

Origin: In the Ybor City area of Tampa, Florida, this sandwich can be traced back to the 1880s, when many Cubans immigrated there to work in the cigar factories. A real Cuban sandwich is almost impossible to find outside of Tampa or Miami. Why? Because Cuban bread contains lard, it must be made fresh daily, which makes it difficult to distribute.

In St. Louis, Missouri, a woman must be fully clothed to be rescued by firemen.

## WEDGE
**Ingredients:** Various meats, very thinly sliced, stacked, folded, and cut in half with the halves served at a 90-degree angle
**Origin:** Not only the name of a sandwich, it's also the name of a delimaster's illusionary trick of manipulating thinly sliced meats to make portion sizes look larger than they really are. This sleight-of-hand has been handed down through generations of deliworkers, primarily in Westchester County, north of New York City.

## PO' BOY
**Ingredients:** It can feature crawfish, shrimp, fried oysters, catfish, crab, deli meats, or meatballs on a baguette. Served "dressed" with lettuce, tomato, and mayonnaise, or "undressed," meaning plain
**Origin:** The po'boy was invented in the Cajun section of New Orleans in 1929. Two brothers, Clovis and Benjamin Martin, took pity on striking transit workers (Benjamin was a former streetcar conductor) and gave these "po'boys" sandwiches made of leftovers from their restaurant. Shellfish was abundant and cheap at the time, and became the main ingredient. Today, any long sandwich served in New Orleans is considered a po'boy, even one with deli meats. However, outside of New Orleans, it usually refers only to sandwiches containing seafood.

## DAGWOOD
**Ingredients:** Anything and everything readily available that can fit between two slices of bread. A true Dagwood is built to such a humongous size that it is nearly impossible to take a bite
**Origin:** The only food that Dagwood Bumstead, husband of Blondie in the popular comic strip, knew how to prepare was a mountainous pile of dissimilar leftovers precariously arranged between two slices of bread. The sandwich became synonymous with the character and took his name.

\*　　\*　　\*

"It requires a certain kind of mind to see beauty in a hamburger bun."
                                    —**Ray Kroc, chairman of McDonald's**

---

**Although 90% of people in the U.S. say adultery is wrong, the adultery rate is about 70%.**

# AUNT SHARI'S AMAZING POWERS

*Our Aunt Shari loves magic tricks and these classics are some of her favorites. Can you guess how they work? (Answers are on page 514.)*

P**EEK-A-BOO**
"I have X-ray vision," Aunt Shari told me. "It's not like Superman's—I can't see through walls, or steel, or anything like that—but I *can* see through paper."

"I don't believe you," I said.

"Okay," she said. "You call out the names of five of your friends. I'll write each one down on a piece of paper, then fold it up and put it in a bag. Then you reach in and grab one, and I'll tell you what name is written on it before you even take it out of the bag."

"You're on!" I said. Aunt Shari got a paper bag, some paper, and a pencil. I called out the names of five of my friends—Steve, Mike, Lara, Dave, and Marilyn—and she wrote each name down on a separate piece of paper, folded it up, and put it in the bag. Then she handed me the bag. I reached in, grabbed one, and said, "Okay."

Aunt Shari stared long and hard at the bag, then she looked up at me and said, "The name on the paper is…'Steve.'"

I pulled out the paper and unfolded it. "It says 'Steve!'" I said.

"You see? X-ray vision!" she said as she took back the bag. How'd she do that?

## PSYCHIC TATTOO

"Hey, would you like a psychic tattoo?" Aunt Shari asked me.

"Sure, why not?" I said.

So Aunt Shari got a felt-tip pen and a drinking glass, which she filled with water. Then she went into her cupboard and came back with a sugar cube, on which she wrote a big letter "U" (for Uncle John) with the felt-tip pen. She dropped the sugar cube into the glass of water, then took my hand in hers and placed it over the glass. "The sugar cube will dissolve, but by the time it does," she told me, "my psychic powers will have transferred the

'U' from the cube to your palm."

Aunt Shari held my hand over the glass until the cube melted into a little pile of sugar at the bottom. The "U" looked like it had melted away too…but when Aunt Shari let go of my hand and I looked at my palm, there it was! The "U" was now on my palm.

How'd she do that?

## FULL OF HOT AIR

"I also have telekinetic powers," Aunt Shari told me. "I can use my mind to move objects, start cars, fight forest fires, inflate balloons, you know, that kind of thing. Here, I'll show you."

She went to her cabinet and got out a balloon and a soda bottle that was covered in aluminum foil all the way up to the lip of the bottle. She put them on the kitchen table.

"I can inflate this balloon using only my brain," she said, stretching the opening of the balloon over the lip of the bottle and letting it snap into place, sealing it over the bottle.

"But psychic brain waves alone aren't enough to inflate a balloon, because they scatter off in every direction," Aunt Shari explained. "That's what the foil is for—it catches the brain waves like an antenna and focuses them into the balloon. I'll hold the balloon upright, so the captured brain waves will go straight up into the balloon. Ready?" she asked. She closed her eyes in concentration, then lifted the droopy part of the balloon and held it straight up over the bottle. And sure enough, it began to inflate.

How'd she do that?

## MATH PSYCHIC

"Now I'm going to have you solve a math problem using numbers you choose. I'll use my psychic powers to guess the answer in advance, before you even pick your numbers," Aunt Shari told me. She closed her eyes and thought for a moment. Then she wrote a number down on a piece of paper (without showing me), put the paper in an envelope, licked the flap, and sealed it shut.

Then, handing me a pencil and another piece of paper, she said, "Pick a three-digit number, one in which each digit is different. Don't tell me what it is. Write it down." I picked 489 and wrote it on the piece of paper.

---

Figure this one out: What word is synonymous with both "solve" and "shape?" A: Figure.

"Now reverse the digits and subtract the smaller number from the larger one. If the answer is only two digits long, add a zero in front. In other words, if the answer is 24, write down 024."

Since 489 reversed is 984, I subtracted 489 from 984 and got 495. I wrote it down.

"Now take your answer, reverse it, and add those two numbers together."

I reversed 495 to get 594, and added them together to get 1,089.

Aunt Shari handed me the envelope. "Open it," she said. I did—the number written on the paper was 1,089.

"Wow!" I told her. "Do it again!"

"Naaah," she replied. "My psychic powers are pooped."

How'd she do it?

## KEEP THE CHANGE

"That was pretty cool, but how do I know you're *really* a psychic?"

Aunt Shari gave me one of her looks and then said, "I guess I have enough psychic powers left to do one more trick." Reaching into her change jar, she pulled out three coins—a penny, a nickel, and a quarter—and laid them out on the kitchen table.

"I'm going to turn around, and when I do, I want you to pick one of the coins and touch it. Press down on it and keep your finger there while I read your mind. Concentrate! It'll take me a little while, but I'll be able to tell you which coin you picked."

Once her back was facing me, Aunt Shari said, "Okay." I picked the quarter and pressed my finger down on it, concentrating hard. Less than a minute later she said, "Okay, take your finger off." I did and she turned around to face me.

"I must be more tired than I thought," Aunt Shari said, "either that or you weren't really concentrating. Anyway, I didn't get much of a reading. The coins are going to have to whisper the answer in my ear." She picked up the penny and held it to her ear for a moment; then she did the same thing with the nickel and the quarter. "You chose the quarter," she said.

How'd she do that?

*To find out how Aunt Shari did these*
*tricks, turn to page 514.*

---

According to surveys, washing dishes is the most disliked household chore.

# FOUNDING FATHERS

*More stories about some famous names you probably
know...and their origins, which you probably don't.*

## RINGLING BROTHERS

When a circus came to their hometown of McGregor,
Iowa, in 1870, the Ringlings, like a lot of kids, were
inspired to put on a show: their pet goat (named Billy Rainbow)
performed tricks in a tent the boys made themselves. Most kids
probably would have stopped after a performance or two, but the
seven Ringling brothers—Alf, Gus, Al, Charles, Henry, Otto, and
John—never did. Their first professional circus, put on in Bara-
boo, Wisconsin, on May 19, 1884, was tiny in comparison to the
shows being put on by P. T. Barnum and James Bailey. But the
brothers kept at it, doing much of the work themselves and plow-
ing all of their profits back into the business. By 1907 they were
big enough to buy the Barnum & Bailey Circus outright. They ran
it as a separate business until 1919, when they merged the two cir-
cuses as the "Ringling Brothers and Barnum & Bailey Combined
Shows, the Greatest Show on Earth."

## CHARLES MERRILL AND EDMUND C. LYNCH

In 1907 Merrill, a recent college graduate working on Wall Street,
happened to meet Lynch, a soda fountain equipment salesman, at
the 23rd Street YMCA in New York City. They became friends
and when Merrill formed his own brokerage firm, Charles E. Merrill & Co., in 1914, he asked Lynch to join him. After a few
months of convincing, Lynch finally agreed. But it wasn't until
1915 that the firm changed its name to Merrill, Lynch & Company. By 1941 it was the largest brokerage firm in the United States.

## ALLAN AND MALCOLM LOUGHEAD

In 1912 Allan and Malcolm borrowed $4,000 and built a seaplane,
called the Model G. They began giving aerial sightseeing tours of
the San Francisco Bay in California. Four years later the brothers
formed an aircraft manufacturing company and began making
planes full-time. There was just one problem: their last name was
easy to mispronounce, and the brothers were worried that cus-

---

Pop quiz: Are there more red stripes or white stripes on the American flag? A: Red, 7-6.

tomers would mistakenly refer to their airplanes as "lugheads" or "logheads." Why take a chance? The brothers decided to spell the company's name the same way that their last name was pronounced: *Lockheed*. In 1995 the company merged with Martin Marietta to form Lockheed Martin, one of the largest aerospace companies in the world today.

## DAVID ABERCROMBIE AND EZRA FITCH

In 1892 hunter and outdoorsman David Abercrombie opened a store in Manhattan that manufactured and sold sporting goods. One of his regular customers was Ezra Fitch, a New York attorney who was so bored with law that he spent as much time as he could fly-fishing and hiking. Abercrombie was his outdoor gear supplier, and he enjoyed the equipment so much that he talked Abercrombie into letting him buy into the business. In 1904 Fitch became a partner in the store, but the partnership didn't last long: Abercrombie wanted to keep the store the way it was, Fitch wanted to expand. Abercrombie resigned in 1907 and Fitch stayed on, outfitting such luminaries as Theodore Roosevelt, Amelia Earhart, and arctic explorer Robert Peary. The business went bankrupt in 1977 and was sold to another sporting goods chain; in 1988 it was purchased by the Limited, which turned it into a clothing company.

## WILLIAM FOX

William Fox was born Wilhelm Fried to Hungarian immigrants who came to the United States in 1879, where he got his start in New York City's garment industry. By 1904 he'd saved enough money to buy a penny arcade, which he later converted into a movie theater. From there he expanded into film production and distribution, and by 1929 his company was worth $200 million ...until the stock market crashed. In just two days, Fox Studio's stock had dropped from $119 a share to $1. Fox was forced to sell his stake in the company in the early 1930s, but the studio kept his name and in May 1935 it merged with 20th Century Studios to become 20th Century Fox. (And in 1986 it added the Fox Television Network.)

\*   \*   \*

**A Bloody Terrible Joke:** Why was the blood donation unsuccessful? It was all in vein.

---

What is the lowest number, when spelled out, that uses every vowel? One thousand twenty-five.

# IT'S A WEIRD, WEIRD WORLD

*Proof that truth is stranger than fiction.*

## DRIVING ME NUTS

"After accepting a German man's kind offer to tow his broken car, a stranded Polish motorist was taken on a terrifying high-speed joyride at speeds of 100 mph. The 36-year-old German tied a cable to the stranded car, and proceeded to hurl down the motorway at high speeds. The motorist, who remained inside his vehicle during the tow, flashed his lights and honked his horn at the speeding driver to stop. Police said the Pole was finally able to bring the German motorist to a halt by swerving his car back and forth. The German was taken to a psychiatric clinic."

**—Reuters**

## QUICKER PICKER-UPPER

"Computer programmer Steve Relles, of Delmar, New York, has the poop on what to do when your job is outsourced to India. For the past year Relles has made his living scooping up dog droppings as the 'Delmar Dog Butler.' 'My parents paid for me to get a degree in math and now I am a pooper scooper,' said the 42-year-old father of two. Relles, who lost his programming job three years ago, now has over 100 clients who pay $10 each for a weekly yard-cleaning. 'It sure beats computer programming because it's flexible,' Relles said. 'And I get to be outside.'"

**—The Houston Chronicle**

## BUTT I WAS JUST JOKING

"Police arrested a man who dropped his pants in the crowded lobby of the St. Louis County Courthouse and made photocopies of his buttocks. Police found Daniel Everett holding two copies he had already made. He was making a third. 'What did I do? What did I do?' witnesses said Everett asked police. Everett, 38, said the copies were intended as a practical joke for his girlfriend."

**—USA Today**

---

Nice kitty: The Des Moines Zoo once used a tiger as a watchdog.

# CRAZY FOR
# STAR WARS

*When Star Wars was released in 1977, it became a
cultural phenomenon. Twenty-eight years later, in May
2005, the hype once again reached a fervor with the release of
Revenge of the Sith. Thousands of crazed fans lined up for weeks
in advance to see Anakin Skywalker finally turn into Darth Vader, proving
that we didn't have to go to a galaxy far, far away to see some strange creatures...*

## THE DARK SIDE

At movie theaters worldwide on May 19, 2005, opening night for the final *Star Wars* episode, *Revenge of the Sith*, looked like Halloween in springtime: Kids were dressed up as Jedi knights; women wore their hair in Princess Leia–like buns; Imperial stormtroopers ushered viewers into the theaters; and several Darth Vaders wandered through the crowds in their shiny black helmets. But a few of the Vaders were up to no good. One showed up at a premiere of *Sith* in Springfield, Illinois, calmly walked into the theater lobby, pushed an employee away from the counter (apparently he didn't have the Force), and stole all the cash from the register. Then he went back outside, where he blended in with all the other Darth Vaders. The following night, another robber—this one wearing black pants, a *Star Wars* T-shirt, and a Vader mask—used a stun gun to rob a pizza delivery man in Kissimmee, Florida. Both Darths got away.

## USE THE FIRE EXTINGUISHER, LUKE!

Two die-hard *Star Wars* fans in England tried to stage (and film) their own lightsaber battle. The pair of wannabe Jedis, a 20-year-old male and his 17-year-old female friend, built their makeshift lightsabers out of two discarded fluorescent light tubes. Bad idea: they poured gasoline into the tubes and lit them on fire. Early on in the battle, their tubes collided and shattered—splattering them with glass and flames. Both were hospitalized with severe burns...just like Anakin Skywalker!

---

Yum! Pork-stuffed crickets are a popular snack in Burma.

## THIS ISN'T THE THEATER YOU'RE LOOKING FOR

On May 25, 1977, the original *Star Wars* premiered at Hollywood's Grauman's Chinese Theater. For weeks afterward, crazed fans lined up to see the movie. So what better place to see the final *Star Wars* film than in the theater where it first played? One problem: the final *Star Wars* film wasn't going to be playing at Grauman's. Not knowing this, hardcore fans started lining up seven weeks before opening day—and most shuffled away somberly when they were told (weeks later) that *Sith* was opening at another theater. Unwilling to admit defeat, though, eleven indignant fans stayed put.

"We've heard all this before," said fan Sarah Sprague, speaking of the false rumors that circulated prior to the first two prequels. But this one wasn't a rumor. Twentieth Century Fox had signed a deal with another theater. A fan organization called LiningUp.net staged a protest. Said one angry member, "Grauman's is the *Star Wars* mecca. The studios knew we were going to line up here, made the decision to show the movie elsewhere, allowed us to line up for weeks, and then told us for sure the movie wouldn't be playing here. Then they offered us seats at a nearby theater, only to retract their offer a week later. It isn't right. We just want to see the movie." Ultimately the Dark Side prevailed—they were forced to wait in line at the other theater and miss the opening-night showings.

\* \* \*

## C-3PO FACTS AND GOSSIP

• C-3PO has the first line in the first *Star Wars* ("Did you hear that? They've shut down the main reactor!") and the last line in the last one ("Oh no!").

• Anthony Daniels, on getting the part: "I was quite insulted to be offered a role as a robot; I was a serious actor. I wasn't going to be in some weird American movie as a robot, yet my agent insisted."

• Kenny Baker (R2-D2), on Daniels: "He's been such an awkward person over the years. If he just calmed down and socialized with everyone, we could make a fortune touring and making personal appearances. I've asked him four times now but the last time he looked down his nose at me like I was a piece of s\*#@ and said, 'I don't do any of these conventions—go away, little man.'"

---

The sound a grasshopper makes is called *stridulation*.

# FRONTIER WOMEN

*It took a lot to survive on the frontier. Most histories of the Wild West focus on men—cowboys, gunfighters, chiefs—and ignore the fact that women could be powerful, influential, and hell-raising, too.*

CALAMITY JANE (1852–1903)
**Claim to Fame:** Soldier, caregiver, hell-raiser
**Her Story:** Born Martha Jane Cannery in Missouri, she was one of the most famous American women of the 19th century. Yet it's difficult to know for sure exactly what she actually *did.* Why? Because much of her legend comes from pulp-fiction writers, as well her own trumped-up autobiography. And then there were her days of touring with Buffalo Bill's Wild West Show, where Jane told many more tall tales about her rugged life. Here's some of what she claimed:

• She was married to Wild Bill Hickok and had his child.

• She was a scout for General Custer.

• She was a Pony Express rider.

• The name "Calamity Jane" was given to her by an army captain who she rescued single-handedly in an Indian fight.

Historians doubt these claims. But what makes Jane so interesting is that she could have told the truth and would still have been considered an amazing woman. Here's what *is* known:

• She was an expert horsewoman and sharpshooter.

• She often dressed as a man and fought Indians.

• A hard drinker who chewed tobacco (and cussed a lot), she was highly respected by the men she rode with.

• During a smallpox epidemic in Deadwood, South Dakota, in 1876, Jane nursed many of the sick back to health.

Most likely, Calamity Jane got her nickname simply because trouble seemed to follow her everywhere. In the end, alcoholism got the better of her—she died penniless at 51 years old.

## NELLIE CASHMAN (1845–1925)
**Claim to Fame:** Humanitarian, entrepreneur, adventurer

**Her Story:** Cashman emigrated to Boston from Ireland with her sister and mother in the mid-1860s. An adventurer at heart, Cashman heard stories of the Gold Rush and decided to go west. She boarded a ship, sailed down the Atlantic coast to Panama, crossed the isthmus on a donkey, then set sail for San Francisco. But she didn't settle there—Cashman wanted to go where the action was, so in 1872 she moved to Nevada and worked as a cook in various mining towns while panning for gold. Using the little money she earned, she opened her first boardinghouse in Panaca Flat.

### Frontier Angel

Once the boardinghouse was up and running, Cashman sold it, joined a group of 200 gold prospectors, and headed for Cassiar, British Columbia. She opened another boardinghouse there, then moved on to Victoria. But as a devout Catholic, Cashman's desire to help people was as strong as her love of adventure. Shortly after arriving in Victoria, she got news of a scurvy epidemic in Cassiar. She hired six men and hauled in 1,500 pounds of food and supplies—a trip that took 77 days, often through blizzard conditions. She nursed 100 men back to health and received the first of many nicknames, "Angel of the Cassiar." Other names given to her in time: "Frontier Angel," "Saint of the Sourdoughs," "Miner's Angel," and "the Angel of Tombstone."

All across the West, from Fairbanks, Alaska, to Tombstone, Arizona, Cashman was responsible for establishing restaurants, hotels, grocery stores, hospitals, and churches. Charitable almost to a fault, she would sooner give a free meal to a hungry man than try to make a profit. Along the way, Cashman had many male suitors, but she turned them all down. When, in 1923, a reporter asked her why, she replied, "Why child, I haven't had time for marriage. Men are a nuisance anyhow, now aren't they? They're just boys grown up."

Nellie Cashman lived a long, hard life that never saw her slow down. She died at the age of 79—after contracting pneumonia on a 750-mile dogsled journey across Alaska.

### OTHER FRONTIER WOMEN

• **Libby Smith Collins.** Like Nellie Cashman, Collins proved that a woman was capable of running a business. Her birthdate is unknown, but she came west with her parents sometime in the

1850s. After her husband, a cattle rancher, fell ill in 1888, Collins took it upon herself to transport their herd from Montana to the stockyards of Chicago. She almost didn't make it: the railroad company wouldn't let her board—it was against regulations for an unaccompanied woman to ride on a train. Collins fought the rule, got it changed, and made a tidy profit in Chicago. She took the trip alone every year after that, earning her the nickname "Cattle Queen of Montana." A movie by that title was released in 1954, based on Collins's life and starring Barbara Stanwyck and Ronald Reagan.

• **Cattle Kate (1861–1889).** Born Ella Watson, Cattle Kate is more famous for the way she died than the way she lived: she was lynched by a vigilante mob in 1889 for alleged cattle rustling. After setting up a cattle ranch in Sweetwater Valley, Wyoming, Kate had tried to register a brand with the state, but the Wyoming Stock Growers Association used their power to squash small-time ranchers. So Kate bought a brand from a neighboring farmer and began homesteading her land. This infuriated the big ranchers, who claimed ownership over the entire Sweetwater Valley. So a group of them took the law into their own hands and hanged Kate and her husband, Jim Averell. No one was ever tried for the crime.

• **Pearl Hart (1870)** The only woman convicted of stagecoach robbery was Canadian-born Pearl Hart. She and a partner named Joe Boot held up a stagecoach in Arizona in 1899 (reportedly because Pearl needed money for her dying mother). They got caught, and newspapers ran with stories of the "Lady Bandit." Hart gained even more notoriety from her disdain for authority: "I shall not consent to be tried under a law in which my sex had no voice in making!"

She was sentenced to five years in prison in Yuma, Arizona, but served only three. She claimed that she was pregnant, so they released her early. After that, Hart was never heard from again.

\* \* \*

"Women have a right to work whenever they want—as long as they have dinner ready when you get home."　　—**John Wayne**

Even for sharp cheese? A dull knife can slice cheese thinner than a sharp one.

# HI PHI

*Anyone who's read Dan Brown's best seller* The DaVinci Code
*is probably familiar with what Brown and others call a "mystical"*
*number that shows up with remarkable regularity in nature, art,*
*music, and architecture. Some even call it a "cosmic blueprint."*
*Some of Brown's claims are far-fetched, but some aren't—*
*they're real…and fascinating. The number is known*
*as Phi, a modern term for a very old concept.*

**T**AKE A NUMBER
The story starts with Euclid, a Greek mathematician who
lived in the 3rd century B.C., considered by experts to be
the most important mathematician in history (his book *Elements* is
still referenced today—2,000 years after he wrote it). Euclid wanted to find the point on a line that divides that line into two segments with a special relationship: the ratio of the entire line to the
large segment is equal to the ratio of the large segment to the
small segment. He found it, and called his discovery *extreme and
mean ratios*. Here's what it looks like:

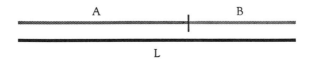

The ratio of line L to segment A is the same as the ratio of segment A to segment B, or L/A = A/B.

The ratio can also be expressed as a number: 1.61803398875…
(the number is *infinite*—the digits go on forever). To meet Euclid's
requirements, line L must be 1.618… times larger than segment A
and segment A must be 1.618… times larger than segment B.
(Euclid didn't use the number, he explained it with an equation.)

**THE DIVINE PROPORTION**
In 1509 Italian mathematician Luca Pacioli published a treatise
entitled *De Divina Proportione* (illustrated by Leonardo daVinci) in
which he gave the ratio the name *divina proportion*, because, he
said, "just as God cannot be properly defined, nor understood

---

**According to experts, camels have the worst breath in the animal kingdom.**

through words, likewise this proportion can never be designated through intelligible numbers." Since then the ratio has been given many names, such as the Golden Section, the Golden Mean (from Euclid's "extreme and mean ratio"), and the Golden Ratio.

## GOLDEN DISCOVERIES

• **Leonardo Fibonacci,** a 12th-century mathematician, developed an amazing sequence of numbers. The sequence starts with zero and one, and continues by adding the two previous digits.

0, 1, 1, 2, 3, 5, 8, 13, 21, 34, 55... and so on.

• **Robert Simson,** a Scottish mathematician, proved in 1753 that the ratios of successive Fibonacci numbers moved closer and closer to the mysterious Golden Ratio.

Fibonacci had found the sequence by computing how fast a pair of rabbits could multiply under ideal conditions. The answer is his number sequence, and since his sequence is so related to the Golden Ratio—the Golden Ratio was believed to have a mysterious presence in the natural world.

## NUMBER BUILDER

Around the turn of the 20th century, American mathematician Mark Barr gave the Golden Ratio the name it is often referred to today—*Phi*. He named it in honor of the Greek sculptor Phidias (500 B.C.–432 B.C.), who he was convinced used the ratio in his sculptures. Others claim that Phi was used in ancient art and architecture because it has a naturally balancing and pleasing aspect to it. (Some mathematicians dispute these claims, attributing them to coincidence.) A few examples:

• The Egyptians may have used Phi in the design of the pyramids. The Great Pyramid of Khufu (3200 B.C.) appears to have been designed so that the ratio of the height of its triangular face to half the side of the base is equal to Phi.

• Many art historians are convinced that Phidias applied the Golden Ratio to his design of sculptures for the Parthenon. The dimensions of the Parthenon itself follow the Golden Ratio of Phi.

• Other buildings that seem to utilize the Phi ratio: the Cathedral of Notre Dame in Paris and the UN building in New York City.

A rhinoceros beetle can push 850 times its weight, equivalent to a man pushing a tank.

• DaVinci may have used Phi to define the proportions of his painting of *The Last Supper*, as well as the face of the *Mona Lisa*, and his classic drawing known as *Vitruvian Man* was an effort to prove that the ideal human body is made of building blocks whose proportional ratios always equal Phi.

• The famous opening notes of Beethoven's 5th Symphony ("duh-duh-duh-duuuuhh") occur not only in the first and last bars but also exactly at the Phi point of the symphony.

• Antonio Stradivari, still considered the greatest violin maker ever, placed the f-holes in his violins according to Phi ratios.

## NATURAL WONDERS

The Phi ratio is frequently found in nature, which may explain much of the mysticism surrounding Phi. Some examples:

• The number of petals on a flower are, for some reason, very often a Fibonacci number. Black-eyed susans and chicory flowers have 21 petals; plantains have 34; daisies have 89.

• The ratio between the number of male and female bees in a beehive can be shown to be related to Phi.

• A nautilus shell is a spiral. The ratio of each spiral's diameter to the next is Phi. It's the same for the rate of curve of a DNA spiral.

• The number of and configuration of leaves on the stems of many plants can be measured in Phi ratios.

• A sunflower's seeds grow in opposing spirals on the flower. The number of seeds in each row grows at the Phi ratio. This is also true of pinecones and pineapples.

Think it has no application to your life? The dimensions of a Kit Kat candy bar are in a Phi ratio, as is the *National Geographic* logo. Trek mountain bikes are proportioned according to Phi, too. Need another example? So is your Visa or MasterCard.

\*     \*     \*

"I may not have gone where I intended to go, but I think I have ended up where I needed to be."

—Douglas Adams

First primates in space: Two spider monkeys named Able and Miss Baker.

# NUDES & PRUDES

*So what side of the debate do you take—*
*are you offended by public nudity, or are you*
*offended by people who are offended by it?*

**N**UDE: When the Boise, Idaho, City Council passed an ordinance outlawing total nudity in public except in cases of "serious artistic merit," Erotic City Gentleman's Club (a strip joint) responded with "Art Nights." On Monday and Tuesday nights they passed out sketch pads and pencils so that patrons could draw the strippers as they danced. "We had a lot of people," owner Chris Teague told reporters, "drawing some very good pictures."

**PRUDE:** So did Art Night work? Nope: In April 2005, Boise police raided Erotic City on Art Night and cited three of the nude dancers. "The law clearly states that the exemption does not apply to adult businesses," says Lynn Hightower, spokesperson for the Boise Police Department. "If it were an art studio and models were actually posing, that would be one thing. These women weren't posing." Erotic City says it will fight the charges in court...but the dancers will have to wear pasties and G-strings until further notice.

**NUDE:** When Stu Smailes died in 2002 at the age of 69, he left the city of Seattle $1 million to buy a new fountain. There's a catch—Smailes's will stipulates that in order for Seattle to claim the money, the fountain must include "one or more *unclothed*, life-size male figure(s)." Furthermore, it must be designed in "the classical style"—in other words, no cheating by making it unrecognizably abstract. "Smailes was a very funny man," said his attorney, Tim Bradbury. "He had a very strong sense of humor."

**PRUDE:** Satirical news anchor Jon Stewart's book *America (The Book)* spent more than 15 weeks on the *New York Times* bestseller list and was named Book of the Year by *Publishers Weekly* magazine...but that didn't stop eight southern Mississippi libraries from banning it. Reason: the satirical book contains a phony photograph of all nine Supreme Court justices in the nude. "We're not an adult bookstore," says Robert Willits, director of the Jackson-George Regional Library System. "Our collection is open to the entire public."

**NUDE:** As of January 2005, the Houston Police Department is relaxing its requirement that undercover vice officers remain fully clothed while trying to bust brothels that masquerade as spas, massage parlors, and "stress relief clinics." The no-nudity policy made it easy for the prostitutes to spot undercover cops: all they had to do was ask customers to disrobe before propositioning them—anyone who didn't was obviously a cop. Now, says Harris County District Attorney Ted Wilson, disrobing "is something the officers can do, if necessary, to gather sufficient evidence."

**PRUDE:** In March 2005, Texas State Representative Al Edwards introduced a bill in the state legislature to reduce funding to state schools that permit "sexually suggestive" cheerleading at athletic events. "It's just too sexually oriented, you know, the way they're shaking their behinds and going on, breaking it down," Edwards told a reporter. "And then we say to them, 'Don't get involved in sex unless it's marriage or love, it's dangerous out there.' And yet the teachers and directors are helping them to go through those kinds of gyrations."

**NUDE:** Tired of watching CNN and FoxNews? If you live in Europe and subscribe to satellite TV, now you can watch Naked News on the Get Lucky TV channel. On Naked News, strippers read the news as they strip. Caveat: if the news is *really* bad, you won't get to see much nudity. "We are quite sensitive to certain issues, one, of course, being death," says stripper/news anchor Samantha Page. "We try to be as respectful as we can, and what we tend to do is leave our clothes on."

**PRUDE:** In 2003 the owner of the Station Cafe in Berlin, Connecticut, posted a gag sign outside his business advertising "Naked Karaoke." The bar owner, Marty St. Pierre, was only joking, but when the town hall threatened to fine and even arrest him if he held the event, he decided to fight back. He filed suit against the town and won…and attracted more than 120 participants to his first Naked Karaoke night.

---

Heavy metal: Steel floats in mercury.

# WELCOME TO NUNAVUT

*Geography quiz: Who's the biggest landowner in North America? Bill Gates? The Rockefeller family? Not even close—the Inuit of Canada. They recently reclaimed ownership over a giant portion of northern Canada. Here's the fascinating story.*

## PEOPLE OF THE NORTH

About 1,300 years ago, a small civilization developed on the coast of the Bering Sea in northwest Alaska. The Thule culture was built around the hunting of sea mammals, primarily whales. They lived in permanent villages along the coast and had a wide variety of sophisticated tools: dogsleds, seal skin umiaks and kayaks, harpoons, knives, snow goggles, combs, and sewing gear made from bone and ivory. Thule culture thrived there for about 200 years. Then they got some help from Mother Nature.

About A.D. 1000, the Northern Hemisphere experienced a warming trend that resulted in less ice on the Arctic Sea. This allowed the Thule to expand to Alaska's north coast, then east along Canada's. And they did expand: within just 200 years the Thule inhabited a region that stretched from Alaska all the way across northern Canada, and even into Greenland. (The name "Thule" comes from an ancient site found in Thule, Greenland.) But they would grow to their largest numbers in northern Canada, where their descendants still live today. Their native Canadian neighbors, the Algonquin Indians, called them "Eskimos," which linguists believe refers to snowshoes, but they called themselves "Inuit"—the People.

## NEW NEIGHBORS

The Inuit thrived in the far north for the next several centuries. Evidence suggests that sometime in the 13th century they had their first contact with Europeans, encountering Viking settlements on Greenland. There may have even been some trade between the two groups, but the Vikings were gone from the island by the 1400s and the Inuit had it to themselves.

In the 1500s and early 1600s, contact increased as Europeans pushed farther into North America. Most of the meetings were unfriendly, with several skirmishes and deaths on both sides. But in the later part of the century, the Hudson's Bay Company of England set up a number of trading posts, and trade between the two groups began on a regular basis. Through the 1700s the Inuit regularly exchanged furs of animals such as seals, wolverines, and arctic foxes for manufactured European goods such as tools, hunting gear, and wool blankets.

If that trade seemed beneficial at first, over time it proved disastrous. Hunting with rifles and steel traps was a lot easier than using spears and bows and arrows, but it caused animal populations to plummet. The Inuit relied on those animals not only for trade but also for clothing and shelter. When the animals began to disappear, the Inuit became increasingly dependent on European goods, while at the same time having less to offer for them. They began a century-long slide into dependency, poverty, and despair.

## THE NORTHWEST TERRITORIES

While they were losing their traditional way of life, the Inuit were also losing control of their land. By the mid-19th century, the Hudson's Bay Company "owned" most of modern-day Canada, including virtually all Inuit lands. In 1870 the company's land was sold to the newly formed Dominion of Canada and designated as the Northwest Territories (NWT). The Inuit lands, as well as those of many other native tribes, ended up as part of the territory.

The Inuit were just one small group in the vast territory and had almost no say in the government. Over the decades large chunks of the region gained independent governing powers as they became the provinces of Manitoba, Saskatchewan, and Alberta, as well as the Yukon Territory, but the rest remained under the control of a federally appointed commissioner. Even after power was transferred to an elected assembly in 1967, the Inuit were still outnumbered and outvoted by the whites and other natives who lived in the non-Inuit lands to the south and west. The Inuit did not trust that the government understood their problems or was responsive to their needs.

They wanted their land back.

## TIME TO SPLIT

The concept of splitting the NWT into Inuit and non-Inuit areas first surfaced in the early 1960s. It didn't make much headway until a landmark Canadian Supreme Court decision in 1973: The Nisga'a Indians of British Columbia argued that they had an "aboriginal claim" to Canadian territory since they had been there for so much longer than Europeans. The court agreed. And that was enough for the Inuit Tapirisat of Canada (ITC), an organization that represents the rights of Canadian Inuit, to begin a formal push for a separate Inuit territory within Canada.

In 1976 the Canadian government agreed to enter into negotiations with the ITC for the creation of a territory that would be known as Nunavut, which means "our land" in Inuktitut, the Inuit language. It turned out to be a long, slow process. It took until 1982 for a vote on the idea to go to the people. It passed. Then they had to work out the details. That took another ten years. In 1992 the final agreement was put to a vote…and passed. The following year the Canadian government ratified the agreement.

## ALMOST HOME

The Canadian government agreed to a triangle-shaped Inuit territory in north-central and eastern Canada, more than 770,000 square miles in size—roughly the same size as western Europe. The Inuit would gain outright title to 135,000 square miles of the territory; the rest would remain the property of the federal government, but the Inuit would have the right to hunt and fish on the land. The federal government also retained control of the mineral rights to all but 14,000 square miles of the territory, but the Inuit would be guaranteed a royalty on any oil or minerals extracted from Nunavut. In addition, the Canadian government agreed to pay the Inuit more than $1 billion Canadian to settle any and all remaining territorial claims.

It still took another six years to set up the new government, but finally, on April 1, 1999, the Nunavut Territory came in to being and the Inuit, who had been there for 1,000 years, had their land back. Paul Okalik, a 34-year-old who that same year had become the first Inuit lawyer in Canada's history, was elected Nunavut's first premier.

## NUNAVUT FACTS

• Nunavut may be as big as western Europe and the largest territory in Canada, but only 29,000 people live there in only 28 isolated and largely icebound communities.

• Eighty percent of the people in Nunavut are Inuit.

• Nunavut is nearly as big as Alaska and California combined.

• The northernmost town in the territory, Alert, is the northernmost inhabited town in the world. It is less than 600 miles from the North Pole.

• Nunavut is the largest area in the world to be governed by aboriginal people.

• Six thousand people live in the capital city, Iqaluit, which means "many fish," on the eastern shore of Baffin Island. The only way to get there is by boat or airplane, and there are no street numbers or even any street names—except for one: the Road to Nowhere.

\*     \*     \*

## PAPER OR PLASTIC?

*Some items and prices from a 1961 grocery store flyer.*

5-piece Wrench Set: 97¢
Men's Cotton Pajamas: $1.00
Grass Seed, 5 lb.: 88¢
Deluxe Rubber Bathmat: 58¢
Ladies Socks: 25¢
Asparagus: 29¢/bunch
California Oranges: 10 for 45¢
Good 'N' Rich Cake Mix: 7¢
Ritz Crackers: 33¢
Waldorf Toilet Tissue: 35¢
Kellogg's Corn Flakes: 2 for 25¢
Pillsbury Flour, 5 lbs: 39¢
Corn: 5 ears for 29¢
Coffee: 57¢/lb.

Rib Roast: 69¢/lb.
Bumble Bee Tuna: 3 cans for $1
Hydrox Cookies: 39¢
Wisk, ½ gallon: $1.39
Celery: 17¢/bunch
Sirloin Steak: 89¢/lb.
Haddock Fillet: 38¢/lb.
Chuck Roast: 34¢/lb.
Jumbo Insulated Picnic Bag: 88¢
Philadelphia Cream Cheese: 29¢
Kosher Salami: 69¢/lb.
Chicken: 25¢/lb.
Tomatoes: 2 cartons for 25¢
Peaches, 29-oz. Cans: 4 for 98¢

Still, it's worth it: Ancient Greeks believed drinking beer would cause leprosy.

# FROSTED LUNGS AND HALIBUT HEADS

*Here are a few Alaskan terms Uncle John picked up the year he wintered in Anchorage with the white eyes and the scissor bills. Enjoy!*

- **Squaw candy.** Dried, smoked salmon. Squaw candy was one of the preserved foods that helped Alaskans survive the long, hard winter months.

- **Boomer.** Someone who comes to work in Alaska only during economic booms, such as during the construction of the Alaskan pipeline.

- **Nooshnik.** An outhouse.

- **Frosted lungs.** A pain in the chest similar to frostbite that you get when breathing air that is colder than −30°F.

- **White eye.** A dog with one white eye and one normal eye.

- **Bear insurance.** A gun brought with you during outdoor activities such as fishing or hiking, to protect yourself if you are attacked by a bear.

- **America.** The other 49 states, also known as "outside." (Alaska didn't become a state until 1959, and it took the old-timers a while to get used to the idea.)

- **The Banana Belt.** The area around Anchorage and Cook Inlet—comparatively warmer than the rest of the state.

- **Skunk bear.** A wolverine. (Looks kind of like a bear, smells like a skunk.)

- **Greasy thumb.** Greedy, dishonest. During the gold rush of 1897, miners often paid for things by holding open their pouch of gold dust and letting a merchant or bartender reach in and take a pinch. Dishonest merchants greased their index finger and thumb to increase the amount of gold that stuck.

- **Candlefish.** A species of fish so oily that, when dried, it can be lit with a match and used as a candle.

- **Salmon cruncher.** A derogatory Caucasian term for the Inuit.

- **Halibut head.** Derogatory Inuit (Eskimo) term for Caucasians.

- **Scissor bill.** Halibut head.

# THE PAJAMA REPORT

*We've written about "Underwear in the News" in previous Bathroom Readers. We thought we'd dress up a little for this one.*

## PAJAMA PROTEST

P"Johannesburg, South Africa, nurses are wearing pajamas and nighties to work to demonstrate the need for a higher uniform allowance. They vowed to continue until their demands are met, citing a yearly figure of 54 rand ($9) for shoes. Officials said the protest was a potential security problem as it made it difficult to distinguish between patients and nurses, meaning anyone could walk into the hospital pretending to be a nurse. A spokesman for the North West health department complained that the protest was 'confusing patients and turning our facilities into bedrooms.'"

—Reuters

## ARMED AND PAJAMEROUS

"A bank robber adopted an unusual disguise when he held up a bank in Bexley, Ohio. Police say the man walked into National City Bank on Saturday wearing blue and white checkered pajamas, and bedroom slippers open at the heels. He didn't have a mask. Of the man's outfit, Sgt. Bryan Holbrook of the Bexley Police Department said: 'It was a little unusual, yes, but then robbing banks is an unusual practice anyway.'"

—Whiteboard News

## LIFE-SAVING PAJAMAS

"Belgian researchers believe that pajamas based on space technology could provide a breakthrough in unlocking the mysteries of Sudden Infant Death Syndrome (SIDS). The prototype pajamas include five sensors, which monitor the baby's breathing and heartbeat, connected to a small detection unit that triggers an alarm if it detects any abnormalities. The technology was developed by Verhaert, a European systems development group, which helped to design and manufacture special suits to monitor the vital signs of European astronauts."

—Wired News

---

Only four days of every year are exactly 24 hours long.

## ON SECOND THOUGHT...

"In February 2001, Girl Scout officials of the San Jacinto Council near Houston announced that this year's father-daughter event would be a 'pajama party' dance in which fathers and the girls, aged 11–17, would come dressed in sleepwear. After some complaints ('It would attract every pervert in the city,' said one mother), the council changed the dress code to sweatsuits."

—*News of the Weird*

## JUST PLANE NUTS

"An airline passenger wearing only a pair of pajama bottoms stole a baggage tractor at Atlanta's main airport and drove it onto an active runway. City police say Robert W. Buzzell, 31, walked out through an exit door that had an alarm at Hartsfield-Jackson Atlanta International Airport. The man was stopped by mechanics who asked him for an employee identification card. When he couldn't provide one, they called police. Buzzell, who had a ticket for a Delta flight, was jailed on charges of unlawful interference with security and reckless conduct."

—*CBS News*

## PAJAMA POLICE

"The days of rolling out of bed and rolling into class are coming to an end. Pajamas, the preferred attire of some sleepy students, are no longer allowed in Hillsborough County, Florida, schools. 'There's no reason to wear pajamas to school,' said James Ammirati, assistant principal at Stewart Middle School. Sleepwear is popular school attire, especially during cold weather and on exam days, students say. Nevena Novakovic, 17, a junior at Robinson High School in Tampa, doesn't like the new ruling. 'I think as long as you don't look like a hootchy mama,' she said, 'you should be able to wear whatever.'"

—*St. Petersburg Times*

\*     \*     \*

In 1992 Ernest Hemingway's sons established Hemingway, Ltd., to license their father's name. Two official items you can buy: Hemingway pajamas and a Hemingway shotgun. (Hemingway killed himself with a shotgun in 1961...while wearing his pajamas.)

---

If it takes a second to vacuum one square foot, it would take 12 years to vacuum Ohio.

# THE VAMPIRE SLAYER

*Many people have a favorite book, movie, or TV show
that nobody else seems to appreciate. And then one day it's
considered a "classic." Here's the story of an underrated
television show that became a cult and critical smash.*

## FIRST BLOOD

After graduating from Wesleyan University in 1987 with a degree in filmmaking, Joss Whedon went to Hollywood to write for television. Doors were already open for him—his grandfather wrote for *Leave It to Beaver* and his father wrote for *Golden Girls* and *Benson*—so Whedon was able to land jobs on the sitcoms *Roseanne* and *Parenthood*. But he found the work dull and uncreative. He wanted to develop his own characters, in his own style. He wanted to do something different.

So he decided to write a movie script that would follow a classic horror film formula, but with a couple of major differences.

• First, it was funny and the dialogue was snappy and fast-paced.

• Second, Whedon flipped the character structure. The young blond girl who typically appeared in horror movies as a hysterical, screaming victim, was the hero. Men were helpless victims, not the heroes.

• To make it even more ironic, Whedon named his heroine the cutsiest, anti–action hero name he could imagine: Buffy Summers.

• The plot of *Buffy the Vampire Slayer*: a high-school cheerleader dates boys, attends class...and fights vampires, demons, and werewolves. And at the end, Buffy ends up not a hero, but an outcast when she burns down her school gym because it's full of vampires.

## A LOT AT STAKE

Twentieth Century Fox bought Whedon's script, but it perplexed them. It wasn't a straight horror or action movie and it wasn't a straight comedy, either. It was about seemingly ditzy teenagers, but they talked like sophisticates from a 1940s Spencer Tracy / Katharine Hepburn movie. It also had an unhappy ending and an unlikely hero. Result: they made Whedon rewrite *Buffy* as a light

---

**A standard Oreo is 29% cream, 71% cookie.**

comedy with cartoonish violence, no edge, and a weak, ditzy heroine. In other words, it became exactly the kind of movie Whedon was trying to parody. Fox's changes didn't work. Released in the summer of 1992, *Buffy the Vampire Slayer* bombed.

## BIG SCREEN, LITTLE SCREEN

Whedon was bitter that Hollywood had ruined his creation. He stopped trying to pitch ideas to the studios and became a screenwriter-for-hire, doing script-doctor work throughout the 1990s.

Meanwhile, *Buffy* was selling well on home video and Fox wanted to capitalize on its success. Fox executive Gail Berman remembered reading Whedon's original script in 1992 and asked Whedon if he'd be interested in resurrecting *Buffy* for a TV show. He was, but on one condition: he would be head writer and executive producer, ensuring the series wouldn't again stray from his original darkly comic, feminist angle. Berman agreed and a new series—a sequel to the film—was begun. Buffy (now played by Sarah Michelle Gellar) attends high school in Sunnydale, California, which sits on a "hellmouth," a gateway to the world of demons and vampires.

Eleven episodes were filmed in 1996. The only problem: the show didn't fit any category, so no network wanted to air it. After months of lobbying both broadcast and cable networks, the young WB Network agreed to air *Buffy* as a mid-season replacement. It premiered in March 1997 to 3.3 million viewers—the WB's biggest audience ever at that time. *Buffy* became the WB's first big hit and actually kept the struggling network afloat.

## THE FORMULA: NO FORMULA

While the original movie was so fluffy that teenagers rejected it, the series followed Whedon's vision and became one of the most influential and talked-about shows on TV. Young viewers liked it because it was hip and never condescending. Viewers of all ages appreciated its originality: no other show at the time combined comedy, horror, melodrama, romance, and action as well as philosophy, feminism, and mythology. Even critics liked it. Joe Queenan of *TV Guide* wrote: "*Buffy* is far from being the stuff of fantasy or mere satire, it is the most realistic portrayal of contemporary teenage life on television today."

After *Buffy*'s success, dozens of teen-oriented shows hit the airwaves in the late 1990s and early 2000s, all heavy on dialogue and wit, and many with a similar supernatural element. *Buffy* also showed that a woman could be the center of an action-oriented series. Among the shows that owe a debt: *Alias, Dawson's Creek, Felicity, The O.C., Tru Calling, Dead Like Me, Wonderfalls, Roswell, Joan of Arcadia, Point Pleasant, Popular, Veronica Mars, Smallville, Gilmore Girls,* and *Charmed.*

## THE DEAD SHALL WALK AGAIN

Because *Buffy* was on a very small network, it couldn't draw huge audiences like *American Idol* or *CSI.* (It never finished higher than 62nd in the ratings.) And because of that, the WB canceled *Buffy the Vampire Slayer* in 2001. Though it had saved the network in its infancy, the show was unceremoniously dropped—not even allowed a final episode to wrap up four years of stories. Fortunately, another small network, UPN, immediately picked it up and ran it for two more years. The modest but loyal audience followed. They've made *Buffy* a pop cultural phenomenon: there are countless *Buffy* books, comics, and Web sites. There's even talk of another big-screen version, featuring the TV series' cast.

Joss Whedon got the last laugh. While Fox tinkered with his movie script and failed, he got to do *Buffy* the way he wanted and it was a huge success. And because *Buffy* worked so well, Whedon now gets creative control on everything he does, which was what he wanted all along.

## BUFFY BITS

• In the 1998 season Buffy, ironically, fell in love with a vampire. That character, named Angel (played by David Boreanaz), was so popular he got his own show, *Angel.* It aired from 1999 to 2004.

• Among the actors who launched their careers on *Buffy:* **Sarah Michelle Gellar** (*Scooby-Doo*), **Seth Green** (*Austin Powers*), and **Alyson Hannigan** (*American Pie*).

• In the episode "Hush," demons that can only be killed by a human scream steal the voices of everyone in Sunnydale, leaving them free to run wild. More than half the episode is dialogue-free. Whedon received *Buffy*'s only major Emmy nomination for this nearly wordless episode—in the writing category.

# AUDIO TREASURES

*Musical taste is very subjective. But how many times have you found yourself in a music store, staring at thousands of CDs by artists you've never heard of, wondering which ones are worth listening to? It happens to us all the time—so we decided to offer a few recommendations. They're not necessarily weird or obscure...just good.*

STEVIE WONDER *Innervisions* (1973) *Soul*
**Review:** "When Wonder discovered that he was stretching the limits of what pop could include, the most visionary of his albums was undoubtedly *Innervisions*, an interconnected suite of songs––many of them segue right into each other—but it's not of the self-indulgent variety implied in the hazy album title." *(The Best Rock N' Roll Records of All Time)*

**ELLA FITZGERALD & LOUIS ARMSTRONG** *Ella and Louis* (1957) *Jazz/Pop*
**Review:** "An inspired collaboration. Both stars were riding high at this stage in their careers. Equally inspired was the choice of material, with the gruffness of Armstrong's voice blending like magic with Fitzgerald's stunningly silky delivery. Gentle and sincere." *(All-Time Top 1,000 Albums)*

**VOICES ON THE VERGE** *Live in Philadelphia* (2001) *Folk/Pop*
**Review:** "Take four up-and-coming female singer/songwriters, put them in a room with some acoustic guitars, and turn on the tape recorder. The disc is not merely a round robin—the women sing and play on each other's songs, expanding one another's styles. It showcases the best of what these women have to offer and lets their hidden talents emerge." *(Rolling Stone)*

**STONE ROSES** *Stone Roses* (1989) *Rock*
**Review:** "As close to perfection as pop gets. The songs are wonder-rockets, a mixture of styles segueing beautifully thanks to production so flawless it's as if the producer was playing a violin. It weaves an atmospheric spell without ever sounding nostalgic." *(Musichound Rock: The Essential Album Guide)*

---

The Grand Canyon gets more snowfall annually than Minneapolis, Minnesota.

**SWAN SILVERTONES** *Love Lifted Me* (1956) *Gospel*
Review: "Some of the best hard-gospel harmonizing from the mid-
'50s, most notably 'How I Got Over' and 'My Rock'—the group's
toughest sides, with firm conviction from lead soloists Solomon
Womack, Claude Jeter, and Paul Owens." (*All Music Guide*)

**ROLLING STONES** *Let It Bleed* (1969) *Rock*
Review: "The record kicks off with the terrifying 'Gimme Shelter,' the song that came to symbolize the death of the utopian spirit of the '60s. But the entire album, although a motley compound
of country, blues, and gospel fire, rattles and burns with apocalyp-
tic cohesion." (*Rolling Stone's Top 500 Albums of All Time*)

**PIXIES** *Doolittle* (1989) *Alternative Rock*
Review: "The band's surf-doom bubblegum never sounded so playful. The swift success was built on two gigantic singles: the puzzling
but catchy 'Monkey Gone to Heaven,' and jaunty pop hit 'Here
Comes Your Man.' But everything about *Doolittle* struck with a
speedy punch and finds its groove in pockets of mysterious wild-
ness." (*Spin's 100 Greatest Albums 1985–2005*)

**YOUSSOU N'DOUR** *Eyes Open* (1992) *World Music*
Review: "N'Dour is a Senegalese singer-songwriter with an amazing voice, but a successful marriage of First and Third World music
is a tricky balancing act. Confident and pointedly cosmopolitan,
*Eyes Open* is an epic-size record that lays claim to a universe of
pop while never dropping its West African accent." (*Rolling Stone*)

**PATTY GRIFFIN** *Living with Ghosts* (1996) *Folk*
Review: "Less a folk album than a rock recording without the
rhythmic clutter. Think Melissa Etheridge with much better
songs." (*Musichound Folk: The Essential Album Guide*)

**MANU CHAO** *Clandestino* (1998) *Latin*
Review: "An enchanting trip through Latin rock, reliant on a
potpourri of musical styles. The best songs benefit from Chao's
freewheeling delivery which incorporates balladry, chorus vocals,
rapping, and spoken-word passages. There are so many great ideas
here that it's difficult to digest in one listen." (*All Music Guide*)

---

A can-do kind of guy: Harry Houdini could open cans with his teeth.

# SECRET SUBWAY

*Contrary to what the history books say, the Interborough Rapid
Transit (IRT) built in 1904 was not New York's first subway.
More than 30 years before, someone built one in secret*

## UNDERGROUND MAN

Alfred Ely Beach (1826–1896) was a patent lawyer, inventor, and the publisher of *Scientific American* magazine.
From his office window in New York City, he could observe pedestrians, horse-drawn carriages, and wagons navigate the congested
streets below. He dreamed of building a luxury transportation system that would travel *beneath* the streets of Manhattan. But Beach
feared interference from City Hall, which was run by the infamously corrupt politician, "Boss" Tweed. Rather than ask permission beforehand, Beach devised a scheme.

In February 1868 he applied for a permit to build an underground "pneumatic dispatch" system, a letter-mailing tube similar
to what drive-through banks use to whisk deposits from cars to the
teller. He chose a location in an area of Lower Manhattan that
was generally deserted in the evenings. Then he made a secret deal
with the owner of Devlin's Clothing Store at the corner of Murray
Street and Broadway to let him use the store cellar as his base of
operations.

## THE BIG DIG

Every night, Beach, his 21-year-old son Fred, and a team of workmen would meet in the merchant's cellar to dig. Equipped with
picks, shovels, wheelbarrows, and a hydraulic boring device that
Beach had designed and built himself, they painstakingly hollowed
out a tunnel nine feet in diameter and a block long. Secrecy was of
the utmost importance: if the political bosses got wind of the operation, the whole thing could be shut down. Rather than risk it,
the unwanted rock and dirt were bagged and whisked away in special wagons with muffled wheels, so as not to make any sound.
Even the lines of track, ties, and railcars were slipped in piece by
piece through the store basement under the cloak of darkness, and
assembled underground.

---

**Wire they doing it? Scottish farmers frequently put braces on the teeth of their sheep.**

It took 58 days to dig the 300-foot-long tunnel to the corner of Warren Street and Broadway. Once the track was laid, the passenger car in place, and the lobby built, Beach installed the piece of equipment that would power his underground railroad. The Roots Patent Force Blast Blower, or "Western Tornado," as the workers called it, was a steam-driven, 100-horsepower wind machine that would blow the train car to one end of the line and suck it back to the other. In test run after test run, the gale force whisked the car quietly along the track at a brisk speed of 10 mph. The air that pushed and pulled the car was vented to the street above, blowing hats off unsuspecting pedestrians' heads.

## BEACH PARTY

Finally the day came for Beach to unveil his magnificent creation. On February 26, 1870, he threw a lavish party and invited all of Manhattan's elite to attend. Those who rode the 22-seat passenger car with its upholstered seats and glass-globed lamps marveled at its luxury. Party guests waited their turn in the elegantly appointed lobby, lounging on velvet settees surrounded by lovely frescoes, a water fountain, and an aquarium filled with goldfish. They listened to music played on a grand piano as they waited to take the nearly silent ride on Beach's pneumatic subway. The next day the *New York Herald*'s headline proclaimed, "Fashionable Reception Held in the Bowels of the Earth!"

Now that his secret was out, Beach felt certain that the public would support a clean, elegant, and comfortable transportation system that ran all the way to Central Park. Of course, the state legislature would want to support it, too. He envisioned it covering five miles and carrying 20,000 passengers a day.

## YOU CAN'T FIGHT CITY HALL

Soon New Yorkers were lining up to take subway rides at 25 cents a trip. They were all for it, but Boss Tweed was against it. When the state legislature passed a bill approving the building of Beach's subway system at the cost of $5 million in private funds, Tweed used his political clout to force Governor John Hoffman to veto the bill. Hoffman then pushed the legislature to give Tweed $80 million in *public* funds to build an elevated railway.

Undaunted, Beach continued to rally the public's support for a subway, and in 1873 (after Tweed was imprisoned for fraud), the air-blown subway was again considered. This time, Beach's nemesis was millionaire financier and Manhattan landlord John Jacob Astor III. Astor worried that tunneling beneath the city streets would collapse many of the buildings he owned aboveground, and was especially concerned about the world's tallest building at the time—Trinity Church with its 281-foot spire.

With Astor and other landlords against him, Beach finally gave up. He closed the pneumatic subway, locked the doors, and walked away. By the time he died in 1896, his elegant subway experiment had been all but forgotten.

## A LAST HURRAH

Elevated trains began carrying passengers in New York City in 1870, and dominated the public transit service for three decades. The first subway—the Interborough Rapid Transit (IRT)—opened in October 1904, carrying 150,000 passengers from City Hall to 145th Street on its first day of operation. Other lines soon followed.

In 1912 workers installing the new "BMT" subway line accidentally broke through the wall of Beach's lobby and discovered his secret subway. Chandeliers still hung from the ceiling, and the passenger car, although badly deteriorated, sat poised on the track. The workers took some photos and a plaque honoring Beach's pioneering efforts to build a subway was erected. Then the workers pressed on with their own labors.

What happened to Alfred Beach's secret subway? It's still there at the corner of Warren Street and Broadway, with the lights out and the doors locked, entombed underground.

\*　　\*　　\*

## NOTES FROM THE UNDERGROUND

- World's first subway system: the Tube, built in London in 1863.
- First subway system in the U.S.: Boston's MTA, or "T," in 1897.
- First subway in Latin America: El Subte, Buenos Aires, in 1913.
- Asia's first subway: Ginza Line, built in Tokyo in 1927.

---

The palace of the Sultan of Brunei has 257 toilets (but no *Bathroom Readers*).

# FABULOUS FLOP: THE DELOREAN, PART II

*Here's the second part of our story about one of the most unusual— and unsuccessful—cars ever made. Part I is on page 163.*

## READY...OR NOT

By the start of 1981, the DeLorean Motor Company was up and running and about to manufacture its first cars. When John DeLorean agreed to build his manufacturing plant just out-side Belfast in Northern Ireland, the British government put up $97 million in financing. The first of 500 test cars rolled off the assembly line on January 21, 1981, and by April the company began producing cars for sale. The first DeLorean shipments arrived in the United States in June.

## BAD CARS

As predicted, DeLoreans were overpriced, overweight, and under-powered. The company knew this and had resigned itself to selling an under-performer. But what caught executives—and the first buyers—off-guard was how badly the first cars were constructed. Few if any of the plant workers in Northern Ireland had worked on an assembly line before; many had never even owned a car...and it showed. In one early shipment of 250 DeLoreans, 150 of them wouldn't start; they had to be pushed off the freighter by hand.

And that was just the beginning. Blinkers wouldn't turn on, headlights wouldn't turn off. Windows fell out of the gull-wing doors when drivers rolled them down. The "stainless" steel stained if you touched it or leaned against it wearing a pair of blue jeans. The roof leaked onto the floor mats, which bled permanent black ink onto shoes and clothing. The fuel gauges didn't work, strand-ing motorists when they ran out of gas without warning. The door locks jammed too: at an auto show in Cleveland, a spectator was trapped inside a DeLorean for more than an hour until paramedics pried him out.

The company moved quickly to address these quality-control issues by setting up quality assurance centers in California, Michigan, and New Jersey. Mechanics spent as many as 200 hours—and $2,000 of the company's rapidly dwindling cash—on each car, taking it apart and putting it back together again before it could be shipped to a dealer and sold to the public. This helped fix the quality problem, but the damage to the car's reputation had been done: early word of mouth was devastating.

## BAD BUSINESS

For all his experience at GM, DeLorean managed his senior executives terribly. He hired too many and paid them higher salaries than his company could afford, further draining its cash reserves. Then in the spring of 1981, he tried to restructure the corporation with a new stock offering that would have voided $22 million worth of executive stock options while increasing his own share to $120 million. The British government would have been shafted, too. It had poured nearly $150 million into DeLorean, but the restructuring would have dropped its stake to just $8.4 million.

Betrayed executives began to depart en masse just as the company was gearing up for production. Even DeLorean's personal assistant, Marian Gibson, quit. But before she left, she photocopied as many incriminating documents as she could, then leaked them to a British newspaper and a member of Parliament. When DeLorean's double-dealing became public in October 1981, his relations with the British government quickly soured.

## BAD TIMING

If ever there was a time to *not* start a new car company, the fall of 1981 was it. The United States was sliding deeper into recession, interest rates were up, consumer spending was down, and bad weather was keeping potential customers away from auto showrooms. DeLorean sales peaked at a meager 720 cars in October, then began to drop. By December, dealers were telling the company to hold future shipments until further notice.

Hundreds of unsold DeLoreans began piling up at the factory loading dock and at auto dealerships all over the country. DeLorean's response to the crisis? He doubled production to 80 cars a day, converting cash the company needed to pay its bills into cars it could not sell. Why did he do it? Because his stock offering—the one that enriched him at the expense of his top executives and the British government—was faltering. DeLorean figured if he kept his production numbers high, he could bluff Wall Street into believing the company was healthy enough to invest in. (It didn't work: the stock offering was canceled due to lack of interest.)

## OFF ROAD

By now the company was more than $65 million in debt and nearly out of cash. DeLorean had hoped to raise $27 million through the stock offering, and when that failed he turned to the British government (the one he'd just been caught ripping off) and told them he needed a $65 million line of credit to stay in business—otherwise he'd close the factory and they'd lose their entire investment. But the British had had enough. They not only refused to put any more money into the company, they hired an outside accounting firm to audit its books…and what they found wasn't good. In February 1982, the DeLorean Motor Company was placed under receivership (the British equivalent of filing for reorganization under Chapter 11 of the bankruptcy code). In May the court shut down the assembly line.

DeLorean had precipitated the crisis by turning his company's cash into cars; now he tried to dig himself out by turning the cars back into cash. He dumped 1,374 DeLoreans with a "bulk liquidator" for $12,500 each, less than half their $28,000 purchase price. That raised about $17 million, which went to pay off a delinquent bank loan that threatened to shut the company down for good.

Next, DeLorean sent urgent telegrams to the company's 345 dealers, asking each of them to purchase six cars at rock-bottom prices to help save the company. "Please call or cable what you can do," the telegram ended. "God bless you all." Only one dealer even bothered to reply. "No thanks," he cabled back.

## (DRUG) DEAL OF THE CENTURY

In the fall of 1982, DeLorean came to an agreement with the British receivers: If he could come up with $10 million in cash by October 18, they'd let him reopen his factory. But where would he get the money?

From his neighbor, James Hoffman, that's who. Hoffman's young son was a friend of DeLorean's son, Zachary. The Hoffmans lived down the street from DeLorean's Southern California estate.

---

The villagers of Sao Miguel Island, off Portugal, heat their food over volcanic vents.

What happened next depends on whom you believe. According to DeLorean, Hoffman offered to put together a group of investors who would chip in $15 million to save the car company. All DeLorean had to do was pay Hoffman a $1.9 million "finder's fee" up front. It wasn't until later, DeLorean claimed, that he learned that the "investors" were actually drug dealers, and that the $1.9 million was going to finance the importation and distribution of 220 pounds of cocaine. When DeLorean learned the truth and tried to back out of the deal, Hoffman threatened to kill DeLorean's wife and children.

That's DeLorean's side of the story; Hoffman says DeLorean knew it was a drug deal all along. What everyone agrees on is that DeLorean *didn't* know Hoffman was a government informant and the drug deal was actually an FBI sting.

**THE END**

What's ironic about the drug deal is that: 1) it happened on October 19, one day too late to meet the British government's deadline, and 2) by that point DeLorean was so broke he couldn't even come up with the $1.9 million in cash. So he was going to rip off the drug dealers just like he'd ripped off his executives and the British government, by giving them $1.9 million worth of shares in a worthless shell company instead of cash.

No matter. As far as the FBI is concerned, a drug deal is still a drug deal, even if you're using phony stock to pay for your dope. On the same day the British receivers announced that the factory was closing for good, DeLorean was arrested in a Los Angeles hotel after he was videotaped handling a suitcase filled with cocaine. "This is as good as gold," he told the undercover agents; it came just "in the nick of time."

**AFTERMATH**

John DeLorean beat the rap...not once, but twice. In August 1984, he was acquitted in the drug trial after jurors concluded the government set him up. Then in December 1986, he was acquitted on embezzling and racketeering charges that the government filed against him after it lost the drug trial.

DeLorean never did time, but he never got over the collapse of his auto company, either. His third marriage (to supermodel

Cristina Ferrare) ended in 1984, and his creditors hounded him
for another 15 years after that. He filed for bankruptcy in 1999;
the following year he was evicted from his New Jersey estate. The
house and its contents were auctioned off to pay his creditors.

DeLorean made two more attempts to launch a new automobile company:

• In December 1986 he announced he'd raised $20 million to
build a $100,000 exotic sports car designed by a West German
designer he refused to name.
• In 1999 he announced he was starting an online retail watch
company, DeLorean Time. Proceeds from the sale of the $3,495
stainless-steel watches ($1,750 down, with a 10-month wait for
delivery of the watch) would be used to found a new car company
that would build a "radical new car," DeLorean claimed.

Neither auto company was ever founded; no new cars were
built. And as far as anyone can tell, the watches weren't either.
DeLorean died from complications of a stroke in March 2005. He
was 80 years old.

## AFTER THE AFTERMATH

DeLorean cars fared a little better than their creator. What makes
them different from other classic cars, a 1968 Chevy Camaro convertible for example, is that people knew from the beginning that
DeLoreans would be collectible. So many people bought them and
held onto them, in fact, that their value stagnated for years.

If you're looking to pick up a DeLorean really cheap, though,
you're a few years too late. Values have finally started creeping up,
as fans of the *Back to the Future* films, which featured a DeLorean
time machine, hit their 20s and 30s and can finally afford the cars
they've been dreaming about since they were kids.

In the late 1990s, you could have picked up a DeLorean in
decent shape for about $17,000; today they can cost $30,000 or
more. Take heart, though, there are still plenty to go around: of
the 9,200 DeLoreans that were manufactured, it's estimated that
more than 7,000 of them are still on the road.

\*      \*      \*

**Yugoslav proverb:** "By the side of luck stands misfortune."

# THE MAN WHO SAVED A BILLION LIVES

*Ever heard of Norman Borlaug? Most people haven't,*
*yet he's credited with a truly amazing accomplishment:*
*saving more lives than anybody else in history*

## THE POPULATION BOMB

In his 1968 best seller, *The Population Bomb*, author and biologist Paul Ehrlich wrote that "the battle to feed all of humanity is over." Ehrlich's chilling book predicted that a rapidly growing world population would soon lead to massive worldwide food shortages, especially in third-world countries. World population was just over 3.5 billion at the time and was increasing at a faster rate than food production. "In the 1970s and 1980s," Ehrlich wrote, "hundreds of millions of people will starve to death." Most experts agreed with Ehrlich's dire predictions...but they hadn't anticipated Dr. Norman Borlaug.

## FARM BOY

Borlaug was born in 1914 and grew up on a farm in Saude, Iowa. In 1942 he graduated from the University of Minnesota with PhDs in plant pathology and genetics. In 1944 he was invited by the Rockefeller Foundation, a global charitable organization, and the Mexican government to head a project aimed at improving wheat production in Mexico. His assignment: to develop a more productive strain of wheat that was also resistant to stem rust, a fungal disease that was becoming a major problem in Latin America.

Borlaug chose two locations with an 8,500-foot altitude difference for his testing. He grew and crossbred thousands of different strains of wheat, and worked with the latest fertilizers, looking for plants that could grow in both environments. Reason: they had to be able to grow anywhere.

Over the next several years Borlaug was able to develop hardy, highly productive strains, but he found that the tall wheats he was using would not support the weight of the added grain. So he crossed the tall wheats with dwarf varieties that were not only

---

Church Street? The main street of Barbotan, France, runs through the town's church.

shorter but had thicker, stronger stems. And that was his break-through: a semi-dwarf, disease-resistant, high-output wheat. He worked incessantly to get the seeds distributed to small farmers throughout Mexico, and by 1963 Borlaug's wheat varieties made up 95 percent of the nation's total production, with a crop yield that was more than six times greater than when he'd arrived. Not only could Mexico stop importing wheat, they were now an exporter—a huge boost to any nation's nutritional and economic health, but especially to an underdeveloped one. And now Borlaug wanted to take his high-yield farming global. He wanted, he said, to secure "a temporary success in man's war against hunger and deprivation."

## ANOTHER VICTORY

In 1963 the Rockefeller Foundation sent Borlaug to Pakistan and India, two nations with severe hunger and malnutrition problems. Borlaug's help was resisted at first; there was cultural opposition to new farming methods. But when acute famine struck in 1965 (1.5 million people would die by 1967), the barriers came down. And the results were incredible: by 1968 Pakistan, which just a few years earlier relied on massive grain imports, was entirely self-sufficient. By 1970 India's production had doubled and it too was getting close to self-sufficiency.

At four o'clock in the morning one day in 1970, Margaret Borlaug got a phone call. She raced out to the fields and informed her husband, already hard at work, that he had won the Nobel Peace Prize. "No, I haven't," he said. He thought it was a hoax. But he had indeed won it for having saved the lives of millions—perhaps hundreds of millions—of people in India and Pakistan and for the message it had sent to the world. "He has given us a well-founded hope," the Nobel committee said, "an alternative of peace and of life—the green revolution."

## NOTHING ESCAPES CONTROVERSY

Borlaug had also been working on other grains, such as corn and rye, and in the 1980s began developing more productive strains of rice to increase production in China and Southeast Asia. He was setting up similar programs in Africa, but ran into a major hurdle: environmentalists opposed his methods. Among their charges: spreading the same few varieties of grains all over the planet is

harming biodiversity; huge farms are benefiting from his techniques and killing off the small farmer; inorganic fertilizers used in
the Borlaug method are harmful to the environment; and genetically engineered food is unnatural and potentially dangerous.

"Some of the environmental lobbyists are the salt of the
earth," Borlaug said, "but many of them are elitists. If they lived
just one month amid the misery of the developing world, as I have
for fifty years, they'd be crying out for tractors and fertilizer and
irrigation canals and be outraged that fashionable elitists back
home were trying to deny them these things." He admitted that
he would rather his work benefited small farmers, but added,
"Wheat isn't political. It doesn't know that it's supposed to be producing more for poor farmers than for rich farmers." Supporters
argue that Borlaug's high-yield method has actually been a boon
for the environment, saving hundreds of millions of acres of wild
land from being turned into farms. The controversy continues, but
none of it has stopped Borlaug from his mission.

## KEEP ON PLANTING
In 1984, with the help of Japanese philanthropist Ryoichi Sasakawa,
Borlaug set up the Sasakawa Africa Association (SAA), training
more than a million farmers throughout Africa. Result: using Borlaug seed and methods, cereal grain yields have increased from two-
to four-fold.

As of 2005—at the age of 91—Norman Borlaug is still at it. He
continues to work with Mexico's International Maize and Wheat
Improvement Center, still heads the SAA, runs research programs,
teaches young scientists, gives lectures, and, of course, still works in
the field. Over his 50-plus-year career he has been credited with
saving as many as a billion people from starvation, and has received
numerous international awards. In May 2004, he was presented with
another: at St. Mark's Episcopal Cathedral in Borlaug's college town
of Minneapolis, he was shown their new "Window of Peace." The
Minneapolis Star Tribune described the event: "He gazed upward to
see the sun shining through a 30-foot-tall stained glass window.
There—along with depictions of Mother Teresa, Mahatma Gandhi,
and other modern-day peacemakers—was a life-size likeness of Borlaug, holding a fistful of wheat."

# IT'S A CONSPIRACY!

*If you know anybody who believes any of these theories, please
send them our way. (We're trying to sell an invisible bridge.)*

CONSPIRACY THEORY: John F. Kennedy wasn't assassinated—he's still alive.
DETAILS: In early 1963, President Kennedy became
convinced his enemies (the Mafia, Cuban dictator Fidel Castro,
and elements within the CIA) were out to kill him. So he enlisted
a group of friends and government agents to fake his death and
then hide him overseas, should an attempt on his life be made.
On November 22, 1963, Kennedy was shot in Dallas by Lee Harvey Oswald, a pawn in a murder plot hatched by Castro, the CIA,
the Mafia, FBI chief J. Edgar Hoover, and Robert Kennedy (who
had presidential aspirations and wanted his brother out of the picture). Contrary to news reports, Oswald's bullets didn't actually
kill Kennedy—they left him in a coma. The president was secretly
flown to a hospital in Poland. When he finally emerged from the
coma in the late 1960s, he was crippled, frail, and mildly brain-damaged. Ever since, Kennedy has lived on the Greek island Skorpios in a hospital owned by Greek tycoon Aristotle Onassis (who
also aided in the cover-up by pretending to be Jackie Kennedy's
second husband). Proof? In 1971 the European tabloid *Midnight*
ran a photo supposedly picturing Kennedy, Jackie, and Kennedy's
two nurses going for a walk on Skorpios.
TRUTH: *Midnight* faked the photos and the story. American
author Truman Capote gave the tale a wider audience when he
presented it as his own idea in a 1971 newspaper article. (In
Capote's version, Kennedy never emerged from his coma and
lived in Switzerland, not Greece.) Capote later retracted the
story, admitting that he had intended it as a silly piece of fiction.
Nevertheless, the theory persists to this day.

CONSPIRACY THEORY: Cabbage Patch Kids weren't innocent
dolls—they were actually made to prepare Americans for what
post-apocalyptic humans will look like.
DETAILS: In the early 1980s, President Ronald Reagan feared
that a nuclear war with the Soviet Union was inevitable. Sur-

---

Bug Bomb: When threatened, a bombardier beetle can release a blast of 212°F air from its rear

vivors, if any, would likely be horribly physically deformed; the offspring of nuclear victims would be even more gruesome. So Reagan assigned government scientists to determine what post-apocalyptic humans would look like and to come up with a way to accustom Americans to their appearance. The scientists exposed human test subjects to high levels of radiation, then took samples of their altered DNA, and bred babies. Result: infants with tiny, beady eyes, chubby limbs with undifferentiated fingers and toes, and mashed-in faces. The government then hired Coleco Toys to make dolls based on the infants. Coleco gave the dolls an innocuous name, explained their odd appearance with a fairy tale about the children growing in the ground, and released them to toy stores. The toys were a huge success. Mission accomplished.

**TRUTH:** Cabbage Patch Kids first appeared in the 1901 novel *Mrs. Wiggs of the Cabbage Patch*, about a woman widowed with five children in Cabbage Patch, Louisiana. Georgia doll maker Xavier Roberts began handmaking dolls based on the characters in the novel in 1978—three years before Reagan took office. Coleco bought the rights to mass-produce the dolls in 1983. Richard Joltes, a college student who worked in a West Virginia Sears store in the early 1980s, claims to be the source of the "mutant" theory. Joltes says he hated the dolls, and whenever he sold one he'd tell the customer, "I heard these things were designed to get people used to what mutants might look like after a nuclear war." Soon, other cashiers started doing it, too. Then Joltes told the tale in political science classes during discussions about President Reagan's far-reaching nuclear policy. The legend spread…and mutated.

**CONSPIRACY THEORY:** The Earth is hollow and its core houses a secret, powerful civilization.

**DETAILS:** Immortal reptilian evil beings live at the center of the Earth and all the world's governments answer to them. The evil denizens of the hollow Earth routinely escape to the surface of the Earth, kidnap humans, and torture them for pleasure. In fact, they are responsible for all the chaos and tragedy on the surface. The Nazis were their surface liaisons and traveled to and from the hollow earth via a portal in the South Pole. How is such a vast conspiracy kept under wraps? As previously stated, *all* of the world's governments are under the control of the hollow-Earthers.

**TRUTH:** In 1869 a self-proclaimed "alchemist" named Cyrus Teed founded a cult based on his theories of a hollow-Earth society. (Some sources claim Adolf Hitler was a follower of Teed.) But the main source of the idea was likely the 1940s science-fiction magazine *Amazing Stories*. It ran stories by Richard Shaver about a superior evil prehistoric race that lived in caves inside the Earth and liked to torture humanity. Shaver's proof: he said he often heard "sinister voices," seemingly coming from nowhere, and he figured there was no explanation other than evil beings who lived inside the Earth. Thousands of *Amazing Stories* readers wrote in and said that they, too, had heard the same unsettling voices.

Scientifically, a hollow Earth is impossible. Newton's law of gravity states that if a sphere, such as the Earth, were hollow, its interior would have zero gravity, meaning that if people were in there they'd float around weightlessly. An interior sun (another aspect of the hollow Earth scenario) is equally improbable. One of the reasons life flourishes on Earth is because of its distance from the Sun—just close enough to stay warm and for plants to use its energy to make food via photosynthesis, the basis of the food chain. If there was a sun in the middle of the Earth, not only would it be too hot to sustain life within the hollow core, it would be too hot to sustain life on the Earth's surface.

## A FEW MORE BIZARRE CONSPIRACY THEORIES

• The United States couldn't find weapons of mass destruction in Iraq because they were invisible. In the 1980s, the United States funded Iraq's war against Iran and gave them advanced military techno-logy, including the ability to make objects invisible. Iraqi leader Sadaam Hussein didn't have to give up his stockpile of WMD—he merely made it invisible.

• Conspiracy theorists claim that the Canadian coffee chain Tim Horton's laces its coffee and doughnuts with nicotine and MSG. They say customers aren't loyal—just addicted.

• The same conspiracy theory floated around in the late 1980s, claiming that McDonald's hamburgers were chemically addictive, then again in the 2000s, saying that kids loved Pokémon trading cards because they were addicted to a secret nicotine coating on the cards.

# ACCORDING TO THE LATEST RESEARCH

*So how does a person get a job conducting one of these weird research studies? (If Uncle John ever finds out, he may take a little break from the book business.)*

## CROSSWORDS AND SEX GROW BRAIN CELLS

**Study:** Conducted by Dr. Perry Bartlett of the University of Queensland's Brain Institute, in Australia

**Findings:** In April 2004, Dr. Bartlett announced that mental and physical exercise may delay the onset of brain diseases such as Alzheimer's and Parkinson's by creating and nurturing new brain cells to replace ones that have been lost. Brain cell creation and growth appear to be stimulated by a chemical called prolactin— and prolactin levels rise during mental and physical exertion. (They're also high when you're pregnant.) "Perhaps one should run a long distance or do crosswords," Dr. Bartlett suggests. "Prolactin levels also go up during sex," he says, "so one could think of a number of more interesting activities than jogging in order to regulate the production of nerve cells."

## PARENTS FAVOR CUTE KIDS OVER UGLY ONES

**Study:** Researchers at the University of Alberta in Canada went to 14 different supermarkets and observed the interactions between 400 different parents and their children. They also ranked the "physical attractiveness" of each child on a scale of 1 to 10.

**Findings:** When Mom did the shopping, 13.3% of the children judged "most attractive" were secured with the seat belt in the shopping cart seat; only 1.2% of the "ugliest" children were. With Dad the disparity was even greater: 12.5% of the "most attractive" children were belted in; *none* of the ugliest children were.

• Ugly children were allowed to wander away from their parents more often than attractive kids, and were allowed to wander farther away than attractive children were.

• Good-looking boys were kept closer to their parents than pretty girls were, although the researchers concede that this may be

---

because girls are perceived to be more mature and responsible than boys of the same age.

• What does all of this mean? Scientists aren't sure. Some speculate that evolution may play a role: parents may unconsciously perceive attractive children as being genetically more valuable. But Emory University psychologist Dr. Frans de Waal disagrees. "If the number of offspring are the same for ugly people and handsome people, there's absolutely no evolutionary reason for parents to invest less in ugly kids," he says.

## DUMB BLONDE JOKES SLOW BLONDES DOWN

**Study:** German researchers at Bremen's International University asked 80 women with different hair colors to take intelligence tests, then monitored them carefully as they took the tests. Half of the women were told "dumb blonde" jokes before they took the test. (Jokes like: "Why do blondes open containers of yogurt while they're still in the supermarket? Because the lid says, 'Open here.'")

**Findings:** No word on how well the blondes or anyone else did on the intelligence tests—that wasn't the point, and the university didn't release the results. But it did keep track of how *quickly* the women completed the tests: The blondes who were told dumb blonde jokes took longer to complete their tests than the blondes who weren't told jokes. Did the dumb blonde jokes make blondes dumber? No, the researchers say: the jokes made them more *self-conscious*, which caused them to work more slowly and cautiously so that they wouldn't make mistakes. "The study shows that even unfounded prejudices generally dismissed as untrue can affect an individual's confidence in their own ability," says Jens Foerster, one of the social psychologists who administered the study.

## GERMANS PREFER MONEY TO SEX

**Study:** In December 2004, the German edition of *Playboy* magazine commissioned a poll of 1,000 Germans. The pollsters asked participants if they were given a choice between more free time, more money, and more sex, which one they would choose.

**Findings:** 62% of Germans said cash, 26% said more free time, and only 6% said more sex. (That might explain why Germany has a declining birth rate.)

# BUT WAIT!
# THERE'S *STILL* MORE!

*Here's Part II of the story of Ron Popeil. (Part I is on page 131.)*

*(Part I is on page 131.)*

**A**MAZING SCIENTIFIC BREAKTHROUGH! Ron Popeil wasn't particularly eager to follow in his father's footsteps—or even to be near him for that matter. Born in 1935, Ron's early childhood was spent in a boarding school (where his parents never visited). At age seven, he went to live with his grandparents, and didn't reunite with his father in Chicago until he was 16. At that point he was immediately put to work doing demonstrations of Popeil products at Sears and Woolworth's.

One day while at Chicago's Maxwell Street Marketplace, an outdoor bazaar, he had a revelation: Popeil suddenly felt he could convince total strangers to buy anything, if he were willing to give it his all. He realized he had to go into business for himself.

In 1951, at the age of 16, Popeil bought a gross of products—vegetable choppers and shoe shine kits—from his father (who sold them to Ron at normal supplier prices, making a full profit). The younger Popeil then set up a booth at the Maxwell Street market on a Sunday afternoon and hawked wildly. By the end of the day, his pockets were stuffed with cash.

He continued performing demonstrations for his father's company, set up permanently just inside the front door of Chicago's Woolworth's. At a time when the average American earned $500 a month, Popeil was making over $1,000 a week. In the summer, he even went on the county fair circuit. By dealing with customers one-on-one, he learned to anticipate what kind of objections or questions people might have to his products. Popeil honed his pitch, learning to answer those questions before they were even asked.

## NOT AVAILABLE IN STORES!

In 1964 Ron Popeil went out on his own. He founded Ronco Teleproducts with his college roommate, Mel Korey. Rather than make their own products like the Popeil brothers did, Ronco contracted with other companies, avoiding the headaches and overhead of operating a factory. Popeil found a television station in Tampa, Florida, that charged $500 to produce an ad. (He made four: a 30-second, a 60-second, a 90-second, and a 120-second.) The product: the Ronco Spray Gun, a garden hose nozzle with a chamber inside to hold soap, car wax, fertilizer, or insecticide. The first commercial ran in Illinois and Wisconsin, near Popeil's Chicago base, to save shipping costs. They sold over a million Spray Guns.

Ronco's next success was London Aire Hosiery, women's nylon stockings "guaranteed in writing" not to run. Their durability was tested in the commercial, as they were subjected to a nail file, a scouring pad, and a lit cigarette. Ronco began manufacturing its own items in 1967 with the Cordless Power Scissors (they were battery-operated, but Popeil called them "cordless electric" to describe it and all future battery-operated Ronco products). All of the ads featured Ron Popeil himself. Doing his own ads saved on production costs, but it also made good business sense: Popeil had hawked so many items at fairs and stores that he was a natural salesman, and no one could sell his products better than him. He didn't even need a script. Ronco products earned $200,000 in 1964, its first year. By 1973 Ronco had annual sales of $20 million.

### SUPPLIES ARE LIMITED!

Among the many Ronco gadgets of the 1970s:

• **Smokeless Ashtray** (1970). An ashtray with a cylinder above it, which houses a "cordless electric" filtering fan.

• **Pocket Fisherman** (1972). A portable, retractable fishing rod.

• **Presco-Lator** (1976). A plastic version of a French press–style coffeemaker. It bombed because it hit the market at the same time as the Mr. Coffee coffeemaker.

• **Mr. Microphone** (1978). A wireless transmitter inside a microphone. It broadcast the user's voice to any properly tuned FM radio up to 100 feet away.

• **Inside-the-Shell Egg Scrambler** (1978). An egg is impaled on the device's needle. The needle spins inside the shell to create a perfectly blended egg without having to use a mixing bowl.

- **Sit-On Trash Compactor** (1978). It worked without electricity: the user sat on a plunging platform that squished the garbage.

- **Food Dehydrator** (1979). A product of the health food craze of the 1970s, it made fruit leather, beef jerky, banana chips, and yogurt.

## OPERATORS ARE STANDING BY!

But in the early 1980s, Ronco started falling apart. From 1982 to June 1983, sales dropped 31 percent. And that same year one of their biggest retailers—Woolco—closed all its stores. Then in a few months, claiming they were owed $2 million, three companies that made products for Ronco filed suit in bankruptcy court to force Ronco to sell off its assets and pay its debts. But Ronco also owed $8 million to First National Bank of Chicago and Wells Fargo Bank. (Business was so bad, Ronco had been operating on credit.) Popeil had no choice but to declare Ronco bankrupt.

The banks planned to auction off Ronco's assets, but before they could, Popeil offered $2 million of his own money to buy the company back. The banks refused and held the auction, but got a high bid of only $1.2 million, so they sold it back to Ron Popeil, who spent the next year doing what he'd done as a teenager: in-person demonstrations at department stores and county fairs.

## EASY PAYMENT PLAN

The story might have ended there. But in 1984, the same year Popeil filed for bankruptcy, the FCC deregulated TV advertising. Ads no longer had to be under two minutes in length, which gave birth to a new form of advertising: the infomercial. Suddenly, products that had relied on rapid-fire pitches in short commercials (kitchen gadgets, exercise equipment, car waxes) were being pitched in half-hour advertisements designed to look like real TV programs. Broadcast and cable networks used infomercials to fill holes in their schedules, usually late at night and on weekends.

When Ginsu knives became the first major product sold this way (over $50 million in sales), Popeil realized the way to rebuild Ronco was through infomercials. "The longer you have to talk, the better chance you have of selling something," Popeil said in 1985. He went into semi-retirement in 1987, leaving day-to-day operation to others while he continued the role of TV pitchman.

Beginning with a redesigned Food Dehydrator in the early 1990s, Ronco has used infomercials exclusively. One product sold was GLH Formula #9, an aerosol can of hair-thickening powder, better known as "hair in a can" (Popeil sprayed it on his own bald spots in the infomercial). Another was the Showtime Rotisserie, a compact countertop rotisserie cooker. Popeil calls it his best invention and has sold three million units to date. But unlike the early days, Popeil now sells only items he's personally developed. "I'm an inventor first and a marketer second," he says. "Other people in our business take the spaghetti approach. They throw a lot of stuff against the wall and hope something sticks."

\*       \*       \*

## CON LETTER

An old man lived alone in the country. He wanted to plant a tomato garden, but it was difficult work, and his only son, Vincent, who used to help him, was in prison. The old man described the predicament in a letter to his son.

> Dear Vincent,
> I'm feeling bad. It looks like I won't be able to put in my tomatoes this year. I'm just too old to be digging up a garden. I wish you were here to dig it for me.
> Love, Dad

A few days later he received a letter from his son.

> Dear Dad,
> Sorry I'm not there to help, but whatever you do, don't dig up that garden. That's where I buried the BODIES.
> Love, Vincent

At 4 a.m. the next morning, FBI agents and local police arrived and dug up the entire area without finding any bodies. They apologized to the old man and left. That same day the old man received another letter from his son.

> Dear Dad,
> Go ahead and plant the tomatoes now. That's the best I could do under the circumstances.
> Love, Vinnie

---

Most popular flowers grown in American gardens: Sunflowers, zinnias, and impatiens.

# THE DIVINE WIND

*If you study history, you may find instances where it seems that fate really can intervene and miracles really do happen. But don't expect that miracle, or you may be disappointed...as this story attests.*

## KING OF THE WORLD

When it came to wealth and power, Kublai Khan had it all. In 1274 the Mongol emperor's dominion stretched for thousands of miles across Asia. His army was the best equipped and best trained in the world. Disciplined and battle-hardened, the Khan's soldiers also had the 13th-century equivalent of a super weapon—a burning cannonball full of gunpowder called a *teppo* that they could hurl with devastating efficiency against an enemy. With all of this military power, the great Khan wasn't content to just rule—he wanted new worlds to conquer. So he set his sights on Japan.

The Japanese must have seemed an easy mark. They fought with antique weaponry—bows and arrows, swords, bamboo spears, and wooden shields. What's more, a century of constant warfare between rival warlords had left Japan's armies exhausted and weak.

Knowing this, Kublai Khan assembled a substantial attack force—a fleet of 900 ships and 40,000 soldiers—and had them set sail for Japan. The armada was met by 10,000 samurai on the beach at Hakata Bay on the island of Kyushu. But the samurai, who excelled in individual combat, were no match for the organized tactics of the Mongols. Defeat seemed certain.

## A LUCKY WIND

Then a miracle occurred: a violent storm overwhelmed the Mongol fleet, sinking 200 ships and drowning 13,000 men. Japan was saved.

When the defeated survivors returned to China, a furious Kublai Khan vowed revenge. And so, five years later, the Mongols invaded again, this time stronger than ever. The Khan's Northern Fleet had 900 ships and 40,000 soldiers. The Southern Fleet was even larger, with 3,500 ships and 100,000 soldiers. In the summer of 1279, the armada sailed once again for Hakata Bay.

---

Find 'em all: In the *Godfather* movies, oranges represent an upcoming death (or close call).

The Japanese warlords knew that the only way to stop the Mongol force was on the beach, before their dreaded artillery could be hauled ashore and put into action. They built a defensive wall 13 miles long bordering the bay—a first for the Japanese, who had never used fortifications before.

The Northern Fleet reached Japan first. When the initial wave of Mongol soldiers came ashore, they were startled to find the entrenched samurai waiting for them behind their wall. The fighting was fierce, lasting for days, but the Japanese defenders held fast. When the Mongols couldn't secure the beach, they retreated to their ships. But despite their victory, the samurai had little opportunity to celebrate: the huge Southern Fleet had arrived, and now the combined armada was sailing off to the south to renew the attack. And this time they were going *around* the wall.

The Japanese samurai were desperate. Although they had fought magnificently, they were badly outnumbered and, without the protection of the wall, they were exposed to the full onslaught of the Mongol invaders. As they waited on the beach to fight what they were sure was their last battle, all the samurai could do was pray for deliverance.

Amazingly, it came.

## SAVED...AGAIN

Out of the south a typhoon swept up and ripped through the invading armada. The devastation was astonishing. Almost 4,000 ships sunk and 100,000 soldiers were lost. The Japanese were jubilant. A "divine wind" had saved them from invasion, not once, but twice. Over time the legend grew: the divine wind would protect them from foreign invaders forever.

Six hundred fifty years later the Japanese empire was once again in dire straits, facing invasion as Allied forces closed in during the final days of World War II. In a desperate attempt to turn the tide of war, the Japanese military sacrificed 5,000 young and untrained pilots in suicide missions against Allied warships.

Their last-ditch effort to save Japan failed, but the suicide bombers became known by the Japanese word for "divine wind"— *kamikaze*.

# SPY HUNT: GRAY DECEIVER, PART III

*Here's part III of our story on one of the biggest mole hunts in FBI history. (Part II is on page 342.)*

## FINGERED

The FBI mole hunters had never suspected Robert Hanssen of spying before, but all residual doubt that he was their man disappeared when the KGB officer who sold them Hanssen's file began to interpret the file's contents.

What about that mysterious sealed envelope marked "Don't Open This"? The FBI waited until the retired KGB officer arrived to open it. The officer explained that when the spy left documents and computer discs at a dead drop, he wrapped them in two plastic garbage bags to protect them from the elements. The envelope contained one of the spy's garbage bags. The KGB officer explained that only he and the spy had touched the bag; if Hanssen was the spy (and wasn't wearing gloves when he wrapped the package), it would likely contain his fingerprints.

The agents took the bag to the lab and succeeded in lifting two fingerprints from the bag. As they expected, the prints were Hanssen's. Every piece of evidence in the KGB file pointed to him and him alone. He even had a thing for diamonds and strippers, just as Russian sources had been reporting for years.

## GRAYDAY

The investigators put aside their investigation of GRAY DECEIVER, gave Hanssen the nickname GRAYDAY, and started investigating him. They arranged for Hanssen to be promoted to a new job at FBI headquarters, where he could be closely watched by hidden cameras. Then they tapped his office phone and searched his laptop computer. They couldn't bug or search his house—his wife and two of his six kids still living at home were never gone long enough—but when a house across the street from Hanssen's was put up for sale, the FBI bought it, moved in, and began watching Hanssen from there. Whenever Hanssen left home, undercover

FBI agents secretly followed him.

This time, the mole hunters' work paid off: after about three months of constant surveillance, on the afternoon of February 18, 2001, Hanssen was caught red-handed leaving a package of computer discs and classified documents in a dead drop in Foxstone Park near his home in Vienna, Virginia. A payment of $50,000 in cash was retrieved from another dead drop in a nature center in Arlington, Virginia.

The evidence against Hanssen was overwhelming, and he knew it. He confessed immediately and later agreed to a plea bargain in which he was spared the death penalty in exchange for cooperating fully with the FBI investigation into his crimes.

Hanssen admitted that he'd been spying off and on for more than 20 years. He started in 1979, quit in 1981 when his wife caught him (a devout Catholic, she made him go to confession but never turned him in), started again in 1985, quit when the Soviet Union collapsed in 1991, and started again in 1999. He continued spying until his arrest in 2001.

## GRAYBOOB

The FBI had long assumed they were hunting a master spy, someone who knew how to cover his tracks and would be very hard to catch. They formed that impression over time as they failed to collect any incriminating evidence against Kelley (other than his jogging map), even though they were certain Kelley was the spy.

But as the investigation into Hanssen continued, the mole hunters realized just how wrong they'd been. Hanssen was smart enough not to tell the Russians his real name, but he was no master spy—in fact, he could have been caught years earlier if the people around him had been paying attention and doing their jobs. Over the years Hanssen left so many clues to his spying that he practically glowed in the dark.

✔ He used FBI phone lines and answering machines to communicate with his KGB handlers in the 1980s.

✔ When the KGB paid him cash, Hanssen sometimes counted the money at work, then deposited it in a savings account *in his own name,* in a bank less than a block from FBI headquarters in Washington, D.C.

Native to Indiana? A species of spider, *calponia Harrisonfordi,* is named for Harrison Ford.

✔ At a time when he made less than $100,000 a year, Hanssen kept a gym bag filled with $100,000 in cash in his bedroom closet. One time he left $5,000 sitting on top of his dresser. His brother-in-law, Mark Wauck, also an FBI agent, saw the unexplained cash and reported it to his superiors, also noting that Hanssen had once talked of retiring to Poland, which was then still part of the Soviet bloc. An FBI agent retiring to a Communist country? The FBI never investigated the incident.

## THE PERSONAL TOUCH

✔ The FBI, and even the KGB, had assumed that Hanssen never met with any Russian agents, but they were wrong. Hanssen launched his spying career in 1979 by walking right into the offices of a Soviet trade organization that was known to be a GRU (the military version of the KGB) front and offering his services, even though he knew the office was likely to be under surveillance. When he made his first contact with the KGB in 1985, he did so by sending a letter through the U.S. mail to a known KGB officer who lived in Virginia. Both approaches were incredibly foolhardy, but Hanssen got away with it both times.

✔ In 1993 Hanssen botched an attempt to resume spying for GRU when he walked up to a GRU officer in the parking lot of the man's apartment building and tried to hand him a packet of classified documents. The officer, thinking it was an FBI sting, reported the incident to his superiors at the Russian Embassy, who lodged a formal protest with the U.S. State Department. The FBI launched an investigation—which Hanssen closely followed by hacking into FBI computers—but the investigation was unsuccessful.

In 1992 Hanssen hacked into a computer to gain access to Soviet counterintelligence documents. Then, fearing he might be caught, he reported his own hacking and claimed he was testing the computer's security. His colleagues and superiors believed his story and were grateful to him for pointing out the weakness in the system. The incident was never investigated.

## AT THE STATE DEPARTMENT

But perhaps the most inexplicable breach of security came in 1994, when Hanssen was transferred to an FBI post at the State Department's Office of Foreign Missions. As the Justice Department later described it, Hanssen was "wholly unsupervised" by either the State Department or the FBI for the next six years. In that time he didn't receive a single job performance review. Hanssen spent much of his time out of the office visiting friends and colleagues; when he did go to the office he spent his time surfing the Internet, reading classified documents, and watching movies on his laptop. Then he resumed spying for the Russians.

✔ In 1997 Hanssen asked for a computer that would connect him to the FBI's Automatic Case Support System (ACS) and got it, even though his job didn't call for it. Soon after he got the computer, Hanssen was caught installing password breaker software that allowed him to hack into password-protected files. When confronted, Hanssen said he was trying to hook up a color printer. His story went unchallenged and the incident was never investigated.

✔ Using the ACS systems, Hanssen downloaded hundreds, if not thousands, of classified documents and gave them to the Russians. At the same time, he repeatedly scanned the FBI's files for his own name, address, and the locations of his various dead drops to check whether the FBI was onto him.

✔ He also stumbled onto the FBI's investigation of Brian Kelley. Assuming that Kelley, too, was a mole, he warned the Russians about the investigation. Then he did what he could to keep the FBI focused on Kelley, so that he could continue his own spying.

## SUMMING IT UP

In the years that Hanssen spied for the Russians, he handed over thousands of America's most important military and intelligence secrets. He revealed the identities of scores of secret Russian sources, at least three of whom were executed, and he caused hundreds of millions of dollars in damage to American intelligence programs. Hanssen also sold computer software to the Russians that allowed them to track CIA and FBI activities. Someone in Russia then sold it to Al-Qaeda, which may have used it to track the CIA's search for Osama Bin Laden.

Hanssen was paid $600,000 for his efforts (and promised that another $800,000 was waiting for him in a Russian bank). He is the most damaging spy in FBI history and possibly in the history of the United States.

## FAILING GRADE

After Hanssen's arrest, the inspector general of the Justice Department launched an investigation into how the mole hunt had gone so wrong and how Hanssen had been able to spy for so long without attracting suspicion.

In August 2003, the inspector general issued a scathing report condemning the FBI mole hunters for focusing on the CIA without seriously considering the possibility that the mole might be in the FBI, especially since most of the biggest secrets known to have been compromised had come from the FBI. (The mole hunters' explanation for how CIA agent Brian Kelley could have known so many FBI secrets: they thought he was seducing female FBI employees and selling *their* secrets to the Soviets.)

## THE HONOR SYSTEM

The inspector general's report also faulted the FBI for "decades of neglect" of its own internal security. Before Hanssen's arrest, the Bureau operated on what was effectively the honor system: in his 25-year career, Hanssen never once had to take a lie detector test or submit to a financial background investigation, which might have turned up the KGB cash he was depositing in banks near FBI headquarters in his own name.

Hanssen had virtually unlimited access to the FBI's most sensitive material—over the years he handed over thousands of original, numbered documents to the Soviets and no one had noticed they were missing. He also had unrestricted, unmonitored access to the ACS computer system, which gave him access to thousands more documents. The ACS software did have an audit feature that would have revealed Hanssen's searches for classified information or for references to himself, but the audit feature was rarely, if ever, used. Hanssen knew it and felt secure enough to conduct thousands of unauthorized and incriminating searches over the years.

## AFTERMATH

• **The FBI.** No one involved in the Kelley/Hanssen mole hunt was disciplined or fired from the FBI, although several agents were promoted. The FBI says it has tightened security since the Hanssen arrest. The Bureau's ACS computer system was scheduled to be replaced by a new $170 million software program called Virtual

Case File in 2003. As of January 2005 only 10 percent of the system was in place, and the system was so flawed that the FBI was weighing whether to scrap the entire project and start over again.

- **Robert Hanssen.** On July 6, 2001, Hanssen pleaded guilty to 15 counts of espionage, conspiracy to commit espionage, and conspiracy; he was sentenced to life in prison without the possibility of parole. He was supposed to cooperate with U.S. investigators, but he flunked a lie detector test when he was asked, "Have you told the truth?" So instead of being sent to a high-security prison, where he would have had some freedom of movement, he was assigned to a "supermax" prison in Florence, Colorado, where he is confined to his soundproof 7' x 12' cell for 23 hours a day.

- **Bonnie Hanssen.** Because she cooperated with investigators and passed a lie detector test that showed she had no knowledge of her husband's espionage after 1981, Bonnie Hanssen was allowed to collect the widow's portion of her husband's pension and to keep their three cars and family home.

- **Brian Kelley.** After Hanssen's arrest, Kelley was completely exonerated. He returned to the CIA and received an apology from the FBI. He did, however, lose his covert status when his identity was revealed by an investigative reporter writing a book about the Hanssen case. At last report he was still working at the CIA, teaching spy catchers how to avoid making the same mistakes that were made when he was targeted by the mole hunters.

After Kelley's identity was revealed in 2002, he went public with his concern that nothing had changed at the FBI and that the same mistakes could happen again. The mole hunters "were so overzealous, so myopic," he told the *Hartford Courant* in 2002. "If these abuses happen to us, what chance does the average citizen have to protect their civil liberties?"

\*     \*     \*

**A Sandwich Is Born.** During World War II, Americans soldiers stationed in Europe found three items in their ration kits: peanut butter, jelly, and bread. One day, legend has it, some soldier put the three together. Proof? There is no written record of the PB&J sandwich before the war, and after the war sales of peanut butter and jelly skyrocketed in America.

# SMUDGERS & SLEEPERS

*A few more bits of top-secret spy lingo.*

• **Terminated with extreme prejudice:** When a spy agency executes one of its own spies for betraying the agency. (As opposed to just firing—terminating—them.)

• **Fumigating:** Searching a home or office to remove or neutralize any listening devices, or "bugs."

• **The British disease:** A reference to several members of the British upper classes who betrayed their country by becoming spies for the USSR after World War II.

• **Sleeper:** A dormant spy; sometimes an employee of a government agency who won't begin spying until he or she is promoted to a position with access to classified information.

• **Smudger:** A photographer.

• **Case of the measles:** An assassination made to look like a death from accidental or natural causes.

• **Shopworn goods:** Spy information so old or out of date that it's completely useless.

• **Jack in the box:** A fake torso, sometimes inflatable, that's put in a car to fool surveillance teams about how many people are riding in it.

• **Backstopping:** Creating fake background material (employers, phone numbers, etc.) to enhance the credibility of a spy's cover.

• **Spy dust:** Invisible powder the KGB sprinkled on door knobs, inside cars, etc., so that they could track diplomats and suspected spies as they moved around Moscow.

• **Cover:** The fake identity that a spy assumes to blend in with his or her surroundings.

• **Overhead:** Planes or satellites that spy from the sky.

• **Cannon:** Spies are sometimes paid large sums of cash. A cannon is a professional thief hired by an intelligence agency to steal the money back.

• **The Farm:** Camp Peary, the 10,000-acre facility near Williamsburg, Virginia, where CIA agents get their spy training.

---

No takeout? Polar bears roam an average 5,500 miles every year in search of food.

# VIVA LA REBELLION!

*You know about the colonists' revolt against British rule in 1776, and the Confederate secession from the United States in 1861, but what about some of America's lesser-known coups and rebellions?*

## THE WHISKEY REBELLION (1794)

**Background:** Staggering under a huge national debt after winning the Revolutionary War, the federal government looked for any revenue source they could find...including a tax on liquor. The large distilleries had well-established political connections, ensuring that their taxes remained low—six cents a gallon (about a dollar in today's money). Small distillers and farmers, however, had no such connections and had to pay a tax of nine cents for every gallon of whiskey they produced.

**Rebellion:** At the time, western Pennsylvania was the frontier, so far from civilization that the only way for farmers to get their grain to market was to distill it into spirits. Furthermore, most farmers couldn't have paid even if they'd wanted to—they had very little money. Result: "revenooers" in the western counties were harassed, beat up...and seldom paid.

**Result:** President George Washington conferred with his treasury secretary, Alexander Hamilton. Keeping in mind the chaos of Shays' Rebellion (page 269), they decided to draw a line in the sand in Pennsylvania and make an example of those farmers. Washington summoned the protesters to federal district court; they responded by setting up camps in the Monongahela Valley near Pittsburgh. Faced with several thousand armed tax protesters, Washington temporarily became a general again, leading 13,000 troops from several states' militias to western Pennsylvania accompanied by Hamilton and General "Lighthouse Harry" Lee. It was the largest army ever commanded by Washington, and it was the first and last time that a sitting president would personally command an army in the field.

In the face of that kind of force, the tax protesters backed down. Two of the leaders of the revolt were convicted of treason, but were pardoned by Washington. The tax? Although it stayed on the books until 1802, the government gave up trying to enforce it.

There are about 6 million miles of paved roads in the U.S.

## DENMARK VESEY'S INSURRECTION (1822)

**Background:** In 1800 Denmark Vesey of Charleston, South Carolina, became much luckier than most slaves: he won $1,500 in a street lottery ($22,000 today), enough to buy his freedom and still have enough left over to open a carpentry shop. But despite his new freedom, Vesey still identified with the enslaved. He founded a Black Methodist church in 1816 (it had 3,000 members), only to have it closed by white authorities for teaching the Bible story of Moses' Egyptian slave rebellion.

**Rebellion:** Inspired by the slave revolt that created the nation of Haiti in 1804, Vesey began plotting. He amassed arms from Haiti and, drawing on his standing in the black community, recruited former members of his congregation for a massive slave revolt. About 9,000 slaves and freed blacks were ready for the revolution. On July 14, 1822, they would seize armories, bridges—and guardhouses—and kill all of Charleston's whites.

**Result:** What is most surprising is how long the conspiracy progressed without being discovered. As the day approached, though, a slave betrayed the plot to his master, and Charleston was suddenly overrun with white soldiers. Vesey, knowing all was lost, released his followers and burned his lists of names. He and hundreds of other blacks were arrested. The trial stunned and terrified white South Carolinians, who were convinced that they were beloved by their slaves. Testimony indicated that virtually all of the slaves who were approached pledged cooperation, even though it meant killing the families they worked for.

After the trial, 43 conspirators were deported, 35—including Vesey—were hanged, and laws were passed to further restrict the freedom of slaves and free blacks. Accounts of the plot and trial were suppressed in the South for fear of giving other slaves ideas, but the word still got out. Over the following decades, the Vesey Insurrection inspired several other slave revolts, and even the battle cry of the first black regiment to fight in the Civil War: "Remember Denmark Vesey of Charleston!"

## THE DORR REBELLION (1841–42)

**Background:** Thomas Wilson Dorr holds a unique place in Rhode Island history: he was elected governor, charged with treason and jailed, yet ultimately managed to convince his opponents that he'd been right all along.

The son of a wealthy family, Dorr was elected as a Whig to the state legislature in 1834. Although not directly affected by them, he fought for liberalization of the state's voting laws, which stated that only white males who owned $134 worth of land were eligible to vote. At one time most of the state's residents had been farmers, but with industrialization, people flocked to the cities, and eventually only 40 percent of white men were qualified to vote.

**Rebellion:** Dorr was convinced that this was unfair and unconstitutional. Other states had adopted universal suffrage for white men by 1840…except Rhode Island. Convinced that the existing power structure would never change the law of its own volition, Dorr called a "People's Convention." The convention had no legal authority, but in short order it drafted a new (illegal) constitution allowing white men to vote after a year's residency, held its own statewide (illegal) election, and elected a new (illegal) state government with Dorr as governor.

**Result:** When word reached Governor Samuel Ward King that Dorr was claiming the governorship, he declared martial law and accused Dorr of treason. Dorr's reformers attempted to raid an armory in Providence, but were repelled by loyalists, including Dorr's father and uncle. Somehow a cow got shot in the confusion (the only casualty), and Dorr's forces retreated…and then fell apart. Governor King issued a warrant and $5,000 reward for Dorr's arrest. Dorr fled the state.

Later that year, the Rhode Island General Assembly decided that perhaps there was some credence to Dorr's position, after all, and called a constitutional convention to change the voter requirements. New election laws—requiring a $1 poll tax, but not land ownership—took effect in May 1843. Dorr assumed he'd be able to return to his home state. Instead, he was arrested, charged with treason, convicted, and given a life sentence of solitary confinement and hard labor.

The harshness of the sentence angered the public and after a year the legislature voided his sentence. A few years later, they restored all of his civil rights. Although vindicated and freed, Dorr died a broken man two days after Christmas 1854.

# TINY BUBBLES

*Here at the BRI, we love accidental inventions...especially when the accident turns out to be a party favorite. Here's the bubbly history of the sparkling drink we all know as champagne.*

## A PLACE CALLED CHAMPAGNE

The story of champagne (the drink) starts in Champagne (the place). It's a hilly, barren district around the Marne River in the far north of France. Fossil evidence shows that wild grape-vines have been growing in the region for more than one million years. Exactly when people started making wine from them is unknown, but records show that the Romans began serious cultivation of vineyards there as far back as 50 B.C. By the 12th century, the Champagne district had become a major crossroads of northern Europe and word of the region's wines began to spread. By the 15th century wine had become the area's most important commodity, and by the 16th century, royal houses all across Europe were drinking the wines of Champagne.

## HAPPY ACCIDENT

Champagne's northern location (its latitude is about that of New-foundland) means a short growing season, and that short season has everything to do with the "invention" of champagne. As in any wine-producing region, at the end of the season Champagne's grapes were picked, pressed, casked, and allowed to ferment. Wine fermentation occurs when yeast in the grape skins convert the sugar in the grape juice to alcohol—and carbon dioxide. This process requires fairly warm temperatures, but in Champagne it was stunted because of early cold. When it warmed up the next spring, the fermentation started again—*and that was the key.* Normally wine only goes through the fermentation process once, but that second fermentation of Champagne's wines created additional carbon dioxide, which created additional bubbles. Just why this hadn't been noticed before remains a mystery.

Why not before? One possible explanation has to do with Champagne's winemaking and bottling process. Traditionally, green grapes were used to make white wines and red (or black)

grapes were used to make red wines. But around 1660 the winemakers in Champagne discovered how to make a light-colored
wine from a dark grape, specifically from the pinot noir grape.
This new "gray" wine—*vin gris*—became popular in London.
What many historians believe happened was that the casks were
stored in the cold all winter, then shipped in the spring, just as the
second fermentation was starting. When the wines arrived in England, they were quickly bottled and corked (the English had corks,
the French did not), so the second fermentation continued in the
bottle. Result: the bubbles were captured. The vintners thought it
was a disaster...but the English loved it.

The champagne industry had begun.

### THE DOM

Why were there bubbles? How could winemakers produce them
with consistency? And how could they keep the bottles from
exploding? No one knew the answers to these questions. Champagne needed a master.

In 1668 the Benedictine monk Dom Pierre Pérignon became
cellar master and treasurer of Saint-Pierre d'Hautvillers abbey in
Champagne. At first he hated the *mousse* (bubbles), regarding
them as a sign of inferior wine and a flaw to be eliminated. He was
unsuccessful, but in the meantime he improved every step of the
abbey's winemaking: he greatly improved cultivation practices;
imported thicker bottles from Spain and corks from England; and
invented the tied-on metal cap to keep the corks on, leading to a
significant decrease in losses from prematurely popped bottles. He
is also credited with being the first vintner to make a blend—a
*cuvée*—of wines from different grapes and vineyards that resulted
in a superior product. By the time Dom Pérignon died in 1715,
what he learned had been passed along to other winemakers in
the region. There was still much improvement to come, but he
had laid the foundation for the future of champagne.

### FIRMLY GRASP THE CORK...

Over the next 150 years, the development of the champagne business progressed slowly, but a few events helped set the stage for an
explosion of success.

• In 1715 Phillipe became king of France, and because he loved champagne, its popularity soared. Around the same time, chemist Jean-Antoine Chaptal discovered what caused champagne's second fermentation: the residual sugar left in the bottle through the winter. He started the practice of adding sugar to the wine in the spring—still an important part of the champagne process today.

• In 1729 Nicolas Ruinart made his first recorded sale of champagne. (Today the House of Ruinart is the world's oldest official champagne house.) Fourteen years later, Claude Moët started the House of Moët and began traveling the world, spreading the champagne gospel. By the end of the 18th century, 300,000 bottles of sparkling Champagne wines were being sold every year.

• In 1823 the cellar master at Veuve Cliquot invented "riddling," a process that removed sediment from the wine, greatly improving its appearance and desirability. Also at this time, the corking and muzzling processes were mechanized.

### AND POP!

In 1836 pharmacist Jean-Baptiste François invented the *sucrooenomètre*, a device that measured the amount of sugar in wine. Champagne vintners could now determine the exact amount of sugar needed to stimulate the second fermentation. Bottles lost to bursting dropped to 5 percent (from as high as 30 percent) and for the first time, a relatively uniform product could be marketed.

The changes and improvements finally came to a climax in the 1840s when champagne sales soared around the world. Result: vintners in the area virtually stopped making still (un-bubbly) wines—champagne was a better seller. By 1853 annual sales had reached 20 million bottles. By 1861 the United States alone was importing 11 million, and that market rose to 17 million just 10 years later. The industry would see few bad years until 1914.

### BUBBLY GOES FLAT

The first half of the 20th century was a bad time for champagne makers. Most of northern France was a battlefield during World War I, with more than 40 percent of the Champagne vineyards completely destroyed by the war's end. During the same time period they lost two of their biggest customers: the czarist regime was toppled by the Russian Revolution of 1917, and in 1918, the United States passed the 18th Amendment—Prohibition—making the

A champagne cork leaves the bottle at approximately 60 mph.

sale of alcohol illegal. Then in 1929 the stock market crashed and the Great Depression began, followed by World War II.

But through it all, champagne refused to disappear. The champagne houses became organized, establishing strict rules of quality and working internationally to promote their wines. It worked. By 1950 sales were back up to 33 million bottles. By 1964 sales rose to 70 million. In 2004, Champagne's winemakers sold an estimated 300 million bottles—170 million in France alone.

## CHAMPAGNE FACTS

• Three types of grapes are blended to make champagne. Pinot Noir, and Pinot Meunier (black grapes), Chardonnay (a white grape). The blends are the secrets of each champagne house. Some use as many as 40 different wines to make a single champagne.

• Why does champagne intoxicate so quickly? The carbon dioxide is instantly absorbed by the stomach wall, which accelerates circulation once in the bloodstream, speeding the alcohol's journey to the brain. (Little wonder champagne is such a party favorite).

• Barbe-Nicole Clicquot Ponsardin took over her husband's small wine business after his death in 1805 and made Veuve Clicquot ("Widow Clicquot") one of the biggest names in the business. (In the film *Casablanca*, Rick asks Ilsa to stay for some champagne. Her response? "If it's Veuve Clicquot, I'll stay.")

• Ever wonder why there are no Italian, German, or Spanish champagnes? Many nations have agreed to make it illegal for any but the vintners of Champagne, France, to use the term *champagne*. To this day, only the United States, Canada (except for the province of Quebec), and some Asian countries use the term "champagne"—everywhere else it's called "sparkling wine."

• The ancient Romans began the serious cultivation of grapes in Champagne, and gave the region another (unintended) boost. They quarried the area's chalky hills for blocks, leaving extensive networks of caves up to 300 feet deep and many miles in length. These caves are still used today for the fermenting of champagne. There are a billion bottles in storage there at any given time.

• Winston Churchill's rallying cry to British troops in World War I: "Remember gentlemen, it's not just France we are fighting for, it's champagne!"

---

"I could not live without champagne. In victory I deserve it, in defeat I need it." —Napoleon

# LIFE IN 1966

*It's amazing how much things have changed in 40 years.*

**Vital Stats:** World population: 3.4 billion. (It's now 6.4 billion.)

• Average yearly wage: $4,938

• 40 percent of women work outside the home.

• Life expectancy: 70.2 years. (Today it's about 78.)

• A postage stamp cost 5¢; a gallon of gas, 32¢; a McDonald's hamburger, 15¢; a movie ticket, $1.09; and a gallon of milk, 99¢.

**Television:** *The Dick Van Dyke Show, The Flintstones,* and *Mr. Ed* end their runs. *Dark Shadows, Batman, The Monkees, That Girl, The Newlywed Game,* and *Star Trek* debut. Canada gets color TV.

**Top Grossing Movies:** *Thunderball, Dr. Zhivago, Who's Afraid of Virginia Woolf?,* and Disney's *That Darn Cat!*

**Sports:** England wins the soccer World Cup; the Baltimore Orioles win the World Series; the Boston Celtics win their eighth consecutive NBA title; golfer Jack Nicklaus wins his third Masters. The first NFL Super Bowl is still a year away.

**New Books:** *Valley of the Dolls* by Jacqueline Susann and *Quotations from Chairman Mao* are now among the top 10 bestsellers of all time.

**Music:** The Beach Boys' *Pet Sounds,* The Beatles' *Revolver,* Bob Dylan's *Blonde on Blonde.* #1 single: "The Ballad Of The Green Berets" by Barry Sadler.

**News:** In *Miranda v. Arizona,* the Supreme Court rules that police must inform suspects of their rights before questioning.

• First African-American Senator: Edward Brooke from Massachusetts.

• More than 300,000 American troops are fighting in Vietnam.

• First African-American professional coach: Bill Russell of the Boston Celtics.

• The Black Panther Party forms in Oakland, California.

**Science:** Russia's unmanned *Luna 9* lands on the moon, as does the U.S.'s *Surveyor I.*

**Deaths:** Walt Disney, Buster Keaton, Elizabeth Arden, Lenny Bruce, Sophie Tucker, and author Evelyn Waugh.

---

**Have you?** 14% of Americans say they've skinny-dipped with the opposite sex at least once.

# ASHES TO ASHES

*When a BRI staffer suggested an article about the history of cremation, everybody said "ew!" But hey—death is a part of life, something we all have to deal with. (Ew!)*

## FIRST FLAME

In 1873 Sir Henry Thompson, a prominent English physician and surgeon to Queen Victoria, attended the Vienna Exposition. There he saw a cremating oven invented by an Italian professor named Brunetti, along with the ashes of someone who had been cremated in the device. Thompson was so impressed that when he returned home he founded the Cremation Society of England and began lobbying to make cremation a socially acceptable alternative to burial, the standard practice in Christian countries. (While cremation was not expressly forbidden by most Christian churches, it was discouraged out of the fear that destroying the body by fire would prevent it from being reunited with the soul on Resurrection Day.)

## NO VACANCY

The foundation of the Cremation Society was timely. England's population was booming, which meant more people dying, and existing graveyards simply could not accommodate them all. In large cities tne problem was particularly acute: one Parliamentary investigation found that while London had only 200 acres of graveyards within the city limits, 50,000 bodies were being buried in them every year. The graveyards were so overcrowded that you literally could not bury one person without digging up another. The smell of decomposing remains in graveyards was so overpowering that grave diggers were said to be "drunkards by force." The graveyards of the late 19th century were serious public health hazards.

It was no coincidence that the earliest proponents for cremation were physicians like Henry Thompson who claimed that cremation was "a necessary sanitary precaution against the propagation of disease among a population daily growing larger in relation to the area it occupied."

## OLD FLAMES

But was cremation even legal in Britain? Nobody knew for sure. There weren't any laws on the books that forbade it, but there weren't any that allowed it, either. With the exception of epidemics and other emergencies when burial was not possible, cremation had fallen out of practice for more than 1,000 years.

The ancient Greeks had practiced cremation as a battlefield necessity—the only way that the bodies of heroes killed in faraway lands could be returned home was by reducing them to ashes. Over time, as cremating bodies on top of giant funeral pyres became increasingly associated with heroism, it became the customary way of disposing of the dead. The Romans adopted the practice from the Greeks, but when the Roman Empire converted to Christianity, cremation was abandoned in favor of burial. (Another practical reason: erecting enormous funeral pyres had gotten so out of hand that supplies of wood were beginning to run short.)

## LEGAL QUESTIONS

As a pillar of the British medical establishment, Thompson had access to some of the best legal minds in the country. When they concluded that there was nothing in the law that forbade cremation, the society started raising money to purchase a suitable site on which to build a crematorium. The bishop of Rochester blocked the society's attempt to build one on donated land inside a Church of England cemetery in London, so they bought land next to a cemetery in Woking, southwest of London, and built it there. Woking was connected to London by train, which would make transportation of remains for cremation fairly easy.

By early 1879, the crematorium was ready for testing, and on March 17 England's first modern cremation took place when a dead horse was put to the flames. It went off without a hitch—the horse was totally consumed, save for a couple of pounds worth of bone fragments, in a little over two hours. The combustion was so complete that almost no smoke or odor escaped up the chimney.

The Cremation Society was ready to repeat the experiment with a human body, but the horrified citizens of Woking, led by a local vicar, fought to have the crematorium shut down. They appealed to the British government, which had its own concerns that cremation might be used by murderers to destroy evidence of their crimes. After considering the issue, the government decided to ban cremation unless and until the British Parliament expressly permitted the practice. The Cremation Society resigned itself to the decision but began lobbying for a change.

## FIRE FIGHT

Then in 1882, a man named Captain Hanham asked the society to cremate both his wife and his mother, as they had requested in their wills. The society forwarded Hanham's request to the government, which refused to allow it. Infuriated, Captain Hanham built a crematorium on his own estate and did the job himself. The Hanham cremations received a lot of press attention, but the British government declined to prosecute Captain Hanham. (When he died a year later, he was cremated there, too.)

The next step toward legalization came in 1884, after an eccentric 84-year-old Welsh physician named Dr. William Price tried to cremate the body of his five-month-old son. An outspoken proponent of cremation, Dr. Price decided to dispose of his son's remains in as public a fashion as possible, cremating the linen-wrapped body in an open fire in plain view of a church just as the congregation was leaving Sunday-evening church services. The horrified crowd pulled the body from the flames before it was consumed, and then chased Dr. Price back to his house and tried to kill him. His mistress held them off with a shotgun until the police came and hauled him off to jail.

Price went on trial in Cardiff, Wales, and in February 1884 the court found him not guilty, ruling that cremation is legal "provided no nuisance is caused in the process to others." Dr. Price was released from jail, but another eight weeks passed before he was allowed to finish cremating his son's remains. (In the meantime he kept them under his bed.)

## BURNING OPPORTUNITY

Now that a court had ruled in favor of cremation, the Cremation Society declared that it was willing to cremate anyone who made such a request in their will. And on March 26, 1885, a "well-known figure in literary and scientific circles" named Mrs. Pickersgill became the first non-horse to receive a modern cremation in England.

Cremation may have been legal, but it still took a long time for the practice to be accepted. Only three people were cremated in all of England in 1885, and it wasn't until 1902 that Parliament passed a law explicitly allowing it. Today, however, more than 60 percent of English people are cremated when they die.

The first American crematorium opened in Washington, Pennsylvania, in 1876, but cremation has taken much longer to catch on in the United States than it did in England. Today only about 20 percent of Americans are cremated, compared to more than half in Germany, Denmark, and other European countries. Japan beats them all—in a land where cemetery space is very scarce, more than 96 percent of people are cremated.

## OTHER WAYS TO GO

*Still not convinced that cremation is right for you? Here are some other ways of disposing of your remains:*

• **Platforms.** The Sioux Indians placed their dead on high platforms that protected them from animals on the ground but allowed carrion-eating birds to feed on the remains. Some Aboriginal tribes in Australia left their dead in trees.

• **Freeze-Drying.** A newer method is immersing a body in liquid nitrogen until it is frozen solid, then smashing it into tiny pieces and freeze-drying them. (It hasn't caught on yet.)

• **Electroplating.** In 1891 Dr. Varlot of France developed a method by which a corpse could be dipped in silver nitrate, then exposed to phosphorus and finally a copper sulphate solution, resulting in a body electroplated with copper. Varlot hoped to use the method to preserve dead bodies until science progressed to the point that they could be resuscitated. (It hasn't caught on, either.)

• **Dead-Acid Batteries.** An atheist named Jimmy Loizeau has proposed using the stomach acid from a deceased person to create a battery, which could then be used to power a flashlight. "Even if the flashlight is off, the bereaved may be comforted in the fact their loved one's electrical potential can be summoned at the flick of a switch," Loizeau writes. Loizeau also proposes adjusting the menus of "last suppers" to include foods likely to "promote acid production" so that the batteries will last longer.

# SAVANT SYNDROME

*In the 1988 movie* Rain Man, *Dustin Hoffman played an autistic man with amazing abilities. His performance won an Oscar and introduced millions of people to one of the most mysterious conditions known to medicine.*

## ISLANDS OF BRILLIANCE

I • Ellen Boudreaux is blind and has never seen a clock. Yet this California resident always knows exactly what time it is, down to the precise second her favorite TV show begins. It's almost as if she has a digital clock in her brain.

• Leslie Lemke, of Arpin, Wisconsin, was born blind with severe mental disabilities, but can play any piece of music on the piano after hearing it just once.

• Alonzo Clemens, of Boulder, Colorado, struggles to express himself with a vocabulary of barely 100 words, yet he can sculpt a perfect clay likeness of a horse in less than an hour. His work is sold in art galleries worldwide.

These people are living examples of a condition known as *savant syndrome*. As defined by Dr. Darold A. Treffert, the world's leading expert on the subject, savant syndrome is "a rare but spectacular condition" in which people with developmental disorders have "astonishing islands of ability, brilliance, or talent" that make them stand out from the crowd.

Savants possess remarkable skills in number and calendar calculation, art and music, mechanical aptitude, and feats of memory. They're called *splinter skills*, because they exist in such dramatic contrast to their owner's physical and mental disabilities. Savants are often obsessed with memorizing facts such as sports and music trivia, map details, or history; counting things such as license plate numbers; or have quirkier habits, such as cataloging vacuum cleaner sounds. The most frequent expression of savant ability is in music, often found combined with blindness and perfect pitch.

## THEY'RE NO IDIOTS

Until recently, people with this condition were known as "idiot savants," a term coined in 1887 by Dr. J. Langdon Down (also

---

The mountain on the Paramount logo is modeled on Utah s Mount Ben Lomond.

known for identifying Down syndrome). Down combined the then-accepted medical term for low IQ with the French word *savant*, which means "knowledgeable one." The phrase has fallen into disuse, partly because of the pejorative nature of the word "idiot"—but mostly because it doesn't really describe most people with this condition. Although roughly half of the world's savants suffer from some degree of mental disability, few are clinically "idiots" (IQ below 25). There is also a significant relationship between savant syndrome and autism—1 of 10 persons with autism has savant skills, a phenomenally high proportion—and many autistic savants have higher than average, or even genius-level, IQs.

## PASSING THE TEST-OSTERONE

One particular statistic about savant syndrome—that it's six times more common in males than females—has led to a provocative theory about its cause. Many experts believe the syndrome stems from damage to the left half of the brain, due to a congenital defect or physical injury, resulting in an overcompensation by the right half of the brain.

In the 1980s, neurologists Norman Geschwind and Albert Galaburda proposed a theory suggesting that the culprit causing this disorder is testosterone. The left half of the brain develops later than the right, which exposes it to possible fetal injury for a longer time. The male fetus starts producing the male sex hormone testosterone at eight weeks. But the hormone is also neurotoxic, which means it's poisonous to nerve cells. Geschwind and Galaburda have suggested that this hormonal flooding of the underdeveloped left hemisphere could be responsible for the brain damage that leads to savant syndrome.

## FAMOUS SAVANTS

• **Thomas Fuller (1710–1790).** An 18th-century black slave from Alexandria, Virginia, who could, according to the doctor who studied him, "comprehend scarcely anything more complex than counting." But when the doctor asked him how many seconds were lived by a man who died at the age of 70 years, 17 days, and 12 hours old, Fuller took only 90 seconds to come up with his answer: 2,210,500,800. When told he was wrong, Fuller pointed out that the doctor had forgotten to include the 17 leap years that would have occurred in 70 years.

• **"Blind Tom" Bethune (1849–1908).** He was so mentally disabled that he could barely put together a coherent sentence, yet he could play more than 5,000 pieces on the piano. Born a slave on a Georgia plantation, Tom was considered too simpleminded to do any work. Although he had never touched a piano before, at four years old he startled his master when he sat down and suddenly started playing. He became a concert pianist, learning his classical repertoire after hearing each piece only once. At a concert early in his career, he was challenged by local musicians to prove his uncanny ability to play by ear. They played two brand-new compositions, which he repeated flawlessly. From then on the "challenge" became a regular part of his performances.

• **James Henry Pullen (1835–1916).** A deaf mute from London, at the age of seven he could only speak one word, but he could carve model boats out of wood. Pullen spent most of his life in asylums, particularly one called Earlswood, where he was encouraged to develop his woodworking skills. Pullen was moody and prone to fits of anger, but he was a gifted carpenter, crafting beautiful furniture and marvelous carved boats of his own imagining. His masterpiece: a model of the sailing ship *Great Eastern*. It took seven years to carve and was accurate down to the rivets. Pullen became known as the "Genius of Earlswood," his work attracting the attention of England's rich and famous, including the future king Edward VII.

• **Kim Peek.** Born in 1951 with an enlarged head and without a *corpus callosum*, the tissue that connects the right and left hemispheres of the brain. At 16 months, Kim could memorize any book that was read to him. By the time he was three, he was looking up words in the dictionary (he didn't learn to walk until he was four). Obsessed with numbers, he would read telephone directories, then add the columns of telephone numbers. When riding in a car he'd total the license plate numbers of passing cars.

Known as "Kimputer" to friends and family, Kim is a walking databank, rattling off facts about British monarchs, horse racing, the Bible, baseball, composers, movies, the space program, authors, geography, and literature. He can recall, word for word, every book he's ever read—all 9,600 of them. Dustin Hoffman met Kim while doing research for *Rain Man*, and was so impressed by Kim's abilities that he told him, "I may be a star but you are the heavens."

# FIRST GLASS

*From where you sit, you can probably see several pieces of*
*glass: a window, the bathroom mirror, maybe even a*
*glass shower door. Here's the BRI's history of glass.*

## ANCIENT GLASS

Glass has existed for millions of years. Whenever natural events involving super-high temperatures—volcanic activity, lightning strikes, or the impact of meteorites—cause certain types of rocks to melt, fuse, and then cool rapidly, glass is formed. Fossil evidence shows that Stone Age humans used this natural glass to make tools, such as spearheads and cutting instruments, as far back as 9,000 years ago. (Better dating techniques may eventually push that date back much further.) Obsidian, the shiny, black glass formed when lava cools quickly (as when flowing into water), was widely used by ancient people for these purposes.

After thousands of years of using naturally-formed glass, humans finally discovered how to make it—probably by accident. The Roman historian Pliny wrote in A.D. 77 that Phoenician sailors placed "stones of soda ash" into a fire (presumably to rest their pots on) on a sandy beach. They later found a "hard, smooth stone" in the ashes. That's one possible scenario, given that sand, soda ash (sodium carbonate), and heat are all ingredients for making glass. Another possibility is that potters inadvertently let some sand drift into their kilns, where it stuck to the wet clay, accidentally creating a hard, smooth glaze on the pottery when the baking was done.

However glassmaking was first discovered, historians agree that it happened about 6,000 years ago. The story of glassmaking after that is one of continuous technologic change: refining the recipe to create new types of glass, learning to shape it into new forms, and finding new and better uses for it.

## GETTING INTO SHAPE

The first known methods used for shaping molten glass into objects were *drawing* and *casting*.

- **Glass drawing.** A metal hook is used to pull molten glass out of a tank while it is a very thick, red-hot liquid. In this state the glass can be drawn—much like taffy—into long thin strands, which are allowed to harden into rods or are cut into decorative beads while still soft.

- **Glass casting.** Molten glass is poured into a form and allowed to harden. The earliest glass molds were probably made of sand.

These methods are believed to have been first used by Sumerians in ancient Mesopotamia (Iraq and Syria) more than 5,000 years ago. Glass beads and simple cast pieces dating to approximately 3500 B.C. have been found in the region, and glassmaking instructions have even been discovered in ancient Sumerian texts. This new technology was passed around on trade routes to neighboring societies, and over the next 2,000 years, simple glassmaking spread across Mesopotamia and the Middle East.

## CUP RUNNETH OVER

The next big leap for glassmaking was using it to make containers. Around 1500 B.C., Egyptian glassmakers discovered that they could dip solid cylinders of silica paste (made of crushed sand and water) into molten glass. They allowed the glass to harden and then broke the core out—thus making the first known glass containers. The method was improved by pouring molten glass over compacted sand forms, and later by another technique, known as glass pressing: molten glass was poured into a mold, and another mold was then pressed down into it. (This is still how many bottles are made today, but the process is done mechanically.)

A huge improvement over wood or clay containers, glass was put to many uses: as bottles for perfumes, dyes, and cosmetics; or as containers for carrying and preserving food and beverages such honey and wine.

## ANCIENT BLOWHARDS

Around 30 B.C., craftsmen in Phoenicia (Lebanon and Syria) discovered that if they blew through a hollow metal tube into a lump of molten glass, it would inflate and take shape. Glassmaking would never be the same. It quickly changed from the limited use of crude molds to the seemingly infinite possibilities of glassblow-

---

According to historians, Asians didn't kiss until the practice was introduced by Westerners.

ing. Craftsmen could now produce a greater variety of wares for a greater variety of uses. And they could do it faster, easier, and cheaper than ever before.

At that time, Phoenicia was part of the Roman Empire. The Romans embraced the new technology and over the next several centuries spread it throughout their empire, including the Middle East, North Africa, and almost the whole of Europe. Glassblowing would remain the dominant way of making glass in these regions for almost the next 2,000 years.

## CLEARING UP

Certain qualities of glass—color, transparency, and heat resistance, to name a few—are determined by the ingredients that are mixed with the silica. Through experimentation, these recipes gradually improved, and around A.D. 100 in Alexandria, Egypt, manganese oxide, a commonly found mineral, was added to the mix. Result: a formula for nearly transparent glass. This soon led to the use of glass for windows (although only in the most important buildings in the most important cities, like Rome and Alexandria). Early windows were usually cast, but some may have been made from *rolled glass*: molten glass poured on a flat surface and rolled out like dough. Either way, the first glass windows were thick, cloudy, and uneven—but they let in light and kept the weather out.

The fall of the Roman Empire in the fifth century marked the beginning of the Dark Ages in Europe and a near-halt in the progress of glassmaking. But by the seventh century, new Muslim empires began to flourish in Asia and Africa. Over the next several centuries, Arab artisans, especially those from Syria, became the world's premier glassmakers. They made huge advances in cutting, engraving, and coloring techniques, as well as inventing ways to paint, enamel, and gild glass. Intricately decorated, multicolored, gilded glass pieces from this era—especially vases in a wide variety of shapes—have been found in all parts of the Arab world. Even after dominance in the trade would shift back to Europe, European glassmakers were greatly influenced by the artistic and scientific advances of their Arab counterparts.

## VENETIAN GLASS

Nobody knows exactly when glassmaking began in Venice, but by

1224 the city's glassmakers had already formed a guild to protect their trade. By 1291 there were so many Venetian glassmakers that the furnaces were causing fires all over the city, which prompted the city council to move them all to the nearby island of Murano. This actually helped the guilds—they were better able to hide their advances from competitors. By the 14th century Venetian glassmakers were the world leaders in all aspects of the craft, including mastering the ingredients for making colored glass. For instance, the right amount of cobalt resulted in a deep blue glass; manganese made yellow or purple. One of their more significant achievements was the development of the clearest glass at that time, *cristallo*. And that led to the first glass lenses, developed in the Netherlands in 1590, which would eventually lead to the invention of eyeglasses, the telescope, and the microscope.

## THE INDUSTRIAL REVOLUTION AND BEYOND

As with many other crafts, the change to factory-made, mass-produced glass meant a fatal blow to an artisan's craft that had been practiced for thousands of years, but it also meant great leaps forward in quality.

• In 1820 a mechanized process of bottle production was introduced in the United States, greatly increasing the public's familiarity with the use of glass.

• In 1876 John Jacob Bausch and Henry Lomb started Bausch and Lomb in Rochester, New York. They developed and refined many types of lenses for use in microscopes, eyeglasses, and magnifiers.

• In 1915 Corning Glass made the first heat-resistant glass for cookware, calling it Pyrex, from *pyro*, the Greek word for "fire."

• In 1919 Henry Ford borrowed from a French invention, putting two layers of glass together with a very thin layer of cellulose in between. The resulting two-ply sheet was transparent and shatterproof. Ford ordered this "safety glass" put on all his cars. (Safety glass is made basically the same way today.)

• In 1926 Corning developed the "399" or "Ribbon" machine to make lightbulbs. It was soon capable of making 400,000 bulbs a day, more than five times the amount made by previous machines —which made lightbulbs affordable for ordinary households.

• In 1959 Britain's Alastair Pilkington invented the "float process" for making sheet glass. A sheet of molten glass is drawn from a tank, then floated over the surface of a tank of molten tin and allowed to cool. This results in the smooth, lustrous, and consistent finish that consumers now expect—and take for granted—in windows. Nearly all sheet glass made today uses the float process.

• In 1970 Corning developed a workable silica optical fiber, an idea that had been around for decades. Used mostly for data transmission, this breakthrough jump-started the "fiber-optic" age.

## GLASS PRESENT AND FUTURE

What's next? A fairly recent development: "smart glass," or glass coated with different substances that make it react to outside stimuli. You've probably seen *photochromic* glass—glass that responds to light—in self-darkening sunglasses. *Thermochromic* glass does the same thing in response to heat, and *electrochromic*, the most promising, responds to electricity; a flick of a switch can change the opaqueness of the glass or how it reflects light. Other techniques can even change the color of glass.

The science of glassmaking continues to advance. New methods are being discovered to produce glass faster and better; more uses for it are being found in computers, medical devices, and communications, to name a few. Thousands of years have passed since the discovery of that strange stone in the ashes of a fire. Who knows what uses the future holds for that simple but elegant substance—glass.

\*　　\*　　\*

## PAST-EGO EXPERIENCE

The 2003 book *Unlock Your Secret Dreams* by Craig Hamilton Parker unlocks some "past life" secrets of several stars:

• Sylvester Stallone believes in reincarnation and is convinced he was guillotined during the French Revolution.

• Englebert Humperdinck believes he was a Roman emperor.

• Tina Turner says she was told by a psychic that she's the reincarnation of Hatshepsut, a female pharaoh in ancient Egypt.

• John Travolta believes he was once Rudolph Valentino.

# HARD-BOILED

*Here's the story of Dashiell Hammett,
the king of the crime novel.*

Samuel Spade's jaw was long and bony, his chin a jutting v under the more flexible v of his mouth. His nostrils curved back to make another, smaller, v. His yellow-grey eyes were horizontal. The v motif was picked up again by thickish brows rising outward from twin creases above a hooked nose, and his pale brown hair grew down—from high flat temples—in a point on his forehead. He looked rather pleasantly like a blond satan.

He said to Effie Perine: "Yes, sweetheart?"

She was a lanky sunburned girl whose tan dress of thin woolen stuff clung to her with an effect of dampness. Her eyes were brown and playful in a shiny boyish face. She finished shutting the door behind her, leaned against it, and said: "There's a girl wants to see you. Her name's Wonderly."

"A customer?"

"I guess so. You'll want to see her anyway: she's a knockout."

"Shoo her in, darling," said Spade. "Shoo her in."

Those are the opening lines from *The Maltese Falcon*, Dashiell Hammett's 1930 novel, voted one of the 100 best novels in the English language by the Modern Library, and the one for which he's most famous. Hammett's looks were a far cry from Sam Spade's: he was thin—and his short white hair and little black mustache made him look anything but tough. But like the rugged antiheroes in his detective stories, Hammett lived a hard life, drank heavily, and preferred to work alone. And his character showed in the stories he wrote for *Black Mask* magazine during the 1920s, which established him as the king of the hard-boiled mystery writers and the father of the film noir movie classics that followed. Although Hammett didn't invent crime fiction, he wrote with such skill that his influence dominated it, elevating the genre to an art form. But that's not how it started out.

---

Big Ma-a-a-c: In India, McDonald's has no beef on the menu. (They do serve lamb burgers.)

# PULP FICTION

Cheap adventure stories published in pocket-sized paperback books first appeared the mid-1800s. Publishing firms saved money by printing them on the cheapest paper available, made from pure wood pulp without any rag fiber (hence the term "pulp fiction"). The earliest were Western stories that featured frontier heroes, but as the Wild West was tamed, the cowboy's urban counterpart began to emerge in the form of the streetwise detective. By the 1870s, the detective story had established itself as a genre. Serialized adventures of characters like Old Cap Collier, Broadway Billy, Jack Harkaway, and the mysterious Old Sleuth, Master of Disguise, helped to develop the style. These were hard-fisted, tough-guy heroes who inhabited a dark, urban underworld where violence seemed to be the only means of establishing order.

Crime fiction magazines and dime novels grew steadily in popularity through the end of the 19th century and into the 20th. By the 1920s, there were more than 20,000 magazines in circulation in the United States. Pulp titles like *The Nick Carter Weekly*, *Detective Stories*, *Girl's Detective*, *Doctor Death*, *Argosy*, and *Police Gazette* dominated newsstands during Prohibition, giving rise to a class of working writers who earned about a penny a word, some using several pseudonyms so they could publish more than a million words per year. Hammett wanted to be a part of it.

In late 1923 he arrived at *Black Mask* magazine, which printed "Stories of Detection, Mystery, Adventure, Romance, and Spiritualism." Earlier that year, the magazine had published a story by Carroll John Daly called "Three Gun Terry," considered the first authentic "hard-boiled" detective story. Yet although he didn't invent the style, Hammett quickly dominated it. Over the next seven years he wrote more than 50 stories for *Black Mask*, becoming its premier writer, and helping it become *the* premier magazine of hard-boiled fiction. Hammett's influence was such that other writers accused the magazine's editors of forcing them to copy him.

## DASHIELL HAMMETT, P.I.

So how was Hammett able to bring such an impressive realism to his characters? Experience. Before becoming a writer, he had been a detective—he was an operative with the Pinkerton Agency from 1915 to 1922. Hammett had had many jobs before that: newsboy, freight clerk, laborer, and rail yard messenger, but it was all just to help support his parents and his two brothers.

## SMART KID

Born in 1894, Samuel Dashiell Hammett grew up between Baltimore and Philadelphia. He learned a love of reading from his mother, who was a nurse, and street smarts from his father, who was a farmer, gambler, occasional politician, and notorious womanizer. Although he never finished high school, young Hammett was a voracious reader. And after spending time on the road with his father, he was also streetwise. So when Hammett arrived at the Pinkerton office in Baltimore to take a clerk job, his bosses soon recognized that this 21-year-old kid would make a great field operative. They placed him under the wing of one of their best private eyes, James Wright, who taught Hammett the ins and outs of "tailing a perp and bringing him in." Wright was the inspiration for the Continental Op, the hero of Hammett's early stories.

Little is known about Hammett's days as a Pinkerton operative. Most biographers agree that he embellished his tales to help create a mystique about himself. In his book *Shadow Man*, author Richard Layman says that Hammett "in a half self-serving, half playful manner, characteristically amplified his stories, rewriting, revising, even inventing accounts of his experiences." What *is* known, however, is that Hammett was a master at tailing suspects. According to one colleague, Dash (as he was known to friends) once followed a man through six small towns without ever being detected. He was quickly rising through the agency ranks, primed to become one of Pinkerton's best. Everything changed when he chose to fight in World War I.

## A LIFELONG CONTRACT

Hammett enlisted in the army in 1919 and served as a sergeant in the ambulance corps, but was discharged a year later when he contracted first tuberculosis and then the Spanish flu. The diseases would plague him for the rest of his life, not only putting a halt to his detective and military careers, but also affecting his relationships with women. (While recovering, he married a nurse named Josephine Dolan, but because TB is contagious, in 1926 she was advised by doctors to take their two daughters and leave him.)

Hammett did go back to Pinkerton after he recovered, but he grew disillusioned with the Pinkerton style of law enforcement after an incident in Montana. The story goes that he was offered $5,000 to kill Frank Little, a labor boss who was organizing miners. Hammett refused, but Little was ultimately captured by five men—allegedly Pinkerton *ops* (short for "operatives")—and hanged from a railroad trestle in Butte. Hammett biographer Diane Johnson writes:

> Perhaps at the moment he was asked to murder Frank Little, or perhaps at the moment that he learned that Little had been killed, possibly by other Pinkerton men, Hammett saw that he himself was on the fringe…and was expected to be, according to a kind of oath of fealty that he and other Pinkerton men took. He also learned something of the lives of poor miners, whose wretched strikes the Pinkerton people were hired to prevent, and about the lies of mine owners. Those things were to sit in the back of his mind.

Not only was Hammett at odds with his Pinkerton bosses because of his idealism and growing distrust of authority, but his chronic TB made it impossible for him to endure assignments that often took place on long, cold nights. He left the agency in 1922 to find something that required less physical effort.

## PEN IN HAND

Unemployed and disabled, Hammett took a job as an ad writer for a San Francisco jewelry store, but found the work unfulfilling. He wanted to write about something that he knew, that he was passionate about. Being a fan of detective stories—but disappointed by their lack of authenticity—Dashiell Hammett decided to create the detective that he was never able to be in real life.

"Your private detective does not," he said, "want to be an erudite solver of riddles in the Sherlock Holmes manner, he wants to be a hard and shifty fellow, able to take care of himself in any situation, able to get the best of anybody he comes in contact with, whether criminal, innocent bystander, or client." So Hammett started pounding out the dark characters and vigilante justice that expressed his cynical views of the world of crime and punishment. Just as he had impressed the Pinkertons with his skill and wit a few years before, he equally impressed the editors at *Black Mask* with his descriptive prose and tight storytelling.

## MEAN STREETS

After Hammett's highly successful run with *Black Mask*, he published his first full novel, *Red Harvest*, in 1929. Drawing on his strike-breaking experience with Pinkertons, Hammett used his Continental Op character to narrate the tale of a corrupt and lawless Montana mining town in the aftermath of a violent labor clash. Just a few months later, Hammett and the Continental Op were back with *The Dain Curse*. Without stopping for a rest, he then banged out *The Maltese Falcon* in time for a spring 1930 release.

Considered his finest novel, *The Maltese Falcon* introduced Sam Spade, who became one of America's best-known fictional heroes during the tough times of the Great Depression. In a decade that saw a high rise in crime—especially in the nation's cities—readers looked up to Spade. He was tough but full of integrity and got results from playing by his own rules. Spade's world was violent, unsympathetic, and full of irony and black humor. Readers ate it up. Sam Spade went on to star in radio dramas, comic books, and on film. Three different movies were made of *The Maltese Falcon*; the classic 1941 Humphrey Bogart version was the third.

## EASY STREET

The 1930s was a good decade for Hammett. He was rich and famous (and single), hopping back and forth between Manhattan and Los Angeles to attend star-studded parties with the likes of Harpo Marx, Jean Harlow, F. Scott Fitzgerald, and William Faulkner. Hammett drank and partied for days at a time. But he was also writing. He would work on movie scripts, first at Paramount and later at MGM—where he was paid $2,000 per week. In 1934 he published his fifth and final novel, *The Thin Man*, which spawned a series of films starring William Powell and Myrna Loy. He wrote script stories for three *The Thin Man* sequels but found writing for Hollywood less rewarding than writing novels. So he worked as little as he could get away with and drank heavily. Result: Hammett garnered an "unreliable" reputation among the film studios. His earlier impressive productivity soon fizzled into nothing. He wanted to get away from detective fiction and write more serious novels, but could never bring himself to do it. "I quit writing because I was repeating myself," he later explained. "It is the beginning of the end when you notice that you have style."

Perhaps Hammett could have written the Great American Novel had he not become such a raging alcoholic. His daughter Jo Hammett recounts in her biography, A *Daughter Remembers*, that the drinking "turned my father maudlin, sarcastic, and mean." He lost focus, starting many projects and finishing none of them.

But with a steady stream of royalties coming in, he didn't have to work, so in the 1940s Hammett became involved in leftist politics. Still stung from his strike-breaking days in Montana, Hammett became a civil rights activist and staunch opponent of Nazi Germany. Despite his age—he was in his 40s—he reenlisted to serve in World War II. They shipped him off to the Aleutian Islands (in Alaska), where he spent nearly three years editing a newspaper for the troops and helping train young writers to be good news correspondents. Hammett said later that this was the last happy time of his life.

## LEFT OUT

When he returned home, Hammett found himself ostracized from the industry that made him famous. Moving further to the fringe, he became vice-chairman of the leftist Civil Rights Congress in 1948, an organization that the FBI called "subversive." He also quit drinking that year, but the damage had been done—his immune system was shot, making him continuously sick with a hacking cough that was as unpleasant for Hammett as it was for those around him.

Downtrodden and out of the public eye, in 1951 Hammett was ordered to turn over a list of names of contributors to the Civil Rights Congress. But he refused. Following in the footsteps of the Continental Op and Sam Spade, he remained loyal and didn't "rat them out." Taking the Fifth, Hammett was charged with contempt of court and thrown into federal prison for five months. When he got out, he was informed by the IRS that he owed hundreds of thousands of dollars in back taxes. They garnisheed all his income from new publications or productions of his previous work. His days of being the toast of Tinseltown now seemed like ancient history. Hammett was broke and alone, and his health was deteriorating. He took a job in New York teaching creative writing just to pay the bills.

## THE LAST CHAPTER

In 1953—at the height of the United States' anti-Communist era—Hammett was called before Senator Joseph McCarthy's House Un-American Activities Committee. McCarthy aide Roy Cohn repeatedly asked Hammett if he was a Communist. Hammett repeatedly said no. "Were you a Communist when you wrote these books?" "No." "Has any of the money you made from these books financed any Communist organizations?" "Not to my knowledge." Without an admission or evidence, McCarthy could do nothing to Hammett, but the damage had been done.

Financially in ruin, Hammett had a major heart attack in 1955. He was unable to care for himself, and was taken in by a longtime friend and confidant, writer Lillian Hellman. She moved him into her Park Avenue apartment where she saw to his needs while he edited her plays. Hammett contracted lung cancer and died in 1961 at the age of 67.

## EPILOGUE

"He very much wanted to be remembered as an American writer," wrote his daughter Jo Hammett. "He was always very proud of his heritage, and it shows in his treatment of the language. Few people have written American speech as well as he did."

But more than just an American writer, Dashiell Hammett wanted to be remembered as a true American. As a veteran of two World Wars, he requested that he be buried at Arlington National Cemetery. FBI Director J. Edgar Hoover objected but was overruled. Hammett's headstone, located in Section 12 of the cemetery, simply reads:

**Samuel D. Hammett**
**Sergeant, U.S. Army**
**1894–1961**

\*     \*     \*

## TOLD YOU!

Research shows that when people see upside-down writing in a book, 99% of the time they will turn the book over.

---

It takes 8,000 workers to run and maintain the Panama Canal.

# CLASSIC HAMMETT

*Dashiell Hammett's style has inspired so many writers,*
*actors, and filmmakers that it's nice to go to the source*
*himself to read some of his grittiest crime prose.*

Poisonville is an ugly city of forty thousand people, set in an ugly notch between two ugly mountains that had been all dirtied up by mining. Spread over this was a grimy sky that looked as if it had come out of smelters' stacks.
**—Red Harvest**

On Spade's desk a limp cigarette smoldered in a brass tray filled with the remains of limp cigarettes. Ragged grey flakes of cigarette-ash dotted the yellow top of the desk and the green blotter and the papers that were there. A buff-curtained window, eight or ten inches open, let in from the court a current of air faintly scented with ammonia. The ashes on the desk twitched and crawled in the current.
**—The Maltese Falcon**

Out of the moving automobile a man stepped. Miraculously he kept his feet, stumbling, sliding, until an arm crooked around an iron awning-post jerked him into an abrupt halt. He was a large man in bleached khaki, tall, broad, and thick-armed; his grey eyes were bloodshot; face and clothing were powdered heavily with dust. One of his hands clutched a thick, black stick, the other swept off his hat, and he bowed with exaggerated lowness before the girl's angry gaze.

The bow completed, he tossed his hat carelessly into the street, and grinned grotesquely through the dirt that masked his face, a grin that accented the heaviness of a begrimed and hair-roughened jaw.

"I beg y'r par'on," he said. "'F I hadn't been careful I believe I'd a'most hit you. 'S unreli'ble, tha' wagon. Borr'ed it from an engi—eng'neer. Don't ever borrow one from eng'neer. They're unreli'ble."

The girl looked at the place where he stood as if no one stood there, as if, in fact, no one had ever stood there, turned her small back on him, and walked very precisely down the street.
**—Nightmare Town**

Geckos, when startled, make a noise that sounds like "Eeek!"

**I was leaning against the bar** in a speakeasy on Fifty-second Street, waiting for Nora to finish her Christmas shopping, when a girl got up from the table where she had been sitting with three other people and came over to see me. She was small and blonde, and whether you looked at her face or at her body in powder-blue sports clothes, the result was satisfactory. "Aren't you Nick Charles?" she asked.

I said: "Yes."

She held out her hand. "I'm Dorothy Wynant. You don't remember me, but you ought to remember my father, Clyde Wynant. You—"

"Sure," I said, "and I remember you now, but you were only a kid of eleven or twelve then, weren't you?"

"Yes, that was eight years ago. Listen: remember those stories you told me? Were they true?"

"Probably not. How is your father?"

*—The Thin Man*

**"Don Wilson's gone** to sit at the right hand of God, if God doesn't mind looking at bullet holes."

"Who shot him?" I asked.

The grey man scratched the back of his neck and said: "Somebody with a gun."

*—Red Harvest*

"You ought to have known I'd do it." My voice sounded harsh and savage and like a stranger's in my ear. "Didn't I steal a crutch from a cripple?"

*—The Continental Op, "The Gutting of Couffignal"*

"Do you think he'll play ball with you after he's re-elected?"

Madvig was not worried. "I can handle him."

"Maybe, but don't forget he's never been licked by anything in his life."

Madvig nodded in complete agreement. "Sure, that's one of the best reasons I know for throwing in with him."

"No it isn't, Paul," Ned Beaumont said earnestly. "It's the very worst. Think that over even if it hurts your head. How far has this dizzy blond daughter of his got her hooks into you?"

*—The Glass Key*

---

The original recipe for Peking duck was 15,000 words long.

# AMAZING ESCAPES

*Disasters happen all the time—floods, crashes, etc.
As the following stories indicate, it takes at least one
of two things to survive an otherwise certain
death: a clear head or a stroke of luck.*

## SPIT BACK OUT

When the British passenger ship *Lusitania* was sunk by a German sub off the coast of Ireland in 1915, less than half of the 1,959 people onboard survived. One who did was a woman named Margaret Dwyer. As the ship's massive deck went underwater, hundreds of people started swimming for their lives. Unfortunately, most were sucked down by the undertow—including Dwyer. But unlike the others, she was pulled down into one of the smokestacks. When the rushing water hit the burning coal, it erupted into a huge explosion of steam, pushing Dwyer out of the water and up into the air. She landed back in the ocean, singed and sooty, but alive. She was then pulled to safety by a rescue boat.

## EXPRESS ELEVATOR

July 28, 1945, was a foggy Saturday morning in New York City. Betty Lou Oliver, an elevator operator at the Empire State Building, was standing at her post on the 80th floor of the skyscraper. At 9:40 a.m., a B-25 bomber lost in the fog slammed into the 79th floor at more than 200 mph. The impact shook the entire building and sent flames and airplane parts flying throughout the offices. Fourteen people, including the plane's three crewmen, were killed instantly. Yet Oliver, who was one floor above, survived the initial impact—only to be severely burned by the ensuing fire. When rescuers arrived, they told those who could still walk to take the stairs down, then they transported the injured in the elevators, believing they were still operating normally. They weren't. One of the plane's engines had fallen down the shaft, severely weakening the cables.

Oliver was given first aid, taken to the 75th floor, and then placed in an elevator car by herself. Shortly after the doors closed, she heard a very loud *snap* and immediately felt the car picking up speed. The elevator's cables had been severed in the crash. With little else to do, Oliver curled up in a ball and prayed as the elevator plummeted more than 1,000 feet down to the basement.

An hour later, rescuers reached the mangled car and cut a hole in the top. To their amazement and relief, they found Oliver badly injured…but alive. What saved her? It was later determined that all the cables below the elevator bunched up as it approached the bottom, thereby cushioning her fall. She made a full recovery.

## FANTASTIC GYMNASTICS

In 1933 a bus transporting seven Japanese acrobats on a mountain road near Tokyo went out of control and rolled off a high cliff. As the bus tumbled down the mountainside, it hit a large rock in the middle of the cliff. The impact slowed the bus just long enough for the agile acrobats to jump out of the windows to safety in a nearby tree. They clung for their lives as they watched the doomed bus, with the driver still inside, complete its descent to the rocks below.

## A FAILURE TO COMMUNICATE

Returning from a night raid over Germany in 1940, an RAF bomber was hit by gunfire and started going down. In the back of the plane, the gunner, Sgt. Roger Peacock, knew the plane was descending fast, but didn't hear an order to bail out, so he asked over the interphone, "Should I bail out?" He got no reply. *They must be too busy wrestling with the controls*, he thought. So he asked again…and again. Still, no reply. By then, the bomber was in a nose dive. Peacock made his way to the front of the plane and discovered that he was alone. He quickly bailed out, but saw right away that he was barely 100 feet above the ground—too close for his parachute to fully open and slow him down.

Peacock was sure he was going to die, but just then the bomber crashed into the ground below and exploded. The rush of heat from the fireball inflated Peacock's parachute and pushed him high up into the air. He landed softly, a safe distance from the wreckage. Five minutes later, the dazed sergeant watched as two other crewmen floated down to earth. It turned out that the pilot *had* given the order to bail out, but Peacock hadn't heard it.

## FLY AWAY HOME

At 10:00 p.m., Sunday, November 10, 2003, Carol Watts went to bed in her home in Tuscaloosa County, Alabama. Her husband, Walter, had decided to stay up and watch the news because severe thunderstorms were on their way. A short time later Walter went upstairs, got Carol out of bed, and helped her to a bathroom in the middle of the house. As the two huddled in the bathtub, the wind outside picked up and suddenly a deafening roar was heard, as everything began to shake and rattle. "The house just exploded," Carol later recalled. "The next thing I remember I was sitting straight up in a field." Disoriented, Carol didn't know where she was until a bolt of lightning lit up her surroundings: she was across the street in a pasture, 250 yards from her home. Walter had landed nearby, and although he had a puncture wound in his head, he was still conscious. It took the couple a few minutes to realize the magnitude of what had just happened to them: they had been sucked up into the vortex of a tornado and lived to tell about it.

The Watts were taken to a hospital, where they were treated for numerous burns, broken bones, and lacerations, but both made a full recovery. They built a new home just up the hill from where their old one used to stand.

\*     \*     \*

## CARS YOU'RE UNLIKELY TO SEE IN AMERICA

*Believe it or not, all these model names are real:*

| | |
|---|---|
| Nissan Homy | Suzuki Mighty Boy |
| Toyota Deliboy | Toyota Urban Supporter |
| Honda Life Dunk | Daihatsu Naked |
| Volugrafo Bimbo | Honda Today Humming |
| Renault Twingo | Toyota Synus |
| Nissan Sunny California | Mitsubishi Lettuce |
| Honda Vamos Hobio | Isuzu Begin Funk Box |
| Isuzu Elf Van | Honda Fit |
| Suzuki Cappuccino | Mazda Bongo Friendee |

Witchcraft was a criminal offense in the United Kingdom until 1951.

# THE MINISERIES

*The sweeping saga and disastrous demise
of a once-grand television tradition.*

E PISODE ONE: THE ENGLISH INVASION
American television series have traditionally followed a
standard formula: each week characters get a problem, solve
it, and learn a valuable lesson. A series could go on like that for
hundreds of episodes. British TV was different: dramatic series
were serialized and usually ran for about six episodes. Especially
popular in this format were adaptations of classic novels.

The first "novel for television" broadcast in the United States
was 1967's English-made *The Forsyte Saga*. The 26-part series—a
decades-spanning story of a prominent British family—was a big
hit for the young, struggling National Educational Television network (later PBS) and would lead to one of PBS's signature shows,
*Masterpiece Theatre*, a showcase for multiple-part literary adaptations, usually made in England.

It also led American commercial networks to test the idea of
long-format television with made-for-TV movies broken up into
shorter episodes. Examples: a seven-hour adaptation of the Leon
Uris novel *QB VII* (ABC, 1974) and the six-hour biblical epic
*Moses the Lawgiver* (CBS, 1975).

But the miniseries wouldn't become a TV force until CBS's
vice president of programming, Fred Silverman, left to join rival
network ABC in 1975. Silverman had a knack for predicting hit
shows (he'd picked *All in the Family*, *The Waltons*, and *Scooby-Doo,
Where Are You?*) and he thought the miniseries made great ratings
sense. Unlike other TV shows, Silverman reasoned, viewers would
have to watch every episode. He also figured that if the network
aired a miniseries during Sweeps Week (when networks set advertising rates and try to lure the most viewers with splashy programming), it could provide a huge ratings boost. Silverman called it
"Event Television."

**EPISODE TWO: THE SAGA BEGINS**
Silverman and ABC produced the first American miniseries, *Rich*

Man, Poor Man, which aired in 1976. The 12-hour saga told the story of two brothers over a period of 30 years and featured Nick Nolte in his first lead role. Silverman's hunch paid off—*Rich Man, Poor Man* averaged a whopping 27 million viewers and was the second most watched show on TV for the year. Executives at all three broadcast networks (ABC, CBS, and NBC) noticed; "Event Television" meant big ratings.

### EPISODE THREE: ROOTS

Silverman's next "event" would be the most popular miniseries of all time—and possibly the most memorable TV show ever—*Roots*. Based on Alex Haley's autobiographical novel, *Roots* traced the history of an African family through slavery to the present day. The all-star cast included Ben Vereen, Lou Gossett Jr., O. J. Simpson, Robert Reed, Todd Bridges, Edward Asner, Maya Angelou, John Amos, Richard Roundtree, and LeVar Burton.

Miniseries episodes were being run in regular weekly time slots, but *Roots* aired on eight consecutive nights because ABC executives didn't think a program about African-American history could hold a broad audience over several weeks. They were wrong: more than 130 million viewers watched at least some of *Roots*. The final installment, airing on January 30, 1977, is still the third highest rated program in TV history.

### EPISODE FOUR: AFTER ROOTS

From the late 1970s to the early 1980s, miniseries were common fare on television, though not all were as successful as *Roots*. The networks quickly learned what kinds of miniseries succeeded: stories about the Old West, the Bible, a powerful family, or a major war. Some of the most popular of the period include:

• *Holocaust* (1978). One of the first American productions to address Nazi atrocities and also one of the first times schoolchildren were actually assigned TV viewing as homework.

• *Jesus of Nazareth* (1977). A reverent film that was so well received that it was expanded from four to six hours and still runs on cable TV every Easter.

• *Shogun* (1980). Based on James Clavell's novel, starring Richard Chamberlain as an English captain shipwrecked in feudal Japan.

A 2½-hour version was released theatrically in Japan.

• *The Thorn Birds* (1983). Spanning 60 years, Richard Chamberlain played a priest torn between his vow of celibacy and his passionate love for a woman he raises from childhood.

• *V* (1983). Alien spaceships loom over U.S. cities, planning to devour humanity in this sci-fi allegory of Nazism.

## EPISODE FIVE: THE END IS NOT THE END

Two World War II miniseries adapted from Herman Wouk novels ended the heyday of the miniseries. *The Winds of War* was a 14-hour, $40 million project that took nearly a decade to film...and it only covered the first two years of World War II. It was a hit in the spring of 1983, so ABC approved a sequel. *War and Remembrance* (1988) was even bigger, costing a record $110 million, but its lackluster ratings told their own story: miniseries had become too expensive to produce; audiences were no longer captivated.

By the late 1980s, broadcast TV networks were fighting for audiences against hundreds of new cable channels as well as home video. Result: very few major minis were produced after the *War* years. CBS and NBC aired a few small, four-hour miniseries, but nothing approaching a *Roots*. ABC, however, wasn't yet ready to let go of the high-profile mini. Filming budgets shrank considerably, but ABC continued to make miniseries thanks to a partnership with horror author Stephen King. He would be the creative force behind seven moderately successful ABC miniseries in the 1990s, including *It*, *The Tommyknockers*, and *The Stand*.

People don't gather for "Event Television" anymore. TV shows can be taped, TiVoed, or rented on DVD, but the miniseries didn't die—it still lives on cable. Since 2000, HBO, Showtime, and the Sci-Fi Channel have produced many acclaimed miniseries on par with *Roots*, including *Band of Brothers*, *From the Earth to the Moon*, and *Angels in America*. The secret to their success? Frequent re-airings.

## MINI-DISASTERS

Not all miniseries attracted record-breaking audiences and truckloads of Emmys. Here are a few clunkers.

• *Beulah Land* (1980). Life on a pre–Civil War Southern plantation, viewed through rose-colored glasses. Features many extremely happy and satisfied slaves.

• *The Last Days of Pompeii* (1984). Ancient Rome meets *Peyton Place*. People engage in lurid behavior of all kinds until the volcano instantly kills them all. One of Sir Laurence Olivier's last roles.

• *Amerika: It Can't Happen Here* (1987). Russian communists take over the United States. Over the two years it took to film *Amerika*, U.S.-Russia tensions had thawed so considerably that the miniseries was irrelevant by the time it aired.

• *Fresno* (1986). A comic send-up of 1980s TV soaps like *Dallas*, starring Carol Burnett and Dabney Coleman as the heads of two rival, raisin-growing families in "America's 64th largest city."

• *Sins* (1986). Joan Collins (*Dynasty*) produced it and played the lead role, a woman separated from her family by death and war. (Collins was twice the character's age.)

• *Scarlett* (1994). In this *Gone With the Wind* sequel, Timothy Dalton and Joanne Whalley stand in for the long-dead Clark Gable and Vivien Leigh.

• *The 10th Kingdom* (2000). A man and his daughter are trapped in an alternate universe where trolls and giants threaten the kingdoms of Snow White, Cinderella, and Little Red Riding Hood.

\* \* \*

## POT LUCK

On July 23, 2005, Leah Robles and her husband Richard spent five hours at the Presbyterian Intercommunity Hospital in Whittier, California. Leah was more than nine months pregnant and thought she was about to have her baby. But hospital staff told her no, she wasn't ready to deliver and sent her home. Less than an hour later the mom-to-be went to the toilet and her husband heard her yell, "I'm having the baby!" He said "No you're not, honey. Come back to bed." Then Leah looked down—and saw Richard Robles III in the toilet. Dad ran in, scooped the baby out, dried him off, and called 911. Firefighters said the boy was fine. (The parents said they'd be talking to the hospital staff again.)

# PHONOGRAPH WARS

*Remember when people listened to records? How about when the records were shaped like toilet paper rolls? This is the story of how a handful of innovators battled each other to dominate the industry they were creating.*

## THE WIZARD OF MENLO PARK

Although he's best known for his work on the lightbulb, Thomas Edison was also driven by a desire to develop the technological ability to record and play back sound. But it wasn't so he could listen to music—he had no particular interest in music. When he invented the phonograph in 1877, he saw it as a new office tool for secretaries to use when taking dictation. In fact, he didn't even think there would be much of a market for the new contraption, and he shelved it for ten years while he worked on more lucrative projects (like the lightbulb). Then in 1887 he got word that a rival research lab was trying to steal his idea.

## HOW IT WORKED

Edison's phonograph recorded sound onto a tinfoil cylinder—about the shape and size of an empty toilet-paper tube. The cylinder was mounted on a hand-cranked screw shaft. The rest of the machine consisted of a steel needle, or *stylus*, attached by a wooden arm to a large speaker cone. Cranking the screw shaft while speaking directly into the speaker caused the arm to vibrate and the stylus to move up and down through the rotating tinfoil cylinder. Putting the needle back at the beginning of the cylinder and cranking at the same speed reproduced the recorded sound.

In 1887 a rival company, Volta Labs, received patents on a machine they called a *graphophone*. It was exactly like the phonograph except that it used a waxed paper cylinder in place of Edison's tinfoil. Unwilling to stand by while another company brought his invention to market, Edison bought them out, incorporated the wax cylinder into his design, and released his Perfect Phonograph in 1888 to wide acclaim. People bought it for business use, but also for the novelty of hearing their own voices come out of a machine. Edison had won the opening skirmish of the phonograph wars.

---

There is a Swiss Army knife with 31 features, including a tool for emergency tracheotomies.

## ANOTHER RIVAL

While Edison was busy buying out Volta Labs, a German American named Emile Berliner was quietly developing an alternative to the phonograph. Patented in 1887, Berliner's gramophone was quite different from the phonograph. For starters, it played flat disc records instead of cylinders. They also featured a new type of sound groove: lateral grooves that caused the stylus to vibrate from side to side at a uniform depth—instead of up and down, like Edison's vertical "hill and dale" grooves. The most important difference, however, was that Berliner's machine did not record sound. All it could do was play pre-recorded records. While Edison's phonograph was an office tool, the gramophone was designed for home entertainment.

To make a gramophone recording, a zinc master disc was coated with a mixture of beeswax and jellied gasoline. After a recording stylus carved lateral grooves into the mixture, the disc was submerged in a vat of acid, which etched the grooves into the zinc. The master was used to cast a metal negative, which was then used to press the grooves into a hard rubber disc. One negative could be used to stamp out hundreds or thousands of identical copies of the original record.

In 1890 Berliner started the U.S. Gramophone Company, at first selling records, but no players. His first customers: toy companies that sold nursery rhyme records with "talking dolls." The dolls had small gramophones built into them. Then he introduced an adult version. Those first records were seven inches in diameter and only had sound on one side. They played at a speed of 30 revolutions per minute, and like Edison's cylinders, held two minutes of sound.

## THE BIRTH OF THE MUSIC INDUSTRY

While Berliner was putting the finishing touches on the gramophone, Edison was running into difficulties. As much as he wanted to see his invention put to serious use as a business tool, he was soon forced to concede that the public wanted to entertain themselves with it. Right from the start, enterprising saloonkeepers and shop owners installed phonographs to attract customers. If ready-to-play recordings of popular music were made available, people would buy them in droves.

Look out! Mt. Everest is moving northeast at a rate of 2.4 inches per year.

In response to this demand, Edison developed a way to mass-produce pre-recorded cylinders and introduced the first coin-operated jukeboxes in the early 1890s. Edison was clueless, though, when it came to show business: he believed that the technology was the selling point, and he viewed pre-recorded music as a demonstration tool or novelty product. He wouldn't even print song titles on his cylinders.

## ROLL ON COLUMBIA

Edison clearly didn't appreciate the possibilities presented by growing demand for pre-recorded music. Inevitably, one of his regional distributors became fed up and split off from him to better serve that market. Columbia Records, today the oldest brand name in continual use in the recording industry, severed all ties with Edison in 1893 and soon became his closest rival. In going head to head with Edison, Columbia had one distinct advantage: it recognized that the selling point was the music, not the brand name. By catering to the customers' musical tastes and by promoting specific singers and songs, Columbia was able to outflank Edison. These cylinders were sold in cardboard cans and gave rise to the term "canned music."

Edison responded with technical improvements. Early cylinders could only be played a few dozen times before the phonograph's heavy steel stylus wore out the grooves. Edison developed a more durable cylinder that could be played over 100 times, but Columbia trumped him by introducing a line of "indestructible" celluloid plastic cylinders. But by 1901 Columbia was losing interest in cylindrical records. Why? Emile Berliner's gramophone was beginning to catch their attention.

## EMILE BERLINER VS. THE WORLD

After selling more than 1,000 gramophones and 25,000 records in 1894, Berliner was poised to challenge Edison and Columbia for a place at the top of the young industry. Instead, he was kept sidelined for the rest of the decade by a series of vicious legal battles.

Businessmen from all over saw the profitability of the new "talking machines," and many tried to move in and dominate the market. First, an outfit calling itself the Standard Talking Machine Company introduced a line of records that were direct copies of

Berliner's originals. No sooner had Berliner succeeded in shutting them down when another group—the American Talking Machine Company—came along selling Berliner's patented technology under the rights of the old Volta Labs "graphophone" patents. Berliner sued and eventually won (based on the difference between his lateral groove system and the vertical cut grooves described in the graphophone patent), but he had spent more time in the court-room than the boardroom and his profits were dwindling.

Before he had a chance to take a breath, Berliner found him-self in court again. This time he was being sued by the *National* *Talking Machine Company*, which produced records under the brand name Zonophone. Universal was started by a man named Frank Seaman, one of Berliner's distributors. Using Columbia's cylindrical record patents, Seaman's group managed to get a fed-eral injunction forcing Berliner to stop production in 1900.

But Berliner wouldn't give up.

In 1901 he joined forces with a fourth company, the *Consoli-dated* Talking Machine Company, and countersued with a vengeance. When the dust settled, the impostors were shut down and Berliner and his new partners won all of National's assets—including the right to use the name Zonophone. In honor of the victory, Berliner's new company called itself the *Victor* Talking Machine Company.

## PRESSING ON

Victor now set out to become the most popular brand of records and players on the market. It became the first company to sign top singing stars such as Enrico Caruso, Jimmie Rodgers, and Dame Nellie Melba to exclusive contracts—using their star power to sell Victor records. In addition, they introduced the Victrola line—record players built into fancy wooden cabinets that became status symbols in American living rooms.

Columbia, meanwhile, started producing flat disc records alongside their cylinder catalogue. Why were flat discs better?

• They took up less storage space than cylinders.

• They could be kept in "albums" that fit neatly on bookshelves.

• The uniform depth of their lateral grooves prevented them from skipping as easily as cylinders.

- They had better sound quality, especially after Victor switched from rubber discs to a material called shellac.

The way was clear for flat records to dominate the market.

## AND THE WINNER WAS...

Not Edison. One of his greatest attributes as an inventor was his stubbornness to see a project through to completion. But it was a bad quality for a businessman who needed to cater to his customers' changing tastes. Edison clung to the cylinders for so long that soon his only sales were to older customers who were as stubborn as he was and refused to purchase new record players.

In 1912 Columbia ceded what little remained of the cylinder market to Edison and put all their efforts into discs. In a move that came too late, that same year Edison introduced the Edison Diamond Disc system, the finest-sounding—and most expensive—system of its day. The sound quality was so good that during barnstorming demonstration tours, audiences were often unable to tell the difference between the record and the real thing.

The problem, however, was that his new system was incompatible with any other company's records. Diamond Discs were a quarter-inch thick and continued to make use of vertical "hill and dale" grooves. And Edison still hadn't grasped that it was the music that sold records. Nobody wanted the best player money could buy if it limited their record selection to Edison's inferior music catalog. Though he eventually developed an adaptor that could be used to play other companies' records, Edison simply did not have the show business savvy to compete with Columbia and Victor.

## SWAN SONG

Finally, in 1929 Edison made a feeble effort to begin producing what, by then, had become the standard record format: a 10-inch, 78 rpm record with lateral grooves that held four minutes of sound. These "Edison Needle Cut" records were of good quality, but his heart wasn't in it. Later that year, America's greatest inventor admitted defeat and withdrew from the record business once and for all. The Edison phonograph factory was converted to produce radio receivers. His only victory in the record wars was a symbolic one: by the time he quit the business, "phonograph" had become the standard American term for any type of record player.

---

The Moon's pull on Earth changes by 23% over the course of a monthly lunar cycle.

## THE BATTLE RAGES ON

Throughout the 1930s and '40s, Columbia and Victor (which had merged with the Radio Corporation of America to become RCA Victor) fought for technical supremacy. Speeds of 33⅓ and 45 rpm replaced the 78; vinyl replaced shellac as the material from which records were made; and in 1951, the first "stereophonic" records were introduced.

Grooved records that produced sound by causing a stylus to vibrate would remain the dominant recorded music format until 1983. That year, magnetic tape cassettes outsold disc records for the first time. In 1988—exactly 100 years after Edison sold his first phonograph—digital compact discs outsold vinyl records for the first time and condemned them forever after to antique or novelty status.

\* \* \*

## MORE DUMB CROOKS

• **Ear It Is.** "German police charged a man with drug possession when he entered a police station to check if he was on their wanted list. 'I suppose he may have heard he was wanted for some offense and just wanted to see if the police had anything on him,' said Volker Pieper, a spokesman for police in the city of Kassel. 'It didn't go quite as he had planned.' As the 33-year-old man, a known drug abuser, questioned police, an officer noticed a suspicious lump stuck in his ear which turned out to be a gram of heroin. Police confiscated the drug before filing charges." (Reuters)

• **Did I Say That?** "Dennis Newton was on trial for the armed robbery of a convenience store when he decided to fire his attorney and represent himself. Oklahoma City District Attorney said Newton was doing a decent job until the store manager testified that Newton was indeed the robber. Newton jumped up, accused the woman of lying and said, 'I should have blown your [expletive] head off.' The defendant paused, then added, 'If I had been the one that was there.' The jury deliberated for 20 minutes before returning a verdict of guilty, recommending a sentence of 30 years." (*Deseret News*)

# THE LITTLE RASCALS HALL OF FAME

*More than 175 kids appeared in the* Our Gang *films between 1922 and 1944. Only 41 had major roles and even fewer became famous. Here are some of our favorites.*

**P**ETE THE PUP
• The dog you remember as Pete, the one with the circle around his eye, was actually the third dog to be featured in the *Our Gang* series. The first was also named Pete (no circle); he appeared in the 1923 film *The Cobbler*. A dog named Pal appeared in several *Our Gang* films in the mid-1920s.

• When Pal left the series, producer Hal Roach selected one of Pal's puppies to replace him. That dog was the one who became famous as Pete. How'd he get a circle around his eye? Purely by chance: before starring in the *Our Gang* series, he played a dog named Tige with a circle around his eye in the *Buster Brown* children's film series. When Roach selected Pete for the *Our Gang* cast, he told the film crew to wash off the circle, but it wouldn't come off—it had been painted on with permanent dye. "What the hell," Roach replied, "leave it on."

• Since the dogs that played Pete could be replaced every few years, he became the longest-running character in the film series, lasting from 1927 until 1938.

**ALLEN "FARINA" HOSKINS** (105 *Our Gang* films from 1922–1931—more than any other kid in the series)
• Farina got his name because a studio executive thought he was as "chubby and agreeable as breakfast mush." The character that William "Buckwheat" Thomas made famous is modeled after Farina, and he was named after a cereal grain, too.

• Farina isn't as well known as Spanky, Alfalfa, or Buckwheat are today, but in his day he was the most popular *Our Gang* character. His salary showed it, too—at his peak he made $250 a week, more than any of the other kids, who started out at $40 a week.

---

**Some species of moth send out jamming signals that confuse bat "radar."**

## JOE COBB (86 films, 1922–1929)

The original fat kid in the series, Joe stumbled into show business while vacationing in Los Angeles with his family in 1922. He and his dad decided to visit Hal Roach Studios one afternoon. Joe caught the eye of the casting people as they were heading off for lunch; they cast him right on the spot and he began working in his first silent movie that afternoon. He made his first *Our Gang* short, *The Big Show*, shortly thereafter.

## ERNIE "SUNSHINE SAMMY" MORRISON (28 films, 1922–1924)

Ernie, who was black, was already a star at Hal Roach Studios when he was cast in the first *Our Gang* comedy in 1922. He was the most popular character in the earliest *Our Gang* films, but he left after just two years when he was offered more money to perform in vaudeville. In the 1940s he starred in several of the Dead End Kids/East Side Kids films.

## BOBBY "WHEEZER" HUTCHINS (58 films, 1927–1933)

Two-year-old Bobby got his nickname, "Wheezer," his very first day on the set—he was so excited to be there that he ran around until he lost his breath and started wheezing.

## NORMAN "CHUBBY" CHANEY (18 films, 1929–1931)

When Joe Cobb grew too old for the series in 1928, the studio launched a nationwide publicity campaign to find a new fat kid. Eleven-year-old Norman Chaney reportedly beat out 20,000 other entrants for the part. His response when told he'd won the part: "Mister, are you just kidding me because I'm fat?"

## MATTHEW "STYMIE" BEARD (36 films, 1930–1935)

• The kid with the trademark bowler hat (a gift from Stan Laurel of Laurel and Hardy fame) replaced Allen "Farina" Hoskins when Allen got too old for the series. The studio had already tested 350 kids for the part when Matthew arrived at the studio for his screen test. He never had to take it—as soon as director Bob McGowan saw him he shouted, "That's who I want! Sign him up for five years."
• Matthew's character was originally named "Hercules." But he was fascinated by the movie-making process, and his curiosity fre-

quently interfered with, or "stymied," the film's progress, which earned him the new nickname.

• When Beard died in 1981, he was buried with his bowler hat.

## TOMMY "BUTCH" BOND (27 films, 1932–1940)

Tommy was discovered by a Hal Roach Studios talent scout while walking down a Dallas street with his mother. He played two characters in the series: Tommy (1932–34) and Butch (1937–40).

## GEORGE "SPANKY" MCFARLAND (95 films, 1932–1942)

• Three-year-old George had already appeared in a Wonder Bread ad when his aunt sent his photograph to Hal Roach, who liked what he saw and ordered a screen test. It went so well—the cameraman ran around the lot telling people, "You've got to see this!"—that George was immediately signed to a five-year deal.

• George's screen nickname was going to be "Sonny" until a writer overheard his mother threaten him with a spanking by saying, "Spankee, spankee, mustn't touch."

• George reportedly learned how to do his double-take reaction shots from comedian Stan Laurel.

## WILLIAM "BUCKWHEAT" THOMAS (93 films, 1934–1944)

So was the Buckwheat character a boy or a girl? It depends on what film you're watching: William was actually the third actor to play the character; the first two were girls, and at first the character's gender was ambiguous. Carlena Beard (Matthew Beard's sister) played Buckwheat in two films; a young girl named Willie Mae Taylor played the character in three others.

## EUGENE "PORKY" LEE (43 films, 1935–1939)

• Eugene joined the cast after his mother mailed a photograph of him to the studio; Hal Roach thought he looked like Spanky and would make a good little brother.

• When Eugene became too big to continue with the series, he was replaced by Bobby Blake.

## BOBBY BLAKE (40 films, 1939–1944)

• Many *Our Gang* stars had fond memories of the experience, even if the typecasting later hurt their careers. Not Blake—he came from an abusive home and deeply resented being denied a normal childhood. "I wasn't a child star, I was a child laborer," he says.

• Blake's career path was the opposite of many of the Little Rascals. He signed on in 1939, after Hal Roach sold the *Our Gang* franchise to MGM. The series was heading downhill, and Bobby (who used his real name, Mickey Gubitosi, before adopting the stage name "Bobby Blake" in the early 1940s) appears in many of the worst films of the series. But he went on to have one of the most successful post–*Our Gang* careers of all. As an adult, Robert Blake won critical acclaim for his portrayal of a death-row killer in the 1967 film *In Cold Blood,* and won an Emmy for his work on the 1970s cop show *Baretta.*

## WILLIAM "FROGGY" LAUGHLIN (29 films, 1940–1944)
Laughlin's scratchy, "froggy" voice wasn't his real voice—it was just a trick that he did for his character. His real voice was normal.

## DARLA HOOD (52 films, 1935–1941)
• Three-year-old Darla, an Oklahoma native, was in New York with her singing instructor when the Edison Hotel's bandleader unexpectedly invited her onstage and asked her to sing. Her performance thrilled the audience—including *Our Gang* casting director Joe Rivkin, who happened to be there that evening. He arranged for a screen test, and when that went well, signed Hood to a seven-year contract at a starting salary of $75 a week.

• Like a lot of the *Our Gang* child actors, Hood had trouble finding film work as an adult. She eventually went into background singing and commercial voice-over work; for a time, hers was the voice of the mermaid in the Chicken of the Sea tuna commercials.

## CARL "ALFALFA" SWITZER (61 films, 1935–1940)
• Carl's father lost his foot in an accident and had trouble finding work, so Carl and his older brother, Harold, sang at auctions, country fairs, and other venues to help make money for the family.
• In 1934 the family went to California to visit relatives; while there they decided to see if they could get an audition for Carl

and Harold at the Hal Roach Studios. They couldn't—but the studio commissary, the Our Gang Cafe, was open to the public, so the boys went in one afternoon during the lunchtime rush and started singing. Hal Roach was so impressed that he signed them both and wrote their act into the next film, *Beginner's Luck*.

• Roach considered naming Carl's character "Hayseed," but later settled on "Alfalfa," which was taken from a character in a silent film that Will Rogers had made for the studio.

• Carl had a reputation as a prankster and a troublemaker. Once, he got mad at the director and urinated on the hot studio lights, shutting down production until the smoke (and the stink) cleared the studio. "They had to open the doors of the stage and run the big fans through there the rest of the day to get the smell out," Robert Blake recalled. "Alfalfa could be a devil."

• One of the running jokes with Alfalfa's character was that he sang off-key but thought he was a great crooner. Tommy "Butch" Bond claims in his memoirs that Switzer *wasn't* in on the joke. "He believed he could sing," Bond writes. "That's what made him so funny. He thought his off-key was on-key. Of course it didn't help that people on the set told him he had a voice. He took them at their word, though they were joking and knew that the audience would howl with laughter on hearing his rendition of 'Let Me Call You Sweetheart' or some other poor, mangled song."

• Carl's "crooning" came back to haunt him when he outgrew the *Our Gang* series and tried to audition for older parts. "They used to say to him, 'Hey Alfalfa, sing off key for us.' It used to drive him crazy," Darla Hood told Leonard Maltin in his book *The Little Rascals: The Life and Times of Our Gang*.

\*　　\*　　\*

## SECRET SERVICE CODE NAMES

Hillary Clinton: *Evergreen*

Barbara Bush: *Tranquility*

Nancy Reagan: *Rainbow*

Rosalynn Carter: *Dancer*

Betty Ford: *Pinafore*

Pat Nixon: *Starlight*

Lady Bird Johnson: *Victoria*

Jacqueline Kennedy: *Lace*

Mamie Eisenhower: *Springtime*

Laura Bush: (*It's still secret.*)

Table talk: Only about a third of the world's population eats with a knife and fork.

# LONGEST LASTING...

*We acted fast and put this page together last.*

...**Echo measured in a building:** 15 seconds, in the Mausoleum in Hamilton, South Lanarkshire, Scotland.

...**Game of Monopoly:** 1,680 hours (more than 70 days).

...**Rainbow:** Residents of North Wales saw a rainbow on August 14, 1975, that lasted three hours.

...**Face-slapping competition:** One held in Kiev, Ukraine, in 1931 lasted 30 hours.

...**TV series:** *Meet the Press* (1947–present).

...**Live burial:** Geoff Smith was buried in a box under a pub in England for 150 days, breaking the record of 101 days (which was set by his mother).

...**Volcanic eruption:** The volcano on the Italian island of Stromboli has been erupting continually since 450 B.C.

...**Pope:** Pius IX reigned for a record 31 years.

...**Continuous musical act:** Les Brown's Band of Reknown played from 1936 until 2000—64 years.

...**Single-family dynasty:** An unbroken line of 36 heirs of Osman I ruled the Ottoman Empire from 1299 until 1922—623 years.

...**Tire fire:** In 1983 nearly 7 million tires on a West Virginia ranch burned for more than 9 months. (It took 22 years and cost more than $11 million to clean it up.)

...**Tornado on record:** On May 26, 1917, a tornado traveled 293 miles from western Illinois to eastern Indiana—more than seven hours on the ground.

...**Ice age:** The Huronian ice age began 2.7 billion years ago. It lasted 900 million years.

...**Plant:** "King Clone" is a creosote plant near Barstow, California. It is estimated to be 11,700 years old.

...**Marriage:** John and Amelia Rocchio got married in 1923. He was 19 and she was 17. As of 2005—82 years later—they were still married.

...**Human:** Jeanne Louise Calment of Arles, France, died in 1997. She was 122 years old.

---

**Where's everyone going?** The average American makes 4 car trips a day, for a total of 41 miles.

# ANSWER PAGES

## AUNT SHARI'S AMAZING POWERS
### (Answers for page 409)

**Peek-a-Boo:** Aunt Shari wrote "Steve" on all five pieces of paper. She only pretended to write the other names down when I called them out. Then as soon as the trick was over, she took back the bag before I could discover the secret.

**Psychic Tattoo:** When Aunt Shari picked up the sugar cube to drop it in the glass of water, she made sure to press down on the "U" with her fingertip. That transferred the "U" to her finger. Then when she took my hand, she pressed her fingertip against my palm, and that transferred the "U" from her finger to my palm.

**Full of Hot Air:** This trick required advanced preparation. Aunt Shari knew I was coming over, so she mixed some water with an equal amount of lemon juice, then poured the stuff into the soda bottle until it was about a third full. (The *real* reason she wrapped the bottle in aluminum foil was to keep me from seeing that there was anything in it.) Then she spooned two tablespoons of baking soda into the balloon. When she attached the balloon to the bottle, she made sure not to spill any baking soda into the bottle. Then, when she was ready to do the trick, Aunt Shari lifted the balloon straight up, causing the baking soda to fall into the bottle and mix with the lemon juice and water. The chemical reaction released carbon dioxide, which inflated the balloon.

**Math Psychic:** Aunt Shari knew that whatever numbers I picked, if I did the math calculations correctly, the answer would always be 1,089. That's why she didn't want to do it more than once—if we both got the same answer again, I'd know it was a trick.

**Keep the Change:** When Aunt Shari had me press down on the coin with my finger, she wasn't reading my mind...she was silently counting to 30. She knew that if I held my finger there for 30 seconds, my body temperature would warm the coin up. Then when she pretended not to be able to read my mind, that gave her the excuse she needed to pick up the coins and feel which one was the warmest.

# THE POLITICALLY CORRECT QUIZ #1
### (Answers from page 114)

**1—b)** When the British National Association of Master Bakers protested, the supermarket chain backed down. Gingerbread men are back; Gingerbread persons are banned.

**2—c)** The vote was 4–3, and not everyone is happy with the decision. "I feel like we're living in the middle of a George Orwell novel," says Jap Road resident Jason Marshburn, 31. "It's like me suing Keebler or Nabisco because the word 'cracker' is offensive to us white people."

**3—b)** After spending several hours watching old *Lone Ranger* reruns, the commission concluded that *kemosabe* means "trusty friend," just like the store owner said it did, and ruled in his favor. "Both the Lone Ranger and Tonto treat one another with respect...At no time during the episodes is the term *kemosabe* ever used in a demeaning or derogatory manner."

**4—c)** The school backed down after the incident became public.

**5—b)** The woman, who is now in college, is suing the school district for $50,000. "Her only dance for her senior prom was on the sidewalk to a song playing on the radio," her lawyer says.

**6—a)** Senator Shurden proposes that the chickens wear the gloves, along with tiny vests containing electric sensors that register every blow. "It's like the fencing that you see on the Olympics, you know, where they have little balls on the ends of the swords and the fencers wear vests," Shurden says. "That's the same application that would be applied to the roosters." He says cockfighting was a $100-million business in Oklahoma before it was outlawed in 2002. (At last report the legislation was still pending).

# THE POLITICALLY CORRECT QUIZ #2
### (Answers from page 371)

**1—c)** Someone in the purchasing department took offense at the term, which refers to primary and secondary hard drives. The county's Department of Affirmative Action tried to get the term removed from the packaging of any computer equipment purchased by the county, but backed down in 2004 in the face of strong public ridicule. The controversy was later named "the most egregious example of political correctness in 2004" by the watchdog group Global Language Monitor, beating out such terms as "waitron" (waiter or waitress) and "higher being" (God).

**2—b)** One of the Oglala Sioux Chief's descendants, Harvey White Woman, started a campaign to pressure Crazy Horse Paris to change its name. "When you say the name Crazy Horse, you don't conjure up nightclubs. You conjure up the warrior," White Woman says. (No word on whether White Woman finds his own name offensive.) In 1992 he and other descendants of Crazy Horse sued the makers of the Original Crazy Horse Malt Liquor and won a $150,000 settlement. The company no longer makes the Crazy Horse brand.

**3—c)** Kraft suspended production of the road-flattened candy critters after the New Jersey SPCA threatened to launch petition drives, boycotts, and letter-writing campaigns against the product. "We take comments from our consumers really seriously and, in hindsight, we understand that this product could be misunderstood," a Kraft spokesperson told reporters.

**4—a)** Mercedes-Benz made the concession after receiving complaints from the German chapter of People for the Ethical Treatment of Animals (PETA). "When you consider that the skins of four to fifteen cows are needed for each car this means thousands of cows will be spared," says PETA spokesperson Edmund Haferbeck. So does Mercedes expect to make a lot of leather-free cars? No. "Our customers are more likely to want even more leather at the premium end," says spokesperson Ursula Mertzig-Stein. "But we will make cars without leather on demand."

**5—b)** "Pubescent kids are not going to want to take part in sumo wrestling if they don't look cool," Japan's *Yomiuri Shimbun* newspaper quoted one local amateur sumo official as saying. Too bad: "We have no intention of allowing children in pants into the ring," says an official with Nihon Sumo Kyokai, the national wrestling body.

**6—a)** The BBC ruled that since narcolepsy (excessive sleepiness) is a serious sleep disorder, *TV's Greatest Moments* should not have made fun of sufferers.

**7—b)** Sure, ladies' nights are popular. Sure, they're profitable. But

J. Frank Vespa-Papaleo, director of the State Division on Civil Rights, says they're illegal in New Jersey because they go against the "important social policy of eradicating discrimination."

**8—b)** The company agreed to make the change after Norwegian Prime Minister Kjell Magne Bondevik accused the furniture giant of showing only men putting the furniture together. "IKEA will now review its instructions leaflets to get a more even balance between men and women," a company spokesperson told reporters. "I myself have great problems screwing together such furniture," the prime minister says.

# WORD GAMES
## (Answers from page 305)

### 1. By the Numbers
GENERATION
- 1234 = GENE
- 456 = ERA
- 567 = RAT
- 890 = ION

### 2. Sum Fun
When written out, the words form anagrams of each other.
ELEVEN PLUS TWO
TWELVE PLUS ONE

### 3. Painful Words
HEARTACHE and HEADACHE

### 4. Looking Back
They both contain all five vowels, which appear in reverse order.

### 5. Magic Words
They all change pronunciations when the first letter is capitalized.

### 6. Branching Out
MAPLE
OAK
ELM
BONSAI
PINE
ASPEN
BAMBOO

### 7. Another Magic Word
NOWHERE becomes...
NOW HERE

### 8. Weighty Riddle
TON

# BRAINTEASERS
**(Answers from page 162)**

**1. A Thousand Squares**
Inside a roll of toilet paper

**2. Horse Sense**
The younger son jumped on his brother's horse and went as fast as he could, ensuring that his own horse would be last.

**3. Wrong Way Corrigan**
He was on foot.

**4. Holed Up**
Julia brought a bucket of sand from the sandbox and poured it very slowly into the hole, giving the baby bird plenty of time to stay on top of it. When the level rose high enough for the bird to be reached, one of the grownups gingerly returned it to its nest.

**5. Dollars to Dogs**
Five cents

**6. Pressing Riddle**
A keyboard

# PLOP, PLOP, QUIZ, QUIZ
**(Answers for page 188)**

1) Maxwell House coffee
2) Allstate insurance
3) Perdue chickens
4) Brylcreem
5) Federal Express
6) Schlitz beer
7) Hebrew National hot dogs
8) Alka-Seltzer
9) Morton's salt
10) American Express
11) Packard
12) Remington shavers
13) Timex
14) AT&T
15) Yellow Pages
16) Energizer batteries
17) Marlboro cigarettes
18) Bactine ointment
19) Milk
20) Cattlemen's Beef Board
21) Delta Airlines
22) Bartles & Jaymes wine coolers
23) Chrysler Cordoba
24) General Foods International Coffees
25) Irish Spring soap
26) Pepsi
27) Motel 6
28) DuPont

There are more than half a million fast-food restaurants in China. KFC is the most popular.

# FINGER LICKIN' QUIZ
### (Answers for page 334)

1) Pantene shampoo
2) Bounty paper towels
3) Burger King
4) Nike
5) Underwood ham
6) Chiffon margarine
7) Anacin
8) Tareyton cigarettes
9) Braniff Airlines
10) Alka-Seltzer
11) Lucky Charms
12) Hallmark
13) Secret deodorant
14) KFC
15) Virginia Slims cigarettes
16) General Electric
17) Doublemint gum
18) Pontiac
19) Miller Lite beer
20) Rolaids
21) Lay's potato chips
22) Peter Paul Mounds
23) Calgon soap
24) LifeCall
25) Ajax laundry detergent
26) Coca-Cola
27) Johnson's baby shampoo
28) Pillsbury Poppin' Fresh Dough
29) Reebok

# SPELLING QUIZ
### (Answers from page 212)

1. c) Millennium; 2. b) Dumbbell; 3. c) Separate; 4. c) Necessary; 5. c) Minuscule; 6. a) Accommodate; 7. b) Liaison; 8. c) Harass; 9. a) Occurrence; 10 . a) Embarrass; 11. c) Independent; 12. c) Questionnaire; 13. b) Broccoli; 14. b) Recommend; 15. c) Sincerely; 16. a) Kindergarten; 17. c) Supersede; 18. a) Grammar; 19. b) Referred; 20. b) Immense

# BRITS VS. YANKS
### (Answers for page 89)

1. u)  2. h)  3. j)  4. r)  5. b)  6. q)  7. w)  8. d)
9. t)  10. a)  11. e)  12. f)  13. l)  14. s)  15. v)  16. n)
17. c)  18. o)  19. p)  20. g)  21. k)  22. m)  23. i)

"You can't depend on your eyes when your imagination is out of focus." —Mark Twain

# UNCLE JOHN'S BATHROOM READER CLASSIC SERIES

Find these and other great titles from the *Uncle John's Bathroom Reader* Classic Series online at **www.bathroomreader.com**. Or contact us at:

Bathroom Readers' Institute
P.O. Box 1117
Ashland, OR 97520
(888) 488-4642

Hiya, Sam!

# THE LAST PAGE

**F**ELLOW BATHROOM READERS:
The fight for good bathroom reading should never be taken loosely—we must do our duty and sit firmly for what we believe in, even while the rest of the world is taking potshots at us.

We'll be brief. Now that we've proven we're not simply a flush-in-the-pan, we invite you to take the plunge: Sit Down and Be Counted! Become a member of the Bathroom Readers' Institute. Log on to *www.bathroomreader.com*, or send a self-addressed, stamped, business-sized envelope to: BRI, PO Box 1117, Ashland, Oregon 97520. You'll receive your free membership card, get discounts when ordering directly through the BRI, and earn a permanent spot on the BRI honor roll!

---

If you like reading our books...
VISIT THE BRI'S WEB SITE!
*www.bathroomreader.com*

- Visit "The Throne Room"—a great place to read!
  - Receive our irregular newsletters via e-mail
    - Order additional *Bathroom Readers*
      - Become a BRI member

*Go with the Flow...*

---

Well, we're out of space, and when you've gotta go, you've gotta go. Tanks for all your support. Hope to hear from you soon. Meanwhile, remember:

*Keep on flushin'!*